PRAISE FOR S

"*Soccernomics* is the most intelligent boo............ten about soccer."
—*San Francisco Chronicle*

"Quite magnificent—a sort of *Freakonomics* of soccer."
—Jonathan Wilson, *The Guardian*

"Many explanations [of England's poor form] can be found in the book *Soccernomics* in a segment entitled 'Why England Loses.' (This is well worth a read for any English football fan; essentially, you overvalue your football heritage and undervalue the benefits of innovation.)"
—Stephen J. Dubner, coauthor of *Freakonomics*

"Fascinating." —VanityFair.com

"The authors take what 'everybody' knows about success and failure in soccer and subject it to rigorous empirical analysis embedded in good stories that carry the narrative along….Highly recommended. All readers."
—*Choice*

"It's a really good book. If more people read it, they'd understand some of the reasons why England [doesn't] win. Everyone can have an opinion, but they back it up with stats." —Jamie Carragher, Liverpool F.C.

"*Soccernomics* [is] a sharply written and provocative examination of the world's game seen through the prism of economics and statistical data. It demolishes almost everything that most soccer fans believe about the game and how professional soccer teams should operate."
—*Globe and Mail* (Canada)

"Oh, Rooney's the best. [My son] Ben thinks that England might be in the top four, but that's it. He knows the starting lineup of every European team. We're reading this very interesting book about [soccer] together."
—Lorrie Moore, author of *A Gate at the Stairs* and *Birds of America*

"With *Soccernomics*, the *Financial Times'* indispensable Simon Kuper and top-flight sports economist Stefan Szymanski bring scrupulous economic analysis and statistical rigor to a sport long dependent on hoary—and, it seems, unfounded—assumptions....Gripping and essential."
—Slate.com, Best Books of 2009

"[The book] is a sporting tale in the *Freakonomics* mode of inquiry, using statistics to come up with fascinating conclusions."
—*Independent* (UK), Best Books of 2009

"[Szymanski and Kuper] entertainingly demolish soccer shibboleths....Well argued and clear headed."
—*Financial Times*, Best Books of 2009

"Using data analysis, history and psychology, [*Soccernomics*] punctures dozens of clichés about what it takes to win, and who makes money in soccer—and in sports in general."   —*Associated Press*

"There just aren't that many interesting, intelligent, analytical books about the world's most popular game, but this is one."   —*Blogcritics*

"A must read for any fan of the business of soccer."
—Footiebusiness.com

"*Soccernomics*...tackles the soccer world's most probing questions with a dispassionate analysis based on economic formulas, which separate fact from accepted-as-fact myths perpetuated by legions of fans."
—Forbes.com

"It's quite a book....*Soccernomics* explains how the lessons of *Moneyball* (sports teams are not completely rational) apply to the world's favorite sport."   —*Huffington Post*

"[Kuper and Szymanski] do for soccer what *Moneyball* did for baseball. It puts the game under an analytical microscope using statistics, economics, psychology, and intuition to try to transform a dogmatic sport."
—*New York Times*

"It's a fascinating book with the potential to effect genuine change in the sport." —*Booklist* (starred)

"Small book, big wallop!…Enthusiastically recommended to all soccer fans, general and specialized, as well as those thinking of becoming one."
—*Library Journal*

"[Kuper and Szymanski] have created a blend of *Freakonomics* and *Fever Pitch*, bringing surprising economic analysis to bear on the world's most popular sport.…This mix of economic analysis and anecdote makes for a thought-provoking, often amusing read. Here, at last, is a British answer to Michael Lewis's baseball-meets-cash bestseller *Moneyball*."
—*Bloomberg News*

"[Kuper and Szymanski] combine their skills to entertaining and mostly convincing effect." —*Economist*

"If you're a football fan, I'll save you some time: read this book…compulsive reading…thoroughly convincing." —*Daily Telegraph* (UK)

"Szymanski has recently published the best introduction to sports economics…while Kuper is probably the smartest of the new generation of super-smart sportswriters." —*Observer* (UK)

"[Kuper and Szymanski] basically trash every cliché about football you ever held to be true. It's bravura stuff…the study of managers buying players and building a club is one you'll feel like photocopying and sending to your team's chairman." —*Metro* (UK)

"More thoughtful than most of its rivals and, by football standards, positively intellectual.…Kuper, a brilliantly contrary columnist, and Szymanski, an economics professor…find plenty of fertile territory in their commendable determination to overturn the lazy preconceptions rife in football." —*The Times* (UK)

"Kuper and Szymanski are…a highly effective and scrupulously rational team, combining the former's detailed and nuanced understanding of European football with the latter's sophisticated econometric analysis. With a remarkable lightness of touch, they demonstrate the limits of conventional thinking in football, as well as the real patterns of behaviour that shape sporting outcomes."   —*Prospect* (UK)

"Books about sport are a bit like players—some are pretty dreadful, most are about the same standard and so don't really stand out, and occasionally one comes along that excels to the point that they change the way you watch and think about the game. *Soccernomics* by Simon Kuper and Stefan Szymanski is such a book….Any fan of the Socceroos who reads *Soccernomics* or indeed any sports fan ready to take on board new ways of thinking might, like me, never look at a penalty kick or a league table and certainly not follow a major international tournament quite the same way again."   —Peter Newlinds, *ABC News* (Australia)

"Should still be compulsory reading for all poor suffering England fans."
—Jim O'Neill, former chairperson of
Goldman Sachs Asset Management

SOCCERNOMICS

ALSO BY SIMON KUPER

Retourtjes Nederland (Atlas, 2006)

Soccer Against the Enemy (Nation Books, 2006)

Soccer Men: Profiles of the Rogues, Geniuses, and Neurotics Who Dominate the World's Most Popular Sport (Nation Books, 2011)

Ajax, the Dutch, the War: The Strange Tale of Soccer During Europe's Darkest Hour (Nation Books, 2012)

Spies, Lies, and Exile: The Extraordinary Story of Russian Double Agent George Blake (New Press, 2021)

The Barcelona Complex: Lionel Messi and the Making—and Unmaking—of the World's Greatest Soccer Club (Penguin Press, 2021)

ALSO BY STEFAN SZYMANSKI

Fans of the World, Unite! A Capitalist Manifesto for Sports Consumers (with Stephen F. Ross; Stanford University Press, 2008)

Il business del calcio (with Umberto Lago and Alessandro Baroncelli; Egea, 2004)

National Pastime: How Americans Play Baseball and the Rest of the World Plays Soccer (with Andrew Zimbalist; Brookings Institution, 2005)

Playbooks and Checkbooks: An Introduction to the Economics of Modern Sports (Princeton University Press, 2009)

Winners and Losers: The Business Strategy of Football (with Tim Kuypers; Viking Books, 1999; Penguin Books, 2000)

Money and Soccer (Nation Books, 2015)

It's Football, Not Soccer (and Vice Versa) (with Silke-Maria Weineck; Perverse Books, 2018)

City of Champions: A History of Triumph and Defeat in Detroit (with Silke-Maria Weineck; New Press, 2020)

Crickonomics (with Tim Wigmore; Bloomsbury Books, 2022)

SOCCERNOMICS

Why European Men and American Women Win
and Billionaire Owners Are Destined to Lose

Simon Kuper and Stefan Szymanski

2022 World Cup Edition

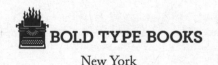

BOLD TYPE BOOKS
New York

Cover design by Pete Garceau
Cover Image © iStock / Getty Images
Cover copyright © 2022 by Hachette Book Group, Inc.

Bold Type Books
30 Irving Place, 10th Floor New York, NY 10003
www.boldtypebooks.org
@BoldTypeBooks

Printed in the United States of America

First US edition: October 2009
2018 Word Cup Edition: April 2018
2022 World Cup Edition: October 2022
Originally published in the United Kingdom by Yellow Jersey Press.

Published by Bold Type Books, an imprint of Perseus Books, LLC, a subsidiary of Hachette Book Group, Inc. Bold Type Books is a co-publishing venture of the Type Media Center and Perseus Books.

The Hachette Speakers Bureau provides a wide range of authors for speaking events. To find out more, go to www.hachettespeakersbureau.com or call (866) 376-6591.

The publisher is not responsible for websites (or their content) that are not owned by the publisher.

Library of Congress Cataloging-in-Publication Data

Names: Kuper, Simon, author. | Szymanski, Stefan, 1960- author.
Title: Soccernomics : why European men and American women win and
    billionaire owners are destined to lose / Simon Kuper and Stefan Szymanski.
Description: 2022 World Cup edition. | New York, N.Y. : Bold Type Books,
    [2022] | Includes bibliographical references and index.
Identifiers: LCCN 2022019359 | ISBN 9781645030171 (trade paperback) |
    ISBN 9781645030188 (epub)
Subjects: LCSH: Soccer—Social aspects.
Classification: LCC GV943.9.S64 K88 2022 | DDC 796.334—dc23/eng/20220609
LC record available at https://lccn.loc.gov/2022019359

ISBNs: 9781568584256 (2009 paperback), 9781568587011 (2012 paperback),
    9781568584812 (2014 paperback), 9781568587516 (2018 paperback),
    9781568588865 (2018 e-book), 9781645030171 (2022 paperback),
    9781645030188 (2022 e-book)

LSC-C

Printing 1, 2022

From Simon:

To Pamela

(who doesn't know about soccer,
but knows about writing) for her astonishing tolerance.

And to

Leila, Leo, and Joey,

for all the smiles.

From Stefan:

To my father

We never saw eye to eye,
but he taught me to question everything.

CONTENTS

PART II The Fans
Loyalty, Suicides, and Happiness

PART III Countries
Rich and Poor, Tom Thumb, England, Spain, Palestine, and the Champions of the Future

1

DRIVING WITH A DASHBOARD

In Search of New Truths About Soccer

Some years ago, the data department at Manchester City carried out a study of corner kicks. City hadn't been scoring much from corners, and the analysts wanted to find out the best way to take them. They watched more than four hundred corners, from different leagues, over several seasons, and concluded: the most dangerous corner was the inswinger to the near post.

The beauty of the inswinger was that it sent the ball straight into the danger zone. Sometimes an attacker would get a head or foot to it and divert it in from point-blank range. Sometimes the keeper or a defender stopped the inswinger on the line, whereupon someone bashed it in. And occasionally the ball just swung straight in from the corner. Of course, you wouldn't want to take every corner as an inswinger. It's smart to hit the odd outswinger, too, just to keep the opponents guessing. This is what's known as a mixed strategy. But all in all, the analysts found that inswingers produced more goals than outswingers.

They took their findings to the club's then manager, Roberto Mancini, who, like almost all managers, is an ex-player. He heard them out politely. Then he said, in effect, "I was a player for many years, and I just know that the outswinger is more effective." He was wrong, but we can understand why he made the mistake: outswingers tend to create beautiful goals (ball swings out, player meets it with powerful header, ball crashes into net), and beautiful goals stick in the memory. The messy goals generally produced by inswingers don't.

At first, Mancini didn't change his thinking. But sometime around 2011, when City was again having trouble with corners, his assistant David Platt came to chat with the club's data department. The analysts told Platt about the corners study. They heard nothing more about the matter, but soon they noticed that City had begun taking inswinging corners. In the 2011–2012 season, City scored fifteen goals from corners, more than any other team in the Premier League. Ten of those goals came from inswingers, including the header from Vincent Kompany against Manchester United that effectively sealed the title for City.

It's a story that captures where soccer is heading. On the one hand, the March of the Geeks has advanced quickly since we first published *Soccernomics* in 2009. Soccer is becoming more intelligent. The analysts who now crunch "match data" at almost all big European clubs (and at many smaller ones) are just one symptom of the shift.

Today's plugged-in clubs know stats like pass-completion rates in the final third of the field, miles run in each phase of the game, and pace of sprints for all their players. These numbers increasingly inform decisions on which players to buy and sell.

On the other hand, as Mancini's initial rejection of the data about corner kicks shows, there is still widespread suspicion of numbers in soccer. Statisticians don't always make the best communicators. Baseball has had its *Moneyball* revolution, but in soccer the transformation is still in its first phase.

This new, updated, expanded edition of *Soccernomics* uses data to clarify our thinking on topics ranging from tackles through transfers and to why England still loses and why the US men's team hasn't yet started winning. We have new chapters on the fiasco of the European Super League and on why men's soccer should pay billions in reparations to the female game, along with an afterword arguing that despite the damage done by COVID-19, the game has never had it so good. We have also expanded our thoughts on some mystifying questions, such as "How do clubs use data to judge, buy, and sell players?" and "How powerful are agents in the transfer market?" In every chapter of the book we have found stories and analyses to update and new ideas to add.

Over the years we've watched fans and media shift to our point of view on certain issues: most people now recognize that hosting big tournaments doesn't make you rich and also that the Premier League isn't holding back the England team. (We wish we could claim responsibility for shifting global opinion, but we can't.) On other issues we've corrected our own thinking somewhat. In 2009 we were confident that the rest of the world would soon catch up with the best Western European nations. That hasn't happened, so we've had to rethink what's going on. We're with the economist John Maynard Keynes: when the facts change, we change our minds.

It's a long way from *Soccernomics'* beginnings in the Istanbul Hilton one winter's day in 2007. From the outside, the hotel is squat and brutalist, but once the security men have checked your car for bombs and waved you through, the place is so soothing that you never want to go home again. Once you've escaped the fourteen-million-person city, the only stress is over what to do next: a Turkish bath, a game of tennis, or yet more overeating while the sun sets over the Bosporus? For aficionados, there was also a perfect view of the Besiktas soccer stadium right next door. And the staff were so friendly; they were even friendlier than ordinary Turkish people.

The two authors of this book, Stefan Szymanski (a sports economist) and Simon Kuper (a journalist), met here. Fenerbahce soccer club was marking its centenary by staging the "100th Year Sports and Science Congress" and had flown us both in to give talks.

The two of us had never met before, but over beers in the Hilton bar we found that we thought much the same way about soccer. Stefan, an economist, has been trained to torture the data until they confess, and Simon, a journalist, tends to go around interviewing people, but those are just surface differences. We both think that much in soccer can be explained, even predicted, by studying data—especially data found outside soccer. We decided to write a book together.

When we began writing, Stefan lived in London and Simon in Paris, so we spent a year firing figures, arguments, and anecdotes back and forth across the English Channel. As we talked more and began to think harder about soccer and data, we buzzed around all sorts of questions. Why was soccer such a terrible business? Might the game somehow deter people from killing themselves? And are fans really monogamous?

Applying data to these questions felt like a new project. Until very recently, soccer had escaped the Enlightenment. Soccer clubs are still run mostly by men who do what they do because they have always done it that way. These men used to "know" that Black players "lacked bottle," and they therefore overpaid mediocre white players. Today they discriminate against Black managers, buy the wrong players, and then let those players take corners and penalties the wrong way. (We can, incidentally, explain why Manchester United won the penalty shoot-out in the Champions League final in 2008. It's a story involving a secret note, a Basque economist, and Edwin van der Sar's powers of detection.)

Entrepreneurs who dip into soccer also keep making the same mistakes. They buy clubs, promising to run them "like a business," and disappear a few seasons later amid the same public derision as the previous owners. Fans and journalists aren't blameless, either. Many media headlines rest on false premises: "Newcastle Lands World Cup Star" or "World Cup Will Be Economic Bonanza." The game is full of unexamined clichés: "Soccer is becoming boring because the big clubs always win," "Soccer is big business," or "The big money will turn fans off." None of these shibboleths have been tested against the data.

Most male team sports have long been pervaded by the same overreliance on traditional beliefs. Baseball, too, was until quite recently an old game stuffed with lore. Since time immemorial, players had stolen bases, hit sacrifice bunts, and been judged on their batting averages. Everyone in the sport just knew that all this was right.

But that was before Bill James came along. He hadn't done much in life beyond keeping the stats in the local children's baseball Little League in Kansas and watching the furnaces in a pork-and-beans factory. However, in his spare time he had begun to study baseball statistics with a fresh eye, and he discovered that "a great portion of the sport's traditional knowledge is ridiculous hokum." James wrote that he wanted to approach the subject of baseball "with the same kind of intellectual rigor and discipline that is routinely applied, by scientists great and poor, to trying to unravel the mysteries of the universe, of society, of the human mind, or of the price of burlap in Des Moines."

James told us that baseball set the trend for the global data revolution because the game's record keepers had begun gathering stats in the nineteenth century—before stats were gathered for almost any other human activity. James explained: "So when the computer revolution started 100 years later, we were ahead of the game. We had 100 years of really interesting data to play around with. So the analytical revolution hit in baseball before places where sensibly you would think it would hit."

In self-published mimeographs masquerading as books, the first of which sold seventy-five copies, James began demolishing the game's myths. He found, for instance, that an extremely telling statistic in batting was the rarely mentioned "on-base percentage"—how often a player manages to get on base. James and his followers (statisticians of baseball who came to be known as sabermetricians) showed that time-honored strategies like sacrifice bunts and base stealing didn't make any sense.

His annual Baseball Abstracts turned into real books; eventually, they reached the best-seller lists. One year the cover picture showed an ape, posed as Rodin's "Thinker," studying a baseball. As James wrote in one Abstract, "This is outside baseball. This is a book about what baseball looks like if you step back from it and study it intensely and minutely, but from a distance."

Some Jamesians started to penetrate professional baseball. One of them, Billy Beane, general manager of the little Oakland A's, is the hero of Michael Lewis's earth-moving book *Moneyball* and the film of the same name starring Brad Pitt. In recent years Beane, like so many Americans, has become a soccer nut. He has spent a lot of time thinking about how his insights into baseball might apply to soccer, and he now invests in multiple European teams. (We'll say more later about Beane's gaming of baseball's transfer market and its lessons for soccer.)

For several seasons, Beane's Oakland A's did so well using Jamesian ideas that eventually even people inside baseball began to get curious about James. In 2002 the Boston Red Sox, owned by the commodities trader John Henry, appointed him senior baseball operations adviser. That same year, the Red Sox hired one of James's followers, the twenty-eight-year-old Theo Epstein, as the youngest general manager in the history of the major leagues. (Beane had said yes and then no to the job.) The "cursed" club quickly won two World Series, the first since 1918, and another two in the following decade. Today, large statistical departments are the norm at Major League Baseball clubs, and Henry owns Liverpool FC as well as the Red Sox. Now soccer has embarked on its own Jamesian revolution.

A NUMBERS GAME

It's strange that soccer always used to be so averse to studying data, because one thing that attracts many fans to the game is precisely a love of numbers.

The man to ask about that is Alex Bellos. He wrote the magnificent *Futebol: The Brazilian Way of Life* but also several books about math. "Numbers are incredibly satisfying," Bellos tells us. "The world has no order, and math is a way of seeing it in an order. League tables have an order. And the calculations you need to do for them are so simple: it's nothing more than your three-times table."

Although most fans would probably deny it, a love of soccer is often intertwined with a love of numbers. There are the match results, the famous dates, and the special joy of sitting in a coffee shop with your phone in the morning "reading" the league table. Fantasy soccer leagues are, at bottom, numbers games.

In this book we want to introduce new numbers and new ideas to soccer: numbers on suicides, on wage spending, on countries' populations, on passes and sprints, on anything that helps to reveal new truths about the game. Although Stefan is a sports economist, this is not a book about money. The point of soccer clubs is not to turn a profit (which is fortunate, as few of them do), nor do we get particularly excited about any profits they happen to make. Rather, we want to use an economist's skills (plus a little geography, psychology, and sociology) to understand the game on the field and the fans off it.

Some people may not want their emotional relationship with soccer sullied by our rational calculations. On the other hand, the next time their team loses a penalty shoot-out at the World Cup, these same people will probably be throwing their beer bottles at the TV, when instead they could be tempering their disappointment with some reflections on the nature of binomial probability theory.

We think it's a good time to be rewriting this book. The amount of information available is expanding exponentially. In recent years the world has entered the era of "big data." The phrase describes the unprecedented mountain of information that is now collected every day. This information comes mostly from the internet (from innumerable search terms, social-media accounts, and emails) and from sensors that are attached to ever more physical objects—among them, soccer players during training sessions. We have much more data to help us understand events than human beings could gather using only their eyes and ears. Moreover, all these data can be stored and faithfully reproduced, without the annoying tendency that humans have to misremember or just plain forget. Artificial intelligence can identify patterns in data sets that would not be visible to a person "reading" the data. We believe that the data revolution enhances the capacity of humans to make good decisions. Note that we say *enhances*, not *replaces*. Cyborgs replacing humans is, for now, still science fiction. But humans can make better decisions if aided by data analysis.

That's true in soccer, too. For the first time in the game's history, there are a lot of numbers to mine. Traditionally, the only data that existed in the game were goals and league tables. (Newspapers published attendance figures, but these were unreliable.) In 1979, after Steve Daley became the first English player to be transferred for more than a million pounds, from Wolves to Manchester City (where he flopped), the British Treasury considered a tax on soccer transfers. The problem was that it couldn't find any reliable financial data on the topic. In the end, a young bureaucrat had to page through the Rothmans Football Yearbook to work out, more or less, how much clubs had spent on transfers the previous season.

Today the game is drowning in information. Data companies such as Opta can collect millions of observations (facts) about a single game. Clubs, which used to rely on gut alone, now use the new stats to analyze games and players. Every day, data analysts collect ever more information about every player's every move on the field, on the training ground, and even in bed—they know how well he slept last night.

Academics are pitching in as well. When Stefan went into sports economics, at the end of the 1980s, only about twenty or thirty academic articles on sports had ever been published. Now countless academics work on soccer. Many of the new truths they have found have not yet reached most fans. Much of what we argue in the book—for instance, that a club's wage bill is an excellent predictor of its league position—is taken from Stefan's academic work. Other insights come from his colleagues' work. Generally speaking, we are more confident of what we assert when it is backed up by research that we believe is credible: the methods are clear, the data is adequate, and the results are carefully explained and preferably peer-reviewed. You could still disagree with the work, but it has a solid foundation. Peer-reviewed academic research is, for us, the gold standard.

However, this book is more than just academic work rewritten for laypeople. Simon has been covering soccer as a journalist for over thirty years. He has met and interviewed many of the people who have shaped the modern game. This kind of knowledge is not always susceptible to formal statistical tests, but it is knowledge just the same. It informs our understanding of the sport. For instance, Simon came up with our theory of soccer networks: that Western Europe keeps winning World Cups because the countries of this little region are constantly exchanging know-how with one another. We have much less data for this theory than, say, for Stefan's insight that coaches have little impact on results. However, we think that the network theory is plausible—and Stefan has set his economist's brain to developing it. We think that our combination of data and experience is the best way to understand social activities.

Like Stefan, Simon has also drawn on the knowledge of his colleagues—the growing number of people who write soccer books. When Pete Davies published *All Played Out: The Full Story of Italia '90*, there were probably only about twenty or thirty good soccer books in existence in English. Now—thanks partly to Davies, who has been described as John the Baptist to Nick Hornby's Jesus—there are thousands in untold languages. Simon, in his office in Paris, has a library containing a large proportion of them. Many of these books contain truths about the game that we try to present here.

What has happened in soccer mirrors a trend across all sports. In 2009 Michael Lewis wrote: "The virus that infected professional baseball in the 1990s, the use of statistics to find new and better ways to value players and strategies, has found its way into every major sport. Not just basketball and [American gridiron] football, but also soccer and cricket and rugby and, for all I know, snooker and darts—each one now supports a subculture of smart people who view it not just as a game to be played but as a problem to be solved."

In soccer these smart men (it's still part of the game's own "ridiculous hokum" that they have to be men) have even begun taking key roles at some of Europe's biggest clubs. European soccer, professional on the field for over a century, is finally creaking into professionalism off the field, too. Given the global obsession with the game, there could come a time when some of the best and brightest young people are working in the front offices of soccer clubs. Already, the rising generation of club executives understands that in soccer today, you need data to get ahead. If you study figures, you will see more and win more.

One early harbinger of the Jamesian takeover of soccer was the Milan Lab. Soon after it began work, AC Milan's in-house medical outfit found that just by studying a player's jump, it could predict with 70 percent accuracy whether he would get injured soon. Later the Lab began testing, almost day by day, each player's muscle weaknesses, the movement of his eyes, the rise and fall of his heart rate, his breathing, and many other obvious and less obvious indicators. Jean-Pierre Meersseman, the Lab's cigarette-puffing director, was given a power of veto over the club's prospective signings. "The last signature on the contract before the big boss signs is mine," he told us in 2008. By 2013, the Lab had performed 1.2 million physical tests on Milan's players, collected millions of pieces of data on computers, logged even the slightest injury to every player, and in the process had stumbled upon the secret of eternal youth.

Most of Milan's starting eleven who beat Liverpool in the Champions League final of 2007 were thirty-one or older: Paolo Maldini, the captain, was thirty-eight, and Filippo Inzaghi, scorer of both of Milan's goals, was thirty-three. (After the final whistle, Inzaghi still had enough juice to kick a ball around on the field for fun.) In large part, that trophy was won by the Milan Lab and its database. It is another version of the March of the Geeks story. AC Milan later reduced the Lab's funding and power. However, other big clubs all over Europe now lead the data-driven quests to reduce injuries and to predict which twelve-year-old will grow up to be the next Erling Haaland. Meersseman says that data-driven scientists seem to be better than experienced youth coaches at making those predictions: "In soccer, they say, 'You know about football or you don't.' And when you go and test the ones who 'know,' it's surprising how little they know. It's based on the emotion of the moment."

What started in Istanbul in 2007 as a book idea has turned into a long-term collaboration. These days our contact is transatlantic: Simon is still mostly in Paris, but Stefan is now at the University of Michigan. And we have kept rewriting and updating this book. It has sold well over 250,000 copies in more than two dozen languages. We've had the chance to influence the opinions of lots of people, some of whom work in the game.

All the while, we have continued to distrust every bit of the game's ancient lore, and we have tested it against the numbers. As Meersseman says, "You can drive a car without a dashboard, without any information, and that's what's happening in soccer. There are excellent drivers, excellent cars, but if you have your dashboard, it makes it just a little bit easier. I wonder why people don't want more information."

We do.

PART I
The Clubs

---

*Racism, Stupidity, Bad Transfers, Capital Cities,
the Leicester Fairy Tale, and What Actually Happened
in That Penalty Shoot-Out in Moscow*

2

GENTLEMEN PREFER BLONDS

How to Avoid Silly Mistakes in the Transfer Market

In 1983 AC Milan spotted a talented young Black forward playing for Watford, just outside London. The word is that the player the Italians liked was actually John Barnes, but they confused him with his Black teammate Luther Blissett. Whatever the truth, Milan ended up paying Watford a "transfer fee" of £1 million (then about $1.5 million) for Blissett.

As a player, Blissett became such a joke in Italy that the name "Luther Blissett" is now used as a pseudonym by groups of anarchist writers. He spent one unhappy year in Milan before the club sold him back to Watford for just over half the sum it had paid for him. At least that year gave soccer one of its best quotes: "No matter how much money you have here," Blissett lamented, "you can't seem to get Rice Krispies." More on the beloved breakfast cereal later.

In the decade through summer 2021, clubs spent a total of $48.5 billion on international transfers, reported FIFA. The sum includes the world-record fee of $263 million that Paris Saint-Germain paid Barcelona for Neymar in 2017.*

---

* A note about currencies: almost always in this book we have cited sums of money in dollars. When converting from pounds or other currencies, we have used the dollar equivalent at the time the sum was spent. (A British pound bought more US dollars in 2011 than in 2022, for instance.)

We want to say right at the start of this chapter that the transfer system is evil. It's essentially a system of human trafficking that gives many people the power to control where a player works. Imagine for a moment that this applied to your own career. Imagine that if you wanted to change jobs, your employer could stop you from moving for up to three years. In the meantime, the employer could threaten to make you do a job well below your qualifications, which could make your skills atrophy. These are the conditions under which soccer players work.

The transfer system allows employers to extort a fee for letting soccer players move. That doesn't happen in any other industry we know of. When a player changes clubs, his agent and club manager (and who knows who else besides?) might dip their paws into the deal. The money that these criminals siphon out of the game is money that ought to go to the employee. And if the player's interests clash with theirs, he risks being mentally or physically abused. Workplace harassment is inevitable in a system that treats players as tradeable commodities.

The way to end these horrors is to close down the transfer system. In 2015 FIFPro, the international players' trade union, asked the European Competition Authority to do exactly that.

Some people will retort that making every player a free agent every season of his career would only serve to make multimillionaires even richer. But, in fact, most players aren't rich. A majority of FIFPro members earn less than $65,000. Many earn much less. So don't think of Messi or Kylian Mbappé, but of struggling family breadwinners in the US or Croatia with short careers.

Some fans fear that their clubs would collapse without income from transfers. However, the reality is that a large fraction of the money simply circulates among the big clubs, as Stefan pointed out in a study commissioned by FIFPro to support its case.

If the transfer system is abolished, there will be far fewer opportunities for stealing. True, if all players become free agents, some will move even more often than they do already. However, others will prefer the stability of staying with the same club as long as they are fairly treated. No longer will agents and managers have an incentive to move players in order to make some illegal cash.

The transfer system seems necessary to most people because it is familiar, and abolishing it seems like a step in the dark. We don't think abolition is nearly as risky as it sounds, but that is beside the point. Soccer's system of "buying" and "selling" players is unjust.

But for now, it exists. And our focus in this chapter is on its inefficiency—how badly most clubs buy and sell, and how they could make better decisions. Much of the money thrown around in the transfer market is wasted. In fact, the net amount that almost any club spends on transfer fees bears little relation to where it finishes in the league.

This conclusion is based on data, which we've been updating with every edition of *Soccernomics*. In the first edition we looked at the spending of forty English clubs between 1978 and 1997. For this edition we looked at the transfer spending of clubs in the English Premier League and Championship between 2011 and 2020. We rely on the published, independently audited financial statements of the clubs to measure net spending on transfer fees. Technically, net spending is identified as "additions to intangible fixed assets" less "book value of disposals of intangible fixed assets" and "profit on sale of player registrations." (The player registrations are the intangible fixed assets—i.e., the contracts that tether a player to the club.)

In other words, we don't rely on the figures quoted in the media. That's because there is a lot of hype in soccer, as in any sport, and you can't really be sure where that information comes from. Audited financial statements are much more reliable. Skeptics will say that the clubs could misrepresent the data to the auditors or even that auditors might lie (which has been known to happen, even though it's a criminal offense). But since the introduction of UEFA's Financial Fair Play Regulations in 2011, big clubs also have to supply their transfer data to UEFA's regulatory body, which can bring in its own independent auditors to review the data and sanction clubs that engage in deception. All in all, the financial statements are the best source of financial information about soccer clubs.

Of course, when a player is acquired via a transfer, the hope is that he will perform for the club over a period of years, so the net spending in any one year will bear little relationship to success in that year. But if you average success over a decade (measured by average league position), and average net transfer spending over a decade, then any long-term relationship should be detectable. What we find is that net transfer spending explains very little of the total variation in league position. The correlation, such as it is, merely reflects that big clubs tend to be bigger net spenders than small clubs. Beyond that, transfer spending doesn't tell you much.

By contrast, clubs' spending on salaries is extremely telling. The size of their wage bills explained a massive 92 percent of variation in their league positions back in 1978–1997, and we show almost exactly the same result below using data for the Premier League and the Championship (the second tier of English soccer) for the decade through 2020. See Figure 2.1 and Table 2.1. In that period, wage spending explained more than 90 percent of the variation in league position.

Obviously, we don't believe that if you took a random bunch of players and doubled their salaries, they would suddenly play twice as well. It's not that high pay *causes* good performance. Rather, we think that high pay *attracts* good performers. Manchester City can afford to pay Kevin De Bruyne's wages, whereas little Burnley cannot. And if you have De Bruyne and other good players, you will win matches. Rich clubs pay high salaries to get the best players.

In short, wage spending is a much better predictor of success than transfer spending. But what, you might argue, if you added net transfer spending to wage spending? Wouldn't that help you explain a bit more of the variation? It turns out that the answer is no. Anything that net transfer spending can explain is already captured by wage spending.

There's an important point we'll come back to later: talk to clubs, and they'll tell you that if a player's performance improves (let's say he stars in the Champions League), the club will preemptively increase his wages to limit his incentive to seek a transfer. That helps explain why wages are such a reliable indicator of quality: new information about ability is incorporated quickly into wages. (There is a similar effect in share prices in the stock markets.) But these wage rises also explain why it's so hard to profit from player trading. Even if you really have spotted a quality in a player that everyone else missed, one senior analyst from a big club told us ruefully, you'll soon have to pay more when the world discovers you were right. Of course, it doesn't work the other way around: if a player performs worse than expected, the club doesn't get to cut the contracted wage. True, players do get paid bonuses linked to performance, but these make up a small percentage of total pay.

FIGURE 2.1. Premier League and Championship teams 2011–2020: performance and wage expenditure

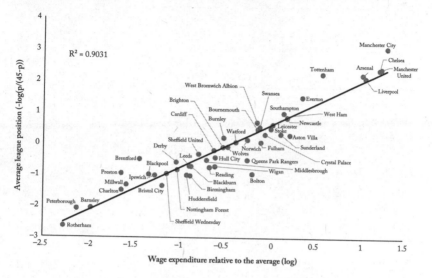

To sum up: wages buy success (something Stefan has been banging on about since his first published article on soccer, in 1991). We have yet to see anyone produce a credible alternative theory. Did Manchester City or Roman Abramovich's Chelsea hire great managers who won titles but then also decided out of the goodness of the owners' hearts to pay the players exorbitant wages? No, they had to hire players whose pay predicted their ability to win games.

True, some players are paid either more or less than they are worth. In fact, it's an agent's job to persuade clubs to pay excessive salaries. The former Dutch defender Rody Turpijn has written up a lovely vignette showing how this works. In 1998 the young Turpijn's career at Ajax Amsterdam was falling apart. The player had just one big thing going for him: he was represented by Mino Raiola, a chubby little Dutch-Italian former pizza restaurateur who was becoming one of Europe's most powerful agents.

Raiola and Turpijn drove to a motorway hotel (classic venue of soccer deals) to meet the chairman of the small Dutch club De Graafschap. Raiola kicked off by impressing the chairman with some gossip about Juventus's

TABLE 2.1. The more you pay your players, the higher you finish: 2011–2020

Club	Wage spending relative to the average	Average league position	Club	Wage spending relative to the average	Average league position
Manchester City	3.65	2	Sheffield United	0.46	26
Manchester United	3.44	4	Hull City	0.55	27
Chelsea	3.36	4	Brentford	0.24	28
Tottenham	1.78	4	Queens Park Rangers	0.78	28
Arsenal	2.80	4	Middlesbrough	0.50	28
Liverpool	2.88	5	Derby	0.36	29
Everton	1.43	8	Leeds	0.42	30
Southampton	1.16	12	Blackburn	0.42	30
Newcastle	1.21	13	Wigan	0.55	30
West Ham	1.21	14	Reading	0.52	31
West Bromwich Albion	0.86	15	Huddersfield	0.36	31
Leicester	1.03	16	Preston	0.20	32
Swansea	0.89	16	Bolton	0.82	32
Stoke	1.01	17	Sheffield Wednesday	0.32	33
Bournemouth	0.87	17	Blackpool	0.26	33
Sunderland	1.13	19	Nottingham Forest	0.40	33
Crystal Palace	0.94	19	Ipswich	0.28	33
Aston Villa	1.24	19	Birmingham	0.42	33
Burnley	0.60	20	Millwall	0.21	35
Norwich	0.78	21	Bristol City	0.31	36
Fulham	0.90	22	Charlton	0.20	37
Watford	0.69	22	Barnsley	0.14	40
Wolves	0.63	23	Peterborough	0.12	40
Brighton	0.60	24	Rotherham	0.10	42
Cardiff	0.54	25			

Pavel Nedved. Then the chairman wrote on a piece of paper the salary he was offering Turpijn. It was more than Turpijn earned at Ajax.

But to Turpijn's surprise, Raiola shouted: "Do you know what he earns at Ajax? This isn't a serious offer! Come, Rody, we're not going to waste our time on this." Raiola stood up as if to walk out, so Turpijn hesitantly rose, too. The chairman anxiously persuaded them to sit down. Twenty minutes later, Raiola had negotiated a lucrative four-year contract. As Turpijn wrote years later in the Dutch literary magazine *Hard Gras*, that meeting secured his future "for just about the rest of my life."

So Turpijn was overpaid. However, the overpayment didn't last. Over his four years at De Graafschap, it became clear that he wasn't worth the salary. When his contract ended, the club let him go. Rather than joining another club at a lower and more rational wage, he retired from soccer at age twenty-five and happily went off to university. The salary market had corrected itself.

Conversely, in 2012 the teenage Paul Pogba was underpaid at Manchester United relative to what he could be earning at other clubs. Raiola, who represented him, too, went to Alex Ferguson to negotiate a higher salary. Raiola, who died in 2022, reconstructed the pay talks for us:

FERGUSON TO RAIOLA: I don't talk to you if the player is not here.
RAIOLA: Get the player out of the locker room and sit him here.
Enter Pogba.
FERGUSON TO POGBA: You don't want to sign this contract?
POGBA: We're not going to sign this contract under these conditions.
FERGUSON TO RAIOLA: You're a twat.
Raiola was unfazed, partly because he didn't know the word.
RAIOLA: This is an offer that my chihuahuas—I have two chihuahuas—
  don't sign.
FERGUSON: What do you think he needs to earn?
RAIOLA: Not that.
FERGUSON: You're a twat.

Ferguson's published verdict on Raiola: "I distrusted him from the moment I met him." Pogba left for Juventus, which paid him what he was worth. Once again, the salary market had corrected itself—but in this case upward rather than downward.

And so, over the long run most soccer players earn what they deserve, at least measured by their contribution to winning matches. (If you measured their contribution to society, you would probably end up with very different salaries, but that's true of almost every profession from bond trader to nurse.) Generally, a player's salary is a good gauge of his ability to play soccer. The same is true at a team level: the higher the total wage bill, the better the squad, and the higher the team will finish in the league.

At this point the reader may be jumping up and down and shouting, "But what about Leicester?" In 2016 the club defied odds of five thousand to one against (for the handful of punters who bet on this outcome preseason) to win the only English title of its 132-year history, despite having the Premier League's fifteenth-highest wage bill. To find a comparable achievement, you would need to go back to Brian Clough and Peter Taylor's triumphs with Derby County in 1972 and Nottingham Forest in 1978.

The popular theory of Leicester's title at the time was that it was mostly down to the coach, Claudio Ranieri, who had supposedly instilled the players with the self-belief and will to win but was too modest to claim any credit. We would instead identify two main causes of Leicester's victory: 1. A very good goalkeeper and defense. 2. Luck.

Let's start with luck. Leicester won the title without performing exceptionally. The team's goal difference that season was plus thirty-two (scored sixty-eight goals, conceded thirty-two). On average over the previous ten seasons, the English champions had a goal difference of plus fifty-three. Only one champion in the previous thirty-nine years had scored fewer goals than Leicester: Manchester United in 1992–1993, with sixty-seven goals.

So Leicester didn't perform as well as the typical champion. The team's goals for and goals against were both two standard deviations better than its expected performance, which is a fancy way of saying much better than expected but not amazing. Nobody might have noticed Leicester except for another random event: all the usual title contenders had bad seasons simultaneously. That allowed an overachieving mid-table team to end up champion. It's reasonable to expect an outcome like that once every fifty years or so. Leicester's triumph was an extreme random event. These things happen. In a single season the correlation between salaries and league position is weaker than over the long term. That's because in such a short period, luck plays a big role in performance. Injuries, dodgy referees, poor form, and any host of other factors cause big swings in performance from year to year. For any one given season, clubs' wage spending explains only about 70 percent of the variation in league position.[1] In the short term, a team can therefore get a big lift from luck.

Yet the human mind tends to resist the notion of luck, of stuff just happening. Even Einstein said, "God does not play dice with the universe." Instead, most people like to seek explanations in human actions: Ranieri suddenly reveals himself as a genius.

We are not denying that Leicester played remarkably well that season. Patrick Lucey, of the data science company STATS in Chicago, has written a paper pinpointing exactly why. He says that while Leicester's attacking stats were unexceptional, the team "had by far the most effective defense." In fact, its defensive numbers were the best of any club in the previous five Premier League seasons. STATS calculates that the keeper, Kaspar Schmeichel, saved about 4.6 goals more than expected over the season—better than any other keeper in the division except Watford's Heurelho Gomes. (It seems that the richest English clubs had been missing some tricks on the goalkeepers' transfer market.) Meanwhile, Leicester's defense did a very good job of forcing opponents to try difficult passes from wide areas. And Leicester had a couple of excellent pass interceptors. STATS ranked Manchester City's Nicolas Otamendi first in the league for improbable interceptions, but Leicester's Christian Fuchs was third and N'Golo Kanté fifth.

The little French midfielder Kanté was clearly crucial. As Steve Walsh, who was Leicester's assistant manager and chief scout, famously remarked, "People think we play with two in midfield, and I say 'No.' We play with Danny Drinkwater in the middle and we play with Kanté either side, giving us essentially 12 players on the pitch." The next season at Chelsea, Kanté ran more kilometers than any other player in the Premier League except Tottenham's Christian Eriksen. He won another league title and was voted England's Players' Player of the Year. In other words, excellent players win titles, and they rarely need managers to inspire them.

Leicester hasn't shocked the world again. The team just doesn't spend enough. True luck (i.e., statistical randomness) tends to even out over the years. So if you track each club's performance over a longer period—fifteen or twenty years, say—then salaries explain about 90 percent of the variation in league position. Leicester in 2015–2016 was an exception.

Simon's colleagues at the *Financial Times* ranked sixty-nine clubs from Europe's biggest leagues by how well they did relative to their wage bills from 2011 through 2015. Atlético Madrid emerged from the exercise as "Europe's 'smartest' spending club," and Everton, Spurs, and Southampton also excelled. Among the worst underachievers were Cesena, Queens Park Rangers, and the two Milan clubs. Real Madrid and Paris Saint-Germain also ranked in the *FT*'s bottom fifteen, largely as an effect of "the sheer size of their wage bills."

But on the whole, the market for players' wages is pretty efficient: the better a player, the more he earns. By comparison, as we will show in this chapter, the transfer market is inefficient. Much of the time, clubs buy the wrong players. Even now that they have brigades of international scouts, they still waste fortunes on flops like Blissett.

As a case study of bad transfer policy, let's take Liverpool from 1998 through 2010. The club's managers in this period, Gérard Houllier and Rafael Benitez, kept splashing out on big transfer fees, yet Liverpool hardly ever even threatened to win the league. Jamie Carragher, who played for Liverpool throughout these years, provides a dolefully comic commentary on some of the club's misguided signings in his excellent autobiography, *Carra*:

- "Sean Dundee was not a Liverpool footballer."
- "The signing I didn't rate was Sander Westerveld....I thought he was an average goalkeeper who seemed to think he was Gordon Banks."
- "What about Josemi? He struggled to find a teammate six yards away. Djimi Traore had the same weakness."
- "To be blunt, [Christian] Ziege couldn't defend."
- "The names El-Hadji Diouf and Salif Diao now make the legs of the toughest Liverpudlians shudder in fear....The first concern I had with Diouf is his pace. He didn't have any....Do you remember being at school and picking sides for a game of football? We do this at Liverpool for the five-a-sides. Diouf was 'last pick' within a few weeks."

- "'You paid ten million for him and no one wants him in their team,' I shouted to Gérard."
- "If Diouf was a disappointment, Diao was a catastrophe....But even he wasn't the worst arrival of this hideous summer [of 2002]. Houllier also signed Bruno Cheyrou."
- On the expensive French striker Djibril Cissé: "He was supposed to be a strong, physical target man who scored goals. He was neither one nor the other."
- "The greatest disappointment was Fernando Morientes....He was a yard off the pace."

When Benitez replaced Houllier in 2004, writes Carragher, the Spaniard encountered "a host of poor, overpaid players and expectations as great as ever." But the new man didn't do much better than his predecessor. Carragher's book is gentler with Benitez than with Houllier, presumably because the Spaniard was still his boss when he wrote it, but the waste of the Benitez years is remarkable. Most strikingly perhaps, in 2008 Benitez handed Tottenham Hotspur £20 million (then about $40 million) for the twenty-eight-year-old forward Robbie Keane. The much-touted fact that Keane was a lifelong Liverpool fan turned out not to help much. Six months after buying the player, Benitez decided that Keane wasn't the thing after all and shipped him back to Tottenham (which itself would soon regret buying him) at a loss of £8 million (then about $14 million). Virgin Trains took out newspaper advertisements that read "A Liverpool to London return faster than Robbie Keane."

For all the spending, most of Liverpool's best performers during the Houllier-Benitez years were homegrown players who had cost the club nothing: Steven Gerrard, Michael Owen, and Carragher himself. Another stalwart for a decade, center back Sami Hyppiä, had come for only $4.1 million from little Willem II in the Netherlands. In short, there didn't seem to be much correlation between transfer spending and quality.

In October 2009, after Benitez's sixth and last summer masterminding Liverpool's transfers, Britain's *Sunday Times* newspaper calculated the damage. It found that in those six years at Anfield, Benitez had spent £122 million (about $220 million) more than he had received in transfer fees. Alex Ferguson's net spend at Manchester United in the same period was only £27 million ($49 million), yet in those years United had won three titles to Liverpool's none. Arsène Wenger at Arsenal had actually received £27 million ($49 million) more in transfer fees than he had spent during the period, the newspaper estimated. From 2005 through 2009, Benitez had outspent even Chelsea on transfers. Yet at the end of this period he had the nerve to complain, "It is always difficult to compete in the Premier League with clubs who have more money." Ferguson later commented that he hadn't been able to see any "strategy" in Benitez's buying. "It amazed me that he used to walk into press conferences and say he had no money to spend," Ferguson wrote in his 2013 autobiography. "He was given plenty. It was the quality of his buys that let him down. If you set aside Torres and Reina, few of his acquisitions were of true Liverpool standard. There were serviceable players—Mascherano and Kuyt, hard-working players—but not real Liverpool quality." (Mind you, with hindsight, Ferguson's assessment of Mascherano wasn't perfectly judged either.)

Benitez's failure at Liverpool was partially disguised by one night in Istanbul: the victory in the Champions League final of 2005, after having been 3–0 down to Milan after forty-five minutes. However, as we'll discuss later in the book, a large chunk of luck is involved in winning knockout competitions—even leaving aside the fact that Benitez got his tactics wrong going into the game and had to turn his team upside down at halftime. The most reliable gauge of a team's quality is its performance in the league, and here Houllier and Benitez failed. Their expensive transfers didn't bring commensurate results. If you add in agents' fees, taxes on transfers, and the constant disruption to the team, all this wheeling and dealing helps explain how Liverpool got left behind by Manchester United. To quote Carragher, "As I know to my cost at Anfield, having money is no guarantee of success. The skill is spending it on the right players."

The question, then, is what clubs can do to improve their status. If you are a club owner who has this knowledge of the relative importance of wages and unimportance of transfers, how can you win more matches? The obvious answer is to spend less of your income on transfers and more of it on wages. In general, it may be better to raise the pay of your leading players than to risk losing a couple of them and have to go out and buy replacements. Benitez had a net transfer spend of minus $220 million in six years. If he had merely balanced his transfer budget in that period, let alone made a profit as Wenger did, he could have raised his team's salaries by $36 million a year. In the 2008–2009 season, that boost would have given Liverpool a slightly larger wage bill than Manchester United. United won the title that year.

Big clubs that repeatedly make bad transfers can undo the advantages of their high wage bills. As we said, net transfer spending is in general a bad predictor of results, and one way this shows up is in the under-performance of some teams that are big spenders in the transfer market. Table 2.2 shows the transfer spending of the "big six" English clubs over the decade 2012–2021, based on the transfer data in the financial statements.

The last two columns of the table are the most telling ones. They measure net spending per year—i.e., how much each club spent on transfer fees minus how much it received for selling players. Manchester United spent $122 million per year (net) in the transfer market, close to Manchester City's $140 million average, but managed a league position of only 3.8, compared with City's 1.8 average—equivalent to a gap of two

TABLE 2.2. Average annual transfer spending of the Premier League "big six," 2012–2021

Club	Transfer spending (in USD millions*)	Transfer revenue**	Average net spending	Average league position
Tottenham	95	61	34	4.5
Liverpool	135	64	70	4.5
Arsenal	133	54	79	4.8
Chelsea	202	107	94	4
Manchester United	180	58	122	3.8
Manchester City	207	67	140	1.8

*Converted at £1 = $1.30.

**Book value of disposals of intangible fixed assets plus profits on disposals.

league places in every season. In the eight seasons after Alex Ferguson's departure, from 2014 through 2021, all that spending—together with one of the highest wage bills—bought United just one second-place finish in the Premier League and seven finishes below that. In that period the club never got beyond the quarterfinals of the Champions League. In particular, the purchase of Pogba in 2016 from Juventus for a then world-record fee of £89 million never quite panned out.

Chelsea did as well as United while spending substantially less, whereas Arsenal and Liverpool all look rather similar. This may be changing—if we averaged over the last five years, Liverpool would look much better and Arsenal much worse—but short-term averaging has a tendency to be misleading. What does stand out is the remarkable economy of Tottenham, retaining a consistent place in the Big Six while spending well below its rivals in the transfer market.

Soccer clubs need to make fewer transfers; they buy too many Dioufs. But they will keep buying players, and the transfer market is probably the area in which clubs can most easily improve their performance. They need to learn from the few clubs and managers who have worked out some of the secrets of the transfer market.

Any inefficient market is an opportunity for somebody. If most clubs are wasting most of their transfer money, then a club that spends wisely is going to outperform. Indeed, a handful of wise buyers have consistently outperformed the transfer market: Brian Clough and his assistant-cum-soul mate Peter Taylor in their years at Nottingham Forest, Wenger during his first decade at Arsenal, and, most mysteriously of all, Olympique Lyon, which rose from an obscure provincial club to a period of dictatorial rule over French soccer. From 2002 through 2008, Lyon won the French league seven times running. That era is now over, and the club subsequently made mistakes as it tried and failed to compete with clubs with much higher revenues, such as Real Madrid and Manchester United. Lyon got tempted into paying big transfer fees for supposed "stars"—for instance, gambling $28 million in 2010 on the slow playmaker Yoann Gourcuff. It is now following a new strategy focused on youth development. However, its seven-year reign remains an extraordinary feat. The usual way to win things in soccer is to pay high salaries. These clubs found a different route: they worked out the secrets of the transfer market.

There is a fourth master of the transfer market who is worth a look, even if he works in a mostly different sport across an ocean: Billy Beane, general manager of the Oakland A's baseball team. In *Moneyball*, Michael Lewis explains how Beane for some years turned one of the worst teams in baseball into one of the best by the simple method of rejecting what everyone in the sport had always "known" to be true about trading for players: "Understanding that he would never have a Yankee-sized checkbook, Beane had set about looking for inefficiencies in the game." It's odd how many of the same inefficiencies exist in soccer.

MARKET INCOMPETENCE

If we study these masters of transfers, it will help us uncover the secrets of the market that all the other clubs are missing. First of all, though, we present a few of the most obvious inefficiencies in the market. Although it doesn't take a Clough or a Beane to identify these, they continue to exist.

A New Manager Wastes Money

Typically, the new manager wants to put his mark on his new team. So he buys his own players. He then has to "clear out" some of his predecessor's purchases, usually at a discount.

Strangely, it's Tottenham—during its years under a famously tightfisted chairman, Alan Sugar—that provides the worst example. In May 2000 the club's manager, George Graham, paid Dynamo Kiev $16.5 million—nearly twice Spurs's previous record fee—for the Ukrainian striker Sergei Rebrov. Clearly, Rebrov was meant to be a long-term investment. But nine months later, Sugar sold his stake in Tottenham, whereupon the new owners sacked Graham and replaced him with Glenn Hoddle. Hoddle didn't appreciate Rebrov. The record signing ended up on the bench, was sent on loan to a Turkish team, and in 2004 moved to West Ham on a free transfer.

This form of waste is common across soccer: a new manager is allowed to buy and sell on the pretense that he is reshaping the club for many years to come, even though in practice he almost always leaves pretty rapidly. A terrible example was Paolo di Canio at Sunderland in 2013: in the six months and thirteen games that he managed the club, he spent about $30 million on transfers, brought in fourteen players, and let fifteen leave. When he was sacked, he left his successor, Gus Poyet, a team in last place in the Premier League. Tony Fernandes, the Queens Park Rangers chairman who spent a net $65 million on transfer fees while getting relegated from the Premier League in 2012–2013, told us mournfully, "Sunderland's going through, in some ways, what we went through. The manager comes in, he changes everyone, and Gus Poyet is already saying, 'I want to control the transfer budget.' If you change a manager, I don't care who they are, they're going to have a different opinion, right? Mark Hughes liked a certain player; Harry [Redknapp] doesn't like a certain player."

But why couldn't a chairman just say no to a shopaholic new manager? "You yourself see the results," replied Fernandes, "and you think, 'God, we need some change.'"

A manager typically doesn't care how much his wheeler-dealing costs: he doesn't get a bonus if the club makes a profit. As Billy Beane told us, "When you think of the structure of most sports teams, there is no benefit to a head coach in the National Football League or a soccer manager to think years ahead. The person who has access to the greatest expenditure in the business has no risk in the decision making." He added that the exception to this rule was Wenger. Beane said, "When I think of Arsène Wenger, I think of Warren Buffett [the billionaire investor]. Wenger runs his football club like he is going to own the club for one hundred years."

Stars of Recent World Cups, or European Championships, Are Overvalued

The worst time to buy a player is in the summer when he's just done well at a big tournament. Everyone in the transfer market has seen how good the player is, but he is exhausted and quite likely sated with success. As Ferguson admitted after retiring from United, "I was always wary of buying players on the back of good tournament performances. I did it at the 1996 European Championship, which prompted me to move for Jordi Cruyff and Karel Poborský. Both had excellent runs in that tournament, but I didn't receive the kind of value their countries did that summer.

They weren't bad buys, but sometimes players get themselves motivated and prepared for World Cups and European Championships and after that there can be a levelling off."

Moreover, if you buy a player because of a good tournament, you are judging him on a very small sample of games. Take, for instance, Arsenal's purchase of the Danish midfielder John Jensen in July 1992. The previous month, Jensen had scored a cracking long-range goal in the European Championship final against Germany. Arsenal's then manager, George Graham, told the British media that Jensen was a goal-scoring midfielder.

But he wasn't. The goal against Germany had been a one-off. Jensen would go years without scoring for Arsenal. Over time, this failing actually turned him into a cult hero: whenever he got the ball, even in his own penalty area, the crowd at Highbury would joyously shout, "Shoot!" By the time Jensen left Arsenal in 1996, he had scored one goal in four years. (Arsenal fans printed T-shirts that said, "I was there when John Jensen scored.") Graham's mistake had been to extrapolate from that single famous goal against Germany. This is an example of the so-called availability heuristic: the more available a piece of information is to the memory, the more likely it is to influence your decision, even when the information is irrelevant. Signing these shooting stars fits what *Moneyball* calls "a tendency to be overly influenced by a guy's most recent performance: what he did last was not necessarily what he would do next."

Real Madrid was for many years the supreme consumer of shooting stars (think of James Rodríguez). This is largely because the club's fans demanded it. Madrid probably wasn't even trying to be rational in the transfer market. The club's aim was not to buy the best results for as little money as possible. When it bought James for possibly as much as $103 million in 2014, it may well have suspected it was paying more for him than the benefit it was likely to get in results or higher revenues. But big signings of this type (like Newcastle buying fragile Michael Owen from Madrid for $30 million in 2005) are best understood as marketing gifts to a club's fans, its sponsors, and the local media, which need something to write about during the three-month summer break. As Ferguson explained Real's purchase of Cristiano Ronaldo in 2009, "Madrid paid £80 million [$131.5 million] in cash for him, and do you know why? It was a way for Florentino Pérez, their president, to say to the world, 'We are Real Madrid, we are the biggest of the lot.'"

In 2013 Madrid's purchase of Gareth Bale for $132 million made the same statement. Probably nobody at Madrid believed that the Welshman was twice as good a player as Mesut Özil—sold to Arsenal for half Bale's transfer fee—but he was deliciously new. His record fee and outsized salary only enhanced his glamour. There was a high risk that the money paid would not bring commensurate reward, but Madrid probably didn't care very much. The club is not a business. It's a populist democracy. Few soccer clubs pursue bean-counting quests for return on investment.

Raiola, the agent, was so wary of Real's tendency to buy a player just for his name that in 2016 he advised Pogba not to move there. Real Madrid had just won the Champions League, and Raiola realized that although the club was keen to sign the Frenchman, it didn't actually need him: "Another player for the cabinet. A trophy player, I call it." By contrast, United needed Pogba—or thought it did. As we have noted, he was never as good at United as he had been at Juve.

Buying a big name (even if you don't need him) makes every person in the club feel bigger. Christoph Biermann, in his pioneering German book on soccer and data, *Die Fussball-Matrix*, cites the president of a Bundesliga club who said his coach got very excited whenever the club paid a large transfer fee. Biermann explains: "For this coach it was a status symbol to be allowed to buy players who cost many millions of euros. My car, my house, my star signing!" In short, it's conspicuous consumption. The very pointlessness of the purchase emphasizes that the purchaser is a prestigious high roller who can afford to waste money.

Buying names also gives supporters the thrill of expectation, a sense that their club is going somewhere, which may be as much fun as actually winning things. Buying big names is how these clubs keep their customers satisfied during the summer shutdown. (And some managers buy players to make themselves some illicit cash on the side, as George Graham did when he signed Jensen, but that's another story.)

Yet it turns out that the superstar isn't necessarily the player who has the biggest impact on a team's performance. (Note that Spurs didn't obviously suffer from losing Bale.) Nor, on the other hand, is the team's weakest link the decisive player. Chris Anderson and David Sally argue in their book *The Numbers Game* that the best way to improve a team is to replace the worst player. But when Stefan and his University of Michigan colleague Guy Wilkinson looked at which players in the team had the biggest impact on results, they found it was neither the best nor the worst. Instead, it was the transfer fee of the *second*-best player that was most decisive. Here, they argue, is the best way to allocate a club's transfer budget across the eleven starters:

Best-paid player: 25.76 percent
Number two: 25.76 percent
Three: 18.41 percent
Four: 9.80 percent
Five: 9.80 percent
Six: 9.80 percent
Seven: 0.14 percent
Eight: 0.14 percent
Nine: 0.14 percent
Ten: 0.14 percent
Eleven: 0.14 percent

In other words, they found it would make sense for a club to spend almost nothing on its five cheapest players—who have very little impact on results—and instead to devote about 70 percent of the budget to the three best players. But, in fact, clubs don't do this. Clubs in the Premier League in 2012–2013 typically spent more than 1 percent of the budget even on the team's cheapest player and about 8 percent on the seventh player. In short, they spread the money around more equally than they should. This might be because they think that massive differences in status within a team could unsettle the locker room. It might be because they want to keep some good players in reserve in case the best get injured. Or perhaps there just aren't enough stars in the sport to go around, especially not for smaller clubs, so relatively little money is spent on the top players. Still, we think an innovative club could do well by concentrating its budget upward. Chris Anderson recently added an interesting nuance, saying that rather than target scarce superstars, clubs should try to assemble productive combinations of two, three, or four players. "Who plays well with whom?"

Certain Nationalities Are Overvalued

Clubs will pay more for a player from a "fashionable" soccer country. American goalkeeper Kasey Keller says that in the transfer market, it's good to be Dutch. "Giovanni van Bronckhorst is the best example," Keller told Christoph Biermann. "He went from Rangers to Arsenal, failed there, and then where did he go? To Barcelona! You have to be a Dutchman to do that. An American would have been sent straight back to DC United."

For decades the most fashionable nationality in the transfer market was Brazilian. As Alex Bellos writes in *Futebol: The Brazilian Way of Life*, "'The phrase 'Brazilian soccer player' is like the phrases 'French chef' or 'Tibetan monk.' The nationality expresses an authority, an innate vocation for the job—whatever the natural ability." A Brazilian agent who had exported very humble Brazilian players to the Faroe Islands and Iceland told Bellos, "It's sad to say, but it is much easier selling, for example, a crap Brazilian than a brilliant Mexican. The Brazilian gets across the image of happiness, party, carnival. Irrespective of talent, it is very seductive to have a Brazilian in your team."

That sentiment was dented by the 1–7 loss in the semifinal at Belo Horizonte in 2014. In recent years, Belgians have been coming into fashion, and after the 2014 World Cup, Costa Ricans suddenly became the hot new items in every self-respecting club's wardrobe. After the little country got within a penalty shoot-out of reaching the semifinal, the total value of transfer fees for Costa Rican players moving internationally rose from $922,000 in 2013 to almost $10 million in 2014, reported FIFA TMS, the department of FIFA that oversees international transfers.

A wise club will buy unfashionable nationalities—Bolivians, say, or Belorussians—at discounts.

Gentlemen Prefer Blonds

One big English club noticed that its scouts who watched youth matches often came back recommending blond players. The likely reason: when you are scanning a field of twenty-two similar-looking players, none of whom yet has a giant reputation, the blonds tend to stand out (except, presumably, in Scandinavia). The color catches the eye. So the scout notices the blond boy without understanding why. The club in question began to take this distortion into account when judging scouting reports. We suspect the bias toward blonds disappears when scouts are assessing adult players who already have established reputations. Then the player's reputation—"World Cup hero," say, or perhaps "Costa Rican"—guides the scout's judgment.

Similarly, Beane at the Oakland A's noticed that baseball scouts had all sorts of "sight-based prejudices." They were suspicious of fat guys or skinny little guys or "short right-handed pitchers," and they overvalued handsome, strapping athletes of the type that Beane himself had been at age seventeen. Scouts look for players who look the part. Perhaps in soccer, blonds are thought to look more like superstars. (A converse example is the Mohawk. When Ole Gunnar Solskjaer was still coaching Molde in Norway, he once abandoned a scouting trip after seeing that the player he had come to watch was sporting one. Solskjaer later recalled, "I just said to my scout: 'Let's go home, not interested.' That was a very short scouting trip." It was also very short-sighted one—Solskjaer's visual prejudice might have alerted Manchester United to his mediocrity as a manager.)

This taste for blonds is another instance of the "availability heuristic": the piece of information is available, so it influences your decision. Blonds stick in the memory.

The inefficiencies we have cited thus far are so-called systemic failures: more than just individual mistakes, they are deviations from rationality. There is now a mountain of research by psychologists showing that even when people try to act rationally, they are prone to all sorts of cognitive biases that lead them astray. If decision makers in soccer clubs are aware of these biases, they stand a better chance of avoiding them. All this is what you might call Transfer Market 101. To learn more about how to play the market, we need to study the masters.

Drunks, Gamblers, and Bargains: Clough and Taylor at Forest

Probably nobody in English soccer has ever done a better job of gaming the transfer market than Nottingham Forest's manager Brian Clough (or "Old Big Head," as he fondly called himself) and his assistant Peter Taylor. As manager of Forest from 1976 to 1993, Clough managed to turn the provincial club into European champions while turning a profit on the transfer market (and, as we'll see in the next chapter, making enough on deals to slip the odd illegal bonus into his own pocket on the side).

Clough and Taylor met while playing in a "Probables Versus Possibles" reserve game at Middlesbrough in 1955. They seem to have fallen in love at first sight. Pretty soon they were using their free time to travel around the North of England watching soccer and coaching children together. Taylor never became more than a journeyman keeper, but Clough scored the fastest two hundred goals ever notched in English soccer. However, at the age of twenty-seven he wrecked his right knee skidding on a frozen field on Boxing Day, 1962. Three years later, he phoned Taylor and said, "I've been offered the managership of Hartlepool, and I don't fancy it. But if you'll come, I'll consider it." He then immediately hung up. Taylor took the bait, although to get in he had to double as Hartlepool's medical department, running onto the field with the sponge on match days. It was the prelude to their legendary years together at Derby and Nottingham Forest.

David Peace's novel *The Damned United*—and Tom Hooper's film of it—are in large part the love story of Clough and Taylor. The men's wives have only walk-on parts. As in all good couples, each partner has an assigned role. As Peace's fictional Clough tells himself, "Peter has the eyes and the ears, but you have the stomach and the balls." Taylor found the players, and Clough led them to glory.

The relationship ended in "divorce" in 1982, with Taylor's resignation from Forest. It seems that the rift had opened two years before, when Taylor published his excellent but now forgotten memoir, *With Clough by Taylor*. More of this in a moment, because it is the closest thing we have to a handbook to the transfer market.

But clearly the couple had other problems besides literature. Perhaps Clough resented his partner because he needed him so badly—not the sort of relationship that Clough liked. Indeed, the film *The Damned United* depicts him failing at Leeds partly because Taylor is not there to scout players, and finally driving down to Brighton with his young sons to beg his partner's forgiveness. He finds Taylor doing the gardening. At Taylor's insistence, he gets down on his knees in the driveway and recites, "I'm nothing without you. Please, please, baby, take me back."

And Taylor takes him back and buys him the cut-price Forest team that wins two European Cups. Whatever their precise relationship, the duo certainly knew how to sign players. Here are a few of their coups:

- Buying Garry Birtles from the nonleague club Long Eaton for $3,500 in 1976 and selling him to Manchester United four years later for $2.9 million. A measure of what a good deal this was for Forest: United forked out about $500,000 more for Birtles than it would pay to sign Eric Cantona from Leeds twelve years later, in 1992. Birtles ended up costing United about $175,000 per goal and after two years was sold back to Forest for a quarter of the initial fee.
- Buying Roy Keane from an Irish club called Cobh Ramblers for $80,000 in 1990 and selling him to Manchester United three years later for $5.6 million, then a British record fee.
- Buying Kenny Burns from Birmingham City for $250,000 in 1977. Taylor writes in *With Clough by Taylor* that Burns was then regarded as "a fighting, hard-drinking gambler…a stone [fourteen pounds] overweight." In 1978 English soccer writers voted Burns the league's player of the year.
- Twice buying Archie Gemmill cheaply. In 1970, when Gemmill was playing for Preston, Clough drove to his house and asked him to come to Derby. Gemmill refused. Clough said that in that case, he would sleep outside in his car. Gemmill's wife invited him to sleep in the house instead. The next morning at breakfast, Clough persuaded Gemmill to sign. The fee was $145,000, and Gemmill quickly won two league titles at Derby. In 1977 Clough paid Derby $35,000 and the now-forgotten goalkeeper John Middleton to bring Gemmill to his new club, Forest, where the player won another league title.

If there was one club where almost every penny spent on transfers bought results, it was Forest under Clough. In the 1970s the correlation must have been off the charts: Forest won two European Cups with a team assembled largely for peanuts. Sadly, there are no good financial data for that period, but we do know that even from 1982 to 1992, in Clough's declining years after Taylor had left him, Forest performed as well on the field as clubs that were spending twice as much on wages. Clough had broken the usually iron link between salaries and league position.

Clough himself seemed to think that what explained Forest's success was his and Taylor's eye for players rather than, say, any motivational gift or tactical genius. As Phil Soar, the club's chairman and chief executive for four years at the end of the 1990s, emailed us, "In hours of musings with Clough (I had to try to defend him from the bung charges) I obviously asked him what made this almost absurdly irrelevant little provincial club (my hometown, of course) into a shooting star. And he always used to say, 'We had some pretty good players you know.'"

It's hard to identify all of Clough and Taylor's transfer secrets, and if their rivals at the time had understood what they were up to, everyone would have simply imitated them. Taylor's book makes it clear that he spent a lot of time trying to identify players (like Burns) whom others had wrongly undervalued because of surface characteristics, but then everyone tries to do that. Forest did sometimes splurge on a player who was rated by everybody, like Trevor Francis, the first "million-pound man," or Peter Shilton, whom it made the most expensive goalkeeper in British history.

Yet thanks to *With Clough by Taylor*, we can identify three of the duo's rules. First, be as eager to sell good players as to buy them. "It's as important in soccer as in the stock market to sell at the right time," wrote Taylor. "A manager should always be looking for signs of disintegration in a winning side and then sell the players responsible before their deterioration is noticed by possible buyers." (Or in Billy Beane's words, "You have to always be upgrading. Otherwise you're fucked.")

The moment when a player reaches the top of his particular hill is like the moment when the stock market peaks. Clough and Taylor were always trying to gauge that moment, and sell. Each time they signed a player, they would give him a set speech, which Taylor records in his book: "Son, the first time we can replace you with a better player, we'll do it without blinking an eyelid. That's what we're paid to do—to produce the best side and to win as many things as we can. If we see a better player than you but don't sign him then we're frauds. But we're not frauds." In 1981, just after Kenny Burns had won everything with Forest, the club offloaded him to Leeds for $800,000.

Second, older players are overrated. "I've noticed over the years how often Liverpool sell players as they near or pass their thirtieth birthday," notes Taylor in his book. "Bob Paisley [then Liverpool's manager] believes the average first division footballer is beginning to burn out at thirty." Taylor added, rather snottily, that that was true of a "running side like Liverpool" but less so of a passing one like Forest. Nonetheless, he agreed with the principle of selling older players.

The master of that trade for many years was Wenger. Arsenal's longtime manager was one of the few people in soccer who could view the game from the outside. In part, this was because he had a degree in economic sciences from the University of Strasbourg. As a trained economist, he was inclined to trust data rather than the game's received wisdom. Wenger understood that in the transfer market, clubs tend to overvalue a player's past performance. That prompts them to pay fortunes—in transfer fees and salaries—for players who have passed their prime. FIFA TMS analyzed the pay of players who moved internationally to Brazil, Argentina, England, Germany, Italy, and Portugal in 2012 and found, remarkably, that the average man earned his peak fixed salary at the ripe old age of thirty-two.

Seniority is a poor rationale for pay in soccer (and probably in other industries). All players are melting blocks of ice. The job of the club is to gauge how fast they are melting and to get rid of them before they turn into expensive puddles of water. Wenger often let defenders carry on until their midthirties, but he usually got rid of his midfielders and forwards much younger. He sold Patrick Vieira for $25 million at age twenty-nine, Thierry Henry for $30 million at twenty-nine, Emmanuel Petit for $10.5 million at twenty-nine, and Marc Overmars for $37 million at twenty-seven, and none of them ever did as well again after leaving Arsenal.

The average striker has peaked by age twenty-five, at least as measured by goals scored, as the French economist Bastien Drut has shown—think of Michael Owen, Robbie Fowler, Fernando Torres, and Patrick Kluivert. By contrast, Zlatan Ibrahimovic and Didier Drogba, who improved after their midtwenties, are exceptions, probably because they never relied much on pace in the first place. Yet many clubs still insist on paying for past performance. Forty percent of players bought by Premier League clubs from 2010 through 2016 were signed after passing their prime age, says Blake Wooster, chief executive of 21st Club, which advises soccer clubs. Manchester United's hiring on loan of the twenty-eight-year-old Colombian striker Radamel Falcao just after a severe injury in 2014 was an especially bad decision, as was Chelsea's repetition of United's mistake a year later. English clubs particularly overvalue Premier League experience, says Wooster—it just isn't that important. Ian Graham, Liverpool's powerful director of research, agrees.

The same overvaluation of older players exists in baseball. The conventional wisdom in the game had always been that players peak in their early thirties. Then along came Bill James from his small town in Kansas. In his mimeographs the father of sabermetrics showed that the average player peaked not in his early thirties but at just twenty-seven. Beane told us, "Nothing strangulates a sports club more than having older players on long contracts, because once they stop performing, they become immoveable. And as they become older, the risk of injury becomes exponential. It's less costly to bring a young player. If it doesn't work, you can go and find the next guy, and the next guy. The downside risk is lower, and the upside much higher."

Finally, Clough and Taylor's third rule: buy players with personal problems (like Burns, or the gambler Stan Bowles) at a discount. Then help them deal with their problems.

Clough, a drinker, and Taylor, a gambler, empathized with troubled players. While negotiating with a new player, they would ask him a stock question "to which we usually know the answer," wrote Taylor. It was "Let's hear your vice before you sign. Is it women, booze, drugs, or gambling?"

Clough and Taylor believed that once they knew the vice, they could help the player manage it. Clough was so confident of his psychological skills that in the early 1970s, he even thought he could handle Manchester United's alcoholic womanizing genius George Best. "I'd sort George out in a week," he boasted. "I'd hide the key to the drinks cabinet and I'd make sure he was tucked up with nothing stronger than cocoa for the first six months. Women? I'd let him home to see his mum and his sisters. No one else in a skirt is getting within a million miles of him."

Taylor says he told Bowles, who joined Forest in 1979 (and, as it happens, failed there), "Any problem in your private life must be brought to us; you may not like that but we'll prove to you that our way of management is good for all of us." After a player confided a problem, wrote Taylor, "if we couldn't find an answer, we would turn to experts: we have sought advice for our players from clergymen, doctors, and local councilors." Taking much the same approach, Wenger helped Tony Adams and Paul Merson combat their addictions.

All this might sound obvious, but the usual attitude in soccer is "We paid a lot of money for you; now get on with it," as if mental illness, addiction, or homesickness should not exist above a certain level of income.

It should be added that often the smartest actors in the transfer market are not managers at all but agents. Raiola told us that he tried to decide which club a player should join and then sometimes persuaded the club to make the move happen. In his words, "I always try to formulate a goal with a player: 'That is what we want. We're not going to sit and wait and see where the wind blows.'" For instance, in 2004, when his client Zlatan Ibrahimovic was a wayward young striker at Ajax, Raiola decided that the best place for him to learn professionalism (while earning good money) was Juventus. Juve may believe that it chose Zlatan, but that ain't necessarily so. In 2006 Raiola told his player that Juve's ship was sinking and it was time to join Inter. In 2009 he moved Ibrahimovic to Barcelona, then to Milan, and in 2012 (very much against the player's will) to Paris Saint-Germain. There the Swede earned €14 million (about $18.5 million) per season on a top-class team while underfunded Milan sank.

In 2016 Raiola brought Ibrahimovic, Pogba, and Henrik Mkhitaryan to Manchester United. Why join a club that hadn't qualified for the Champions League and had underperformed for three years? Raiola told us: "Because I think: you have to go to the club that needs you. This club needed them."

He claimed to have foreseen United's need as early as summer 2015, when the club signed the young forwards Anthony Martial and Memphis Depay. Raiola insisted he knew they wouldn't succeed. "Not if you have to perform *now*," he said, slapping a fat fist into a fat hand. "Martial and Depay come in and say, 'We have to carry Manchester United, a giant institution?' So already last year [2015] I told the people at United, 'You'll have to put in a guy like Zlatan to restore the balance. Then the attention goes to Zlatan. He has the experience, and he dares to take the responsibility.'"

Raiola continued: "At clubs that understand me, I have three or four players. Now at United, and before at Juventus, Milan, Paris Saint-Germain." In these cases, he said, he became a club's "in-house consultant." He then effectively shared a seat with the club's top management. No wonder that in 2017, Manchester United paid Everton $97 million for Raiola's client Romelu Lukaku—a move that didn't work out brilliantly, except perhaps for Raiola.

Meanwhile, one of the forwards being replaced by Ibrahimovic and Lukaku at United, Memphis Depay, needed a new club. Memphis, too, relied on his agent, the Dutchman Kees Ploegsma, to be proactive. Ploegsma set up a meeting at the player's mansion outside Manchester with Giels Brouwer, founder of the data company SciSports, reports Simon Zwartkruis in his biography of Memphis. The striker complained to Brouwer that United gave him too many defensive tasks, shrinking his freedom to attack. Brouwer then drew up a data profile not just of Memphis but of all left-sided strikers at big European clubs. He also assessed the tactics of each club's coach to see who would give Memphis the best opportunity to play his favorite game. (We have more later in the book on the growing role of analytics in the transfer market.)

Five clubs made Brouwer's shortlist: Milan, Valencia, Olympique Marseille, Schalke 04, and Olympique Lyon. The best match of all, writes Zwartkruis, was Lyon and its coach, Bruno Génésio. Happily, Lyon, with its characteristic eye for the suitable player, had already told Ploegsma that it was interested in Memphis. In January 2017 he moved to France, where he revived his career and eventually ended up joining Barcelona. The combination of agent, data analyst, and player had become an independent force in the transfer market.

Some readers may be surprised to hear us praise agents, who are always accused of breaking laws and sucking money out of the game. True, some of them are criminals (who often act in cahoots with clubs), but most agents get an unfair rap. We understand why clubs wish they didn't exist. A club would love to be able to tell a twenty-year-old player from a poor background who has never had any financial education, "Here's your contract, congratulations. Now run up and see the chief executive, and he'll tell you your salary." This sort of talk plays well with the fans, who like to think that players shouldn't care about money. However, soccer needs professional agents who will take a closer long-term interest in their players' well-being than any club ever will.

RELOCATION, RELOCATION, RELOCATION: THE RICE KRISPIES PROBLEM

Clough and Taylor understood that many transfers fail because of a player's problems off the field. In a surprising number of cases, these problems are the product of the transfer itself.

Moving to a job in another city is always stressful; moving to another country is even more so. The challenge of moving from Rio de Janeiro to Manchester involves cultural adjustments that just don't compare with moving from Springfield, Missouri, to Springfield, Ohio. An uprooted soccer player has to find a home and a new life for his family and gain some grasp of the social rules of his new country. Yet European clubs that pay tens of millions of dollars for foreign players are often unwilling to spend a few thousand more to help the players settle in their new homes. Instead, the clubs have historically told them, "Here's a plane ticket. Come over and play brilliantly from day one." The player fails to adjust to the new country, he underperforms, and his transfer fee is wasted. "Relocation," as the industry of relocation consultants calls it, has long been one of the biggest inefficiencies in the transfer market.

All the inefficiencies surrounding relocation can be assuaged. Most big businesses know how difficult relocation is and do their best to smooth the passage. When a senior Microsoft executive moves between countries, a relocation consultant helps his or her family find schools and a house and learn the social rules of the new country. If Luther Blissett had been working for Microsoft, a relocation consultant could have found him Rice Krispies. An expensive relocation might cost $25,000, or 0.1 percent of a large transfer fee. But in soccer, possibly the most globalized industry of all, spending anything at all on relocation was until very recently regarded as a waste of money.

Boudewijn Zenden, who played in four countries for clubs including Liverpool and Barcelona, told us this during his stint in Marseille in 2009:

> It's the weirdest thing ever that you can actually buy a player for 20 mil, and you don't do anything to make him feel at home. I think the first thing you should do is get him a mobile phone and a house. Get him a school for the kids, get something for his missus, get a teacher in for both of them straightaway, because obviously everything goes with the language. Do they need anything for other family members, do they

need a driving license, do they need a visa, do they need a new passport? Sometimes even at the biggest clubs it's really badly organized.

Milan: best club ever. AC Milan is organized in a way you can't believe. Anything is done for you: you arrive, you get your house, it's fully furnished, you get five cars to choose from, you know the sky's the limit. They really say: we'll take care of everything else; you make sure you play really well. Whereas unfortunately in a lot of clubs, you have to get after it yourself....Sometimes you get to a club, and you've got people actually at the club who take profit from players.

For any foreign player, or even a player who comes in new, they could get one man who's actually there to take care of everything. But then again, sometimes players are a bit—I don't want to say abusive, but they might take profit of the situation. They might call in the middle of the night, just to say there's no milk in the fridge. You know how they are sometimes.

Raiola laughingly endorsed Zenden's assessment of golden-age Milan: "I always used to say, 'I think they'll come and put a pill on your tongue if you have a headache.' Whereas Inter would say, 'Here's your contract; go and figure it all out yourself.'"

In soccer, bad relocations have traditionally been the norm. In 1961 two fifteen-year-olds from the Northern Irish capital of Belfast took the boat across the Irish Sea to become apprentices with Manchester United. George Best and Eric McMordie had never left home before. When they landed at Liverpool docks, they couldn't find anyone from the club to meet them. So they worked out for themselves how to get a train to Manchester, eventually found the stadium, and wound up feeling so lonely and confused that on their second day they told the club: "We want to go back on the next boat." And they did, recounts Duncan Hamilton in his biography of Best, *Immortal*. In the end, Best decided to give Manchester one last try. McMordie refused. He became a plasterer in Belfast after leaving school, although he did later make a respectable soccer career with Middlesbrough. Just imagine how the botched welcome of Best might have changed United's history.

Yet bad relocations continued for decades, like Gary Lineker and his wife spending their first four months in Barcelona in 1985 in a tiny brown-walled hotel room, or Chelsea signing Dutch cosmopolitan Ruud Gullit in 1996 and sticking him in a hotel in the ugly London dormitory town of Slough, or Ian Rush coming back to England from a bad year in Italy marveling, "It was like another country." Many players down the years would have understood that phrase. In 1995 Manchester City bought the Georgian playmaker Georgi Kinkladze, who spoke no English, and stuck him on his own in a hotel for three months. No wonder his early games were poor. His improvement, writes Michael Cox in *The Mixer*, "coincided with the arrival of two Georgian friends and his mother, Khatuna, who brought some home comforts: Georgian cognac, walnuts, and spices to make Kinkladze his favorite dishes."

But perhaps the great failed relocation, one that a Spanish relocation consultant cited for years after in her presentations, was Nicolas Anelka's to Real Madrid in 1999.

A half hour of conversation with Anelka is enough to confirm that he is self-absorbed, scared of other people, and not someone who makes contact easily. Nor does he appear to be good at languages, because after well over a decade in England he still spoke very mediocre English. Anelka is the sort of expatriate who really needed a relocation consultant.

Real had spent $35 million buying him from Arsenal. The club then spent nothing on helping him adjust. On day one, the shy, awkward twenty-year-old reported to work and found that there was nobody to show him around. He hadn't even been assigned a locker in the dressing room. Several times that first morning, he would take a locker that seemed to be unused only for another player to walk in and claim it.

Anelka doesn't seem to have talked about his problems to anyone at Madrid. Nor did anyone at the club ask him. Instead, he talked to *France Football*, a magazine that he treated as his newspaper of record, like a 1950s British prime minister talking to the *Times*. "I am alone against the rest of the team," he revealed midway through the season. He claimed to possess a video showing his teammates looking gloomy after he had scored his first goal for Real after six months at the club. He had tried to give this video to the coach, but the coach hadn't wanted to see it. Also, the other Black Francophone players had told Anelka that the other players wouldn't pass to him. Madrid ended up giving him a forty-five-day ban, essentially for being maladjusted.

Paranoid though Anelka may have been, he had a point. The other players really didn't like him. And they never got to know him because nobody at the club seems ever to have bothered to introduce him to anyone. As he said later, all that Madrid had told him was "Look after yourself." The club seems to have taken the strangely materialistic view that Anelka's salary should determine his behavior. But even in materialistic terms, that was foolish. If you pay $35 million for an immature young employee, it is bad management to make him look after himself. Wenger at Arsenal knew that, and he had Anelka on the field scoring goals.

Even a player with a normal personality can find emigration tricky. Tyrone Mears, an English defender who spent a year at Marseille, where his best relocation consultant was his teammate Zenden, said, "Sometimes it's not a problem of the player adapting. A lot of the times it's the family adapting." Perhaps the player's girlfriend is unhappy because she can't find a job in the new town. Or perhaps she's pregnant and doesn't know how to negotiate the local hospital, or perhaps she can't find Rice Krispies ("or beans on toast," added Zenden, when told about the Blissett drama). The club doesn't care. It is paying her boyfriend well. He simply has to perform.

Soccer clubs never used to bother with anything like an HR department. As late as about 2005, there were only a few relocation consultants in soccer, and most weren't called that and weren't hired by clubs. Instead, they worked either for players' agents or for sportswear companies. If Nike or Adidas is paying a player to wear its shoes, it needs him to succeed. If the player moves to a foreign club, the sportswear company—knowing that the club might not bother—sometimes sends a minder to live in that town and look after him.

The minder gives the player occasional presents; acts as his secretary, friend, and shrink; and remembers his wife's birthday. The minder of a young midfielder who was struggling in his first weeks at Milan said that when the player came home from training frustrated, lonely, and confused by Italy, his main task was to take the young man out to dinner. At dinner the player would grumble and say, "Tomorrow I'm going to tell the coach what I really think of him," and the minder would say, "That might not be such a brilliant idea. Here, have some more spaghetti alle vongole." To most players, this sort of thing comes as a bonus in a stressful life. To a few, it is essential.

After international transfers became common in the 1990s, some agents began to double as player minders. When the Dutch forward Bryan Roy moved from Ajax to Foggia in Italy in 1992, Raiola's personal service included spending seven months with Roy in Foggia and helping paint the player's house. He later said, "I already realized then that this kind of guidance was very important in determining the success or failure of a player."

Many of Raiola's players treated him as an all-purpose helpmeet. Mario Balotelli once phoned him to say his house was on fire; Raiola advised him to try the fire brigade. Later, Raiola's younger players Facetimed him. He waddled around his office imitating them as they held up their phones to show him the objects they wanted to buy: "'I'm walking through the house. What do you think of it?'" He chuckled fondly. He considered it all part of his job. So it is, now, for most agents. The sports lawyer Daniel Geey writes that "football agency staff members could be tasked with anything: booking holidays, paying utility bills, organizing a taxi to pick up a family member from the airport, even taking the dog for a walk."

Part of the history of soccer is that agents have tended to be smarter than the people who run clubs. Most clubs took a long time to see the value of relocation. Drogba in his autobiography recounts joining Chelsea from Olympique Marseille in 2004 for $44 million: "I plunged into problems linked to my situation as an expatriate. Chelsea didn't necessarily help me." Nobody at the club could help him find a school for his children. All Chelsea did to get him a house was put him in touch with a real estate agent who tried to sell him one for $18 million. For "weeks of irritation" the Drogba family lived in a hotel while Drogba, who at that point barely spoke English, went house hunting after practice.

All Chelsea's expensive foreign signings had much the same experience, Drogba writes. "We sometimes laughed about it with Gallas, Makelele, Kezman, Geremi. 'You too, you're still living in a hotel?' After all these worries, I didn't feel like integrating [at Chelsea] or multiplying my efforts."

Chelsea was no worse than other English clubs at the time. The same summer that Drogba arrived in London, Wayne Rooney moved thirty-five miles up the motorway from Everton to Manchester United and had an almost equally disorienting experience. United had paid $49 million for him but then stuck its eighteen-year-old star asset in a hotel room. "Living in such a place I found horrible," reports Rooney in his *My Story So Far*. The nearest thing to a relocation consultant he found at United seems to have been a teammate: "Gary Neville tried to persuade me to buy one of his houses. I don't know how many he has, or whether he was boasting or winding me up, but he kept telling me about these properties he had."

At a conference in Rome in 2008, relocation consultants literally lined up to tell their horror stories about soccer. Lots of them had tried to get into the sport and been rebuffed. A Danish relocator had been told by FC Copenhagen that her services weren't required because the players' wives always helped one another settle. Many clubs had never even heard of relocation. Moreover, they had never hired relocation consultants before, so given the logic of soccer, not hiring relocation consultants must be the right thing to do. One Swedish relocator surmised, "I guess it comes down to the fact that they see the players as merchandise."

The only relocation consultants who had penetrated soccer happened to have a friend inside a club or, in the case of one Greek woman, had married a club owner. She had told her husband, "All these guys would be happier if you find out what their needs are and address their needs."

Another relocator had entered a German club as a language teacher and worked her way up. She said, "I was their mother, their nurse, their real estate agent, their cleaning lady, their everything. They didn't have a car; they didn't speak the language." Did her work help them play better? "Absolutely." The club was happy for her to work as an amateur, but as soon as she founded a relocation company, it didn't want her anymore. She had become threatening.

So countless new signings continued to flop abroad. Clubs often anticipated this by avoiding players who seemed particularly ill-equipped to adjust. For instance, on average, Latin Americans are the world's most skillful players. Yet, historically, English clubs rarely bought them: Latin Americans don't speak English, don't like cold weather, and don't tend to understand the core traditions of English soccer, like drinking twenty pints of beer in a night. Few Latin Americans adjust easily to English soccer.

Instead of Latin Americans, English clubs traditionally bought Scandinavians. On average, Scandinavians are worse soccer players than Latin

Americans, but they are very familiar with English, cold weather, and twenty pints of beer. Scandinavians adapted to England, so the clubs bought them. But the clubs were missing a great opportunity. Anyone who bought a great Latin American player and hired a good relocation consultant to help him adjust would be on to a winner. Yet few clubs did. Years used to go by without any English club buying a Latin American.

In 2008 Manchester City took a gamble on Robinho. As a Brazilian forward who had had his moments in the World Cup of 2006, he was bound to be overvalued and was also very likely to relocate badly. So it's little wonder that City paid a British record transfer fee of $55 million for him or that eighteen months later it gave up on him and sent him home to Santos on loan. Robinho never returned to English soccer. The experience obviously taught City a lesson because for the next two years the club switched to a policy of buying only players who had already established themselves in England. It also finally began to take relocation seriously.

Bit by bit in recent years, the soccer business has become smarter. Way back in the mid-1990s, Liverpool had become one of the first clubs to hire some sort of employee to help new players settle. Ajax Amsterdam was another pioneer. The woman who first handled relocations at Ajax found that some of the problems of new players were absurdly easy to solve. When Steven Pienaar and another young South African player came to Amsterdam, they were teenagers, had never lived on their own before, and suddenly found themselves sharing an apartment in a cold country at the other end of the Earth. Inevitably, they put their music speakers on the bare floor and cranked up the volume. Inevitably, the neighbors complained. The South Africans had a miserable time in their building until the woman from Ajax came around to see what was wrong and suggested they put their speakers on a table instead. They did. The noise diminished, their lives got easier, and that might just have made them better able to perform for Ajax.

Most clubs in the Premier League now have "player-care officers"—soccer code for relocation consultants. Some of these officers are full-timers, others not. Some do a serious job. Manchester City, in particular, learned from Robinho's failure. When we visited the club's training ground in 2012, on a wall just behind reception we saw a map of Manchester's surroundings, designed to catch the eyes of passing players. The map highlighted eight recommended wealthy towns and suburbs for them to live in; not on the list was Manchester's city center, with its vibrant nightlife.

These recommendations are just the start. City's "player-care department" aims to take care of almost every need that a new immigrant might have, whether it's a nanny or a "discreet car service." Even before a new player signs, the club has already researched his off-duty habits and his partner's taste in restaurants. When he arrives for preseason training, the club might say to him, "Well, you're going to be busy for a couple of weeks, but here's a little restaurant your girlfriend might like." It's not true that behind every successful soccer player there is a happy woman (or man), but it probably does help.

In 2011 City signed the young Argentine striker Sergio Agüero. Nobody doubted his talent. However, many doubted whether he would adapt to English soccer and rainy provincial life. His transfer fee of $61 million seemed a gamble, even for Manchester City. But Agüero scored twice on debut. He finished his first English season with thirty goals, including the last-second strike in the last game of the season against QPR that won City its first league title since 1968. In part, Agüero succeeded thanks to City's excellence at relocation. As Gavin Fleig, the club's head of performance analysis, told us, "The normal transition time for a foreign player is considered in the industry to be about a year. Normally, those players are in a hotel for the first three months. We were able to get from agreeing on a fee to Sergio living in his house within two weeks, with a Spanish sat-nav system in his car, linked to the Spanish community in Manchester. We had our prize asset ready to go from day one."

Then there was City's signing of Kevin De Bruyne from Wolfsburg in 2015. The Belgian was flown to Manchester in a private jet. "It was like in a film," his agent Patrick De Koster later recalled. "We thought we'd have a lot of work finding a new house, opening a bank account, phone cards, a car. But everything was sorted in three hours. Incredible." And City lured Pep Guardiola to Manchester in 2016 partly by building him a custom-made house in the city center.

Raiola said, "In England the clubs have kept getting better at it. But it's just that in Italy it's done in a very Italian way, human: 'Lovely, and we'll go and get a bite to eat, and how are the children?' In England it's much more businesslike. There's something to be said for both ways."

Still, a few clubs continue to undervalue or even neglect relocation. As one player-care officer in the Premier League told us, "Some very well-known managers have said to me they can't understand why you can possibly need it. They have said, 'Well, when I moved to a foreign country as a player I had to do it myself.' Well, yes, but that doesn't mean it's right. You probably had to clean boots, too, but nobody does that now."

THE NICEST TOWN IN EUROPE: HOW OLYMPIQUE LYON BOUGHT AND SOLD

If you had to locate the middle-class European dream anywhere, it would be in Lyon. It's a town the size of Oakland, about two-thirds of the way down France, nestled between rivers just west of the Alps. On a warm January afternoon, drinking coffee outside in the eighteenth-century Place Bellecour, where the citizens are as elegant as the buildings, you think: nice. Here's a wealthy town where you can have a good job, nice weather, and a big house near the mountains.

Lyon also has some of the best restaurants in Europe, known locally as *bouchons*, or "corks." Even at the town's soccer stadium, you can have a wonderful three-course pregame meal consisting largely of intestines or head cheese, unless you prefer to eat at local boy Paul Bocuse's brasserie across the road and totter into the grounds just before kickoff. And then, for a remarkable decade or so, you could watch some very decent soccer, too.

Until about 2000, Lyon was known as the birthplace of cinema and nouvelle cuisine, but not as a soccer town. It was just too bourgeois. If for some reason you wanted soccer, you drove thirty-five miles down the highway to gritty proletarian Saint-Étienne. In 1987 Olympique Lyon, or OL, or les Gones (the Kids), was playing in France's second division on an annual budget of about $3 million. It was any old backwater provincial club in Europe. From 2002 through 2008, Lyon ruled French soccer. The club's ascent was in large part a story of the international transfer market. Better than any other club in Europe, for a while Lyon worked out how to play the market.

In 1987 Jean-Michel Aulas, a local software entrepreneur with the stark, grooved features of a Roman emperor, became club president. Aulas had played fairly good handball as a young man and had a season ticket at OL. "I didn't know the world of soccer well," he admitted to us in 2007 over a bottle of OL mineral water in his office beside the stadium (which he was already aiming to tear down and replace with a bigger one). Had he expected the transformation that he wrought? "No."

Aulas set out to improve the club step-by-step. "We tried to abstract the factor 'time,'" he explained. "Each year we fix as an aim to have sporting progress, and progress of our financial resources. It's like a cyclist riding: you can overtake the people in front of you." Others in France preferred to liken Aulas to "*un bulldozer.*"

In 1987 even the local Lyonnais didn't care much about les Gones. You could live in Lyon without knowing that soccer existed. The club barely had a personality, whereas Saint-Étienne was the "miners' club" that had suffered tragic defeats on great European nights in the 1970s. Saint-Étienne's president at the time said that when it came to soccer, Lyon was a suburb of Saint-Étienne, a remark that still rankles. At one derby after Lyon's domination began, les Gones' fans unfurled a banner that told the Saint-Étienne supporters, "We invented cinema when your fathers were dying in the mines."

Aulas appointed local boy Raymond Domenech as his first coach. In Domenech's first season, OL finished at the top of the second division without losing a game. Right after that, it qualified for Europe. Aulas recalled, "At a stroke the credibility was total. The project was en route."

It turned out that the second city in France, even if it was a bit bourgeois, was just hungry enough for a decent soccer club. The Lyonnais were willing to buy match tickets if things went well, but if things went badly, they weren't immediately waving white handkerchiefs in the stands and demanding that the president or manager or half the team be gotten rid of. Nor did the French media track the club's doings hour by hour. It's much easier to build for the long term in a place like that than in a "soccer city" like Marseille or Newcastle. Moreover, players were happy to move to a town that is hardly a hardship posting. Almost nothing they got into in Lyon made it into the gossip press. Another of Lyon's advantages: the locals had money. "It allowed us to have not just a 'popular clientele' but also a 'business clientele,'" said Aulas.

Talking about money is something of a taboo in France. It is considered a grubby and private topic. Socially, you're never supposed to ask anyone a question that might reveal how much somebody has. Soccer, to most French fans, is not supposed to be about money. They find the notion of a well-run soccer club humorless, practically American.

It therefore irritated them that Aulas talked about it so unabashedly. Aulas's theme was that over time, the more money a club makes, the more matches it will win, and the more matches it wins, the more money it will make. In the short term you can lose a match, but in the long term there is a rationality even to soccer. (And to baseball. As *Moneyball* describes it, Beane believes that winning "is simply a matter of figuring out the odds, and exploiting the laws of probability.... To get worked up over plays, or even games, is as unproductive as a casino manager worrying over the outcomes of individual pulls of the slot machines.")

In Aulas's view, rationality in soccer works more or less like this: if you buy good players for less than they are worth, you will win more games. You will then have more money to buy better players for less than they are worth. The better players will win you more matches, and that will attract more fans (and thus more money) because Aulas spotted early that most soccer fans everywhere are much more like shoppers than like religious believers: if they can get a better experience somewhere new, they will go there. He told us in 2007, "We sold 110,000 replica shirts last season. This season we are already at 200,000. I think Olympique Lyon has become by far the most beloved club in France." Polls suggested that at the time he was right: in Sport+Markt's survey of European supporters in 2006, Lyon emerged as the country's most popular club, just ahead of Olympique Marseille. This popularity was a recent phenomenon. In 2002, when Lyon first became champions of France, the overriding French emotion toward the club had still been "Whatever." The editor of *France Football* magazine complained around that time that when Lyon won the title, his magazine didn't sell. But as the club won the title every year from 2002 through 2008—at the time, the longest period of domination by any club in any of Europe's five biggest national leagues—many French fans began to care about it.

What made the club's rise possible was the transfer market. On this warm winter's afternoon in Lyon, Aulas told us: "We will invest better than Chelsea, Arsenal, or Real Madrid. We will make different strategic choices. For instance, we won't try to have the best team on paper in terms of brand. We will have the best team relative to our investment." Here are Lyon's rules of the transfer market:

Use the wisdom of crowds. When Lyon was thinking of signing a player, a group of men would sit down to debate the transfer. Aulas would be there, along with Bernard Lacombe, once a bull-like center forward for Lyon and France who served from the late 1980s until 2017 as the club's sporting director and then as Aulas's "special adviser." Lacombe was known for having the best pair of eyes in French soccer. He coached Lyon from 1997 to 2000, but Aulas clearly figured out that if you have someone with his knack for spotting the right transfer, you want to keep him at the club for a long term rather than make his job contingent on four lost matches. The same went for Peter Taylor at Forest.

Whoever happened to be Lyon's head coach at the moment would sit in on the meeting, too, and so would four or five other coaches. "We have a group that gives its advice," Aulas explained. "In England the manager often does it alone. In France it's often the technical director." Lacombe told us that the house rule was that after the group had made the decision, everyone present would then publicly get behind the transfer.

Like Lyon, the Oakland A's sidelined their manager. Like Lyon, the A's understood that he was merely "a middle manager" obsessed with the very short term. The A's let him watch baseball's annual draft. They didn't let him say a word about it.

Lyon's method for choosing players is so obvious and smart that it's surprising all clubs don't use it. The theory of the "wisdom of crowds" says that if you aggregate many different opinions from a diverse group of people, you are much more likely to arrive at the best opinion than if you just listen to one specialist. For instance, if you ask a diverse crowd to guess the weight of an ox, the average of their guesses will be very nearly right. If you ask a diverse set of gamblers to bet on, say, the outcome of a presidential election, the average of their bets is likely to be right, too. (Gambling markets have proved excellent predictors of all sorts of outcomes.) The wisdom of crowds fails when the components of the crowd are not diverse enough. This is often the case in American sports. But in European soccer, opinions tend to come from many different countries, and that helps ensure diversity.

Clough and Taylor at least were a crowd of two. However, the traditional decision-making model in English soccer is not "wisdom of crowds" but short-term dictatorship. At many clubs the manager is still treated as a sort of divinely inspired monarch who gets to decide everything until he is sacked. Then the next manager clears out his predecessor's signings at a discount. Lyon, noted a rival French club president with envy, never had expensive signings rotting on the bench. It never had revolutions at all. It understood that the coach was only a temp. OL won its seven consecutive titles with four different coaches—Jacques Santini, Paul Le Guen, Gérard Houllier, and Alain Perrin—none of whom, judging by their subsequent records, was exactly a Hegelian world-historical individual. When a coach left Lyon, not much changed. No matter who happened to be sitting on the bench, the team always played much the same brand of attacking soccer (by French standards).

Emmanuel Hembert grew up in Lyon supporting OL when it was still in the second division. Later, as head of the sports practice of the management consultancy A. T. Kearney in London, he was always citing the club as an example to his clients in soccer. "A big secret of a successful club is stability," Hembert explained over coffee in Paris years ago. "In Lyon the stability is not with the coach but with the sports director, Lacombe."

Even a club run as a one-man dictatorship can access the wisdom of crowds. Ferguson at Manchester United would regularly consult his players on transfers. When he was thinking of buying Eric Cantona from Leeds in 1992, writes Michael Cox, he "asked center-backs Gary Pallister and Steve Bruce for their opinion after Leeds' visit to Old Trafford. Both men suggested he was a difficult opponent because he took up unusual positions." Ferguson bought Cantona. A year later, after United's players unanimously vouched that Nottingham Forest's Roy Keane was top class, Ferguson broke the British transfer record to sign him, too. And most famously, in 2003, on the plane home from a friendly in Portugal, United's defenders told Ferguson what a handful Sporting Lisbon's little-known teenage winger had been. The manager promptly forked out £12.24 million ($20.3 million) for Cristiano Ronaldo.

The best time to buy a player is when he is in his early twenties. Aulas said, "We buy young players with potential who are considered the best in their country, between twenty and twenty-two years old." It's almost as if he had read *Moneyball*. The book keeps banging away about a truth discovered by Bill James, who wrote: "College players are a better invest-ment than high school players by a huge, huge, laughably huge margin."

Baseball clubs traditionally preferred to draft high school players. But how good you are at seventeen or eighteen is a poor predictor of how good you will become as an adult. By definition, when a player is that young, there is still too little information to judge him. Beane himself had been probably the hottest baseball prospect in the United States at seventeen, but he was already declining in his senior year at high school, and he then failed in the major leagues. Watching the 2002 draft as the A's general manager, he "punches his fist in the air" each time rival teams draft schoolboys.

It's the same in soccer, where brilliant teenagers tend to disappear soon afterward. Here are a few winners of the Golden Ball for best player at the under-seventeen World Cup since the 1980s: Philip Osundo of Nigeria, William de Oliveira of Brazil, Nii Lamptey of Ghana, Scottish goalkeeper James Will, Mohammed al-Kathiri of Oman, Sergio Santa-maria of Spain, and the Nigerian Sani Emmanuel. Once upon a time they must have all been brilliant, but none of them made it as adults. (Will ended up a police officer in the Scottish Highlands playing for his village team, while Emmanuel seems to have drifted out of professional soccer at age twenty-three.) The most famous case of a teenager who flamed out is American Freddy Adu, who at fourteen was the next Pelé and Maradona. Ben Lyttleton, our partner in the *Soccernomics* consultancy, points out in his book *Edge* that "it can be a challenge for a youngster who is suddenly successful—maybe even harder than coping with failure." Many gifted teenagers are probably destroyed by acclaim and money.

Yet there's a converse to all these early flameouts: some ugly ducklings become swans. When Helmut Schulte was head of Schalke 04's youth academy, he had to decide the futures of the teenage Manuel Neuer and Mesut Özil. He remembers the fourteen-year-old Neuer as "a totally nor-mal keeper" who, moreover, was small. Schalke's coaches and scouts recom-mended getting rid of him. Schulte agonized over the decision and finally decided to keep him. "I overruled the others on three or four occasions during my time at Schalke, and it never worked out, except with Manuel."

Soon after Neuer's narrow escape, he had a growth spurt and got better. By the time he was about eighteen, he was playing for German national youth teams. Schulte recommended that he be given a senior contract. Schalke's general manager, Rudi Assauer, came to watch the kid at training. It happened that the session was a passing exercise, and Neuer could pass as well as any outfield player. Assauer, whose main criterion was skill on the ball, instantly decided to give him a contract.

The teenage Özil was even skinnier than Neuer. Nor did he seem particularly brilliant. Schalke soon let him go to the smaller local club Rot-Weiss Essen. Later, Schalke was asked whether Özil could train with their youth players in the mornings. "As long as he doesn't disrupt training, he can join in" was the verdict. Like Neuer, Özil belatedly got better. However, when his dad announced, "Mesut isn't a player for Schalke. He's a player for Barcelona or Real Madrid," Schalke coaches laughed at him. In short, when it comes to teenage soccer players, the famous phrase of the Hollywood scriptwriter William Goldman applies: "Nobody knows anything."

Only a handful of world-class players in each generation, most of them creators or forwards—Pelé, Maradona, Rooney, Lionel Messi, Cesc Fabregas, Kylian Mbappé—reach the top by the age of eighteen. Most players get there considerably later. Almost all defenders and goalkeepers do. You can be confident of their potential only when they are more mature.

Beane knows that by the time baseball players are in college—which tends to put them in Lyon's magical age range of twenty to twenty-two—you have a pretty good idea of what they will become. There is a lot of information about them. They have grown up a bit. They are old enough to be nearly fully formed but too young to be expensive stars. FIFA TMS analyzed international transfers to England in 2013 and found that players moving at ages twenty to twenty-two were 18 percent cheaper than players aged twenty-five to twenty-seven. Moreover, the younger players tended to have lower salaries and higher future resale values.

Lyon always tried to avoid paying a premium for an established player's "name." Here, again, it was lucky to be a club from a quiet town. Its placid supporters and local media didn't demand stars. By contrast, as the former president of a club in a much more raucous French city recalls, "I ran [the club] with the mission to create a spectacle. It wasn't to build a project for twenty years to come." A team from a big city tends to need big stars.

Soccer being barely distinguishable from baseball, the same split between big and small towns operates in that sport. "Big-market teams," like the Boston Red Sox and the New York Yankees, hunt players with names. Their media and fans demand it. In *Moneyball* Lewis calls this the pathology of "many foolish teams that thought all their questions could be answered by a single player." (It's a pathology that may sound strangely familiar to European soccer fans.) By contrast, the Oakland A's, as a small-market team, were free to forgo stars. As Lewis writes, "Billy may not care for the Oakland press but it is really very tame next to the Boston press, and it certainly has no effect on his behavior, other than to infuriate him once a week or so. Oakland A's fans, too, were apathetic compared to the maniacs in Fenway Park or Yankee Stadium." But as Beane told us, English soccer is "even more emotional" than baseball. "It's the biggest sport in the world," he said. "And that's the biggest league in the world, and then you put in sixty million people and a four-hour drive from north to south, and that's what you have."

That's why most English soccer clubs are always being pushed by their fans to buy stars. Happy is the club that has no need of heroes. Lyon was free to buy young unknowns such as Michael Essien, Florent Malouda, Mahamadou Diarra, and Hugo Lloris just because they were good. And unknowns accept modest salaries. Like Clough's Forest, Lyon for many years performed the magic trick of winning things without paying silly wages.

Here are a few more of Lyon's secrets during the golden years. First, try not to buy center forwards. Center forward is the most overpriced position in the transfer market, perhaps simply because center forwards are the players who score most and therefore end up on TV. Strikers in general also cost the most in salaries. In Italy's Serie A between 2009 and 2014, forwards earned about 57 percent more than defenders and 34 percent more than midfielders, calculates French economist Bastien Drut.

Admittedly, Lyon "announced" itself to soccer by buying the Brazilian center forward Sonny Anderson for $19 million in 1999, but the club mostly scrimped on the position afterward. Houllier left OL in 2007 grumbling that even after the club sold Malouda and Eric Abidal for a combined total of $45 million, Aulas still wouldn't buy him a center forward.

By contrast, goalkeeper is the most underpriced position in soccer's transfer market. Keepers also earn less than outfield players (according to a study by German economist Bernd Frick), even though they make a very large contribution to results and have longer careers than strikers.

Help your foreign signings relocate. All sorts of great Brazilians have passed through Lyon: Sonny Anderson; the longtime club captain, Cris; the future internationals Juninho and Fred; and the world champion Edmilson. Most were barely known when they joined the club. But as the former president of a rival French club puts it, "They [Lyon] don't select players just for their quality but for their ability to adapt. I can't see Lyon recruiting an Anelka or a Ronaldinho."

And Lyon helped the newcomers to settle. Drogba noted enviously, "At Lyon, a translator takes care of the Brazilians, helps them to find a house, get their bearings, tries to reduce as much as possible the negative effects of moving. . . . Even at a place of the calibre of Chelsea, that didn't exist."

Lyon's "translator," who worked full-time for the club, sorted out the players' homesickness, bank accounts, nouvelle cuisine, and whatever else. Other people at the club educated the newcomers in Lyon's culture: no stars or showoffs.

Sell any player if another club offers more than he is worth. This is what Aulas meant when he said "Buying and selling players is not an activity for improving the soccer performance. It's a trading activity, in which we produce gross margin. If an offer for a player is greatly superior to his market value, you must not keep him." The ghost of Peter Taylor would approve.

Like Clough and Taylor, and like Billy Beane, Lyon never got sentimental about players. In the club's annual accounts it booked each player for a certain transfer value. (Beane says, "Know exactly what every player in baseball is worth to you. You can put a dollar figure on it.") Lyon knew that sooner or later its best players would attract somebody else's attention. Because the club expected to sell them, it replaced them even before they went. Ferguson at United also pursued a strategy of early replacement: "I did feel sentimental about great players leaving us. At the same time, my eye would always be on a player who was coming to an end. An internal voice would always ask, 'When's he going to leave, how long will he last?' Experience taught me to stockpile young players in important positions."

Bringing in replacements before they are needed avoids a transition period or a panic purchase after the player's departure. As Aulas explained, "We will replace the player in the squad six months or a year before. So when Michael Essien goes [to Chelsea for $43 million], we already have a certain number of players who are ready to replace him. Then, when the opportunity to buy Tiago arises, for 25 percent of the price of Essien, you take him."

Before Essien's transfer in 2005, Aulas spent weeks proclaiming that the Ghanaian was "untransferable." He always said that when he was about to transfer a player, because it drove up the price. In his words, "Every international at Lyon is untransferable. Until the offer surpasses by far the amount we had expected."

That leads to Lyon's final insight: don't worry too much about buying or keeping superstars. Media and fans tend to obsess about the team's best player (as Essien was), but in fact you can usually let him go without damaging performance too much.

In general, most clubs don't spend their transfer budgets very rationally. Here, as a free service, are the thirteen main secrets of the transfer market in full:

1. A new manager wastes money on transfers; don't let him.
2. Use the wisdom of crowds.
3. Stars of recent World Cups or European championships are overvalued; ignore them.
4. Both superstars and weakest links are overvalued: your top three players matter most.
5. Certain nationalities are overvalued.
6. Older players are overvalued.
7. Center forwards are overvalued; goalkeepers are undervalued.
8. Gentlemen prefer blonds: identify and abandon "sight-based prejudices."
9. The best time to buy a player is when he is in his early twenties.

10. Sell any player when another club offers more than he is worth.
11. Replace your best players even before you sell them.
12. Buy players with personal problems, and then help them deal with their problems.
13. Help your players relocate.

Alternatively, clubs could just stick with the conventional wisdom.

3

THE WORST BUSINESS
IN THE WORLD

Why Soccer Clubs Haven't Made Money

A man we know once tried to do business with a revered institution of English soccer. "I can do business with stupid people," he said afterward, "and I can do business with crooks. But I can't do business with stupid people who want to be crooks."

It was a decent summary of the soccer business, if you can call soccer a business. People often do. William McGregor, the Scottish draper who founded the English Football League in 1888, was probably the first person to describe soccer as "big business," but the phrase has since become one of the game's great clichés. In fact, McGregor was wrong. For almost all the game's history, soccer was neither big business nor good business. It arguably wasn't even business at all. But that may now be changing. For the first time ever, some of the world's biggest clubs are starting to turn into decent-sized and reasonably well-run businesses.

"BIG BUSINESS"

Few people have heard of United Natural Foods. The company was formed out of a merger of two food distributors in 1996. Today it distributes natural, organic, and specialty foods, and it has done well because of the rise of foodies in North America. Still, it hasn't quite made its way onto the list of the five hundred big publicly traded American companies that make up the S&P 500. Its annual revenues for the year through July 2021 were $27 billion, for net income of $149 million. United Natural Foods, whose headquarters are on Iron Horse Way in Providence, Rhode Island, is not big business. For comparison, Walmart in 2021 had revenues that were twenty times bigger.

But United Natural Foods is a much larger business than any soccer club on Earth. In 2018–2019, the last full season before the COVID-19 pandemic closed stadiums, FC Barcelona's revenues were €841 million, or nearly a billion dollars, according to Deloitte. That's a tidy sum, more than any other club in any sport had ever achieved at that point. However, it's just 4 percent of United Natural Foods' revenues and barely 0.2 percent the size of Walmart's. To put it very starkly, in terms of revenue, Barcelona would have still been only the fifty-second largest company in Finland.

Because almost no clubs are quoted on the stock market anymore, it is hard to work out their value. But we can certainly say that not even Real Madrid, Manchester United, or Barcelona would get anywhere near the S&P 500. In 2021, company number 501 on US stock markets, next in line for inclusion on the index, was Western Union, with a market capitalization (or value) of $7.25 billion. By contrast, Manchester United's market cap was a mere $2.2 billion. There are probably hundreds of companies ahead of it in line.

And if Deloitte ranked clubs by their profits, the results would be embarrassing. Most clubs make losses or meager profits and fail to pay any dividends to their shareholders. They are chasing glory, not riches.

Whichever way you measure it, no soccer club is a big business. Even the world's biggest clubs are dwarfed by United Natural Foods. As for all the rest, Alex Fynn noted in the 1990s that the average English Premier League club had about the same revenue as a British supermarket—not a chain of supermarkets, but one single large British Tesco store. True, Premier League clubs have grown a lot since then. However, Fynn's comparison remains relevant. Costco in 2020 had 560 warehouse stores in the US with average sales of about $250 million each. There are around 700 top-division clubs in Europe, and the Union of European Football Associations (UEFA) reported that their average revenue in 2019 was about $32 million. In other words, a single large supermarket is a bigger business than all but a handful of soccer clubs.

A good way to visualize the size of the soccer industry is to visit the headquarters of UEFA, the European soccer association, in the Swiss town of Nyon. The building has a lovely view of Lake Geneva, but it looks like the offices of a small insurance company. Soccer is small business.

This feels like a contradiction. We all know that soccer is huge. Some of the most famous people on Earth are soccer players, and the most-watched television program in history is generally the most-recent World Cup final. Nonetheless, soccer clubs are puny businesses. This is partly a problem of what economists call appropriability: so far, soccer clubs have not been able to make money out of (haven't appropriated) more than a tiny share of our love of soccer.

It may be that season tickets are expensive and replica shirts overpriced, but buying these things once a year represents the extravagant extreme of soccer fanaticism. Most soccer is watched not from $2,000 seats in the stadium but on a screen—sometimes at the price of a subscription, often at the price of watching a few commercials, or frequently for the price of a couple of beers in a bar. Compare the cost of watching a game in a bar with the cost of eating out or watching a movie, let alone going on vacation.

Worse still, soccer generates little income from reruns of matches. And watching soccer (even on TV) is only a tiny part of a fan's engagement with the game. There are internet sites to be trawled and a growing array of video games to keep up with. Then there is the soccer banter that passes time at the dinner table, by the water cooler, and above all on social media. All this entertainment is made possible by soccer clubs, but they cannot appropriate a penny of the value we attach to it. Chelsea cannot charge us for talking or reading or thinking about Chelsea. As the former Dutch international midfielder Demy de Zeeuw said, "There are complaints that we [players] earn too much, but the whole world earns money from your success as a player: newspapers, television, companies." In fact, the world earns more from soccer than the soccer industry itself does.

BAD BUSINESS

Soccer is not merely a small business. It has also historically been a bad one. Until very recently, and to some degree still today, anyone who spent any time inside soccer soon discovered that just as oil was part of the oil business, stupidity was part of the soccer business.

This became obvious when people in soccer encountered people in other industries. Generally, the soccer people got exploited because people in other industries understood business better. In 1997 Peter Kenyon, then chief executive of the sportswear company Umbro, invited a few guests to watch a European game at Chelsea, the club he would end up running a few years later. After the game, Kenyon took his guests out for dinner. Over curry, he reminisced about how the sportswear industry used to treat soccer clubs. Before the 1980s, he said, big English clubs paid companies like Umbro to supply their clothing. It was obviously great advertising for the gear makers to have some of England's best players running around in their clothes, but the clubs had not yet figured that out. So sportswear companies used to get paid to advertise themselves.

In fact, when England hosted the World Cup in 1966, it hoped merely that its usual supplier would give it a discount on shoes and shirts, "particularly in the opening ceremony…with the Queen present," writes Mihir Bose in *The Spirit of the Game*. As it happened, the English did even better: Umbro offered to supply the team for free. The company must have been pleased when England won the tournament.

Ricky George saw the ignorance of soccer in those days from point-blank range. In 1972, when George scored the famous goal for little semiprofessional Hereford that knocked Newcastle out of the FA Cup, he was working for Adidas as a "soccer PR." His job was to represent Adidas to England players, former world champions like Bobby Moore, Bobby Charlton, and Gordon Banks. There was little need to persuade them to choose Adidas. Most of them wore the three stripes for free anyway. George says, "It is quite a fascinating thing if you compare it with today. There were no great sponsorship deals going on. All that happened is that you would give the players boots. But even then, at the beginning of every season the clubs would go to their local sports retailer and just buy twenty, thirty pairs of boots and hand them out. For a company like Adidas, it was the cheapest type of PR you could imagine."

Only on special occasions did George have to pay players: "When it came to a big international, and the game was going to be televised, my job was to go to the team hotel, hang around there, make myself known, and a couple of hours before the game I would go into the players' rooms and paint the white stripes on their boots with luminous paint so it was more visible. My bosses used to be keenly watching the television to make sure the stripes were visible, and if they weren't, I would be in for bollocking."

For this service, an England player would receive £75 per match, which was then about $200—not a princely sum even in 1972. George recalls, "Bobby [Moore], the most charming of people, didn't take the money on the day of the game. He just used to say to me, 'Let it build up for a few games, and I'll ring you when I need it.' And that's what he did." Then the most famous defender of the era would pocket a cumulative few hundred pounds for having advertised an international brand to a cumulative audience of tens of millions.

Only in the late 1980s did English soccer clubs discover that people were willing to buy replicas of their team shirts. That made it plain even to them that their gear must have some value. They had already stopped paying sportswear companies for the stuff; now they started to charge them.

Over time, soccer clubs have found new ways of making money. However, the ideas almost never came from the clubs themselves. Whether it was branded clothing, the gambling pools, or television, it was usually people in other industries who first saw there might be profits to be made. It was Rupert Murdoch who went to English clubs and suggested putting them on satellite TV; the clubs would never have thought of going to him. In fact, the clubs often fought against new moneymaking schemes. Until 1982, they refused to allow any league games to be shown live on TV, fearing that it might deter fans from coming to the stadium. Clubs couldn't grasp that games on television meant both free money and free advertising. There is now a good deal of research into the question of how many fans are lost when a game is shown on TV. Almost all the evidence shows that the number is tiny and that the gate revenue that would be lost is usually well below the amount that would be made from selling extra matches for television coverage.

It took clubs a long time to realize just how much soccer was worth to television. When Greg Dyke was chairman of the UK's ITV Sport in the 1980s, he offered five big clubs £1 million each (then about $1.65 million) for the TV rights for English soccer. Dyke, who later became chairman of England's Football Association, told us in 2013, "It's funny now, when you look at the money that's involved: these chairmen had eyes bulging. They couldn't believe it." In total, Dyke bought the entire TV rights for English professional soccer for £12 million a year—a bit under $20 million at the time. Soon afterward, he went up to Nottingham to try to talk Brian Clough, Forest's then manager, into coming back on TV as a pundit. When Dyke arrived at the club, Clough came up to him and said, "Thank you. I want to shake your hand, Mr. Dyke, because you're the first person that's given football what it's due: twelve million quid."

In 1992 Rupert Murdoch began paying about $100 million per season for the television rights to the new Premier League. As of 2022, the league is getting twelve times as much a season from British TV companies alone. "I've been screwed by television," admitted Sir John Hall, then the Newcastle chairman, one rowdy night at Trinity College Dublin in 1995. "But I'll tell you one thing: I won't be screwed again."

Or take the renovation of English stadiums in the early 1990s. It was an obvious business idea. Supermarkets don't receive customers in sheds built in the Victorian era and gone to seed since. They are forever renovating their stores. Yet soccer clubs never seem to have thought of spending money on their grounds until the Taylor Report of 1990 forced them to. They did up their stadiums, and bingo: more customers came.

All this proves how much like consumers soccer fans are. It's not just that they come running when a team does well (although they do). But in addition, it seems that soccer can quickly become popular across a whole country. All teams then benefit, but particularly those that build nice new stadiums where spectators feel comfortable and safe. That would explain why the three English clubs whose crowds grew fastest over the 1990s were Manchester United, Sunderland, and Newcastle. Later, when Arsenal moved from Highbury to the much larger Emirates, the new stadium filled up despite the fact that the club stopped winning prizes. In other leagues, clubs such as Juventus, Ajax, and Celtic have also drawn big new crowds to their new grounds. There is such a close link between building a nice stadium and drawing more spectators that the traditional English fans' chant of "Where were you when you were shit?" should be revised to "Where were you when your stadium was shit?"

Yet, like almost all good business ideas in soccer, the Taylor Report was imposed on the game from outside. Soccer clubs are classic late adopters of new ideas. Several years after the internet emerged, Liverpool, a club with millions of fans around the world, still did not have a website. It's no wonder that from 1992 through May 2008, even before the financial crisis struck, forty of England's ninety-two professional clubs had been involved in insolvency proceedings, some of them more than once. The proportions have been even higher in Spanish soccer.

HOW THE TRIBE CHOOSES ITS CHIEFS

Rather than stack up endless examples of the historical dimness of soccer clubs, let's take one contemporary case study: how clubs have traditionally hired the person they believe to be their key employee, the manager. English fans are still asking themselves how Steve McClaren ever got to be appointed England manager in 2006, but in fact it is unfair to single him out. The profusion of fantasy soccer leagues, in which office workers masquerade as coaches, indicates the widely held suspicion that any fool could do as well as the people who actually get the jobs. The incompetence of soccer managers may have something to do with the nonsensical and illegal methods by which they are typically recruited.

Soccer "is a sad business," said Bjørn Johansson, founder of a headhunting firm in Zurich. Like his colleagues in headhunting, Johansson was never consulted by clubs seeking managers. Instead, a club typically chooses its man using the following methods.

The New Manager Is Hired in a Mad Rush

In a panel at the International Football Arena conference in Zurich in 2006, Johansson said that in a "normal" business, "an average search process takes four to five months." In soccer, a club usually finds a coach within a couple of days of sacking his predecessor. "Hesitation is regarded as weak leadership," explained another panelist in Zurich, Ilja Kaenzig, then general manager of the German club Hannover 96. Brian Barwick, the English Football Association's former chief executive, noted that McClaren's recruitment "took from beginning to end nine weeks," yet the media accused the FA of being "sluggish." If only it had been more sluggish. Succession planning, common in business, is almost unheard of in soccer.

One rare slow hire became perhaps the most inspired choice in the game's modern history: Arsenal's appointment of Arsène Wenger in 1996. The Frenchman, working in Japan, was not immediately free. Arsenal waited for him, operating under caretaker managers for weeks, and was inevitably accused of being sluggish. Similarly, in 1990 Manchester United's chairman, Martin Edwards, was derided as sluggish when he refused to sack his losing manager, Alex Ferguson. Edwards thought that in the long term, Ferguson might improve.

The New Manager Is Interviewed Only Very Cursorily

In a "normal" business, a wannabe chief executive writes a business plan, gives a presentation, and undergoes several interviews. In soccer a club WhatsApps an agent and offers the job.

The New Manager Is Always a Man

For over a century it was unthinkable that the manager could be a woman, because stupid fans and players would object. Only in 2014 did Clermont in France's Ligue 2 finally break that taboo, appointing Corinne Diacre. "Hiring a woman as a coach has not changed my daily life," Clermont's president Claude Michy told Ben Lyttleton years later. "The sun still rises in the east. I don't feel like I'm an innovator, just because I hired someone with the competence and the skills to do a job." In 2015 *France Football* voted Diacre best coach in Ligue 2. In her first three seasons the team always finished higher in the table than its budget would have predicted. In 2017 she was named coach of France's women's team. But that was partly because no other team in male soccer—which, after all, is where the money is—seemed to want her. Almost all the world's men's teams still discriminate illegally against women.

In men's soccer the new manager is not only invariably male but also almost always white, with a conservative haircut, between thirty-five and sixty years old, and a former professional player. Clubs know that if they choose someone with that profile, then even if the appointment turns out to be terrible, they won't be blamed too much because at least they will have failed in the traditional way.

The idea is that there is something mystical about managing a team, something that only former players can truly understand. Naturally, former players like this idea. Once, in the 1980s, when Kenny Dalglish was in his first spell managing Liverpool, a journalist at a press conference questioned one of his tactical decisions. Dalglish deadpanned, in his almost impenetrable Scots accent, "Who did you play for, then?" The whole room laughed. Dalglish had come up with the killer retort: if you didn't play, you couldn't know.

A former chairman of a Premier League club told us that the managers he employed would often make that argument. The chairman (a rich businessman) never knew how to respond. He hadn't played, so if there really was some kind of mystical knowledge you gained from playing, he wouldn't know. Usually, he would back down.

"Who did you play for, then?" is best understood as a job-protection scheme. Ex-players have used it to corner the market in managerial jobs.

But in truth, their argument never made sense. There is no evidence that having been a good player (or being white and of conservative appearance) is an advantage for a soccer manager. Way back in 1995, Stefan did a study of 209 managers in English football from 1974 to 1994, looking at which ones consistently finished higher in the league than their teams' wage bills predicted. He reported:

> I looked at each manager's football career, first as a player (including number of games played, goals scored, position on the field, international appearances, number of clubs played for) and then as a manager (years of experience, number of clubs played for, and age while in management). Playing history provides almost no guide, except that defenders and goalkeepers in particular do not do well (most managers were midfielders, forwards are slightly more successful than average).

Dalglish finished at the top of Stefan's sample of 209 managers, just ahead of John Duncan, Bob Paisley, George Curtis, Ken Furphy, and Bill Shankly. (Clough wasn't in the sample because no good financial data existed for his clubs, Derby County and Nottingham Forest, or else he'd have surely won. Stefan recently updated his study, and we'll say more about his new findings in Chapter 9.)

Dalglish was a great player and an overperforming manager. However, Bobby Moore, another great player, was 193rd on the managers' list. Taken overall, a good career as a player predicted neither success nor failure as a manager. The two jobs just didn't seem to have much to do with each other. As Arrigo Sacchi, a terrible player turned great manager of Milan, phrased it, "You don't need to have been a horse to be a jockey."

A horse's knowledge doesn't help a jockey. Here is one player turned manager testifying anonymously in *Football Management*, an insightful book by Sue Bridgewater of Warwick Business School: "I got the job and on the first day I showed up and the secretary let me into my office, the manager's office with a phone in and I didn't know where I was supposed to start. I knew about football, I could do the on-pitch things, but I had never worked in an office and I just sat there and I waited for something to happen but no one came in so after a while I picked up the phone and rang my Mum." Even this man's claim that "I knew about football, I could do the on-pitch things" is dubious. Did Diego Maradona know more about the game than Jose Mourinho? Did Roy Keane's knack for geeing up teammates on the field translate once he had become a jockey?

Playing and coaching are different skill sets. Mourinho, who barely ever kicked a ball for money, was, match for match, among the most successful coaches in soccer's history for more than a decade. When rival coach Carlo Ancelotti noted his almost nonexistent record as a player, the Portuguese replied, "I don't see the connection. My dentist is the best in the world, and yet he's never had a particularly bad toothache." Asked why failed players often become good coaches, Mourinho said, "More time to study." They also have to have provided some evidence that they are good coaches because nobody is going to hire them based on their playing careers.

The problem with ex-pros may be precisely their experience. Having been steeped in the game for decades, they just know what to do: how to train, who to buy, how to talk to their players. They don't need to investigate whether these inherited prejudices are, in fact, correct. Rare is the ex-pro who realizes, like Billy Beane at the Oakland A's, that he needs to jettison what he learned along the way. As Lewis writes in *Moneyball*, "Billy had played pro ball, and regarded it as an experience he needed to overcome if he wanted to do his job well. 'A reformed alcoholic,' is how he described himself." Even Ancelotti seems to have changed his mind about the usefulness of a playing career. Once a canny midfielder with Milan, and now a long-standing A-list coach, he told us in 2013, "Experience as a player can help you just in one situation: I can understand what the players are thinking. But the job is different. You have to study to be a manager."

In the world's most innovative soccer country, Germany, ex-players have now lost their monopoly on managerial jobs. In the German soccer federation's annual training course to certify professional coaches, an average of sixteen of the twenty-four places are reserved for people who didn't play professionally. The man who runs the course, Frank Wormuth, told the Dutch website DeCorrespondent.nl that although it helps to know "the smell of the stables" in professional soccer, "that's only one aspect of being a coach. How are you pedagogically, analytically, communicatively? Ex-pros often have less of an eye for that."

Successful German coaches of recent times include Thomas Tuchel, who played eight games in the Second Bundesliga; Roger Schmidt, who was a manager in a car factory; and Julian Nagelsmann, who didn't play a single professional game either before becoming coach of Hoffenheim at age twenty-eight. In 2022, age thirty-four, he was managing Bayern Munich. Nagelsmann's career would have been unthinkable in all other major soccer countries. It's their loss.

But even outside Germany, former great players like Keane, Ruud Gullit, Marco van Basten, Frank Lampard, and Tony Adams are no longer in demand as managers of serious clubs. This looks like another indication that soccer is becoming less stupid.

Immediate Availability

The new manager is appointed either because he is able to start work immediately (often as a result of having just been sacked), because he has achieved good results over his career, or, failing that, because he achieved good results in the weeks preceding the appointment. McClaren became England manager only because his team, Middlesbrough, reached the UEFA Cup final in 2006 and avoided relegation just as the English Football Association was deciding who to pick. By the time Middlesbrough was thumped 4–0 by Sevilla in the final, McClaren already had the job.

The problem is that there is a lot of randomness in short-term results. The underlying patterns can be identified only once you let the law of large numbers do its work. Match results (like daily movements in share prices) are a random walk, and only after many observations can you start to see the trend. Consider the other main candidates to manage England in 1996: Bryan Robson, Frank Clark, Gerry Francis, and the eventual choice, Glenn Hoddle. All of them faded out of the profession fairly quickly, and none had his last job in the Premier League. They were in the frame in 1996 because they had had good results recently, had been good players, and were English—another illegal consideration in hiring.

Star Power

The new manager is traditionally chosen not for his alleged managerial skills but because his name, appearance, and skills at public relations are expected to impress the club's fans, its players, and the media. It was brave of Milan to appoint the unknown Sacchi, and Arsenal the unknown Wenger. Tony Adams, Arsenal's then captain, doubted the obscure foreigner on first sight. In his autobiography, *Addicted*, the player recalls thinking, "What does this Frenchman know about soccer? He wears glasses and looks more like a schoolteacher. He's not going to be as good as George. Does he even speak English properly?"

A manager must above all look like a manager. Clubs would rather use traditional methods to appoint incompetents than risk doing anything that looks odd.

BAD STAFF

The most obvious reason soccer was such an incompetent business for so long is that soccer clubs tended to hire incompetent staff. The manager is only the start of it. Years ago, Simon recalls, I requested an interview with the chairman of an English club quoted on the stock market. The press officer asked me to send a fax (a 1980s technology revered by soccer clubs well into the twenty-first century). I sent it. She said she never got it. On request I sent three more faxes to different officials. She said none arrived. This is quite a common experience for soccer journalists. Because soccer clubs are the only businesses that get daily publicity without trying to, they treat journalists as humble supplicants instead of as unpaid marketers of the clubs' brands. The media often retaliate by being mean. This is not very clever of the clubs because almost all their fans follow them through the media rather than by going to the stadiums.

A month after all the faxes, I was granted permission to send my request by email. When I arrived at the club for the interview, I met the press officer. She was beautiful. Of course she was. Traditionally, soccer clubs recruited the women on their office staff for their looks and the men because they had played professional soccer or were somebody's friend.

When Mino Raiola entered soccer as an agent in his early twenties, straight out of his family's restaurant business, he "was not impressed at all," he told us:

> It's a closed world, with a gigantic potential, and where a lot of money circulates, but it's often managed by people of whom I think, "What the fuck?" It's hard to understand that on the field there are people who have made it through sweat and tears, through a certain natural selection—but not at the top, in the boardroom. That's very strange.
>
> You have to have done something in the soccer world to get another job in the soccer world. The average level in the soccer world is low, and why is it low? Because we don't want outsiders to influence and change or improve our soccer world.

A clever person who has never played professional soccer can (after rigorous study) become a brain surgeon, but however long that person studies, they can never become coach of Ajax Amsterdam, marveled Raiola. "That's ridiculous, isn't it?" When a soccer director's job opens up, he notes, it's rarely advertised publicly. Nor do many clubs or federations scour the world for the best possible candidate. "No," scoffed Raiola, "we'll take someone from within our own ranks. Incest makes this world weak."

This is all the more bizarre because it would be easy for soccer clubs and federations to recruit excellent executives. Professors at business schools report that many of their MBA students, who pay up to $80,000 per year in tuition fees, dream of working in soccer for a pitiful salary. Often, the students beg clubs to let them work for free as summer interns.

The clubs seldom want them (although here again, as the soccer business gradually gets smarter, more MBAs are creeping in).

If you work for a soccer club, your goal is generally to keep working there, not to be shown up by some overeducated young thing who has actually learned something about business. In part, this is because much of the traditionally working-class soccer industry distrusted education. In part, Emmanuel Hembert told us when he was at A. T. Kearney, it is because many clubs are dominated by a vain owner-manager: "Lots of them invested for ego reasons, which is never a good thing in business. They prefer not to have strong people around them, except the coach. They really pay low salaries." If you work for a soccer club as anything but a player or manager, you typically get paid in stardust.

Historically, only Manchester United recruited respected executives from normal industries (such as Peter Kenyon from Umbro). Only after about 2010 did most of the other biggest European clubs start to do so, too.

Baseball for a long time was just as incompetent. In *Moneyball* Lewis asked why, among baseball executives and scouts, "there really is no level of incompetence that won't be tolerated." He thought the main reason was "that baseball has structured itself less as a business than as a social club.... There are many ways to embarrass the Club, but being bad at your job isn't one of them. The greatest offense a Club member can commit is not ineptitude but disloyalty." Club members—and this applies in soccer as much as in baseball—are selected for clubbability. Clever outsiders are not clubbable, because they talk funny and go around pointing out the things that people inside the club are doing wrong. "It wasn't as simple as the unease of jocks in the presence of nerds," wrote Lewis, but that unease does have a lot to do with it.

The staff of soccer clubs traditionally tend not merely to be incompetent; they are also often novices. This is because staff turnover is rapid. Whenever a new owner arrives, he generally brings in his cronies. The departing staff rarely join a new club because that is considered disloyal (Kenyon, an exception, was persecuted for moving from United to Chelsea), even though players change clubs all the time. So soccer executives are always having to reinvent the wheel.

Worse, the media and fans often make it impossible for clubs to take sensible decisions. They are always hassling the club to do something immediately. If the team loses three games, fans start chanting for the club to sack the coach or buy a new player, in short tear up the plans it might have made a month ago. Tony Fernandes, the Malaysian businessman who had run a tight ship at his airline, AirAsia, couldn't do the same after taking over QPR in 2011. "Two things are different from AirAsia," he told us in 2013. "One is I can control almost everything in AirAsia. You can do whatever you want in football, but it's up to the eleven guys on the pitch at the end of the day, right? The second thing is, you have a very vocal bunch of shareholders—called fans. Everyone has an opinion. The plans get thrown out of the window when you start losing. The excitement you get when you win a football game is unbelievable. The downside is that when you lose you want to kill yourself."

"Consumer activism in this industry is extreme," agreed A. T. Kearney in its report "Playing for Profits." Hembert says, "The business plan—as soon as you sign a player for £10 million, you blow up your business plan. Commercial employees have to fight for £100,000 of spending here or there, but then suddenly the club spends £10 million."

Or more. Sven Goran Eriksson once flew into Zurich to tell the International Football Arena a "good story" about his time managing Lazio. "The chairman I had was very good," Eriksson recalled for an audience of mostly Swiss businessmen. "If I wanted a player, he would try to get that player. One day I phoned him up and I said: 'Vieri.'"

Christian Vieri was then playing for Atlético Madrid. Eriksson and Lazio's chairman, Sergio Cragnotti, flew to Spain to bid for him. Atlético told them Vieri would cost 50 billion Italian lire. At the time, in 1998, that was nearly $29 million. Eriksson reminisced, "That was the biggest sum in the world. No player had been involved for that." He said the talks then went more or less as follows:

CRAGNOTTI: That's a lot of money.
ERIKSSON: I know.

At this point, Atlético mentioned that it might accept some Lazio players in partial payment for Vieri.

CRAGNOTTI: Can we do that?
ERIKSSON: No, we can't give away these players.

CRAGNOTTI: What shall we do then?
ERIKSSON: Buy him.
CRAGNOTTI: OK.

Eriksson recalled in Zurich, "He didn't even try to pay forty-nine. He just paid fifty."

Nine months after Vieri joined Lazio, Inter Milan wanted to buy him. Once again, Eriksson reported the conversation:

CRAGNOTTI: What shall I ask for him?
ERIKSSON: Ask for double. Ask one hundred.
CRAGNOTTI: I can't do that.

Eriksson recalled: "So he asked for ninety. And he got ninety. That's good business." (Or the ultimate example of the greater-fool principle.)

Someone in the audience in Zurich asked Eriksson whether such behavior was healthy. After all, Lazio ran out of money in 2002 when Cragnotti's food company, Cirio, went belly-up. Cragnotti later spent time in prison, which even by the standards of Italian soccer is going a bit far. Eriksson replied: "It's not healthy. And if you see Lazio, it was not healthy. But we won the league. And we won the Cupwinners Cup. We won everything."

The point is that soccer clubs, prompted by media and fans, have a tendency to make financially irrational decisions in an instant. They would like to think long term, but because they are in the news every day, they have ended up fixating on the short term. As the British writer Arthur Hopcraft wrote in his book *The Football Man* in 1968, "It is the first characteristic of football that it is always urgent." Ferran Soriano, chief executive of Manchester City, advises, "Do not take decisions on a Monday" (i.e., based on the weekend's result). However, taking decisions on a Monday is the nature of professional soccer.

An executive with an American entertainment corporation tells a story about his long-arranged business meeting with Real Madrid. His company was hoping to build a relationship with the club. But on the day of the meeting, Madrid ritually sacked its manager. The usual chaos ensued. Two of the club officials scheduled to attend the meeting with the American executive did not show up.

Chris Anderson entered soccer specifically with the aim of making the game smarter. Once a semiprofessional goalkeeper in Germany, he became a professor of political science at Cornell University, but his life changed in 2009 when his wife gave him a copy of *Moneyball*. Anderson read it open-mouthed. He began blogging about soccer data. Soon he was being asked to consult clubs. He wrote his book *The Numbers Game* and in 2015 gave up his tenured job at Cornell to become managing director of Coventry City in England's League One. He lasted only eleven months at Coventry, but he came away with some insights into why clubs don't think very hard. Anderson told the world-class Dutch sportswriter Michiel de Hoog that he hadn't come across a single truly innovative club anywhere in soccer. A club could potentially use all the new knowledge from physiology, psychology, sports data, organizational science, and so on, and come up with a completely different way of doing things, but, said Anderson, "No one has really taken it and run with it."

Why not? Anderson identified various reasons:

1. "Time is the great luxury in football," he told de Hoog. Coventry often played two matches a week. That constant pressure dissuades clubs from trying anything new.
2. European soccer clubs can be relegated, which means financial disaster. Clubs in American sports leagues are free from that pressure, which is why you find innovators at some NBA teams, such as the Houston Rockets and the Philadelphia 76ers.
3. If you do everything the same as all the other clubs, then you can't be blamed or humiliated if things go wrong.
4. Most soccer clubs are packed with people who have always done things the old way. So everyone keeps doing the same things they have done forever, even if those things have never worked particularly well.
5. A "masculine culture" in the "working-class" soccer industry encourages stubbornness and certainty, argues Anderson. He says that in recent years the game's insiders, the gnarled old ex-players-turned-coaches, have become scared of losing their power to eggheaded data whizzes. That has made some of them even more stubborn.

Anderson had concluded that the clubs with the most freedom to innovate were new creations with no preexisting culture, such as RB Leipzig, which was founded in 2009 and now regularly qualifies for the Champions League. But in the rest of the industry, he said, two basic rules applied: "When you're doing well, why change? And when you're doing badly, why change?"

NOT BUSINESSES AT ALL

When businesspeople looked at soccer, they were often astonished at how unbusinesslike the clubs were. Every now and then one of them would take over a club and promise to run it "like a business." Sugar, who made his money in computers, became chairman of Tottenham Hotspur in 1991. His brilliant idea was to make Spurs live within its means. Never would he fork out 50 billion lire for a Vieri. He was dismayed to discover that managers regularly stole from their clubs in the form of bungs (bribes, mostly paid by agents who wanted the manager to make a particular transfer). After Newcastle bought Alan Shearer for $23 million in 1996, Sugar remarked, "I've slapped myself around the face a couple of times, but I still can't believe it."

He more or less kept his word. In the ten years that he ran Spurs, the team lived within its means. But most of the fans hated it. The only thing Spurs won in that decade was a solitary League Cup. It spent most of its time in the mid-table of the Premier League, falling far behind its neighbor Arsenal. Nor did it even make much money: about $3 million a year in profits in Sugar's first six years, which was much less than Arsenal and not very good for a company its size. Sugar's Spurs disappointed both on and off the field, and its experience also illustrated a paradox: when businesspeople try to run a soccer club as a business, not only does the soccer suffer, but so does the business.

Other businesspeople pursued a different strategy. They assumed that if they could get their clubs to win prizes, profits would inevitably follow. But they too turned out to be wrong. Even the best teams seldom generated profits. We plotted the league positions and profits of all the clubs that played in the Premier League from 2010 through the 2019–2020 season in Figure 3.1. The figure shows how spectacularly unprofitable the

FIGURE 3.1. Pretax profit/loss of Premier League clubs by league position, 2011–2020

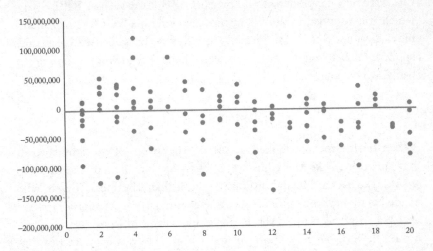

soccer business has been. Each point on the chart represents the combination of profit and position for a club in a particular year. One obvious point to note is that half of the dots fall below zero on the profit axis: these clubs were making losses. But the figure also shows that there was barely any connection between league position and making money. Although there is some suggestion that a few clubs at the top of the table made big profits, the chart also shows that some clubs in these positions had big losses. Manchester United's consistent profitability is clearly exceptional. In the thirty years before being taken over by the Glazer family in 2005, the club generated more than £250 million (about $400 million) in pretax profits while also winning eight league titles. Indeed, other American owners might never have bothered buying into English soccer without United's example. Arsenal was also profitable year in, year out, before the COVID-19 pandemic.

Our graph shows that for most English clubs there was not even a connection between changing league position and changing profits. Looking at just the top two divisions from 2010–2011 to 2019–2020, we find that in 45 percent of all cases, when a club changed its league position, its profits moved in the opposite direction: higher position, lower profits, or lower position, higher profits. Only 55 percent of the time did profits and position move in the same direction. Had there been no correlation at all between winning and making profits, that figure would have been much the same, namely, 50 percent. Clearly, winning games is not the route to making money. Rather, the effect often works the other way around: if a club finds new revenues, that can help it win matches.

For almost all of soccer's history, it proved nearly impossible to run a club like a solid, profit-making business. This is because there were always rival owners—the Abramoviches; the Qatari royal family at PSG; or the longtime ruling family of Libya, the Gadhafis, who owned a chunk of Juventus—who didn't care about profits and spent whatever it took in the hope of winning prizes. All other club owners were forced to keep up with them. If one owner refused to pay large transfer fees and salaries, somebody else would, and that somebody else would get the best players and win prizes. The consequence is that the biggest slice of money that soccer makes is almost always handed over to the best players. As A. T. Kearney said, you could even argue that soccer clubs are nothing more than vessels for transporting soccer's income to players. Hembert explained: "The players are a key factor in winning, and also in the ego, in pleasing the fans. And they all have pretty savvy agents who are able to maximize their bargaining power."

This meant that even the cautious Sugar type could not make decent profits in soccer. In fact, because his team won fewer matches than its free-spending rivals, some fans deserted him. That ate further into his profits. From 1991 to 1998, average attendance in the Premier League rose 29 percent, but Tottenham's crowds fell 5 percent.

"I thought we could make it [QPR] profitable, definitely," Fernandes admitted to us. "I haven't yet," he added, laughing. Even in the 2011–2012 season, when the club survived in the Premier League, it lost £22.6 million (about $36 million). The next season, when it kept buying players but got relegated regardless, it lost a lot more. "On the pitch it was just a disaster," said Fernandes. He mused: "Football has survived on benefactors. Shareholders coming in and pumping money in, and then the next sucker comes in and pumps money in." Did he consider himself a sucker, a benefactor, or a businessman in soccer? "Now I would define myself as a sucker," he replied. "And benefactor. And I hope I will become a benefactor-stroke-businessman." He hasn't. Over the 2010s, QPR lost about $350 million.

In fact, very few club owners in history have even aspired to act like businesspeople. Stefan and the Spanish economist Pedro Garcia del Barrio (of the Universidad Internacional de Cataluña) studied the behavior of Spanish and English clubs between 1993 and 2005 to see whether the clubs were chiefly pursuing profits off the field or victories on it.

If a club wanted to make profits, clearly it would have to spend less than it earned. That would mean limiting its players' wages. Any club that paid players less would suffer on the field because as we have seen, paying high wages wins soccer matches. It's a trade-off: if you want glory, you have to forget maximizing profits. If you want maximum profits, give up hope of glory. Stefan and Pedro estimated, for instance, that if Barcelona wanted to maximize profits, it would have to aim to finish fifteenth in the league because it would need to slash its wages. A profit-driven Real Madrid should expect to finish a mere seventeenth, just above the relegation spots. Most other teams—such as Atlético Madrid, Athletic Bilbao, Sevilla, and Villareal—would maximize their profit potential by playing in the second division. There they could save a lot of money on players' wages.

On the other hand, if a club's main aim was to win matches, it would have to spend every cent it earned (and borrow more besides). So what were clubs chasing, profits or wins?

Stefan and Pedro estimated how each club in the top two Spanish divisions would have behaved on average in the 1994–2005 period if it were pursuing profits and how it would have behaved if it wanted wins. Then they looked at how clubs behaved in real life. Their unambiguous finding: clubs didn't care about profits. They were spending what it took to win games. "On average," Stefan and Pedro concluded, looking at ten years of league tables, "the Spanish teams were twelve places above their profit-maximizing position over the sample period, but less than half a place below their win-maximizing position." In short, club presidents were spending way more than they would have done if they were hardheaded businesspeople out to make profits. Although many of the presidents were in fact hardheaded businesspeople in real life, they weren't treating their soccer clubs as businesses. Nor was there any sign that any other actors—lending banks, say—were pressuring them to make profits.

Building magnates like Florentino Pérez and Jesús Gil y Gil seemed especially prone to blowing what looked like absurd sums of money on players. Possibly they were pursuing a business logic after all: they may have reasoned that making a name in local soccer would help them befriend bankers and get planning permission from local government for their construction projects. That would have boosted their nonsoccer businesses. Fred Wilpon, the real estate developer who took over the New York Mets, discovered that a similar effect operated in baseball. To quote a profile of Wilpon in the *New Yorker*, "He didn't anticipate that owning the Mets would boost his seemingly unrelated business interests. 'No one had heard of us before we bought the Mets, and afterward the change was dramatic. . . . I don't think someone has not returned one of my telephone calls in thirty years. It's a small club, owning a baseball team, and people want to be near it.'"

Owning a soccer team might help the owner's other businesses, but all Spanish soccer clubs tended to pursue wins rather than profits. In a sense, they had to. If your rivals are spending whatever it takes to win, then you must as well. Any team that pursued the highest possible profits would probably end up being relegated because it wouldn't be spending enough to hire good players. And if the club got relegated, it would lose much of its revenues. So Spanish soccer became an arms race: every club overspent for fear of the neighbors.

No matter how much money Spanish clubs got their hands on, they spent it. In the decade that Stefan and Pedro studied, the average revenues of a club in the Spanish first division (Primera División) rose nearly fourteenfold, from €4.3 million (about $3.6 million) in 1994 to €59 million ($73 million) in 2004. (By 2015, the figure was €130 million, about $143 million.) Yet the share of revenue that clubs spent on player wages didn't drop much throughout the period: in that decade, first-division clubs paid over an average of 62 percent of their revenues to their players. In other words, the clubs weren't able to save all the additional money or do much else with it, such as build new stadiums or cut ticket prices. Most of the money that came in just went straight out again into players' bank accounts. In the second division, a whopping 93 percent of clubs' revenues went to the players. These clubs really were just vessels for transporting money to players. The clubs weren't content with giving the players what money they had. They also gave them money they didn't have, and some clubs ended up seriously in debt.

By the standards of a normal business, this sort of spending is nuts. But for soccer clubs, it made sense: the only way to win matches was to overspend. Historically, almost nobody ran a soccer club to turn a tidy annual profit. And as we'll explain in the next chapter, clubs can safely rack up losses and debts essentially forever. They are bad businesses because they can be bad with impunity.

4

SAFER THAN THE BANK
OF ENGLAND

Why Soccer Clubs Almost Never Disappear

On September 15, 2008, the investment bank Lehman Brothers collapsed, followed almost immediately by the world's stock markets.

Any soccer club on Earth was a midget next to Lehman. In the fiscal year ending in September 2007, the bank had income of $59 billion (148 times Manchester United's at the time), had profits of $6 billion (fifty times Manchester United's), and was valued by the stock market at $34 billion. If United's shares had been traded on the market at the time, they probably would have been worth less than 5 percent of Lehman's. Yet Lehman no longer exists, whereas United very much does. So does almost every club in Europe that existed in 2008.

In the years before the global economic crisis, people worried a lot more about the survival of soccer clubs than that of banks. Yet it was many of the world's largest banks that disappeared. Then, when the COVID-19 pandemic struck, almost every club in Europe survived playing in empty stadiums for a year. The notion that soccer clubs are inherently unstable businesses is wrong. Although large numbers of them are still incompetently run and many have been loss making for most of the last century or more, they are some of the most stable businesses on Earth. Why do clubs keep going bust? And why do they almost always survive regardless?

First, some facts. In 1923 the English Football League consisted of eighty-eight teams spread over four divisions. In the 2021–2022 season, eighty-five of these clubs still existed (97 percent),[1] and seventy remained in the top four divisions (80 percent). Thirty-eight were in the same division as they had been in 1923. Of the twenty-two teams in the First Division in 1923, only three were playing below the second tier in 2022: Bolton Wanderers and Sunderland in the third tier and Notts County in the fifth tier.

You would have expected the Great Depression of the 1930s, in particular, to pose clubs something of a threat. After all, the Depression bit deepest in the North of England, where most of the country's professional clubs were based, and all romantic rhetoric aside, you would think that when people cannot afford to buy bread, they would stop going to soccer matches.

Crowds in the Football League did indeed fall 12 percent between 1929 and 1931. However, by 1932, they were growing again, even though the British economy was not. And clubs helped one another through the hard times. When Orient in East London hit trouble in 1931, Arsenal wrote its tiny neighbor a check for £3,450 (then about $13,000) to tide it over. Clubs know they cannot operate without opponents, and so, unlike in most businesses, the collapse of a rival is not cause for celebration.

The Depression culled only a couple of clubs. Merthyr Town, after failing to be reelected to the league in 1930, folded a few years later, the victim of economic hardship in the Welsh valleys (as well as competition from far more popular rugby). Wigan Borough went bankrupt a few games into the 1931–1932 season. It left the league, and its remaining fixtures were never played. Aldershot was elected to replace it, and sixty years later, in another recession, it became only the second English club in history to withdraw from the league with fixtures unplayed.

Almost equally hard as the Depression for English clubs was the "Thatcher recession" of the early 1980s. Again, many working-class fans lost their factory jobs. The league's attendance dropped from 24.6 million to 16.5 million between 1980 and 1986. Among those who continued to show up were lots of hooligans. Soccer seemed to be in terminal decline. As Ken Friar, then managing director of Arsenal, put it, "Football is the oddest of industries. It sells one product and has ninety-two outlets for it.

In any other business, if not all ninety-two outlets were doing well, there would be some talk of closing some of them down. But in football, all ninety-two outlets claim an equal right to survive."

During the Thatcher recession, many clubs flirted with going insolvent. Solvency means the capacity to pay your debts—that is, the reasonable expectation that your future income will be enough to pay what you owe. In most European countries, solvency is a basic requirement for doing business. If a company's directors know that it cannot pay its debts—a very common business problem—then legally they should stop doing business until either solvency is restored or the company is shut down. Solvency can be restored if the creditors agree to write off some of their debts. If the creditors won't do that, then the business can be closed, the assets sold, and the creditors paid off as far as is possible.

However, soccer clubs found an ingenious way to survive insolvency: a trick called "phoenixing." It works like this: every English football club is a club but also a public limited company. For instance, Arsenal is also Arsenal Holdings PLC. When the limited company is heavily in debt and goes insolvent, there's an easy solution: simply dissolve the old company and create a new "phoenix" company. So when Bristol City's holding company Bristol City Football Club PLC looked on the point of folding in 1982, taking the ancient club down with it, some local businesspeople created a new holding company called BCFC (1982) PLC. This company became a new Bristol City, a phoenix from the ashes of the old club. The old company was liquidated, and the new one took over almost everything that made up the undying essence of the old club—the name, the stadium, the club colors—but not, crucially, the old club's debts and unaffordable players. On the field, Bristol City lived on.

Other clubs quickly cottoned onto the joy of phoenixing. Between 1982 and 1984, Hereford, Hull, Wolves, Derby, Bradford, and Charlton went through much the same experience as Bristol City. All these troubled clubs survived either by creating a new "phoenix" company (Wolves, Bradford, and Charlton) or by getting creditors to agree to suspend their claims (a moratorium), under the threat that a phoenix might be the alternative. In all cases, the bankrupt company was ditched but the immortal club inside it salvaged.

Phoenixing—the creation of a new company—turned out to be an excellent way to escape creditors. Clearly, there is something suspect about the method, which allowed disastrous directors to avoid the consequences of their decisions. Their clubs survived, but at the expense of creditors (often players, banks, and the taxman), who never saw their money again.

Still, this was just what hapless soccer clubs needed. Many of them struggled in the 1980s, and several survived only thanks to a "sub"—financial support—from the players' trade union, the Professional Footballers' Association. Charlton and Bristol City's neighbor Bristol Rovers had to move grounds because it could not pay the rent. However, nobody resigned from the league.

Soon after the Thatcher recession, a new law made it even easier for British clubs to survive. Historically in Western countries, attitudes to bankruptcy had been harsh. In nineteenth-century England, bankrupts were still being sent to prison. But over time we have become more forgiving. Increasingly, people have come to recognize that bankruptcy can be caused by bad luck as well as bad judgment. As well as relaxing our moral stance, we have discovered some self-interested motives to keep struggling businesses alive: bankruptcy destroys a company's value, often unnecessarily. By the 1980s, the UK's traditional method of liquidation—the bankrupt company's assets were sold, the debts repaid as far as possible, and the company liquidated—had become discredited. Critics said it gave stricken companies little chance to recover. They praised the American approach, which treated failure as a frequently necessary precursor to eventual success. In 1979 the US introduced the now-famous Chapter 11 provisions. These protect a firm from its creditors while it tries to work out a solution that saves the business. Britain—where insolvencies hit an all-time high during the Thatcher recession—wanted some of that. Later, Italy, Germany, Spain, and eventually France adopted some version of the more forgiving "American" bankruptcy laws. This proved a boon to soccer clubs.

The UK's Insolvency Act of 1986 transformed a procedure known as "administration." From then on, when a company went into administration, an independent insolvency practitioner was called in and charged with finding a way to keep the business running while repaying as much money as possible to the creditors. After the new law arrived, stricken soccer clubs typically entered administration, struck deals with creditors, and then swiftly emerged from administration. That's what Tranmere

Rovers and Rotherham United did in 1987, for instance. For most clubs, financial collapse was becoming something of a breeze.

True, Aldershot FC was liquidated in 1992, but supporters simply started a new club almost identical to the old one. The "new" Aldershot Town AFC has a badge that shows a phoenix rising from the ashes. Other tiny British clubs that folded—Maidstone United, Newport County, Accrington Stanley—were also eventually resuscitated and now stumble on somewhere in the semiprofessional or professional game. Accrington Stanley's rebirth was surely the most drawn out: it resigned from the Football League in 1962 with debts of £63,000 ($176,400), got liquidated in 1966, was newly created by fans in 1968, and returned to the Football League in 2006, its brand still very much alive, probably even enhanced by the drama. "Above the turnstiles now, the welcoming sign is 'The Club That Wouldn't Die,'" Accrington's then chairman Ilyas Khan told us proudly in 2012.

The new British law was so kind to insolvent companies that ever more companies decided to enter insolvency. Some did it just to wipe off their debts. The method became increasingly popular even as the economy improved. Company insolvencies in the recession of the early 1980s had run at an average of around ten thousand per year. In the boom period between 1994 and 2001, they ran at sixteen thousand per year. Soccer clubs, too, loved the new law: more of them went insolvent in the 1990s boom than in the early 1980s bust. They rarely even needed to bother to create new "phoenix" companies anymore. Clubs would run up unpayable debts, go insolvent, and, hey, presto, months later would be fine and signing shiny new center forwards again. Better-run rivals complained that insolvency and phoenixing were giving the culprits an unfair advantage. In 2004 this argument prompted the league to introduce a ten-point penalty for clubs that went into administration. Still, it hasn't proved a huge deterrent.

There's something else to note about these near-death experiences: they almost always happen to small clubs. Big clubs hardly ever go bust.

Yes, there was a great kerfuffle in 2010 when Portsmouth FC of the mighty Premier League entered administration. The club had been on much the same journey as Bristol City thirty years earlier, just with larger sums. It had overspent on good players, won an FA Cup, and ended up in trouble. In some ways, Portsmouth's story was familiar: soccer club goes bust and, after many premature reports of its demise, is reborn. The shared fan angst about their club disappearing has a useful psychological function: it's a communal ritual that gives people a chance to join together to affirm their love of the club. After administration, Portsmouth slid down the divisions and spent a few miserable years bumping along in League Two, the bottom tier of English soccer, until getting promoted to League One in 2017. That summer the club was bought by Michael Eisner, former chief executive of Disney, whose estimated net worth is $2.5 billion. Having flirted with disaster, Portsmouth, as of 2022, was still in League One. Like so many clubs that have been through the same experience, it's alive and kicking.

But in another way, Portsmouth's story is exceptional. It's the only club ever to go into administration while playing in the Premier League. There were no less than sixty-seven cases of insolvency in English soccer from 1982 through 2010, and all but Portsmouth involved teams in the lower divisions. That is something that doomsayers should note. They often complain about the debts of rich clubs, like Manchester United. They used to ask how Chelsea would survive if Roman Abramovich were to fall under a bus. Then the unprovoked Russian invasion of Ukraine in February 2022 forced Abramovich out, and it emerged that there were at least fifteen billionaires keen to bid for the club.

In fact, big clubs are not the problem. Across Europe, lower-tier teams live on the edge of insolvency, but top-tier teams, even though they also mostly lose money, seldom become insolvent. The highest risk of all in most countries is to recently relegated teams. This is true even in Germany and France, where strict licensing systems regulate clubs' spending. The Germans, in particular, have been regulating their clubs' spending since the 1960s. Clubs have to submit budgets for each forthcoming season, showing that they aren't spending more on wages than their expected revenues. Only "healthy" clubs get licenses. The French system is similar.

It is often said that these systems save clubs from the financial crises and insolvency so common in England. It is true that German clubs have not gone into insolvency proceedings while playing in the top two divisions, but insolvency is actually a very common event in German soccer. It just usually happens after clubs are relegated from the top two tiers.

Stefan and Daniel Weimar of the German Sports University in Cologne found 105 cases of German clubs being declared insolvent between 1995 and 2017 alone, including nine clubs that had once played in the top division and thirty clubs that had played in the second Bundesliga. This level of insolvency is similar to that of the English game. There are also plenty of instances of insolvency in French soccer.

German and French journalists have paid little attention to these insolvency crises, perhaps because only obscure divisions are affected. When Daniel was about to present the paper on German soccer insolvency at a German conference in 2017, the chair of his session looked at him quizzically and said, "There weren't a lot of insolvencies, right?" Everybody laughed. By the end of the session, they were wondering why they had never heard of the problem. Meanwhile, British journalists have agonized for four decades about insolvencies in British soccer.

Many small European clubs went insolvent in the economic crisis after 2008. In the last edition of *Soccernomics* we identified about a dozen small clubs that "disappeared": UD Salamanca, Lorca, and CD Badajoz in Spain; Evian Thonon Gaillard in France; Haarlem, Veendam, AGOVV, and RBC Roosendaal in Holland; FC Brussels and Beerschot in Belgium; MyPa in Finland; and Gretna in Scotland. When we reviewed this list in 2021, we found that all but Veendam and FC Brussels had been revived in one form or another. Most have similar names and play in the same stadiums as before they "died." Some have merged with other local clubs, and most have relied on the fans for their revival. It's almost impossible to kill off a football club, even if you want to.

Perhaps because English professional clubs are older, more established brands than most Continental teams, even the littlest among them survived the crisis. But if people are determined to worry about clubs going bust, it's the Accrington Stanleys they should worry about, not the Chelseas. And they probably shouldn't worry too much about the issue at all. If European soccer clubs really did collapse beneath their debts, there would now be virtually no European soccer clubs left. "We must be sustainable," clubs say nowadays, parroting the latest business cliché. In fact, they are fantastically sustainable. They survive even when they go bust. You can't get more sustainable than that. Match fixing, say, is a much bigger problem for European soccer than bankruptcy.

Yet the 2008 crisis helped prompt UEFA to make drastic reforms to prevent bankruptcies. Soccer officials had been worrying about the health of numerous clubs since the late 1990s. In many European countries, clubs had long been kept afloat by public subsidies—often, a million here and there from the local town hall. Now these flows were drying up. Would clubs suddenly disappear?

During the economic crisis, UEFA—for decades a sleepy organization—began to wake up. The first thing it realized was that knowledge is power, so, advised by lawyers, it gathered information from clubs about their administrative and financial statuses. It then used this information to argue for European-wide regulation, otherwise known as club licensing. Who should be the regulator? UEFA, of course.

The association's president, Michel Platini, who had taken office in 2007, obsessed about clubs' debts. By 2009, UEFA was ready. Having worked to win the support of the big clubs and national associations, as well as some sympathetic journalists and fan lobby groups, it announced it would begin enforcing a set of regulations called Financial Fair Play (FFP). The aim, UEFA claimed, was to stop clubs from spending more than they took in. Platini sold FFP as a way of restoring European soccer to "good health." Even though clubs weren't disappearing in the economic crisis, he seized on the possibility that they might have. He warned that half of Europe's professional clubs had financial troubles of some kind. "If this situation goes on," he added, "it will not be long before even some major clubs face going out of business."

Platini also seems to have had moral objections to overspending and big money in soccer, perhaps because he himself had played in an era when there was little money in the game. Ultimately, he helped push through the FFP regulations, which came into force in the early 2010s and specified financial rules that clubs must follow. UEFA's stated objectives included introducing "more discipline and rationality in football club finances." (Interestingly, the objectives said nothing about making competition fairer.) Of course, the near-immortality of soccer clubs makes you wonder exactly what problem these rules were meant to solve.

The FFP regulations did do one thing that we applaud: they insisted that every club be solvent. In the past, many insolvent clubs restored their finances by refusing to pay small creditors, banks, and the taxman—daring any of them to take on the label of the creditor that destroyed a club. Very few creditors have chosen to tread this path. No bank manager or tax collector wants to say, "The century-old local club is closing. I'm turning off the lights." And perhaps in the days when there was almost no money in soccer, it didn't matter. Local banks can usually write off a debt of a few tens of thousands of dollars (not much money for even a modestly sized bank).

In recent years, though, clubs' income has started to add up to something. These days, when a club can't pay, lots of creditors get hurt. Often, the victims are small local businesses, such as the grocers who supply clubs with food. Clearly, it's wrong for a club to pay its players millions and then stiff its creditors. So we think it's right that clubs should have to be solvent.

From 2011 to 2013, the four English divisions adopted their own rules to stop their clubs from overspending. The Premier League's rules, called Short Term Cost Control (although often referred to as Premier League Financial Fair Play), involve a complex formula that broadly limits rises in player spending to a fixed amount per year. Spain, too, tried to clamp down on profligate clubs. Indeed, it was La Liga's rules that stopped a massively indebted Barcelona from giving Leo Messi a new contract in 2021.

However, the regulators should have looked more closely at what most clubs' debts actually consisted of. Platini and others fretted that when Chelsea met Manchester United in May 2008 in the final of the Champions League, the two clubs had a combined debt of about $3 billion. Now, it's true that football clubs have a history of being unable to pay their debts. But it's precisely for this reason that banks and other commercial lenders stopped lending to them decades ago, except for the safest of projects. Most of the debts that football clubs have are in fact "soft" loans—meaning that they reflect sums of money spent by the owners, who fondly hope that their clubs will repay them one day. For example, the 2021 financial statements for Fordstam PLC, the company that owns Chelsea FC, showed that the company had debts amounting to £602 million due for payment within one year and £1.19 billion due beyond one year. This amount of debt (£1.79 billion in total, or about $2.3 billion) sounds a little scary against Fordstam's mere £437 million (about

$568 million) of annual revenue until you read the small print. Notes 21 and 22 to the financial statements demonstrated that £1.4 billion (or $1.8 billion) of the debt (78 percent) was in fact owed to "related parties," which is accounting jargon for "yourself." In other words, Abramovich, the owner, had decided to classify $1.8 billion of the money he had put into Chelsea as a (soft) loan. It's soft because lending money to yourself is a fairly meaningless activity (try it).

The "loans" were needed to run the business. If he had wanted his money back, he could in theory have done what any creditor can do—insist on repayment and trigger insolvency proceedings if the money was not forthcoming—but bankrupting his own business would hardly help. The only way for him to get his money back would have been to sell the club. In 2022 he was forced to do so for political reasons, but the British government undertook to make sure that the money went to Ukrainian aid rather than into his pockets.

Soft loans are common at clubs like Chelsea, PSG, and Manchester City, whose owners have global ambitions, but they are also common at the small clubs bailed out by local businessmen. There are only a few clubs that have commercial (i.e., real) debt, and these typically involve cases where big clubs have built stadiums knowing they can easily fill them. (Arsenal and Tottenham are good examples.) Most frustrating of all, for fans, is the case of Manchester United, in which the Glazer family used commercial debt to fund their own purchase of the club, which yielded them huge profits at little or no cost. The only reason that this worked was precisely because the fans love their club. The cruel irony was that there was never any risk of Manchester United losing support, so the banks were quite happy to lend to the Glazers. In 2005 they had used £790 million ($1.4 billion) in borrowed money to buy United. They then took their cut annually out of the business and by March 2022 still owned an asset valued (on the New York Stock Exchange) at $2.4 billion. Money for nothing, as the saying goes. The Glazers successfully monetized the fans' loyalty.

Why do so many soccer clubs go bankrupt? UEFA's Financial Fair Play regulations offer one possible explanation. UEFA's view was that the repeated financial crises of clubs were caused by mismanagement, which stricter regulations could correct.

A second explanation for club bankruptcies draws a parallel with communism. Just as most soccer clubs lose money, so did most state-owned companies under communism. It was the great Hungarian economist János Kornai who hit on the reason why. Kornai was a communist in the 1950s, and he wanted the system to work. But when it didn't, he came up with a four-word explanation: "the soft-budget constraint." Imagine that you are a tractor factory in communist Hungary. Each year the state gives you a budget. But if at the end of the year you've overspent the budget and haven't made any profits, the state just gives you a bit more money to make up the difference. Under communism, bad companies were propped up forever. In other words, the "budget constraint" on communist firms was soft. If they wanted to overspend their budgets, they could. The obvious consequence: unprofitable overspending became rife. Scholars such as Wladimir Andreff and Rasmus Storm believe that the "soft-budget constraint" also explains soccer economics. Like tractor factories in communism, clubs lose money because they can. They have no need to be competent. So high-spending owners and managers drive clubs into bankruptcy, knowing that they will be bailed out.

Both the mismanagement explanation for soccer bankruptcies and the soft-budget-constraint explanation are plausible. But no one has yet tried to test either in any systematic way. Meanwhile, over the last decade, Stefan has developed a third explanation that is consistent with the data.

Stefan had been studying the frequent financial failures of clubs in England, France, and Germany. When he looked at what had happened to clubs in the period before they entered bankruptcy, one thing stood out: in almost every case the performance of the club had been *deteriorating*. In the five years prior to bankruptcy, most clubs achieved lower league positions year on year and frequently endured relegation. This finding in itself challenges the irrationality and soft-budget-constraint theories. After all, if it was excessive spending that drove clubs into bankruptcy, then their league performances should have been *improving* beforehand. (We know that higher spending leads to better league performances in European soccer.)

The biggest factor precipitating bankruptcy is frequently relegation because of the dilemma it creates for the afflicted club. The club knows that revenues will fall in the lower division, often dramatically, so it needs to cut costs, usually by replacing expensive players with cheaper ones. But this cost cutting can start a vicious circle: quite often, a club will get relegated in successive seasons. Players also have contracts, which can be expensive to terminate, and selling players straight after they have visibly failed is never easy when other clubs know you need the money. All in all, the financial crunch of relegation can be disastrous.

However, Stefan argues, the bankruptcy isn't really caused by the relegation itself but by the uncertainty surrounding it—what economists call "shocks." An economic shock is any random event that hits the economy. The shock can be positive (such as an unexpectedly good harvest) or negative. COVID-19, which shut down much of the global economy for a year, is a scarily good example of a negative shock. That was a big one, but shocks can also be very small and localized. A common negative shock for a soccer club is an injury to a star player. The event usually cannot be anticipated, but it will affect team performance. Relegation is also a negative shock because for the most part, clubs do not know that they will be relegated until the very end of the season.

Stefan defined negative shocks to soccer clubs in England as random downward variations from average performances. Then he measured the size of these shocks over many seasons. A negative shock in one season might not be much of a problem. Two consecutive negative shocks were usually manageable. But Stefan found that sequences of three or more negative shocks in consecutive seasons significantly increased the likelihood of bankruptcy. In other words, what bankrupts clubs is not indiscipline and irrational management; it's the difficulty of coping with a series of unfortunate events.

Not surprisingly, we tend to prefer Stefan's theory of bankruptcy. However, the three explanations are not mutually exclusive. Ideally, one would like to test each one using data. But COVID-19 does provide a test of sorts because it was a negative shock to a whole economy, including soccer clubs. Never before had clubs taken such a financial hit; even during world wars and economic depressions, grounds were often full. Big clubs could cope with empty stadiums: fueled by TV revenues, they could still keep their players in Ferraris. But smaller clubs rely chiefly on football's oldest form of financing: butts in seats. Deprived of ticket sales, many clubs faced "an existential threat," said Juve's president Andrea Agnelli in March 2020, when he was also president of the European Club Association. He called the coronavirus "the biggest challenge our game and industry has ever faced."

In summer 2021, UEFA identified forty-eight clubs across the Continent that entered insolvency proceedings or withdrew from their leagues on financial grounds between March 2020 and April 2021. UEFA estimates that the aggregate lost profits of European soccer caused by COVID-19 will be around $6 billion to $7 billion, which will scar clubs for many years to come. So here is a shock that caused widespread bankruptcy. Yet we can identify only two European clubs that stopped playing during the pandemic, and even they were swiftly reborn. Sporting Lokeren in Belgium merged with little Temse into K.S.C. Lokeren-Temse, and it joined the Belgian fourth tier, although there is no doubt that it will rise fast. Meanwhile, in England, Macclesfield Town, which folded in 2020, was bought by a local businessman and rejoined non-league football in 2021—another example of the joys of phoenixing.

Other clubs were bailed out by loans or loan guarantees from local governments (as happened to Schalke 04) or were bought by new owners. In countries including Germany and England, big clubs helped subsidize small ones, in the tradition of Arsenal writing that check for Orient in 1931. Happily, salvation came pretty cheaply. After all, most soccer clubs are tiny businesses that can be bailed out at a low cost. Society swallows the two-bit losses and lets the minnows swim on. In 2020 the English Premier League agreed to a rescue package of £250 million (about $320 million) in grants and interest-free loans for the seventy-two clubs in the English Football League. Compare that sum with the aviation industry: Virgin Atlantic alone needed a $1.5 billion rescue package just to keep going until 2022. In a sense, soccer clubs are too small to fail.

It also helped that their only significant operating cost, the salary bill, could be vastly reduced. Especially in France, many clubs pressured players to accept pay cuts—no great hardship, as wages had spiraled in the thirty years of the TV era.

The simple truth of professional soccer is that most players and managers would, if it came to it, do the job for free. That makes it easy to cut costs in times of crisis. Post-COVID, many small clubs might revert to employing part-time and amateur players, which was the norm across most of Europe for much of football's history. An amateur or part-time team can still be a pillar of a town. Even the biggest German clubs were semiprofessional until 1963.

Look at Bury FC, which folded amid much mourning pre-pandemic in 2019 but almost immediately returned to the tenth tier of English football, probably destined for a steep rise to somewhere near its old perch in League Two. Even in the tenth tier, the penniless club received 750 applications for the job of manager, although the job would have paid next to nothing. The happy truth is that Bury could exist either in the Premier League or as an amateur pub team. That is the ultimate scalability of soccer. "Death" in this sport often simply means downsizing: a club cuts wages, drops down the divisions, and competes at a lower level.

Once again, the comparison between soccer clubs and "real" businesses breaks down. Imagine if other businesses could slash costs like clubs do. Suppose that Ford could sack skilled workers and hire unskilled ones to produce worse cars or that American Airlines could replace all its pilots with people who weren't as well qualified to fly planes. The government would stop it, and in any case, consumers would not put up with terrible products. (President Ronald Reagan did sack striking air-traffic controllers in 1981 and replace them with new hires, but that was something of a one-off.)

Soccer clubs have it easy. Recall that almost every English professional club has survived the Great Depression, World War II, recessions, corrupt chairmen, appalling managers, and the post-2008 economic crisis. By contrast, the economic historian Les Hannah made a list of the top one hundred global companies in 1912 and researched what had become of them by 1995. Nearly half the companies—forty-nine—had ceased to exist. Five of these had gone bankrupt, six were nationalized, and thirty-eight were taken over by other firms. Even among the businesses that survived, many had gone into new sectors or moved to new locations.

What made these nonfootball businesses so unstable was, above all, competition. There is such a thing as brand loyalty, but when a better product turns up, most people will switch sooner or later. So normal businesses keep having to innovate or die. They face endless pitfalls: competitors pull ahead, consumers' tastes change, new technologies make entire industries obsolete, cheap goods arrive from abroad, the government interferes, recessions hit, companies overinvest and go bust or simply get unlucky.

By contrast, soccer clubs are immune from almost all these effects.

A club that fails to keep up with the competition might get relegated, but it can always survive at a lower level. Some fans will lose interest, but clubs have geographical roots. A bad team might find its catchment area shrinking but not disappearing completely.

The "technology" of soccer can never become obsolete because the technology is the game itself. At worst, soccer might become less popular.

Foreign rivals cannot enter the market and supply soccer at a lower price. The rules of soccer protect domestic clubs by forbidding foreign competitors from joining their leagues. English clubs as a whole could fall behind foreign competitors and lose their best players, but foreign clubs have financial problems and incompetent management of their own.

Governments are not about to nationalize soccer.

Clubs often overinvest, but this almost never destroys them—only the wealth of their investors. At worst, the club gets relegated.

A club's revenues might decline in a recession, but it can always live with lower revenues.

In most industries, a bad business goes bankrupt, but soccer clubs almost never do. No matter how much money they waste, someone will always bail them out. This is what is known in finance as "moral hazard": when you know you will be saved no matter how much money you lose, you are free to lose money.

But there's one more element that makes the football business so uniquely sustainable: love. Even terrible clubs tend to have a core fan base of a couple of thousand people who will stick by them no matter what. So viable is the business model of these small clubs that many of them have been around since Queen Victoria's day. Bury, for instance, founded in 1885, hasn't won a national trophy since the FA Cup of 1903. Like nearby Macclesfield and Accrington Stanley, the club is a relic of the Industrial Revolution, left behind in a struggling northern town after the economic tide receded, searching for a modern catchment area in the soccer-satiated region around Manchester. But then, Bury isn't competing with Manchester United. Its fans don't expect trophies. They just need their club to survive and keep providing an extremely local service, essentially forever. Calling this "brand loyalty" is not respectful enough of the sentiment involved. To quote Rogan Taylor, a Liverpool fan and Liverpool University professor, "Football is more than just a business. No one has their ashes scattered down the aisle at Tesco."

5

A DECENT BUSINESS AT LAST?

Be Careful What You Wish For

A few years ago, a rich man sent former Israeli prime minister Ehud Olmert on a mission. The man, whom Olmert would describe to us only as an "Eastern investor" (we think from East Asia), wanted to buy Manchester United. A lot of people do. But for all of them, an early obstacle is the difficulty of actually meeting the Glazer family, which owns the club. The Glazers don't get out much.

That was where Olmert came in. The Glazers are great "friends of Israel," and the Eastern investor suspected they would like to meet the country's former leader. So it proved. A meeting was arranged. At the Glazers' country club in Palm Beach, Florida, Olmert—a United fan since the Munich air crash of 1958—handed the family a check from the investor for about £1 billion ($1.6 billion) to take over United.

Unfortunately, the Glazers said no straight away. "This is the strongest brand name in the sports world," they explained. They also expected the club to just get more valuable. And so far, they have been proven right.

The Glazers have shown how profitable a soccer club can be. Business-minded investors around the world have been following their lead, hoping to make money out of soccer, too. If you want soccer to become a better business, that sounds good. But we think it's bad news. We aren't pleased that some of the biggest clubs might one day become profitable businesses because we believe soccer shouldn't be a business at all.

99

The most lucrative thing that ever happened to the soccer business was television. As long as the audience was restricted to the number of people who could fit inside a stadium, there could never be much money in it. For example, when Arsenal won the English title in 1948, the club's total revenue for the season was £143,021. Allowing for inflation, that's about £5.3 million ($6.8 million) in 2020 money. By 2020, mostly thanks to TV, Arsenal's annual soccer revenues were £343.5 million ($441 million), or sixty-five times higher, despite taking a hit during the COVID-19 pandemic.

As we've seen, television began boosting soccer's revenues in the 1970s, but the big leap happened in the 1990s. Cable and satellite technology, digitization, encryption, and flat-panel display made it possible to broadcast every game and charge customers premium prices for the privilege of watching on seventy-two-inch screens in their own homes. In England the revenues of Premier League clubs jumped more than forty-fold in the thirty years from 1990 to 2019. (The median income of a twenty-two-year-old American is currently $22,000, so the equivalent jump would be to make $880,000 a year by age fifty-two. Think how different that person's life would be.)

TV also turned out to be the greatest showcase the game had ever had. It beamed the best of Western European soccer into living rooms around the world. Pretty soon, some rich foreigners got interested in owning a piece of the action. And for the first few years, at least, most of them weren't interested in making profits.

In 2003 Roman Abramovich bought Chelsea, sealing the deal with the departing owner Ken Bates over a bottle of Evian water in London's Dorchester Hotel. The Russian oligarch was then still happy to talk to journalists. When the *Financial Times* rang, he explained why he had bought Chelsea: "I'm looking at it as something to have fun with rather than having to realize a return. I don't look at this as a financial investment." Abramovich has barely spoken another word in public since, but two things have become clear: (1) Buying a soccer club made this unknown billionaire world famous. (2) As he predicted, the purchase hasn't been a "financial investment." In his first eight years as owner, he sank about $1 billion of his personal fortune into the club, money that is unlikely ever to result in profits.

Despite the losses, Abramovich inspired the era of billionaire "sugar daddies" in soccer. When a man becomes a billionaire, he tends to want to convert some of that money into fun and prestige. A good way of doing that is to buy into sports. Men such as Sheikh Mansour of Abu Dhabi, who bought Manchester City in 2008, aren't like investors in normal businesses. They are willing to lose money just to be part of the game. They have helped drive up wages and salaries for the best players to unprecedented levels. The sums involved don't matter much to the sugar daddies. After all, for Abramovich, signing a striker for $50 million was equivalent to your average person buying a cup of coffee. But, pretty soon, the sugar daddies hit obstacles. Much of European soccer told them "We don't want your money; take it away."

UEFA's FFP rules—supposedly drawn up to stop clubs from going bust—brought in, among other things, the "break-even" rule. This aimed to stop clubs from spending more than they earned. If a club's annual revenues were $400 million, the break-even rule barred it from spending $500 million, even if some sugar daddy wanted to give it the money. This was a downer for the sheikhs looking to splash clubs with their personal fortunes. The break-even rule cemented inequality by making it harder for smaller clubs to compete with the established giants.

In previous editions we expressed our disapproval of the concept. The rule was designed to limit competition, not to keep clubs solvent. Why should a rich owner be prevented from spending his or her own money to assemble a great team? Fans complain about the dominance of the big clubs, but the only inroads in that dominance in recent decades have come through rich individuals buying clubs that were previously also-rans (think Chelsea) or had fallen on hard times (think Manchester City) and then building them up to challenge the aristocrats.

But FFP 1.0 has been a complete failure even on its own terms. It was intended to curb excessive spending. In 2009, before the regulations were applied, clubs spent 63.9 percent of revenues on salaries. In 2019, the last year before the COVID-19 pandemic, the clubs spent—ta-da—64 percent. In 2009, 24.3 percent of clubs spent more than 80 percent of their revenues on wages. In 2019 it was (drum roll, please) 29.3 percent. (These are UEFA's own figures.)

When the pandemic inflicted big losses on most clubs, UEFA relaxed the FFP rules to the point of meaninglessness. Paris Saint-Germain was projected to lose several hundred million euros between 2019 and 2021, and its revenues of €540 million for the 2019–2020 season ranked the club only seventh in Europe. Yet that didn't stop it from signing Messi in 2021 and ousting Barcelona as the club paying the highest salaries in soccer. By then, UEFA was thinking of formally abolishing FFP.

The FFP rules haven't stopped the sugar daddies, because the rules are largely unenforceable. Big clubs like Manchester City have fought UEFA through the courts. You may or may not like Sheikh Mansour, but if he wants to spend his own money on his own club, you can't stop him. Under European law, you cannot prohibit business owners from investing in their businesses, as FFP tried to do. City and PSG were quite happy to defy UEFA and drag it through the courts, knowing that they couldn't lose. Some fans complain that UEFA was too slack in enforcing its rules, but the fact is that the rules were always on shaky legal grounds. After UEFA tried to stop PSG from buying Kylian Mbappé and Neymar simultaneously for well over $400 million in 2017, the Parisians triumphed in court.

What City and PSG have done very publicly is what most European clubs have continued to do on the down-low. As the spending data show, clubs are still throwing money at players in the hope of winning or at least not getting relegated. The choice between a UEFA disciplinary hearing or dropping down a division is really no choice at all.

Americans will point out that US major leagues have salary caps, but that probably wouldn't work in soccer. There are more than seven hundred clubs in Europe's top divisions and several thousand in the lower tiers. They are all in the same competitive pyramid. It's one thing for thirty-two teams in the NFL to agree to a salary cap, but how would that work for, say, two thousand European clubs? Should they all face the same salary cap? For that to have a real effect, Real Madrid's annual player payroll would have to be limited to the same level as, say, that of UE Santa Coloma, ranked by UEFA as Europe's 433rd team. Santa Coloma is a village of three thousand souls in the tiny mountain state of Andorra, which lies between Spain and France. But if we're not going to treat all clubs equally, complaints about excessive spending are mostly cant. The real value of "discipline and rationality" to soccer's old "aristocrats," like Arsenal, Manchester United, and Bayern Munich, is that they limit the potential for new rivals, such as Manchester City and Paris, to rise up and compete.

After a decade of failure, you might think that UEFA would face facts, but not a bit. In August 2021 it announced plans for what one might call FFP 2.0. The idea seems to be to limit wage spending to a fixed percentage of revenues and then tax any spending over this limit and redistribute it to other clubs. Major League Baseball in the US has had a luxury tax since 1996. Teams spending above a given level faced a tax, the proceeds of which were distributed to teams operating in smaller markets. There is little evidence that this improved the competitive balance of baseball, but this is in part because the owners of the clubs that received handouts simply pocketed the money rather than investing in better teams. Given the tendency of soccer clubs to spend all additional revenue on players, UEFA may be hoping for a different outcome.

As with FFP 1.0, the new scheme would theoretically make big clubs more profitable by enabling them to restrain spending (leaving more profit for the owners). But we are skeptical that any of this will ever happen. The big clubs would probably balk if a high salary tax limited their spending. These clubs have a lot of power to tell UEFA where to go. Salary caps are legal in the US, where the law treats agreements between unions and employers as exempt from competition law, but that's not the case in Europe. We look forward to reviewing whatever scheme is adopted ten years from now.

For the moment, European soccer has no strong rules against owners spending their own money. This allows sugar-daddy–funded clubs such as Manchester City and PSG to steal marches on rivals, such as Manchester United, Real Madrid, and Barcelona. No wonder that Qatar's rival, Saudi Arabia, hoping to sportswash its bloody reputation, bought Newcastle United in 2021.

Many fans are sorry that cost control has failed. They regard it as a long-needed dose of sanity. We disagree. We think that cost controls are bad for the game. Even if they did help big clubs make profits, that would be happy news not for fans or players but for a very select set of people: the rich men who own the big clubs. If cost controls were to cut players' wages, there is no reason to think the savings would go back into soccer. More likely, they would go into the offshore accounts of billionaire owners.

A CLUB IS A CASHBOX

Since the 2010s, a new breed of owner has been coming into soccer: businesspeople who want to imitate the Glazers and who, unlike the sugar daddies, hope to make money out of the game. And they don't even need to make profits to do this. There's something else luring these people into soccer: cash. Because the game demonstrates that it's perfectly possible to generate cash even without profits.

It's crucial to understand that the financial losses in many clubs' accounts are often more or less fictional. A big club can report losses and still be in excellent financial health. Manchester United reported a pretax loss of £20 million (about $26 million) in the financial year 2020–2021, but the business was doing just fine, thank you very much. United's EBITDA ("earnings before interest, tax, depreciation and amortization"—the financial professional's preferred measure of profitability) was a very healthy £96 million (about $125 million), even in the aftermath of COVID-19. Clubs like Manchester United can lose money on paper while remaining cash-rich. The key word to grasp here comes from accounting: *amortization.*

Here's how amortization works. Until 1990, a club paying a transfer fee had to report it in its accounts as a one-off expense. If you paid another club $1 million for a player, that meant $1 million less profit for the season. Then, in the 1990s, British and European accounting rules changed. Clubs were allowed to "amortize"—to write off—the cost of a transfer fee over the life of a player's contract. If you paid a $30 million transfer fee and signed the player to a three-year deal, you reported a cost of $10 million in each of the three years of the contract in your accounts. (Once the contract ends and the player is free to walk out the door, he is no longer worth anything to your club.)

Now, player trading can often involve relatively small financial transactions relative to the total amounts you hear reported. When you read a report that club X paid $50 million for player Y, club Z, which sold the player, usually doesn't get that much money. A lot is typically offset by players being traded in the other direction, and payment is contingent on all sorts of things (like the buying team winning the title) that might never end up happening.

Nonetheless, even if no money changed hands, the contract value in the accounts would still be $50 million. The paying club will amortize it over the life of the player contract: $10 million a year, if it's a five-year contract. So when a club reports losses because of heavy amortization, it's quite possible that there was no actual money going out.

And amortization has become a huge item in the financial accounts of big clubs. For example, for the financial year 2018–2019, Premier League clubs reported total revenues of £5.1 billion ($6.8 billion) and operating losses of £424 million ($566 million). But they also reported amortization charges of £1.3 billion ($1.7 billion)—none of which is "real" money actually paid out. Add this back, and the pretax loss turns into a healthy "cash" surplus. Strip out amortization, and you get a better picture of how rich these clubs really are.

Amortization isn't money paid out; it's just an adjustment made by the accountant. Of course, if you did pay out real money to finance all your player transfer spending, then you might well have a cash deficit, but because player registrations are easily traded, they represent assets that are almost as good as cash. In other words, the player you signed for $50 million two years ago can generally easily be sold for the same sum or more whenever you want. In practice, Premier League clubs plus the leading dozen or so continental European clubs have become big cash machines, even though they are not big profit makers.

Cash, in modern finance, means opportunity. A business that generates a lot of cash can borrow a lot of money—as long as the banks think that the cash generation is backed up by a solid business, such as charging people to watch good soccer.

There are many ways to exploit this opportunity. Some owners, like the Glazers, used the club's own cash to buy the club. The Glazers convinced banks that Manchester United was a cash machine. The banks then lent them the money to buy the club. Finally, the Glazers used United's cash to repay most of the debt and interest. Other owners have used the cash opportunity to borrow money to build bigger and better stadiums. Some Premier League owners would like to use the cash to make their league the best in the world.

But as big soccer generates ever more cash, more businesspeople are being tempted in because they want to finance other businesses altogether. Viewed this way, big clubs are becoming like banks. They generate far more cash than they need to finance their operations. Theirs is a world of opportunity.

In short, at the top of the game we are seeing the contours of something new emerge: soccer still isn't big business, but it is finally becoming midsize, attracting profit-seeking new owners. Since we wrote this for our preceding edition, back in 2017, soccer has begun drawing a type of investor that had previously steered clear of the game: private equity.

People who explain finance to people who aren't trained in finance usually like to wrap their explanations up in technical jargon so as to imply their expertise and also your ignorance. Doing so allows them to charge you money for taking care of something you feel you don't understand. But beneath the jargon, most finance is pretty simple. A private-equity firm takes money from investors and uses that money to buy companies that it thinks are undervalued. The firm then manages the companies for a few years by following a simple strategy: find new revenue streams and cut costs, often by brutally sacking staff. The aim is to suck cash out of the business and transfer it into the pockets of their backers. Once that's done, the firm will try to sell a turned-around company to other investors as a more valuable business and make a profit on the deal.

Soccer fans like to grumble that there's a crazy amount of money in the game today. Private equity thinks there is a lot more to be discovered. Private equity, like a lot of finance, is largely governed by herd mentality. Managers of private-equity firms have collectively decided that soccer is a profitable opportunity because they look at examples like the Glazers. Once it became evident that Manchester United was a honeypot for the family, the search was on for other Manchester Uniteds. Bear in mind that many private-equity firms are run by Americans whose familiarity with soccer is limited.

Private-equity firms that have bought into the game include Redbird Capital Partners (which bought 10 percent of Liverpool FC in 2021 and also owns stakes in French clubs Toulouse and Bordeaux), Elliott Management Corporation (owners of AC Milan since 2018), Silver Lake Technology Management (owners of a 10 percent stake in Manchester City since 2019), and NewCity Capital (owners in whole or part of Barnsley FC, FC Thun, AS Nancy, and others). CVC Capital Partners has gone further, spending $2.2 billion in December 2021 to get 8 percent of the revenues of Spain's La Liga for the next fifty years.

So why would private equity want to invest in an industry decimated by the coronavirus? Well, European soccer clubs may be in trouble now, but most of them have existed for a century or more, and it's reasonable to expect that most will be here in a century's time. Soccer in the long term is a stable business because it dominates the sporting landscape in most countries. That fundamental fact is not altered by COVID-19 any more than it was by the Great Flu a century earlier.

Rather, the private-equity funds and other investors see an opportunity in soccer's COVID-induced crisis. While club owners mount up their debts, new investors are willing to come to their rescue in exchange for big stakes in the business. If history is anything to go by, soccer will soon overcome COVID-19, as it has so many catastrophes before, and resume its long-term growth—but now globally. The new investors think soccer has the potential to capture foreign markets in a way that American sports don't. They see the long rise in the Premier League's broadcast income. Soccer is bigger and more durable than possibly even television itself.

These investors hope to take money out of the game. But they may be overlooking something: popularity is just one enduring feature of professional soccer. Another is chronic loss making. Even if a small number of clubs escaped that fate in the 2010s, it's a bold gamble to think this will be true of the game as a whole. Manchester City might become consistently profitable, but Barnsley and FC Thun? AC Milan perhaps, but Nancy and Bordeaux? Anyone can see the attractions of Real Madrid and Barcelona, but CVC's investment in La Liga means handing out large sums to teams such as Cadiz and Getafe.

So the question becomes "How are private-equity investors going to get their money back in five years' time if they're investing in clubs with proven track records of losing money for a century or more?" It's not like we haven't been here before. Stephanie Leach, one of UEFA's senior analysts, wrote her PhD thesis at Imperial College London under Stefan's supervision. They also coauthored an academic paper titled "Making Money Out of Football" that examined the rash of football clubs' stock-market flotations (IPOs) in the mid-1990s. At the time, stock investors were so impressed with Manchester United's successful flotation in 1991, and the Premier League's ballooning broadcast rights, that they thought soccer had become a profitable business. What Stephanie and Stefan showed was that all these flotations failed because nothing had changed about soccer's fundamental economics: when clubs got money from investors, they just spent it on players as they always had. That drove up wages and transfer fees, and even made English soccer more popular, but it did nothing for the bottom line. Within a few years all these clubs had left the stock market, and many had entered insolvency proceedings.

We don't think the private-equity firms will succeed where almost all past investors have failed and manage to make profits from the game. What's more, we don't want them to. We prefer soccer to be loss making. We don't think the advent of profit-making clubs would mean a new "healthy," "sustainable" era in soccer. That's because we do not see the point of enriching the owners.

To imagine what a more profitable future for European soccer might look like, think of Arsenal. The club spends relatively modestly, and inevitably it hasn't won any league titles lately. That's bad for Arsenal's fans, but it's good for the club's American majority owner, Stan Kroenke. When he took over the club in 2011, it was valued at £731 million, or about $1.17 billion. By 2021, after a decade of disappointment on the field but healthy profits off it, *Forbes* valued Arsenal at $2.8 billion.

Arsenal isn't a great soccer club anymore, but it is a good business. This is what a club run as a business looks like: high ticket prices, little desire to win trophies, and big profits. If other leading clubs end up being run like Arsenal rather than like Manchester City, then we predict slower rises in players' wages and a rise in club profits, which would mean more money being taken out of the game by profit-hungry owners.

We prefer people who want to lose money on soccer. Hurrah for the sugar daddies, we say. It's hard to think of any other domain in which organizations actively seek to stop rich people from investing. Not many universities, opera houses, or aid agencies turn away sugar daddies. We think European soccer needs these people.

Sugar daddies are often depicted as a curse on the game. It's easy to see why a Manchester United fan would dislike Manchester City. Setting aside local rivalry, there's the age-old disdain of the aristocracy for the nouveaux riches. City is an upstart that has used a wallet full of foreign currency to barge its way onto the top table. When City won the Premier League in 2012, it did so with several players bought from Arsenal, and at United's expense. Of course United fans oppose sugar daddies.

But why should fans of smaller clubs be so bothered by them? In most walks of life we welcome the outsider who comes in and shakes up the existing order. Taking the aristocrats down a notch is the plot of endless feel-good movies (not to mention the French and Russian revolutions). Why should it be different for soccer? It certainly seems that when a club's fans learn that a sugar daddy is in the offing, they perk up. Finding a sugar daddy is like winning the lottery.

Some argue that the "excessive" spending of sugar daddies drives smaller clubs into bankruptcy. In fact, if anything, the opposite is true. Sugar daddies buy players and then pay them very high wages. The usual argument is that this forces other clubs to pay their players higher salaries to stay. However, (a) this applies only to a small number of players, and (b) no club can be forced to pay more than it can afford. If clubs without sugar daddies try to match the ambitions of clubs with them, that will certainly end in tears, but then that's also the case for clubs that try to compete with aristocrats. Whether you want to be a Manchester United or an oil-funded Manchester City, you'll fail if you're a small club without a sugar daddy.

The problem for small clubs is that they just don't have the resources to compete in Europe with the dominant clubs, and they have not had them for decades. This has very little to do with sugar daddies.

Sugar daddies are good for the soccer economy for one big reason: the cash they inject supports other clubs. Think of the fortunes that Paris Saint-Germain has spent in transfer fees. Some of that money ended up with agents, but by far the biggest chunk has gone to other clubs. Those clubs spent some of that money on players and some on improving training facilities or building better stadiums.

We lament the seizing of so much of the world's wealth by a small number of billionaires—many of them heirs, criminals, or tax dodgers—but it has been good news for soccer. We applaud the removal of Russian oligarchs from soccer in the same way that we are glad to see them driven out of every other business. We don't hold a candle for the mega-rich. But if we are going to let them play an outsized role in our lives, we can live with their blowing their billions on the game.

To understand how sugar daddies help the game, it's instructive to return to the Glazers, because they are on the opposite end of the spectrum. The Glazers make sure that United turns a profit. That might sound "healthy" and "sustainable." However, that profit represents money that the owners can then take out of football. The Glazers sucked something in the order of $1 billion out of United from 2005 through 2015. That's precisely why most United fans resent them.

United's profits would have been welcome had they been reinvested in buying players, building a bigger stadium, or even funding a cut in ticket prices—but then, of course, they would have ceased to be profits. So if sucking money out of clubs is a bad thing, then putting money into clubs is surely a good thing. We have always been happy to see rich owners blow fortunes on building teams. We don't want them to start making profits. We would rather they put the money back into soccer.

Clubs shouldn't be profit-oriented businesses. A club has a different purpose from a company like Apple or Exxon. Companies exist chiefly to turn profits. By contrast, most of a club's customers (its fans), its employees (players and coaches), and usually even its owners would say that it exists to play well and win things, not to make its owners rich. That's why a 1974 report by the British Commission on Industrial Relations quoted an anonymous club chairman as saying, "Any club management which allows the club to make a profit is behaving foolishly."

Traditionally, soccer clubs have behaved more like charitable trusts than for-profit businesses. In the not-so-distant past the English Football Association used to forbid club owners from profiting from their investment. Directors couldn't get paid, and dividends were capped. The aim was to ensure that clubs were run by "the right class of men who love soccer for its own sake." These rules were abolished in the early 1980s. If they still existed, they might have stopped the businesspeople Tom Hicks and George Gillett at Liverpool and the Glazers at United from burdening these clubs with a combined $1.5 billion in debt simply to finance their takeovers.

The business of soccer is soccer. Clubs shouldn't chase profits. Instead, they should invest every cent they have in the game.

Soccer clubs need to know what they are. They shouldn't even aspire to be big profit-making companies like United Natural Foods. Rather, they are like museums: public-spirited organizations that aim to serve communities while remaining reasonably solvent. If soccer ever becomes profitable, fans may end up pining for the days when it was the worst business in the world.

6

SUPER LEAGUE

Why Rich People Don't Always Get What They Want

At 6.10 p.m. East Coast time on Sunday April 18, 2021, football was supposed to change forever. That was when journalists around the world received a press release alerting them to the launch of the European Super League—a closed competition of at most twenty giant clubs, with very limited promotion and relegation. Fifteen of the league's founder clubs would be guaranteed spots in the league every year, no matter how badly they performed, while a few places would be left for those outside the magic circle. Almost all the thousands of other European clubs would be excluded, condemned to minor-league status forever.

The initial dozen founding clubs together looked like an unstoppable force: Real Madrid, Barcelona, Manchester City, Manchester United, Liverpool, Chelsea, Tottenham, Arsenal, Atlético Madrid, Juventus, AC Milan, and Inter Milan. They also had a serious funder: the American bank J. P. Morgan was underwriting the project with $4.8 billion, a sum that the clubs planned to share as a welcome bonus. The plotters seemed to have thought things through: Florentino Pérez, Real Madrid's president and the main mover behind the league, had begun pitching the idea to investors two years earlier. The plan set out revenue-sharing deals and spending limits on players for the next twenty-three years.

So convinced were the founders of the brilliance of their scheme that they hadn't bothered checking with fans to see if they were on board.

The Super League was just going to happen. And then, within forty-eight hours, it was dead, after an unprecedented global supporters' uprising. How could some of soccer's mightiest figures be so swiftly defeated? What does that say about how the game works and will continue to work?

The Super League had been a very long time in coming. "There was a general expectation a little while ago of what was called a Super League, in which all the leading European clubs would play, breaking away from the domestic leagues in their own countries. It has not materialised," wrote the journalist Arthur Hopcraft in 1968.

In the 1980s, Milan's then owner Silvio Berlusconi touted a Super League; among the advisers hired to flesh out of the concept was J. P. Morgan. In the early 1990s, UEFA created the Champions League partly to deter a breakaway by big clubs. In 1999 Stefan published an article with Tom Hoehn that examined the Super League concept in detail. Always, the logic of the idea has been the same: to grow revenues by getting Europe's giant clubs to play one another more often.

And that logic is powerful. In the decade ending in 2021, among the twelve founders of the Super League, those based in different countries played one another just ninety times. If the Super League involved playing each team home and away, the number of games among international rivals would equal ninety *every season*. To sentimentalists who argue that these matches wouldn't be so valuable because scarcity is part of their appeal, we say: Get a grip. Like it or not, the history of the Champions League is a history of expanding competition to create more international matchups, and this has raked in ever more cash. This isn't chiefly about the clubs; it's not about creating rivalry between, say, Manchester City and Juventus. What the league's founders were banking on was the appetite of fans for matchups between players: Messi against Kane, Neymar against Salah, Frenkie de Jong against De Bruyne.

In truth, in 2021 the Super League's ambitions were limited. This wasn't going to be a "European" league, just an Anglo-Spanish-Italian one. The founders had failed to persuade Germany's biggest clubs or Paris Saint-Germain to sign up. Nor was the Super League genuinely "super," given the presence of modern underachievers like Arsenal, Tottenham, and Milan. And it aspired merely to be a sideshow to domestic leagues. The giveaway is that the matches were to be played in midweek. During European weekday evenings, most American fans would be at work and most Asians asleep, which would limit the Super League's TV audiences. Soccer's prime-time slot—weekend afternoons, when all three continents can watch—would remain reserved for domestic leagues.

Nonetheless, the Super League was poised to be the most dramatic transformation in soccer's modern history. With higher revenues, caps on spending, and no risk of relegation, the biggest clubs could finally start making predictable profits. The Super League was a reminder that only economists like competition; businesses generally prefer closed shops.

In some ways the Super League simply imported into soccer one of the dominant ideas of our time: neoliberalism. This is a word that we've always been reluctant to use because it gets slung around all the time as a pejorative for anything commercial. But the launch of the Super League clarified beautifully what *neoliberal* means, at least as we understand it. We define it as the idea that every activity must be run for profit: that every hospital or university or social-media platform should behave like a profit-seeking company. Neoliberalism has had a winning run since Ronald Reagan and Margaret Thatcher began pushing it in the 1980s. The Super League applied neoliberalism to soccer—an activity that, as we have explained, has rarely pursued profits, let alone made any.

Like so many neoliberal ideas, the Super League originated in the United States. American sports leagues—including Major League Soccer—have always been closed, meaning that there is no promotion or relegation. That suits the country's billionaire club owners because it allows them to make even more money. Without any pressure to buy a winning team, and with an artificial nationwide shortage of major-league clubs, American team valuations are astronomical. *Forbes* conducts an annual valuation of professional sports teams. In its most recent estimates the least valuable of the thirty Major League Baseball franchises was valued at $1 billion. *Forbes*'s valuation of Europe's twentieth-biggest soccer club (Ajax) in 2021 was a mere $172 million.

Four of the twelve club owners behind the Super League were Americans: John Henry at Liverpool, Kroenke at Arsenal, Paul Singer at AC Milan, and the Glazer family at Manchester United. All except Singer owned American sports franchises. These men had been brought up without promotion and relegation, and didn't see why it was a big deal. They knew that a closed profit-seeking league might upset sentimental Europeans. But the owners figured: fans will whine for a bit and then they'll get over it.

The big clubs tried to sell their plan with the standard neoliberal arguments. Echoing Thatcher, Florentino suggested that there was no alternative: the Super League was the only way for soccer to escape the debt mountain left behind by the pandemic. "This is not a league for the rich; it's a league to save football," he said. He also suggested the money would eventually "trickle down"—a beloved neoliberal phrase—in the form of "solidarity" fees to smaller clubs in lesser competitions. As Reagan and Thatcher always liked to promise, the poor would benefit from the rise of the rich.

The plan sounded brilliant—until the fans found out about it. It is easy to be cynical about such things, but on the day of the Super League's launch it turned out that most supporters really do love soccer's traditional system. When news of the league first leaked, Gary Neville, the English former Manchester United full-back turned TV pundit, fumed: "The [club owners] are nothing to do with football in this country. There are a hundred-odd years of history in this country from fans who have loved these clubs, and they need protecting." Simon's newspaper, the *Financial Times*, reported: "Clips of his on-air rant went viral on social media and marked 'a turning point,' says an executive involved in Super League talks."

Especially in England, protesters gathered outside the stadiums of the participating clubs. A banner appeared at Liverpool's Anfield reading "SHAME ON YOU—R.I.P. LFC—1892–2021." A Chelsea fan at a demonstration in London waved a sign that read "FOOTBALL BE-LONGS TO US NOT YOU."

And these were supporters of teams that would get into the Super League. As the chair of one Premier League club marveled, "The fans protested for the right to lose." It turned out that supporters saw themselves not simply as individual consumers but as member of a broader community of soccer fans. They were fine with a rich man (he's almost always a man) temporarily running their club, as long as he understood that his main job was to put his money into it. In European soccer the owners are there to serve the fans, not vice versa. You have only to witness the anguish of American fans when an owner moves a team to a more profitable city to know how easily the boot can end up on the other foot.

European fans don't think that soccer is a business. They don't believe that the so-called owner "owns" their club. He is merely the club's steward. He doesn't have a right to join a Super League simply to increase his own wealth. April 2021 was arguably the first mass uprising against neoliberalism. It is intriguing, in fact, that many people seemed more upset about neoliberalism in soccer than in areas such as health care, which has far more tangible effects on their lives.

The fans understood that the new league would blow up soccer's two cornerstones: tradition and competition. From childhood till death, people watch their club playing in the same colors, often on the same grounds, in the same competitions, against the same opponents. As Neville had said, a European Super League would end all that.

But the bit that fans seemed to hate most was the lack of competition. After all, soccer's essential promise—which rests on the promotion-and-relegation system—is that even the smallest club can triumph. Sometimes that promise actually comes true. In 2002 Leicester City was insolvent, in 2009 it was playing in League One—the third tier of English soccer—but it then got promoted twice, and in 2016 it won the Premier League. Promotion and relegation were adopted by the English Football League in the 1890s, and they have been copied by almost every country that plays the game, and by many other sports besides. From a cold economic perspective, the system benefits fans by forcing clubs to keep investing in players or get relegated.

Every club in soccer's pyramid, right down to the lowest level of amateur leagues, has a stake in promotion and relegation. End this system, and you kill hope. You might even kill the clubs as well or simply turn them into farm teams for the big clubs.

This is exactly what happened to baseball, America's most popular sport in the twentieth century. From the 1880s to the 1950s almost every town of any size in the US had a professional baseball team playing in a local league. There were two "major" leagues, the National League and the American League. But there were as many as forty-seven "minor leagues" in 1912 and still well over twenty at the start of the Great Depression in 1930. The Depression shut down a lot of leagues, but later, as the wartime economy boomed, so did baseball. When World War II ended, the minor leagues looked set to revive.

But that's when television arrived. Suddenly, you had the option to watch top-quality baseball in the comfort of your own home rather than go and see a bunch of second-rate players scrap it out in substandard facilities.

By the 1950s, many minor leagues had folded. Those that survived were bought out by major-league teams to become dependent farm teams, playing in competitions that are about as meaningful as international friendlies in soccer. Why did American baseball shrink to a cartel of thirty teams for a nation of 330 million, while Europe maintains over seven hundred professional league clubs in the top tiers alone, for a population just over twice the size?

Promotion and relegation offer the most obvious answer. Top-class soccer on TV in Europe proved just as attractive as top-class baseball in the US. What differed was that American minor-league teams had no hope of ever getting promoted.

The fans' uprising against the Super League took the founding clubs by surprise. Within two days, ten of the twelve had withdrawn from the league, often while uttering self-abasing apologies.

Many people wondered in amazement, "Why such amateurism? Surely the bosses of these giant clubs cannot be idiots?" But, in fact, the Super League's failure does come down in part to soccer's traditional cognitive problems, as outlined in Chapter 3. On the field, the game has always been the purest meritocracy: there are no bad professional soccer players. (We hear your jokes, but really there aren't.) Off the field, though, there is little quality control. As we explained in Chapter 4, punishment for incompetence in soccer is limited. If you mismanage a restaurant, it will go into debt, and eventually the bank will close it down. But if you mismanage a football club, the worst that is likely to happen is relegation. Even if the club goes bankrupt, someone will almost certainly bail it out. Because soccer clubs practically always survive (and big clubs always do), they can afford to tolerate stupidity.

Many of the men behind the Super League weren't selected for their brains. Take Andrea Agnelli, president of Juventus and a prime mover behind the league. He owes his job to his surname: his family has run Juve since 1923. But he came to overestimate himself—a natural consequence of being an Agnelli and spending his life surrounded by bootlickers. His self-image as a thrusting entrepreneur helped fuel the Super League debacle.

Four of the other owners of the twelve would-be Super League clubs were heirs too: the Abu Dhabi royals at Manchester City, the Glazer siblings at Manchester United, Atlético Madrid's chief executive Miguel Gil, and Steven Zhang, Chinese president of Inter Milan, who was appointed by his billionaire father at age twenty-six. Another owner, Kroenke of Arsenal, married the Walmart heiress Ann Walton in 1974. From a distance, you might imagine that these guys are demonic profit-making machines who reason like calculators. Up close, they are less impressive.

Isolated in their mansions, some of them oceans away from their clubs, and even more detached than usual in the era of Zoom, they never seem to have thought of getting fans, politicians, and media onside before launching their Super League. Anyway, most of them look down on fans, politicians, and media. Even after their project went public, they made barely any attempt to sell it beyond an out-of-touch TV performance by Florentino, who explained that young people weren't very interested in soccer.

After this fiasco, it will surely be a long time—well, a few months at least—before anyone is stupid enough to propose a Super League again. But the threat will never entirely vanish. Club owners will continue to yearn for guaranteed profits in an American-style system. We can expect to see imaginative proposals for novel competitions with a closed-league element. The interests of owners will often clash with those of fans, and in the long run, rich people tend to get what they want. Gloriously, however, the Super League debacle of 2021 shows that this isn't always the case.

7

UNBANNED

The Case for Reparations for Women's Soccer

Henry Spelman, one of the first English settlers in North America, described two versions of football, played by Native Americans, that he witnessed in 1609—one version for men and one for women. We have no reason to think that women are any less attracted to playing ball games than men, but when the rules of modern soccer were written down in England in 1863, it was by men who assumed that the game was for men only. Some women saw it differently. In the 1890s, Nettie Honeyball (probably a pseudonym) formed the British Ladies Football Club and played a match against an XI organized by "Mrs. Graham" (definitely a pseudonym), which was attended by twelve thousand spectators.

These female players faced resistance from men. Although the medical profession approved of light exercise for women, soccer was beyond the pale. One letter to the *British Medical Journal* in 1894 warned of the risk of "serious internal displacements.... Nor can one overlook the chances of injury to the breasts." Opinions like this were common and no doubt enabled the men who ran England's Football Association to dissociate themselves from the women's game.

But during World War I, female soccer in Britain in particular launched a challenge to male hegemony. As British women were being drafted into factories to replace the men away at war, they started to organize their own sporting activities around the workplace. Usually, these

took the form of contests to raise money for soldiers. Male soccer officials could scarcely object. At the Dick, Kerr Munitions and Engineering
Works factory in Preston, some female workers began joining the men
in their kickarounds at lunch and teatime. Soon women workers founded
their own team. The Dick, Kerr Ladies would become probably the most
celebrated female team ever (the movie, we should add, is long overdue).

It continued playing after the war, supplying most of the England
eleven for the first international women's match, against France in 1920.
After a much-publicized tour of France, the Dick, Kerr women played at
Everton's Goodison Park on the day after Christmas and drew a crowd
of 53,000—more than almost any men's professional club at the time.
That game poses the great "What if?" of women's soccer. What if female
players had been allowed to prosper? Where would we be now?

The patriarchs of the Football League didn't let it happen. Stung by
the popularity of women's soccer, they set out to ban it. The FA obliged
in December 1921: "Complaints having been made as to football being
played by women, the Council feel impelled to express their strong opinion that the game of football is quite unsuitable for females and ought
not to be encouraged....For these reasons the Council request the clubs
belonging to the Association to refuse the use of their grounds for such
matches." With the war over, women were being sent back to the kitchen.

They couldn't easily fight back. British women had won the right to
vote as recently as 1918, and even then, the franchise originally only extended to women over thirty. Laws against gender discrimination didn't
exist.

The Dick, Kerr players were among the few British women unde-
terred by the FA's ban. They toured the US, where they defeated several
men's teams, and the club survived as Preston Ladies FC until 1965. Lily
Parr, perhaps the team's greatest player, played until 1951 and is celebrated now as a pioneer of the women's game.

But with the men of the FA controlling almost all English soccer
fields, the women's game was exiled to obscure, muddy parks and almost died out. Most football associations around the world followed the
English lead. In Canada in 1922, Norway in 1931, Germany in 1955,
and Denmark in 1963, the men endorsed their own bans on female
soccer. Women who defied the ban were shamed. Prewar players in

Frankfurt were called *Mannsweiber* (roughly, "male women"), says historian Mareike König, who describes the history of women's soccer as one of prohibition and resistance.

These bans are now almost forgotten, but they lasted half a century, and they hamper women's soccer to this day. We will argue in this chapter that what is needed now are reparations: a large-scale program of investment in the women's game, paid from the revenues of the men's game, to redress at least some of the damage.

When feminism revived in the 1960s, so did women's soccer. In 1969 some European women set up their own international federation. They even found a drinks sponsor to back an international tournament the following year. The French and German FAs lifted their bans in 1970, and the English followed in 1971. UEFA suggested that all national associations recognize the women's game.

In those years, there was one country above all others where women's sport took off: the US. The story begins with Bernice Sandler, who graduated from the University of Maryland with a doctorate in education in 1969. After being repeatedly rejected for teaching jobs at universities, she asked in one interview why it was such a struggle. The answer, she later recalled, was that "she came on too strong for a woman." She decided she needed to come on just a tad stronger, and she went to work for an organization called the Women's Equity Action League (WEAL). Here she focused on an executive order issued by President Johnson in 1967, which added "sex" to the requirement that all government agencies and federal contractors grant equal employment opportunity "regardless of race, creed, color, or national origin." Thanks to evidence provided by Sandler and WEAL, Congress introduced an amendment to the Civil Rights Act called Title IX. President Nixon signed it into law in 1972. Title IX required recipients of government funding to maintain records and demonstrate that they weren't discriminating.

Before Title IX, the funding of sports in US schools and universities was highly gendered. Sports for boys had always been central to the US academic curriculum, but not so for girls' sports. According to Sandler, "In the early 1970s the budget for men's varsity sports at the University of Michigan was about $1.1 million. The budget for women's varsity athletics was zero. Women athletes sold apples at football games to pay for their own travel and other expenses."

"At the University of Minnesota," she wrote, "there was no budget for women gymnasts for athletic tape to wrap their wrists or other joints to prevent injury. The male gymnasts were very gallant; they would give their used, sweaty, grungy athletic tape to the women."

No wonder that in 1971 the female participation rate in all high school sports stood at about 7 percent, whereas the rate for boys was around 50 percent. Most academic sports administrators were male and took for granted that sports were a male preserve. Sandler and her colleagues had to drag them through the courts to demonstrate that they no longer had a choice: the law required that male and female sports receive equal funding.

The women won several high-profile victories, and by 1977, women's and girls' participation rates in sports reached 25 percent. Today they are over 40 percent, close to parity with the boys. Girls flocked into almost all school sports except gridiron football, which to this day has no high school teams for girls (although in recent years there has been some talk). And no women's school sport grew faster than soccer.

Meanwhile, outside the US, little changed. In 1971 UEFA appointed a Women's Football Committee composed entirely of men. For the next seven years it proceeded to do more or less nothing before being dissolved.

Only in 1991 did FIFA agree to organize a women's World Cup. The event was staged in China, partly as a nod to the early development of the women's game there, but also because FIFA preferred holding the tournament in a country where there was little chance of global exposure. The patriarchs were playing it safe. However, the inaugural World Cup was a great success. The Chinese organized large crowds, and in the final the US narrowly beat its rival, Norway. "We are not a soccer culture in the United States," said goalkeeper Mary Harvey. "We have an inferiority complex, but now we can say we have a team that is the best in the world. It's a shot in the arm for soccer in America, for men, women, youth teams, all of us."

In 1996 women's soccer became an Olympic sport, and the US women won gold in Atlanta. They then won the 1999 World Cup, also at home, defeating China in the final after a penalty shoot-out. This produced one of the iconic moments in all of American soccer, when the winning goal scorer, Brandi Chastain—one of the all-time greats—took off her top in celebration. The media's focus on Chastain's gesture didn't do justice to a pretty amazing team, but it did raise women's soccer to a level of consciousness that no American team in that sport had ever achieved.

The contrast with basketball is instructive. Basketball is a sport invented in the United States, at which both American men and women have always excelled. Basketball was first played at the Olympics in 1936, and the US men's team has won the gold medal in sixteen out of nineteen attempts. Women's basketball was first played at the 1976 Olympics, and the US women have won in nine out of eleven attempts. In other words, American men and women both rule basketball. But with soccer the story is different: the US men have been consistently mediocre, never close to an Olympic gold medal. More importantly, they've never come close to winning a World Cup since a third-place finish in the inaugural tournament with only thirteen teams way back in 1930.

By contrast, the US women have remained soccer's dominant team. They have won four of the eight women's World Cups, finished runners-up once, and come in third three times. At the Olympics, they have won four golds, one silver, one bronze, and missed out on a medal only once. Roughly speaking, the US women have always reached the semifinals of big tournaments and have won the finals half the time. Their crucial advantage was that whereas Title IX turbocharged American women's soccer, the female game in other countries remained almost unfunded and unknown.

Entering the new millennium, a group of investors in the US put up $40 million to launch the Women's United Soccer Association (WUSA), the world's first professional women's soccer league. Meanwhile, men's Major League Soccer, launched in 1996 with an investment of around $100 million, was struggling. What happened next is illustrative of the uneven playing field on which women compete. When WUSA hit trouble, its investors soon pulled the plug, having sunk a total of $100 million into the venture. MLS faced very similar struggles and was estimated to have lost $350 million between 1996 and 2004, but the investors stuck with it. The men whose wealth determines which leagues live or die in the US believed there was a profitable future in a men's league made up of mediocre Americans and foreign has-beens—but not in a women's league that would include most of the world's best female players, almost all of whom were American. Think of it this way: if someone offered you the chance to take one of two products to market, would you choose the one for which there were dozens of producers better than you, or the one for which you were the best producer on Earth?

In fairness, the US Soccer Federation remained committed to establishing a women's professional league. A second league was launched in 2009 and folded three years later, at which point the federation stepped in and underwrote the creation of the National Women's Soccer League (NWSL) in 2013. This league has proved more durable.

Yet most American media continued to ignore women's soccer. The sports pages of newspapers remained the de facto men's pages. In fact, journalistic attention to women's sports *fell* in the 1990s and 2000s, according to the Center for Feminist Research at the University of Southern California. In 2009 women's sports received 1.6 percent of the total airtime given to American sports.

We authors aren't pretending we have always been exempt from the ambient sexism around soccer. We are part of the problem. When we began kicking balls on European school playgrounds in the 1960s and 1970s, we absorbed the general assumption that soccer was for boys. After all, at the start of this period, women's soccer was still banned. For most of our careers we have taken football's maleness for granted. We have worked on soccer for decades, but until recently we practically ignored the women's game. The first edition of *Soccernomics*, published in 2009, barely mentioned women's soccer. Subsequent editions said only a bit more.

It's reasonable to be irritated by men who don't grasp the magnitude of sexism until they have daughters. Simon is not proud of it, but that's the way it has been for him. When he had children in Paris—first a daughter, then two sons—everyone around him thought it natural that the boys played football. Simon's sons could hone their technique kicking around with their friends on the unofficial "soccer street" beside the local town hall every day. But most girls their age were eager to dissociate themselves from what they considered a male activity: they didn't want to be branded male. If a ball bounced near them, they'd fake exaggerated fear. When Simon's daughter began playing, there were still hardly any girls' teams in Paris, and all her teammates were boys. She was treated like a freak who shouldn't be passed to.

Happily, things have gradually improved. By 2006, FIFA reckoned that the world had 26 million female players—up from approximately zero (officially, anyway) four decades previously.

In Europe the number of female semiprofessionals and full pros more than doubled from 2012 through 2017, to 2,853. On-field standards have kept rising, as Lieke Martens, the Dutch winger voted World Women's Player of the Year in 2017, told us: "You notice it in every position. Defenders get better, midfielders turn away very easily and place passes over forty meters. You see that the pace of play is rising, though it will never be like the men, because men are just faster and more physical. Our keepers said recently, 'You're all shooting harder and more precisely than five years ago.'"

UEFA has set a target of doubling the total number of female players in Europe to 2.5 million by 2024. Whereas the girls of Simon's daughter's generation were shunned, today's six-year-old European girls are being overwhelmed with invitations from their local clubs.

Only a few holdouts still argue that women have no place in soccer. In Britain in 2011, Sky TV commentators were sacked for voicing that view when they didn't realize their microphones were on. The Taliban and Iran's mullahs, who banned women even from watching soccer, would have agreed with them. Almost everyone else now says nice things about the women's game, in public at least. Yet it's remarkable how much pushback female soccer still encounters.

There are constant humiliations. For the 2012 Olympics, Japan's women's team, then the reigning world champions, flew premium economy class to London. The men's team flew business class. As the women's captain Homare Sawa noted, given the status of her team, it should have been the other way around. Japan's FA justified the decision with the argument that the men were professionals and the women weren't, writes soccer historian Alan McDougall. Three years later, the entire women's

World Cup in Canada was played on AstroTurf, a surface that would never be considered for even one game at a men's World Cup. And when the Norwegian Ada Hegerberg was crowned World Women's Player in Paris in December 2018, the French DJ Martin Solveig asked her on stage whether she twerked. (On the other hand, Hegerberg reported that everyone else she encountered in Paris was respectful. The former Brazilian great Roberto Carlos carried around her Ballon d'Or trophy for her, and she ended the night with her parents in a little Iranian restaurant where all the customers and staff wanted to pose with her prize.)

Women players also encounter rather scarier obstacles. The #MeToo movement resulted in the increased reporting of sexual crimes and exposed the systemic abuse of women athletes. In 1986 Larry Nassar became an athletic trainer for the USA Gymnastics team. From 1996 until 2014 he worked as national medical coordinator for USA Gymnastics. During this time he sexually assaulted hundreds of women and girls while senior figures around him covered up and ignored repeated complaints from athletes. USA Gymnastics finally cut ties with Nassar in 2015, but only in 2017, at the height of #MeToo, did the scale of his abuse become publicly known. It also emerged that FBI agents who investigated earlier complaints had played down the allegations and may have falsified statements. Nassar was finally prosecuted and will likely spend the rest of his life in prison. But his case brought to light the fact that even after Title IX, female athletes often play their sports under the tutelage of predators.

In 2021 *The Athletic* website revealed that Paul Riley, coach of the North Carolina Courage team in the NWSL, had, among other things, coerced a player into having sex with him, had forced two players to kiss each other, and had sent those players unsolicited sexual pictures. Riley had previously been fired by the NWSL as coach of the Portland Thorns for "violations of team policy," but the league had not revealed the nature of these violations. Numerous players came forward to report cases of abuse at other teams, and Lisa Baird, the league commissioner, resigned. The NWSL suspended play for five games as it sought to regroup.

A reckoning is happening in women's soccer. Decades after Title IX, an atmosphere of toxic masculinity has survived and has even grown in some quarters as a new front in the culture wars. Criminal abuse is perhaps the most important dimension of this, but disrespect for female athletes has an economic dimension as well. NWSL players generally earn incredibly low salaries by the standards of world-class professional athletes. The league's fixed maximum salary, established in 2020, was $50,000, and the minimum was $16,538. At these wages, most players must either work a second job or rely on someone else for financial support.

Players on the US Women's National Team (USWNT) make a lot more, but since 2016 they have been battling the USSF over equal pay and conditions. The players first challenged the federation before the Equal Employment Opportunity Commission and emerged in 2017 with a much better collective-bargaining agreement, in many cases doubling their payments. Then, in 2019, twenty-eight USWNT players filed a gender-discrimination lawsuit, arguing that the federation's entire structure granted favorable treatment to the men over the women. Winning the case in court was always going to be tough: the legal arguments are complicated, and USWNT and USMNT were paid on different bases (e.g., appearances, results). What's more, taking a simple average of all salary payments, the men's and women's pay looked roughly the same. In 2020 a judge ruled largely in favor of the USSF while leaving some avenues open for the women to pursue their case.

But the biggest impact came in the court of public opinion. Court filings revealed that the USSF's lawyers had argued that women's soccer did not constitute "equal work" when compared with men's soccer. In the lawyers' words, "MNT players have responsibility for competing in multiple soccer tournaments with the potential for generating a total of more than $40 million in prize money for US soccer every four years. WNT players compete in only one soccer tournament every four years that has the potential to generate any prize money at all, and most recently that amounted to one-tenth of the amount the MNT players could generate."

Although this argument worked in court, American soccer opinion was incensed that the all-conquering USWNT could be belittled in this way, especially in comparison with the losers of the USMNT. The USSF's recently elected president, Carlos Cordeiro, abruptly resigned for having let the lawyers make this argument. His successor was Cindy Cone, the federation's first female president. In February 2022 the USWNT players agreed to end the discrimination case in exchange for a $24 million settlement and a pledge from USSF to equalize pay across national men's and women's teams. Equal pay finally arrived in May 2022.

Men's continuing dominance in soccer—just another manifestation of patriarchy—has kept the American women's game from reaching its potential. But this isn't only an American story. If the rest of the world hadn't banned women's soccer, the USWNT might never have become the sport's superpower, and globally the game would have developed much earlier.

Rich women are abused as well as poor ones, and male athletes have been victims of horrific assaults too, as the story of the University of Michigan's athletic doctor Robert Anderson demonstrates. At the same time, economic strength does give you a modicum of protection, or at least some means to fight back. This means that the rampant sexual abuse in women's soccer is also tied, like most problems of the game, to a lack of money. In our predominantly capitalist world, money is a currency of respect.

And money is the point over which many male sympathizers balk: women's soccer, they argue, fails to generate enough revenue because most people are more interested in the men's game. If only the women's game could draw more fans, they say, it would overcome its financial hurdles and gain the respect it deserves. Some people go further: they claim that the men's game is more appealing because men are stronger and run faster than women, dooming the women's game to inferiority. This thinking blames women's soccer itself for its underfunding. Every tub must stand on its own bottom, say the blowhards, and women's soccer simply lacks appeal.

You hear this argument in relation to almost all female sports. The problem is that it is ahistorical. It privileges introspective logic over an examination of what actually happened. (Bad economists make this mistake all the time.) But the facts speak clearly. We know that women's soccer was banned precisely at the moment when it posed an economic threat to the men's game. And we also know that when women's sports aren't banned, they can generate roughly equal interest among fans.

The case in point is tennis. To be sure, female players like Billie Jean King had to fight for financial equality back in the 1970s, but thanks to them, this is scarcely an issue today. It's true that male players can on average hit the ball harder, but there's a lot more to sport than brute force, and women's tennis proves that handily.

If soccer associations tried to ban the women's game today, the response would be rather different than in 1921. It's not just that attitudes have changed but also that the legal weapons available to women have been sharpened. The law in the US and other countries is much tougher now against restraints of trade. Banning women from playing—a violation of antitrust laws—would be straightforwardly illegal.

Any association that tried to impose such a ban, and lost, would find itself on the hook for a lot of money. In the US, each side in the case would assess the economic damages arising from the ban—chiefly lost earnings potential, but also as any knock-on effects. The judge would then decide which side's estimate was most reasonable.

Under US law, the penalty for an antitrust violation is levied at *three times* the value of the damages, the idea being to create big disincentives to violate the law in the first place. It is not possible to bring a retrospective antitrust case against a ban implemented one hundred years ago that lasted half a century and whose consequences still undermine women's soccer today. But it is possible to hazard a guess at the size of the potential damages. Is there any reason to think that women's soccer, poised as it was in 1920 to become a popular source of entertainment in England, the home of the game, would not have grown and spread around the world? This is not about some potential market that had not yet been tapped, but a market that had already been tested and was demonstrating the existence of real demand by regularly selling tens of thousands of match tickets. These revenues would surely have risen over time, as did revenues from men's soccer.

How big would women's professional soccer have become by now without those bans? Tennis is a natural benchmark, for it has had no bans, and women have organized themselves to manage their own competitions and revenues. Beyond the prestigious Grand Slam tournaments, there is an international circuit of professional competition managed by an organization for men's tennis, the ATP, and one for women's tennis, the WTA. In 2019 the ATP reported revenue of $159 million and the WTA $109 million. That sum equaled 69 percent of the ATP's income, or 41 percent of all tennis circuit revenue.

According to Deloitte, European soccer generated around $30 billion in 2019, almost entirely from men's professional soccer. Our argument is not that women's soccer would have necessarily generated additional revenues but that it would have shared the soccer market with the men. Let's say the women would have generated 41 percent of European soccer revenues in 2019 had it not been for the fifty-year ban. That would amount to around $12 billion. If this is a rough estimate of the damage done to women's soccer, then an antitrust court would treble these damages to $36 billion. And that relates just to a single year, whereas the economic harm has persisted for decades.

The ban on women's soccer was so long ago, is so little remembered, and reverberated for so long that it is hard to imagine the extent of the potential suppressed. This little exercise in approximating the damages gives at least some measure of the harm done. Soccer federations today advertise everything they do to promote the women's game, but they fail to acknowledge the harm they did. Men's soccer will never make good in full, but by at least recognizing the harms we can think more honestly about policies to address them.

FIFA could start. It claimed in its 2019 report that "women's football development is one of FIFA's top priorities," yet the $9 million spent directly on women's soccer that year represented less than 2 percent of the total allocated to "development and education." In 2018–2019 FIFA spent more on developing its Football Museum than it did on supporting the women's game.

The women are not to blame. It's the soccer authorities who banned their game and then ignored systematic abuse who need to act. It's time for reparations to build up female soccer to where it always should have been.

8

NEED NOT APPLY

Does Soccer Discriminate Against Black People?

In 1991 Ron Noades, chairman of Crystal Palace, popped up on British TV. "The problem with Black players," explained Noades, whose heavily Black team had just finished third in England, "is they've great pace, great athletes, love to play with the ball in front of them....When it's behind them, it's chaos. I don't think too many of them can read the game. When you're getting into the midwinter, you need a few of the hard white men to carry the athletic Black players through."

Noades's interview was one of the last flourishes of unabashed racism in British soccer. Through the 1980s, racism had been more or less taken for granted in the game. Fans threw bananas at Black players. Pundits like Emlyn Hughes explained the curious absence of Black players at Liverpool and Everton by saying, "They haven't got the bottle." The writer Dave Hill summed up the stereotypes: "'No bottle' is a particular favorite, lack of concentration another. 'You don't want too many of them in your defense,' one backroom bod told me, 'they cave in under pressure.' Then there is the curious conviction that Blacks are susceptible to the cold and won't go out when it rains."

It's clear that English soccer in those days was shot through with open prejudice based on skin color. But what we want to know is whether that racism translated into discrimination: unfair treatment of people. People like Noades may have been prejudiced against Black players, but did they make it harder for these players to get jobs in soccer? The 1980s Black striker Garth Crooks thought they did: "I always felt I had to be 15 percent better than the white person to get the same chance."

Yet the notion of discrimination against Black people clashes with something we think we know about soccer: that on the field, at least, the game is ruthlessly fair. In soccer, good players of whatever color perform better than bad ones. Fans and chairmen and managers may walk around with Noadesian fantasies in their heads, but when a Black player plays well, everyone can see it. As Nick Hornby writes in *Fever Pitch*, in his famous riff on Gus Caesar, "One of the great things about sport is its cruel clarity; there is no such thing, for example, as a bad one-hundred-meter runner or a hopeless center-half who got lucky; in sport, you get found out. Nor is there such a thing as an unknown genius striker starving in a garret somewhere."

In short, it would seem that in soccer there is no room for ideologies. You have to be right, and results on the field will tell you very quickly whether you are. So would clubs really discriminate against Black players at the cost of winning matches? After all, even Ron Noades employed Black players. (He seems to have known something about soccer, too: after leaving Palace he bought Brentford, appointed himself manager, won promotion, and was voted manager of the year in the second division.) In fact, the very success of Black players on the field might be taken as evidence that the opportunities were there.

It's also often hard to prove objectively that discrimination exists. How can you show that you failed to get the job because of prejudice rather than just because you weren't good enough? Liverpool and Everton might argue that they employed white players in the 1980s simply because the whites were better.

Luckily, there is no need to get into a "he said, she said" argument. We have data to prove that English soccer discriminated against Black players. We can show when this particular kind of wage discrimination ended. And we can predict that the forms of discrimination that continue to pervade English soccer today will shift only if the game's authorities take action.

The first Black person to set foot in the British Isles was probably a soldier in Julius Caesar's invading army, in 55 BCE. The "indigenous" English themselves arrived only about four hundred years later, during the collapse of the Roman Empire.

Much later, under Victoria, Britain's own empire ruled a large share of the world's Black people. A few of the better-educated or entrepreneurial ones made their way from the British Raj in India, the Caribbean, or Africa to Britain. Arthur Wharton, born in 1865 in the Gold Coast (now Ghana), became the world's first Black professional soccer player. As well as keeping goal for Preston, he set the world record of ten seconds for the one-hundred-yard sprint.

But until the 1950s, most Britons had probably never seen a Black person. Then, after World War II, hundreds of thousands of colonial immigrants began arriving. The influx was small enough—less than 5 percent of Britain's total population, spread over a quarter of a century—to pose little threat to the concepts of Englishness, Scottishness, or Welshness. Nonetheless, the signs went up in the windows of apartment houses:

NO COLOUREDS

Stefan is the son of an immigrant from Poland who escaped to London in 1940 and joined the British Army to fight the Nazis. Stefan remembers his father telling him about looking for lodging in London in the early 1950s and finding signs in the windows saying:

ROOMS TO LET—NO POLES, NO HUNGARIANS

Not only was this kind of discrimination legal, but Stefan's father accepted it. In his mind, he was the immigrant, and it was his job to fit in. Luckily for him (and for Stefan), he was an educated man, able to find a reasonable job and make a reasonable living. He was also racist. This might sound harsh, but with hindsight, most British adults seemed to be racist in the 1970s, when Stefan was growing up. In the popular comedy series of the time *Till Death Us Do Part*, the hero, Alf Garnett, was a ludicrously prejudiced Londoner who favored labels like "coon," "darky," "Paki," and "the Jews up at Spurs" (Garnett supported West Ham). Not only were these words used on the BBC, but they were also accompanied by canned laughter (the series was such a success that a US version followed, giving birth to Archie Bunker). Admittedly, the joke of the series was ultimately on Garnett, who was regularly exposed to the falsity of his own prejudices. But Stefan used to argue that these labels were offensive. His father took this as evidence of his son's lack of a sense of humor.

It was against this 1970s background of instinctive racism that Black players began arriving in English soccer. Most were the British-born children of immigrants. That didn't stop them from being treated to monkey noises and bananas. (As Hornby notes in *Fever Pitch*, "There may well be attractive, articulate and elegant racists, but they certainly never come to soccer matches.") For a while, neo-Nazi parties even imagined that they could lead a revolution from the soccer terraces.

Given the abuse that the early Black players received, it would have been easy for them to give up on soccer. It was thinkable that they would be driven out of the game. Instead, they stayed, played, and triumphed. In 1978, when Viv Anderson became the first Black man to play for England, it became apparent that children of Caribbean immigrants might have something of a role to play in English soccer. Still, even after the Black winger John Barnes scored his solo goal to beat Brazil in Rio in 1984, the Football Association's chairman was harangued by England fans on the flight back home: "You fucking wanker, you prefer sambos to us."

It's true that today's all-seaters in the Premier League exclude poor people. But the terraces before the 1990s were far more exclusive. Whenever people reminisce about the good old days, when ordinary working people could afford to go to soccer matches, it's worth scanning the photographs of the cloth-capped masses standing on the terraces for the faces you don't see: there are almost no women or minorities.

As late as 1993, you could still witness the following scene in London: a crowd of people in a pub in the central business district, the "City," is watching England-Holland on TV. Every time Jamaican-born John Barnes gets the ball, one man—in shirtsleeves and a tie, just out of his City office—makes monkey noises. Every time, his coworkers laugh. If anyone had complained, let alone gone off to find a police officer and asked him to arrest the man, the response would have been "Where's your sense of humor?" (Hornby's line on this sort of problem: "I wish I were enormous and of a violent disposition, so that I could deal with any problem that arises near me in a fashion commensurate with the anger I feel.") That kind of open racist abuse remains common today in many leagues, from Italy to Russia. In the UK it has mostly been driven out. Nowadays, the police might well arrest that man. More likely, the pub would have kicked him out.

In the late 1980s, Stefan began thinking about the economics of soccer. He was then working for the Centre for Business Strategy at London Business School. Everyone in the center was an economist and therefore tempted to think that markets more or less "worked." The theory was that any businessperson who came up with a brilliant innovation—inventing the telephone, say—would not keep their advantage for long because others would imitate them and compete.

But the economists were interested in the few companies that stayed successful despite competition. Clearly, there must be something to learn from them. Stefan suggested looking for these paragons in soccer. It was obviously a highly competitive industry, yet some clubs succeeded in dominating for years on end. How did they manage to stay ahead for so long?

Stefan enlisted the support of Ron Smith, who had taught him when he was writing his PhD. Smith, as well as being an expert on Marxist economics and the economics of defense, is a well-known econometrician. Econometrics is essentially the art of finding statistical methods to extract information from data—or, as a lawyer friend of Stefan's likes to put it, taking the data down into the basement and torturing them until they confess. Studying the accounts of soccer clubs, Stefan and Ron could see how much each club spent on salaries. The two discovered that this spending alone explained almost all the variation in positions in the English Football League. When Stefan analyzed the accounts of forty clubs for 1978 through 1997, he found that their wage spending accounted for 92 percent of the variation in their league positions.

Clearly, the market in players' pay was highly efficient: the better a player, the more he earned. And this made sense because soccer is one of the few markets that indisputably meets the conditions in which competition can work efficiently: there are large numbers of buyers and sellers, all of whom have plenty of information about the quality of the players being bought and sold. If a player got paid less than he was worth, he could move to another club. If he got paid more, he would soon find himself being sold off again.

But what about the variation in league position that remained unexplained after adjusting for players' pay? If buying talent was generally enough to win titles—as rich-club chairmen like Jack Walker at Blackburn Rovers and Abramovich at Chelsea would soon demonstrate—what else accounted for a team's success? If it was something that was easy to copy—a new tactic, for instance—then other teams would copy it, and the advantage would disappear. That got Stefan thinking about discrimination. What if owners were simply not willing to copy the secret of others' success because they didn't want to hire the kinds of players who brought that success? He began to search for discrimination against Black players.

In most industries there is a way to demonstrate that discrimination exists. Suppose that you could construct a sample of all applicants for a job and also of all their relevant qualifications. If you then found that a much larger proportion of relevantly qualified white applicants received job offers than relevantly qualified Black applicants, you could reasonably infer the presence of discrimination. For example, if 50 percent of whites with doctorates in philosophy got job offers from university philosophy departments but only 10 percent of their Black equivalents did, then you should suspect discrimination.

This is essentially how economists have tried to identify job discrimination. The method also works for wage discrimination. If equivalently qualified Black people (or women, or left-handers, or whoever) get lower wages for equivalent jobs, then there is probably discrimination going on. Researchers have put together databases of thousands of workers, each identified by dozens of relevant qualifications, to test whether discrimination exists. When it comes to ethnic minorities and women, the evidence usually shows that it does.

The problem is that there are few measurable qualifications that make someone a great soccer player. When a company is accused of racism, it often says that although the Black (or Asian, or female) candidates might have possessed some of the relevant characteristics, there were other, less quantifiable characteristics that they didn't have. Intellectually, this point is hard to overturn. Hundreds of cases of racial discrimination have been fought in US courts, and evidence based on the kinds of studies we have mentioned has often run into trouble.

Happily, there is another way to test for discrimination in soccer. Once again, it relies on evidence from the market. As a general rule, the best way to find out what people are up to is to see how they behave when faced with a price. Don't know whether you prefer Coke to Pepsi? Well, let's see what you choose when they both cost the same. (Most people choose Coke.) Do managers prefer white players to Black ones? Well, let's see how they spend their clubs' money.

If clubs discriminate, then they will prefer to hire a white player to an equivalently talented Black player. If they do that, then Black people will find it harder to get jobs as professional soccer players. The Black players will then be willing to accept lower wages than equivalently talented whites. After all, when demand for what we sell is lower, we tend to lower our asking price. So Black players become cheaper than white players. If there is discrimination, we would expect to find Black players earning less than equally talented whites.

If Black players are being discriminated against, that creates an economic opportunity for unprejudiced clubs. By hiring Black players, the club can do just as well in the league as an equivalently talented (but more expensive) team of white players. That means that a simple experiment will reveal whether discrimination exists: if teams with more Black players achieve higher average league positions for a given sum of wage spending, then the teams with fewer Black players must have been discriminating. Otherwise, the whiter teams would have seen that Black players were good value for the money and would have tried to hire them. Then Black players' wages would have risen as a result of increased competition for their services, and the relative advantage of hiring Black players would have disappeared.

Note that the argument is not that some teams hire more Black players than others. That could happen for many reasons. Rather, we can infer discrimination if (a) some teams have more Black players than others and (b) those same teams consistently outperform their competitors at a given level of wage spending.

After Stefan figured this out, he had the luck of running into just the right person. Around that time he was also researching the relationship between the pay of senior executives in the biggest British companies and the performance of their companies. (Very unlike soccer players' wages, there turned out to be almost no correlation between senior-executive pay and the performance of a company's share price, until share options became common in the 1990s. In other words, paying top executives more seemed to do nothing for business efficiency.) Stefan was interviewed for a BBC program by the political journalist Michael Crick. Over time, he and Crick got to talking about soccer.

Crick is a famously thorough researcher. Book reviewers delight in finding errors, no matter how trivial, but they never succeed with Crick's political biographies. And as it happens, Crick supports Manchester United. In 1989 he wrote a fascinating history of the club with David Smith, describing how United packaged its legend for commercial gain. About this time, Crick became interested in whether soccer clubs discriminated in their hiring. Everyone knew of the suspicious cases of the day, chiefly Liverpool and Everton.

Crick began collecting data from the 1970s onward to see which clubs had hired Black players. This was no easy task. How do you decide who is "Black"? Crick took a commonsense approach. He started with the old Rothmans Football Yearbooks, which published a photograph of every English league team. From this he made a judgment as to which players "looked Black." He then followed up by asking clubs and supporters' clubs to fill in any gaps. It took him months to come up with a list of players who, to most fans, would have appeared to be Black. This sounds arbitrary, but it is precisely what was required. Prejudice is based on appearance. For example, several years after Crick did his research, it emerged that the great Manchester United winger Ryan Giggs had a Black father. Giggs even spoke publicly about his pride in his Caribbean ancestry. However, until that point, most people would not have considered Giggs a Black player. He didn't look Black, and for that reason he would have been unlikely to face discrimination. So at least for the purposes of detecting discrimination, Crick was right not to count Giggs as Black.

When Crick told Stefan about his list of Black players, it was a cinch to create a test for discrimination. All that was necessary was to count how many times each Black player had played for his club in a given season. It would then be clear which teams employed a larger proportion of Black players.

Stefan then matched these data with figures on each team's league position and its spending on wages. If there were no discrimination in the market, then wages alone would almost entirely explain league performance. Everything else would just be random noise: "luck." But if Black players were systematically being paid less than equally talented white players, then logically the teams that hired an above-average proportion of Black players would do systematically better than their wage bill alone would predict.

Back in the 1970s, there were very few Black players in English soccer. Combining the data on wages with Crick's database had generated a sample of thirty-nine out of the ninety-two professional league teams. In the 1973–1974 season, only two of these clubs had fielded any Black players at all. By 1983–1984, there were still twenty teams in our sample that did not field a Black player all season. However, at this point there seems to have been a major breakthrough. By 1989, every team in the sample had fielded at least one Black player at some point. By 1992, when the Premier League was founded, only five teams in the sample did not field a Black player that season. This implied that about 90 percent of clubs were putting Black players in the first team. Attitudes were changing. Bananas left the game. When Noades voiced his theories on Black players in 1991, he was widely derided.

It is interesting to look at the characteristics of the Black players in the English game in these years. For purposes of comparison, Stefan constructed a random sample of an equal number of white players with similar age profiles. Almost all the Black players (89 percent) were born in Britain, not very different from the white players (95 percent). Most of the Black players were strikers (58 percent), compared with only 33 percent of white players. There were no Black goalkeepers at the time. Noades would have noted the fact that Black players seemed underrepresented in defense. But then strikers always carry a premium to defenders in the market: it takes more talent to score than to stop other people from scoring.

Certain facts about the sample stood out: the careers of the Black players averaged more than six years, compared with less than four for the whites. And 36 percent of the Black players had played for their countries, compared with only 23 percent of the whites. On this evidence, it looked suspiciously as if the Black players were better than the white ones.

The proof came when Stefan deployed the economist's favorite tool, regression analysis. He used it to isolate the distinct effects of wages and the share of Black players on each club's league performance. What he found was discrimination. The data showed that clubs with more Black players really did have a better record in the league than clubs with fewer Black players, after allowing for wage spending. If two teams had identical annual wage budgets, the team with more Black players would finish higher in the league. The test implied that Black players were systematically better value for money than white ones. Certain teams of the 1980s, such as Arsenal, Noades's Palace, and Ron Atkinson's West Bromwich Albion (this was years before Atkinson racially abused Marcel Desailly on air), benefited from fielding Black players.

The clubs with fewer Black players were not suffering from a lack of information. Anyone who knew soccer could judge fairly easily how good most players were just by watching them play. So the only credible reason that clubs would deny themselves the opportunity to hire these players was prejudice. Clubs didn't like the look of Black players, or they thought their fans wouldn't, either simply because of skin hue or because they perceived weaknesses that were just not there. By testing the behavior of managers against the market, it proved possible to uncover evidence of discrimination.

In soccer you can judge someone's performance only against other competitors. This means that I lose nothing by being inefficient if my competitors are inefficient in the same way as I am. I can go on hiring mediocre players as long as other clubs do, too. As long as all clubs refused to hire talented Black players, the cost of discriminating was low. What the data showed was that by the beginning of the 1980s, so many teams were hiring talented Black players that the cost of discriminating had become quite high. Teams that refused to field Black players were overpaying for white players and losing more matches as a consequence.

Yet some level of discrimination persisted. Even by the end of the 1980s, an all-white team like Everton would cost around 5 percent more than an equally good team that fielded merely an average proportion of Black players. As Dave Hill wrote in the fanzine *When Saturday Comes* in 1989, "Half a century after Jesse Owens, a quarter of a century after Martin Luther King, and 21 years after two American sprinters gave the Black Power salute from the Olympic medal rostrum, some of these dickheads don't even know what a black person is." But by the time Hill wrote that, precisely because soccer is so competitive, more and more clubs had begun to hire Black players. In 1995 even Everton signed the Nigerian Daniel Amokachi. The economic forces of competition drove white men to disregard their prejudices, at least in this particular area.

Quite soon, enough clubs were hiring Black players that they came to be statistically overrepresented in English soccer. Only about 1.6 percent of people in the 1991 British census described themselves as Black. Yet in the early 1990s, about 10 percent of all players in English professional soccer were Black. By the end of the decade, after the influx of foreign players, the share was nearer 20 percent. By 2021, the proportion in the English Premier League was over 40 percent.

So did clubs learn to overcome their prejudices? A few years after Stefan ran his first test for discrimination, he badgered some students who were looking for undergraduate projects into compiling a list of Black players for another six seasons. That took the data set up to the 1998–1999 season. Once again, Stefan merged the data with figures on wages and league performances. Now he could run the regression to the end of the 1990s. For these six additional years, there was no evidence that the share of Black players on a team had any effect on team performance, after allowing for the team's wage bill. In other words, by then Black players were on average paid what they were worth to a team.

Perhaps the best witness to the acceptance of Black players, at least in the job market, is Lilian Thuram. A Black man born on the Caribbean island of Guadeloupe and raised in a town just outside Paris, Thuram played professionally from 1991 to 2008 and became France's most capped player. He won the World Cup of 1998 with that famous multicolored French team. He is also a French intellectual, possibly the only soccer player ever to have spoken the sentence "There's an interesting young ethnographer at the Musée de l'Homme...."

Thuram is acutely sensitive to racism. He now runs an antiracism foundation. Nonetheless, in 2008, in the final months of his long playing career, he insisted to us that soccer was innocent of the sin. Over late-night pasta in an Italian restaurant in Barcelona, he explained: "In soccer it's harder to have discrimination because we are judged on very specific performances. There are not really subjective criteria. Sincerely, I've never met a racist person in soccer. Maybe they were there, but I didn't see it." In fact, he added, "In sport, prejudices favor the Blacks. In the popular imagination, the Black is in his place in sport. For example, recently in Barcelona, the fitness coach said about Abidal [the Black French defender], 'He's an athlete of the Black race.' It's not because he stays behind after training to run. No, it's because he's Black." Note that Thuram wasn't denying the existence of racism in the stands or the media or in the hiring of coaches—an issue we'll discuss in the next chapter. He was talking strictly about the acceptance of Black players by clubs. By the 1990s, discrimination against Black players as measured by salaries had disappeared.

The story of racism in American sports followed much the same arc. Right through World War II, baseball and basketball had segregated Black players into Negro Leagues. In 1947 Branch Rickey of the Brooklyn Dodgers broke an unspoken rule among baseball owners and hired Black infielder Jackie Robinson to play for his team. Robinson eventually became an American hero. However, the costar of his story was economics. The Dodgers had less money than their crosstown rivals, the New York Yankees. If Rickey wanted a winning team, he had to tap talent that the other owners overlooked. Racism gave him an opportunity.

Of course, discrimination against Black players persisted in American sports long after Robinson. Lawrence Kahn, an economist at Cornell University, surveyed the data and found little evidence that before the 1990s baseball teams were withholding jobs or pay from Black players. But he did think they were giving Black players unduly short careers and using them only in certain positions. In basketball, Kahn found wage discrimination. When he repeated his study in 2000, he discovered, like Stefan the second time around, that discrimination was fading. British and American sports were becoming fairer to Black athletes.

Yet racism and discrimination still flourish in parts of soccer. When three English Black players missed penalties in the shoot-out against Italy in the final of Euro 2021, they suffered a torrent of racial abuse on social media. And discrimination can persist even among top decision makers of one of the most successful national soccer federations on Earth.

In April 2011 the minutes of a secret meeting at France's soccer federation were leaked to the French website Mediapart. The meeting, held in November 2010, had begun fairly innocuously. At first the officials had mused about admitting fewer youngsters of double nationality (often French plus African) into the federation's academies. It bothered the officials that some of these youngsters eventually chose to play for Algeria, say, rather than for France. However, the discussion quickly spread to scarier territory: complaints about Black players per se.

France's coach, Laurent "Le Président" Blanc (who had played alongside Thuram in the Black-white-Arab French team of 1998), was quoted as telling the attendees, "You have the feeling that we are producing really only one prototype of player: big, strong, fast…and who are the big, strong, fast players? The Blacks. That's the way it is. That's the way things are today."

According to the leaked minutes, Blanc continued. "I think we need to refocus, above all for boys of thirteen-fourteen, twelve-thirteen—introduce other parameters, adjusted to our own culture.…The Spaniards say to me: 'We don't have this problem. We don't have any Blacks.'" Blanc did add that he was talking about soccer qualities, not color. He wouldn't mind if the whole French team was Black, he said, as long as there was a balance of size and skill.

Even so, it's difficult to know where to start with a critique of his position. Most obviously, Blanc seemed to be conflating the dull, uncreative, physical French style of the time with the presence of Black players. Secondly, the issue of double nationality scarcely mattered: a player of African origin good enough to play for France, like the Senegalese-born Patrick Vieira, will choose France. It's generally only French-raised players overlooked by France, such as Marouane Chamakh (Morocco) or Riyad Mahrez (Algeria), who will represent another country.

Yet some inside the French federation seemed to want to let fewer boys of African origin into the academies. Blocking the pipeline to professional soccer would mean job discrimination against Black players. It would be a return to the practices of English soccer of the 1980s. Nobody—we had previously thought—was barred from top-class soccer in Western Europe anymore because of his skin color. Whereas ordinary Arab and Black people in France struggled to find jobs because of discrimination, we had imagined that Arab and Black soccer players in France did not.

But even before the federation's secret meeting, many French soccer fans had been calling for discrimination. There had long been popular grumbling about the number of nonwhite players on the national team. Every year, France's National Consultative Commission on Human Rights publishes a big survey on racist attitudes. In 1999 a new question was inserted into the survey: Were there "too many players of foreign origin in the French soccer team?" You would not have imagined anyone thought so. The players of foreign origin had just made *les Bleus* world champions. Yet in 1999, 31 percent of respondents either totally or mostly agreed with this statement. In 2000, 36 percent agreed. More than a third of French people did not want this team even when it was the best one on Earth. Jean-Marie Le Pen, then leader of France's racist Front National party, knew exactly what he was doing when he led the grumbles about France's Black players.

As the team began playing worse after 2000 and became Blacker, public disquiet only grew. The philosopher Alain Finkielkraut voiced the thoughts of many French racists (and in France, philosophers are heard) when he complained that the "Black-Black-Black" team had become an international joke.

In 2010 France's coach, Raymond Domenech, omitted three gifted young men of North African origin from his squad for the World Cup: Samir Nasri, Karim Benzema, and Hatem Ben Arfa. Domenech quite likely made his choices without any racist intention. There were soccer-based arguments against each of the trio. Nevertheless, says the French sociologist Stéphane Beaud, author of *Traîtres à la nation?* (*Traitors to the Nation?*), a book on *les Bleus* and ethnicity, Domenech seemed unable to deal with a new, more assertive generation of North African youth.

The *Bleus* of 2010 were different from those of 1998, explains Beaud. The 1998 team had come mostly from stable, fairly comfortably off working-class families not all that far from the French mainstream. Thuram, for instance, had grown up playing for an ethnically Portuguese team in the far-from-deprived Parisian suburb of Fontainebleu. But the 2010 team reflected the later wave of immigration to France: many players were from poorer and broken immigrant families who lived in the ghettos outside France's big cities. These men had grown up at a distance from the white French mainstream. And whereas most of the heroes of 1998 had spent many years earning relatively modest salaries in the French league, getting married, and raising children, the new lot tended to have moved abroad very young, had spent their whole careers playing for top-level teams amid huge stress, and often had chaotic private lives, says Beaud.

The new generation could be harder to deal with for an older white Frenchman like Domenech (himself of Spanish descent). He was furious when Benzema (of Algerian descent) said he didn't want to come on as a sub in a game against Romania. In the minds of many white Frenchmen, the image of *les Bleus* became that of spoiled young globalized multimillionaires slouched on the team bus wearing massive headphones, ignoring fans who had waited hours to see them. And of course, these *Bleus* weren't white.

Popular anger erupted one Sunday night during the 2010 World Cup. French TV showed live how the players, angry with Domenech at their training ground in the South African tourist town of Knysna, reached for an authentically French remedy: they went on strike. They got onto their bus and refused to train. Nicolas Anelka swore at Domenech. The phrase "the bus of shame" entered the French language. Knysna was "a national affair, a political affair," says Beaud. These mostly Black and Brown players were perceived as rejecting France. Worse than losing to Mexico and South Africa, they had (briefly) refused to sweat the blue shirt. France's national anger against the young Black and Arab-origin players echoed the national anger of 2005 against the young Black and Arab-origin rioters in the run-down suburbs of the big cities. "Scum" was what then interior minister Nicolas Sarkozy had called the rioters. In 2010 President Sarkozy instituted an inquiry into the soccer team.

A few months later came the federation's meeting in Paris. In a horrible way it made sense that officials of a national federation should be tempted by discrimination. Clubs are all about winning. However, national teams have an additional function: to incarnate the nation. Many white French people—and of course the federation's officials were overwhelmingly white—seemed to feel that their nation could not be incarnated by a nonwhite team. If the officials had complained about Black players publicly rather than in secret, a lot of French people would have been delighted.

After Mediapart leaked the minutes of the meeting, Thuram broke the unwritten social code of soccer to attack his old teammate Blanc. Three years earlier, Thuram had told us that discrimination in soccer was impossible. Now he argued that Blanc had been guilty at least of "unconscious racism" and promoting "racial stereotypes." If you say that Blacks are stronger and faster than whites, Thuram argued, you open the door to saying that whites are more intelligent than Blacks. Vieira, another Black hero of 1998, complained, too: "I know Laurent Blanc and I don't think he is racist. But I don't understand how any of the officials present at that meeting can stay in their job."

In the end, Blanc and the others did keep their jobs, cleared by a government inquiry, to the joy of most French fans. "I think a similar affair at the Federation is still imaginable," Thuram told us in 2016. The French quotas scandal had changed nothing. Even the Black players stayed on the team—and in 2018 a very mixed French team won the World Cup. They were the best, and that is still (almost always) what matters in soccer.

9

DO COACHES MATTER?

The Cult of the White Manager

Way back in 2005, when Trevor Phillips was head of Britain's Commission for Racial Equality, he identified the most tenacious form of discrimination within soccer clubs: "loads of Black players on the field and none in the dugout."

You might think that just as competition pushed clubs into signing Black players, it would eventually push them into hiring Black managers. But, in fact, the prejudice against Black managers has proved much harder to shift.

Some people argue that since Black and mixed-race people represent only about 5 percent of the British population, the 4–6 percent of Black managers you see in English soccer is not really underrepresentation. But this fails to take account of the way soccer works. Almost every manager is a former professional player. In 2021, 43 percent of players in the English Premier League were Black, and they accounted for 48 percent of goals scored, yet when Patrick Vieira was appointed to manage Crystal Palace that November, he became only the tenth Black manager in the league's thirty-year history. Delroy Corinaldi, who in 2022 founded the UK's Black Footballers Partnership, a pressure group, says that in the Premier League, "Sam Allardyce has had nearly as many roles as the whole Black population."

Possibly the only British club in 2022 that was run mostly by Black men was Queens Park Rangers (QPR) in London. The club's technical director, Chris Ramsey, who entered coaching in the late 1980s, when, he said, "there were literally no black coaches," told us, "There's always a dream that you're going to make the highest level, so naively you coach believing that your talent will get you there, but very early on I realized that wasn't going to happen."

He said discrimination in hiring was always unspoken: "People hide behind politically correct language. They will take a knee and say, 'I'm all for it.' You're just never really seen as able to do the job. And then people sometimes employ people less qualified than you. Plenty of white managers have failed, and I just want to have the opportunity to be as bad as them, and to be given an opportunity again. You don't want to have to be better just because you're Black."

Les Ferdinand is QPR's director of football. When his glittering playing career ended, he worried that studying for his coaching badges might "waste five years of my life," given that the white men running clubs were reluctant to hire even famous Black ex-players like John Barnes and Paul Ince. In Ferdinand's first seven years on the market, he was offered just one managerial job. He suspects that QPR hired him in part because its Malaysian chairman, Tony Fernandes, was a person of color. After the two men met and began talking, recalled Ferdinand, "He said, 'Why are you not doing this job in football?' I said, 'Because I've not been given the opportunity.' The conversations went from there. Had he not been a person of color, I perhaps wouldn't have had the opportunity to talk to him in the way that I did."

And the discrimination runs far beyond the top job, through soccer's entire post-playing career structure. When Stefan analyzed 129 executive, leadership, and ownership positions in English professional soccer in 2021, only two were held by Black or mixed-race people: Ben Robinson, the longtime owner of Burton Albion, and Ryan Giggs, who with some of his former Manchester United teammates co-owns Salford City in the game's fourth tier. Former Black players were also very underrepresented in scouting or junior coaching roles—the sort of entry-level jobs that can eventually lead to managerial posts. As for fitness coaches, we couldn't identify a single Black one in the whole league.

Why has discrimination died on the field in England but persisted off it? Well, playing talent is so transparent that hiring discrimination could no longer hold, but assessments of managerial talent are so subjective that there is ample room to indulge prejudice. As soon as you get to thinking about what it will take to get more Black people into coaching jobs, you confront the great question about soccer coaches: do they really matter? We will argue that the vast majority of coaches or managers (call them what you like) simply don't make much difference. Typical soccer talk vastly overstates their importance. Consequently, the market in soccer managers is much less efficient than the market in players. That means Black people will probably continue to have a hard time finding coaching jobs unless the soccer authorities take compulsory action. We suspect that clubs will drop this form of discrimination only if forced to do so.

Like discrimination against Black players, discrimination against Black managers first became visible in American sports. As early as 1969, the first Black man to play in Major League Baseball, Jackie Robinson, who had become more disillusioned as he grew older, refused to attend Old Timers' Day at Yankee Stadium, protesting the sport's refusal to hire Black coaches and managers.

The issue hit public consciousness in Britain only when the pioneering generation of Black players began to retire (it being an article of faith in soccer that only ex-players had what it took to become managers). The former England international Luther Blissett, who as a player had made that ill-fated transfer to Milan, applied for twenty-two jobs as a manager in the 1990s. He did not get a single interview. Stella Orakwue, who recounts his story in her 1998 book *Pitch Invaders*, concludes: "I feel a British black managing a Premiership team could be a very long way off." Indeed, only in 2008, ten years after she wrote this, did Blackburn give Paul Ince a brief chance. After Ince's appointment, John Barnes, who himself had struggled to get work as a manager in England, still maintained, "I believe the situation for Black managers is like it was for Black players back in the 1970s."

Not even good results with Newcastle could save the Black manager Chris Hughton in 2010: four months after he won the club promotion to the Premier League, with Newcastle safely in eleventh place in the top division, he was sacked. "Regrettably the board now feels that an individual with more managerial experience is needed to take the club forward," the club explained. Newcastle finished the season in twelfth place. Hughton went on to do well at Birmingham, stayed in the Premier League with Norwich (but was sacked regardless), and took Brighton into the top flight in 2017. It's hard to avoid the conclusion that he would have been treated better if he had been white. In the decade from 2010, only one other Black manager was given a serious run of games in the Premier League: the Portuguese Nuno Espirito Santo. He probably benefited from being a foreigner; he could be stereotyped as a sophisticated Continental manager and only secondarily as an untried Black one. He didn't set the Premier League alight, but then very few managers do.

Almost all other soccer leagues remain unwelcoming toward Black coaches. For example, the MLS had just two in its first twenty-one seasons through 2017. As Nelson Rodriguez, former president of the Chicago Fire, said, "I refuse to believe that the best people and best professionals are mostly white males. I would find that an incredible set of coincidences." Yet that remains the basic principle of coach recruitment in soccer.

One argument you sometimes hear is that Black players don't have the motivation or interest to go into coaching. This is another version of the "lazy Black people" racist stereotype. The evidence suggests otherwise. Each national association in Europe runs training programs for coaches, the highest level of which is known as the UEFA Pro License. The English FA started these courses in the early 2000s and has since graduated around four hundred coaches, including David Moyes, Brendan Rodgers, and Gareth Southgate. The UEFA Pro License is the royal road to management. More than 10 percent of the course's graduates are Black, yet many have struggled to find jobs, and they generally have to satisfy themselves with coaching in lower divisions at best. Given the paucity of opportunities, it's remarkable that so many Black people bother to start down this career track at all. As Lilian Thuram told the author Ben Lyttleton, "Sometimes Black players ask themselves, 'Should I become a manager?' But then they think, 'Even if I get my qualifications, who's going to hire me?' I think that in the collective unconscious, we have trouble imagining a Black manager."

Until recently the issue mostly went undiscussed within the European game. Even as senior a club president as Andrea Agnelli of Juventus, who has tried to combat racism in the stands, shrugged when we asked him some years ago why there were so few Black coaches: "I haven't got a clue. I don't think it's to do with discrimination. I have never really thought about the issue." But in the past few years the issue has finally burst into the open. Many of soccer's decision makers will now queasily admit that there is a problem.

An approach that has grabbed attention is the NFL's "Rooney Rule," which requires teams to interview at least two minority candidates from outside the franchise when recruiting a head coach or certain other senior officials. The rule's impact is debatable. There certainly has been a large increase in the number of Black NFL coaches (staffers more than head coaches) since an earlier version of it was introduced in 2003, and this has tempted many observers to conclude that it has been effective. But while more Black coaches are emerging at the lower levels, it's not clear how much they have benefited from the Rooney Rule itself, and Black coaches remain significantly underrepresented given that about 65 percent of NFL players are Black. In early 2022, only two of the thirty-two NFL head coaches were African Americans. A big part of the problem in the NFL, as in English soccer, is the pipeline: Black coaches are underrepresented at the college level, which is the main nursery for coaching talent.

In 2019 the Rooney Rule was made mandatory in the three lower tiers of English professional soccer, though not in the Premier League or anywhere else in Europe. Clubs had to interview at least one Black, Asian, or minority ethnic (BAME) candidate (if any applied) for all managerial and first-team coaching roles. Why didn't the rule noticeably increase minority hiring? QPR's Les Ferdinand told us: "Because there's nobody being held accountable to it. What is the Rooney Rule? You give someone the opportunity to come through the door and talk." Moreover, English football's version of the rule has a major loophole: clubs are exempt if they interview only one candidate, typically someone found through the white old boys' network.

In 2020 the English FA launched the Football Leadership Diversity Code to tackle inequality across senior leadership positions, broader team operations, and coaching roles. Most English professional clubs refused even to sign up for this voluntary code. However, forty did commit to achieving percentage targets for Black, Asian, and mixed-heritage people among new hires: 15 percent for senior leadership and team operations positions, and 25 percent for men's coaching—a discrepancy in goals that itself reflects the problem. These modest targets were further watered down by allowing clubs to adjust their target "based on local demographics." When we asked Les Ferdinand if clubs took the code seriously, he smiled ironically: "From day one *I* didn't take it seriously. Because it's a voluntary code. What's the repercussions if you don't follow the voluntary code? No one will say anything; no one will do anything about it."

The code's first annual report, published in November 2021, suggested mixed results. Many clubs missed the targets, and several Premier League clubs reported zero diversity hires, but the report did claim that over 20 percent of new hires in men's soccer were Black, Asian, or of mixed heritage, which was at least better than historical hiring rates.

You would think that given this job discrimination, unprejudiced clubs could clean up by hiring the best Black (or female) managers at low salaries. A small club like FC Dallas, say, could probably take its pick of the world's Black managers. It could get the best female manager in history. It probably won't, though. That's because the market in soccer managers is so different from the market in players. Markets tend to work when they are transparent—when you can see who is doing what and place a value on it. That is preeminently true of soccer players, who do their work in public. When you can't see what people do, it's very hard to assign a value to their work. Efficient markets punish discrimination in plain view of everyone, so discrimination tends to get rooted out. Inefficient markets can maintain discrimination almost indefinitely.

Wage discrimination among Black soccer players righted itself because the market in players is transparent. It is usually obvious who can play and who can't, who's "got bottle" and who hasn't. The market for players, as we have seen, is so efficient that salaries explain about 90 percent of the variation in clubs' league positions in the long run. If a player is underpaid relative to his contribution to the team, he just gets bid away by another club. That's why the club with the best-paid players typically wins the league and the one with the worst-paid finishes in the cellar.

But if players' salaries determine results almost by themselves, then it follows that the vast majority of managers are not very relevant—much less so than most media and fans imagine. Thomas Tuchel, coach of Chelsea when it won the Champions League in 2021, calls soccer "a players' game," not "a coaches' game."

To grasp the modest significance of head coaches, think of personnel managers of large companies. Did that person cause the success of Apple, Siemens, or Toyota? Well, all big companies need personnel managers, and in theory these people could have a big impact, but on the list of explanations for corporate success, the personnel manager would not typically figure very high.

Players matter much more. Johan Cruyff said when he was coaching Barcelona, "If your players are better than your opponents, 90 percent of the time you will win." There cannot be many businesses in which a manager would make such an extravagant claim. The chief executive of General Motors does not say that the art of management is simply hiring the best designers or software engineers. Instead, CEOs talk about organization or innovation. We typically think of businesses as complex organisms. Yet in club soccer, according to someone as insightful as Cruyff, management is little more than assembling the best employees.

As we'll argue later in the book, we think that managers of national teams have a better chance of making a difference. A manager can outperform when he brings a country foreign knowledge that it didn't previously have. Fabio Capello arguably did that for England and Guus Hiddink for South Korea, Australia, and Russia. These men helped their players access some of the latest Western European soccer know-how. However, it's very rare for such knowledge gaps to exist in a league like England's. All serious English clubs are now stuffed with people from all over the world and have access to current best practice. The Premier League is like a market with almost perfect information. Consequently, few club managers can make much difference.

One common counterargument to ours is that the clubs that pay their players the most also tend to pay managers the most. So the clubs with the best players would also have the best managers. In other words, or so this theory goes, the manager's quality matters a lot.

We believe this argument is false in most cases. First, if some managers are good and others are bad, why do the performances of managers over time vary so much more than the performances of players? Kylian

Mbappé and Harry Kane are always good players. They will have the odd bad match, but nobody ever thinks they are terrible and in need of sacking. In contrast, the history of management is littered with guys appointed as messiahs and sacked as losers a few months later. Most managers' careers seem to follow a random walk: some good seasons, some bad ones. And anyway, how can managers make much difference when most of them now last so briefly in each job? In 1992 the average manager's tenure in English soccer was still 3.5 years. But the fifty-eight managers sacked in the 2015–2016 season—a record high—had been in their posts for an average of just 1.29 years. Of the ninety-two managers of English league clubs in December 2021, only four—Simon Weaver at Harrogate Town, Gareth Ainsworth at Wycombe Wanderers, Sean Dyche at Burnley, and John Coleman at Accrington Stanley—had held their jobs for more than seven years.

Tenure is even shorter in other major soccer countries. The median survival time for head coaches in the top two professional tiers in Germany, France, Spain, and Italy from 2001 through 2015 was just 350 days, according to economists Alex Bryson, Babatunde Buraimo, and Rob Simmons.

Chris Anderson and David Sally challenge our argument about managers in their book *The Numbers Game*. They say that managers matter rather more than we say, and they point to studies of chief executives making a difference in other industries. However, soccer isn't like most other industries. For a start, CEOs in other industries tend to do their jobs for much longer. In 2020 the average tenure of departing chief executives of companies in the S&P 500 was 7.8 years. These people have more time to make a difference than a soccer manager. Secondly, although CEOs in all industries will make speeches about "the talent of our people," individual talent of staff members probably counts for more in soccer than it does at, say, Walmart. For a big retailer, having the right processes and technology is what matters most, and those things are in large part under the CEO's control. But if you want to beat Chelsea, you need eleven excellent players. That helps explain the difference in wages between soccer players and workers in other industries.

Furthermore, the individual soccer manager has probably become even less important in recent years. He rarely decides transfers alone anymore, as used to be the norm. Most managers at big clubs today work with dozens of staffers, from physios to defensive coaches to data analysts. Jürgen Klopp at Liverpool for years outsourced much (perhaps most) of his training and match tactics to his assistant, Željko Buvač. Klopp called him the "brain" of his coaching team.

Arsène Wenger told Arsenal's website this in 2015:

I just compare now to when I started, when I was on my own with my players. Today I have a team of about twenty people around me who take care of the players but also give me information: statistics, the analysis of the game, the quantification of the players' work rate and their performances.

Modern managers have so much information available to them....The modern manager is a guy who selects what is important and leaves what is less important....The manager isn't a lonely man anymore.

At many clubs staffers have been appointed by the club chairman or the technical director and will stay in their jobs long after the manager leaves. Day to day, they may have a bigger impact on results. QPR's owner Tony Fernandes says that coaching staff are "underrated.... I think coaching staff make a big difference."

Most journalists love to focus on great men, but today it probably makes more sense to talk about management teams rather than individual managers. Indeed, you could argue that the main point of the "top job" now is as a focus of competition for other staffers, who can aspire to become manager one day. For instance, Brendan Rodgers, André Villas-Boas, and Steve Clarke all made it from Mourinho's staff at Chelsea to managing big clubs of their own. Clubs themselves increasingly seem to understand the importance of staffers. After Leicester won the title in 2016, several of the club's staffers got lucrative offers from leading clubs. The scout Ben Wrigglesworth jumped to Arsenal, and chief scout Steve Walsh became director of soccer at Everton. On the other hand, no big club seems to have tried to poach the supposed miracle maker, head coach Claudio Ranieri.

The general obsession with managers is a version of the "great man" theory of history, the idea that prominent individuals—Genghis Khan, or Napoleon, or even Ranieri—cause historical change. Academic historians binned this theory decades ago.

WHO ARE THE SPECIAL ONES?

But there is one important caveat to our argument: players' wages don't explain everything about league position—merely almost everything at most clubs. That leaves some room for a few managers to make a difference. The question then is which elite managers finish consistently higher with their teams than their wage bills would predict, not just in one season but for most of their careers. In other words, to borrow a phrase from José Mourinho, who are the special ones?

For an earlier edition of *Soccernomics*, Stefan and the economist Thomas Peeters made some rudimentary calculations to try to identify the best coaches in England between 1973 and 2010. To account for differences in wage spending, they obtained the figures from clubs' financial accounts. This is not as hard as it sounds. All clubs except one were limited companies during this period and therefore obliged by law to file annual accounts with Britain's Companies House. You can obtain copies online (there used to be a small fee, but since 2015 you can download them for free).

That database included about seven hundred managers. However, nearly four hundred of them hadn't even managed thirty professional games—far too short a run on which to evaluate them. Even judging a manager on a couple of seasons isn't entirely fair because that's still a short enough period for luck to play a big role. So Stefan ranked only managers who had worked in the game for five or more full seasons: 251 men. Allowing for wage spending, he produced a statistical estimate of the ability (measured by contribution to winning) of each of them. It must be said that few of the managers who had worked less than five seasons looked like overachievers. Indeed, most of them had drifted out of soccer early because of their poor records. Some of the worst performers exited the profession fastest—but a few survivors seemed capable of producing sustained underperformance.

Malcolm Allison (a feted assistant manager with Manchester City in the late 1960s but a failure as a go-it-alone manager afterward) made our list of shame, as did Alan Mullery, Harry Gregg, and a few lesser-known names it would be kindest not to mention. But even these failures didn't seem to be terrible managers. Their underachievements are not what statisticians call "statistically significant." In simple English: it could have just been chance.

The analysis didn't treat all divisions equally. The ninety-two English professional teams are spread over four divisions. A manager in the bottom tier, League Two, who has the ninetieth budget in England but manages to finish eightieth in the country is doing well. However, a manager with the third-highest budget in England who succeeds in winning the Premier League is probably doing even better. At the top of soccer, competition is fiercer, and the amount of money typically required to jump a place is much higher, so the model gave more credit to overachieving managers in the Premier League than to overachievers lower down. Still, the model did allow for some lower-division managers to reach the top of our rankings.

All in all, somewhere between forty and seventy of the managers in the sample made a positive difference: they usually overachieved with their teams. Note that this is at most 28 percent of the 251 survivors in the database—and these survivors themselves tended to be the elite because underachieving managers rarely last five years in soccer. In other words, of the seven hundred managers we observed for more than thirty games from 1973 through 2010, at most about 10 percent look like overachievers. These managers tend to have stayed in their posts for relatively long periods, which makes sense.

The men whom we identified as the biggest overachievers of this era included many big names. Top was Bob Paisley at Liverpool, followed by Alex Ferguson at Manchester United, Bobby Robson at Ipswich, and Arsène Wenger at Arsenal. Paisley, for those who have not been following English soccer forever, won six league titles and three European Cups with Liverpool from 1974 to 1983, yet he somehow never became the subject of a personal legend.

Of course, there are caveats that apply to our valuations. First, the estimates are not exact. Wenger ranked a touch above Kenny Dalglish in our table, but small differences are unlikely to be significant. Working at Arsenal from 1996 is a different experience from working at Liverpool,

Blackburn, and Newcastle in the 1980s and 1990s. Many other factors besides the manager might have caused each club's overachievement. In the 1980s and 1990s, Arsenal and Liverpool managers looked like over-achievers, but perhaps they were just the lucky beneficiaries of excellent youth-development systems they inherited. Perhaps Liverpool's famous "boot room" of the 1970s and 1980s—the gang of old-time coaches and scouts who would sit around drinking whiskey and scheming for games together—gave Paisley and Dalglish the wisdom of crowds. Quite likely Paisley, Dalglish, Wenger, Benitez, and George Graham landed in help-ful settings. Yet they do seem to have been good managers, too.

Another caveat: our ranking measures only spending on wages, not on transfers. We saw in Chapter 2 that Wenger and Ferguson had relatively low net spending on transfers, which makes their high rankings in our list even more impressive. But we also saw that Benitez blew fortunes on transfers at Liverpool. So although he economized on wages, he didn't get his league positions cheaply.

In fact, all overachieving managers require closer analysis. Just as you cannot sign a player simply on the basis of his match data, you cannot simply hire a manager from our list and sit back and wait for the tro-phies to roll in (although this would certainly be a much better method than hiring a guy because he used to be a good player). Some managers succeeded in circumstances that might not be repeatable. For instance, another overachiever was Bobby Robson at Ipswich in the 1970s, perhaps because he was a rare manager of the time who preferred passing soccer and who scouted on the Continent. Today, he'd have had to find new tricks.

Most of the top-ranked managers in our list worked for the giant clubs, which raises a question about the direction of causation. For sure, the best managers tend to end up at the best clubs. Arsenal hired Wenger after he'd excelled at Monaco; Manchester United signed Ferguson after he'd broken the Celtic-Rangers duopoly with Aberdeen in Scotland. In fact, we might have ranked Ferguson even higher had we been able to include his brilliant Aberdeen years. Unfortunately, we had to omit Scot-tish clubs because the financial data weren't detailed enough. A second reason that managers of giant clubs tend to dominate: by definition, more overachieving clubs end up at the top of the league than at the bottom.

Skeptics may wonder whether a manager of Manchester United can overachieve by much. After all, United has the highest revenues in English soccer. Surely a club that rich ought to be winning league titles? (We must admit that we used to think so ourselves. Simon now blushes with shame to remember that he once wrote that if he managed United, with all its money, he would probably do about as well as Ferguson did.)

In fact, Ferguson does seem to have added value. From 2003 until his retirement in 2013, he consistently had to compete against higher-spending teams. In particular, after Roman Abramovich bought Chelsea, the London club accounted for 14 percent of the Premier League's total outlay on wages from 2004 through 2010—the largest share for any top-division club in the thirty-seven years of our database. In 2003–2004 Abramovich gave his manager Claudio Ranieri a mammoth 16 percent of the Premier League's wage spending. Chelsea's payroll that year was £115 million (nearly $200 million), which was 65 percent higher than the eventual champion, Arsenal. Of course, Ranieri ought to have won the league that season. Yet we have some sympathy for him. Even with the highest wage bill, it's tricky to finish on top if you're competing both against bad luck and the well-funded overachievers Ferguson and Wenger. Still, in the end salaries tend to tell. Chelsea was the country's biggest-spending club for six or seven years until the rise of Manchester City, and Abramovich's money bought him three league titles.

Despite the competition, Ferguson won more than even United's gargantuan wage bill would have predicted. Yet it's hard to work out exactly what he was doing right. If it were obvious, other managers would simply have copied him. Media tend to emphasize his supposedly exceptional motivational skills. But the widespread fascination with motivation in soccer is exaggerated. Almost any player who has risen high enough to play for Manchester United can motivate himself. Most players play for their own careers rather than for a club or manager. Judged every match by millions of knowledgeable observers, they have strong incentives to perform under any manager.

Moreover, it's often the players rather than the manager who shape team tactics. As Peter Schmeichel later said of Eric Cantona's first training session under Ferguson in 1992, "From that day, Manchester United's style of play changed. The arrival of Cantona suddenly made it clear to the coaching staff exactly how the team should play." Still, the failure of Ferguson's successors at United—first David Moyes and then Louis van Gaal, Mourinho, Ole Gunnar Solskjaer, and Ralf Rangnick—leaves the Scot alone on his pedestal.

Wenger's results were awesome in his first decade at Arsenal. But in his later years, from 2006 until the club pushed him out in 2018, his haul of trophies amounted only to three victories in the FA Cup, the consolation prize of modern English soccer. We can explain his decline. When he arrived at Arsenal in 1996, he brought knowledge that nobody else in insular England possessed at the time. "I felt like I was opening the door to the rest of the world," he said later. English soccer then still offered gaping knowledge gaps to exploit. For instance, Arsenal's pre-Wenger diet was suboptimal. Michael Cox writes in *The Mixer*, "They'd enjoy a full English breakfast before training, and their pre-match options included fish and chips, steak, scrambled eggs and beans on toast. Post-match, things became even worse: on the long coach journey back from Newcastle, for example, some players held an eating competition, with no one capable of matching the impressive nine dinners consumed by centre-back Steve Bould."

Wenger introduced dieticians at Arsenal, and when the team stayed in a hotel, he had the minibars in the players' rooms emptied. He was a pioneer in many other areas besides. For instance, he encouraged the use of supplements such as creatine; he was one of the only managers already using statistics to analyze players' performances; and above all, he knew foreign transfer markets. Hardly any other manager in England in the mid-1990s scouted abroad, notes Cox. Middlesbrough had spotted the Brazilian Juninho in 1995 only after he shone for Brazil in a tournament in England, under the eyes of England's assistant manager Bryan Robson, who happened to be Boro's player-manager.

In short, Wenger back then had the rest of the world almost to himself. He seems to have been the only manager in England to realize that Milan's reserve Patrick Vieira and Juventus's reserve Thierry Henry were great players. Spotting that didn't require mystical insight—Vieira convinced the Highbury crowd of the same fact inside forty-five minutes on his debut against Sheffield Wednesday—but none of Wenger's British rivals appeared even to know who Vieira was. So Wenger overachieved magnificently.

His problem was that everyone could see his success. Other managers began to copy his innovations in diet, scouting, and statistics. Meanwhile, like many brilliant pioneers, Wenger seems to have fallen into the trap of becoming more like himself—less willing to learn new tricks or listen to intelligent criticism—as he got older.

Eventually, when English soccer caught up with the world, and everyone had more or less the same knowledge, Arsenal was overtaken by clubs with bigger wage bills. Knowledge gaps inside a league close fast.

However, Wenger's critics were too harsh on him. Given that he was up against several richer clubs and against another great overachieving manager in Ferguson, it would have been astonishing had Arsenal kept winning titles. As he told us in 2020, "Chelsea and Man City came in as well, with superior financial resources. At the end of the day, you know, it is down to how much money you have available to buy players." Obviously, this was a self-justification. But it was also true. Arsenal's board couldn't very well tell the fans, "Forget it. We can't stay ahead of Chelsea, City, and United over a whole season." But the board knew this was true. It didn't expect Wenger to win titles anymore. That's why he was allowed to continue through so many disappointments. It's also why his successors have won nothing either.

So far we've discussed only overperforming managers of giant clubs. However, several overachievers of the 1973–2010 period—men such as Paul Sturrock, Steve Parkin, Ronnie Moore, and John Beck—spent their careers in soccer's lower reaches. None of them has managed a team even in the Football League since 2016. These men were titans of the lower divisions, but hardly anybody higher up pays attention to titans of the lower divisions.

Admittedly, some of them succeeded by playing a long-ball game that might not work at top level. "I think my style of play has been successful in the lower leagues," Sturrock told us cautiously in his bare little office at Southend one winter's night in 2012. Yet most good managers could surely adjust their methods to better players. We suspect these men were undervalued because they didn't physically look the part, lacked charisma, or had had their reputations unfairly tarnished somewhere along the way. Sturrock thought this happened to him during his only stint in the Premier League: his thirteen matches with Southampton in 2004. He won five of those games—pretty good at a small club—but fell out with Southampton's chairman, Rupert Lowe. He never got a chance at the top level again. In his Southend office, he reflected, "'I've been to the show,' as the Americans would say. The one thing I'll say is that I enjoyed every minute of it."

We're not saying Newcastle or Chelsea should have hired one of these tiny giants sight unseen, but it couldn't have hurt to take a look.

For this edition of the book we examined the performances of managers in England's top two divisions from 2010–2011 through 2020–2021. The data include 10,206 games, with 181 managers. Rather than use wage spending to control for player ability, we used Transfermarkt's valuations of each squad at the beginning of each season. Transfermarkt is a website that contains detailed information about teams, players, and staff going back to 2004. It also provides a valuation of individual players, which is generated by fan forums run by subscribers to the site. The valuation data is incredibly accurate as a predictor of performance—almost as good as the players' wages. Indeed, the valuations are so credible that clubs have begun using them as a basis for negotiating transfer fees. We used the ratio of the Transfermarkt valuation for each team to control for players' ability.

We focused on managers with at least thirty games. Only twenty managers in our data were found to have a statistically significant positive effect—just over 10 percent of the total. All the rest were insignificantly different from zero. Our top twenty includes several of the usual suspects (Guardiola, Ferguson, Klopp, Conte, Mancini, Pochettino, Rodgers), some managers whose reputations suffered in recent times but who were still exceptional (Wenger and Mourinho), and some possible pointers for the future. Valérien Ismaël at Barnsley in 2020–2021 and Chris Wilder at Sheffield United from 2017 onward achieved exceptional success relative to their budgets. Two of Brentford's managers, Dean Smith and Thomas Frank, make the list, which reflects that club's innovative managerial culture. And Marcelo Bielsa's achievements at Leeds also receive statistical recognition.

Overall, though, the message from our data is that great managers are rare. Most managers seem to add so little value that it is tempting to think that they could be replaced by their secretaries, or their chairmen, or by stuffed teddy bears without the club's league position changing. All in all, Jamie Carragher gets things about right in his autobiography: "The bottom line is this: if you assemble a squad of players with talent and the right attitude and character, you'll win more football matches than you lose, no matter how inventive your training sessions, what system you play or what team-talks you give. But anything that can give you the extra 10 percent, whether that's through diet, your general fitness or the correct word in your ear, also has merit."

Fernandes of QPR insisted that "managers do play a big part." But he added: "Ultimately, if you have rubbish players, there's nothing a manager can do." Perhaps the main service a manager can perform for his club is to rein in spending on transfers. After all, transfers usually fail, and they waste funds that could have been spent on boosting the all-determining players' wages. Wenger was a better manager than Benitez in part because he blew less of his budget on transfers. But there isn't much else that most club managers can do to push their teams up the table.

THE MARKET IN MEDIOCRITY

For the last few years, Stefan has continued working with Thomas Peeters on managerial performance. Thomas graduated from the University of Antwerp under the tutelage of professor Stefan Kesenne, a pioneer of sports economics in Europe, who died in 2021. Stefan K. asked Stefan S. to sit on Thomas's PhD committee, so a collaboration was born. Now Thomas teaches at Erasmus University in Rotterdam.

He realized that soccer managers offered the perfect opportunity to test a theory developed by the Finnish economist Marko Terviö. The theory had to do with markets for very talented individuals. The problem, Terviö argued, is that firms often have limited incentives to invest in finding these people if their ability is revealed only on the job, because once it is revealed, the stars will sell themselves to the highest bidder. The outcome, Terviö concluded, is underinvestment in finding talent and overinvestment in "mediocrities"—employees who are not terrible but most likely not as good as untried market entrants. This is a form of market inefficiency.

To Stefan and Thomas this sounded just like the market for football managers. Experienced mediocrities—almost all of them white—keep getting hired again after each sacking because clubs are afraid of experimenting with inexperienced entrants. In fact, there is additional fear of experimentation in the market for soccer managers: if an entrant turns out to be very poor and gets his club relegated, then the club might be bankrupted. That encourages clubs to go with tried and trusted mediocrities. All this reinforces discrimination against novice Black candidates.

Using a sample of a thousand managers covering 75,000 games over 37 seasons, Stefan and Thomas generated estimates of managerial ability on a month-by-month basis. They updated their estimates after every month (typically four or five games) to produce a profile of changing ability. And, just as Terviö predicted, they found that lots of managers were mediocre—in the sense that their estimated ability at a point in time was lower than the ability of the average entrant (based on the performance of entrants over the previous five years). Fully a third of managers fit into this category. Most soccer fans will probably recognize this pattern: some managers find job after job in which they are OK but not great.

Again: look at Claudio Ranieri. In 2015, fresh from a disastrous spell with Greece that ended with defeat at home to the miniscule Faroe Islands, he joined Leicester City. At that point he had been a manager for twenty-nine years without any outstanding successes. "He was the perfect loser, with a capital L," says the Italian soccer writer Tommaso Pellizzari. "Everyone in Italy thought he was very nice, polite, kind, but please never call him to my team." Then in Ranieri's first season at Leicester, the club won an utterly unexpected English title. Ranieri himself said there was no explanation for the team's success. He claimed no credit for it. But many people looking for a narrative and a main character attributed the triumph to him, as if at age sixty-four he had suddenly become a genius. *Harvard Business Review* published an article extolling his management skills.

The next season, after just five victories in twenty-five games, Leicester sacked him. If you looked at one club over one season, you might think that Ranieri was a magical motivator. But if you studied his whole career or indeed looked at hundreds of managers over decades, as we have, it becomes hard to believe that these people are the secret to success.

WHAT ARE MANAGERS FOR?

It's doubtful anyway whether many clubs or countries choose a manager chiefly because they think he will maximize performance. Often he is chosen more as a symbolic figurehead than for his perceived competence. In other words, the manager is more of a king, or a head of public relations, than an executive.

When a club appoints as manager a former iconic player such as Solskjaer or Andrea Pirlo, it is not simply betting that he will garner more points than some upstart like Thomas Tuchel. Players are almost always employed because the club thinks they'll help win matches, but that's merely one of the criteria used for hiring managers. This is because a club exists only partly to win matches. Its other job is to embody the eternal spirit of the team or country. Nobody could incarnate Argentina better than Diego Maradona, so he was made manager. Popular white ex-players often get hired because they are easily accepted by fans, media, players, and sponsors. Look at how rapidly recently retired English players like Wayne Rooney, Steven Gerrard, Frank Lampard, and Lee Bowyer were handed managerial jobs without any evidence that they were up to it. (Remember our finding that, in soccer, a good horse doesn't make a good jockey.)

The other criterion in hiring a manager is typically his gift for PR. Image has become all the more important for managers since the 1990s, when soccer became omnipresent on television. Managerial press conferences still attract halls packed with journalists, even though these events are generally streamed online. A manager might not affect his team's result, but after the game he's the person who explains the result to the world. He is the club's face and voice. That means he has to look good—which is why so many managers have glossy, wavy hair—and say the right things.

The forte of most managers is not winning matches but keeping all the interest groups in and around the club (players, board, fans, media, sponsors) united behind them. That's why so many managers are charismatic. Their charisma may not win trophies, but it does help the managers keep support.

The myth of managerial omnipotence has been both good and bad for managers. When the manager became the face of the club, his salary and fame rose. On the other hand, he also became more vulnerable. If the team was losing, the obvious thing to do was to get rid of its symbolic figurehead. Indeed, British club directors in the early twentieth century upgraded club secretaries to the position of manager partly so that when a team's results were bad, the directors would be able to deflect blame from themselves onto a lower-class scapegoat. As Barney Ronay writes in *The Manager: The Absurd Ascent of the Most Important Man in Football*, "The manager was born to be sacked, and sacked with some sense of cathartic public ceremony."

After Mauricio Macri became president of Boca Juniors in Argentina in 1995, he and coach Carlos Bilardo cleared out several popular players. Fans weren't pleased, Macri told us years later: "But fortunately we could put most of the damage on Bilardo because he was a very big figure. He paid the cost. That was very important." Coaches, Macri explained, function as "fuses—when you lose three matches in a row, you fire them." In 2015 Macri parlayed his political savvy into getting elected president of Argentina.

Firing the manager is now a traditional rite, soccer's version of the Aztecan human sacrifice. English clubs spent an estimated $157 million sacrificing their managers in the 2010–2011 season if you add up the cost of compensation, legal fees, and "double contracts" (paying the old and new manager at the same time), according to the League Managers Association. All this money could have been more usefully spent on players' wage bills or on improving stadiums.

As it happens, after the manager is sacrificed, a team's performance does tend to improve briefly. Sue Bridgewater, professor at Warwick Business School in the UK, analyzed sackings in the Premier League from 1992 to 2008 and found that "there is a boost for a short honeymoon period." For instance, after Manchester City sacked Mark Hughes at Christmas 2009, it won its first four games under Roberto Mancini. However, that's not because Mancini or any other new manager can work magic. The short honeymoon is easy to explain. Typically, the average club earns 1.3 points a match. Bridgewater found that an English club usually sacks its manager when it averages only one point a match—that is, at a low point in the cycle. Any statistician can predict what should happen after a low point: whether or not the club sacks its manager or changes its brand of teacakes, its performance will probably "regress to the mean." Simply put, from a low point you are always likely to improve. The club may have hit the low because of bad luck, injuries, or a tough run of fixtures.

In other words, the new manager rarely causes the pendulum to swing. He's just the beneficiary of the swing. Perhaps some players will briefly work harder to impress him, although on that logic clubs should sack managers even more often.

Bridgewater found that three months after a sacking, the typical club averaged the standard 1.3 points a game. "Most studies find that coach dismissals do not improve team performance," say the Dutch economists Jan van Ours and Martin van Tuijl in a study that found the same thing.

Sheikh Mansour, City's billionaire owner, should probably just have stuck with Hughes and waited for results to rebound, but in business doing nothing is often the hardest thing. (And not just in business. Harold Macmillan, British prime minister during the Cuban missile crisis of 1962, mused then "on the frightful desire to do something, with the knowledge that not to do anything…was prob. the right answer.")

Inevitably, Mancini was credited with City's short honeymoon. "Mancini really is magic," proclaimed the *Sun*, and people began to whisper that the Italian might win that season's Premier League. No wonder, because the glossy-haired Italian looked like a manager and boasted a glittering résumé as a player. His salary—like any manager's—therefore reflected his iconic status and his gift for PR as much as his expected contribution to performance.

None of this is good news for Black managers. Because it is so hard to measure a manager's performance, even after complex grinding of stats over many seasons, and because managers simply don't seem to matter much, clubs can continue to discriminate against Black managers without their match results suffering noticeably. Nor are clubs at much risk of being sued for discrimination. No matter what the statistics say, it will always be hard to prove that any club's choice of manager was motivated by prejudice. Intent is very hard to prove, and prejudices may indeed be unconscious. Absent more active intervention, clubs are likely to continue hiring managers based on appearances. Any club appointing someone who is not a white male ex-player with a conservative haircut must worry about looking foolish if its choice fails. Appointing a Black manager feels risky; as John Barnes says, "Black guys haven't proved themselves as managers." White guys have—or at least some of them appear to have.

The market in managers is so opaque that voluntary antidiscrimination codes such as the English FA's are not enough. Voluntary regulation makes it easy for clubs to find excuses to do nothing. We've demonstrated the scale of racial prejudice. A proportionate response is needed. To end discrimination against Black managers, coaches, scouts, and CEOs— essentially, all off-the-field roles—soccer leagues need to introduce compulsory rules. QPR's Chris Ramsey told us: "If there is no revolutionary action, we'll be having this same conversation in ten years' time." And he remembered saying exactly those words ten years before.

10

ISAAC NEWTON, LIVERPOOL, AND THE *MONEYBALL* OF SOCCER

Have Data Analytics Transformed the Game?

In 2015 Liverpool went looking for a new coach. The club conducted "as thorough an investigative process as any soccer club had undertaken to replace a manager," wrote the *New York Times*. At that point, Jürgen Klopp of Borussia Dortmund no longer looked the obvious choice. His team had finished seventh in the Bundesliga that season, and Klopp's star seemed to be fading. Yet Liverpool's director of research, Ian Graham, who has a PhD in theoretical physics from Cambridge University, concluded after intricate data analysis that Dortmund's disappointing results weren't Klopp's fault. Dortmund had just been desperately unlucky. Given the team's quality of chances over the season, Graham's model suggested it should have finished second. So data analytics persuaded Liverpool to hire Klopp.

Then, in 2017, Liverpool's analysts lobbied Klopp to sign the Egyptian winger Mo Salah, who had blossomed on loan at Roma after flopping at Chelsea. "There was something, analytically, that our sports science team saw in him and kept popping his name to the top of the list," Liverpool's chief executive Peter Moore would recall.

Liverpool's analysts hadn't merely identified Salah's individual qualities—which were becoming increasingly obvious as he scored fifteen league goals for Roma that season. They knew that soccer recruitment should aim to find players who will play well together. There's a term they used from statistics, *covariance*, which measures the relationship between two different elements. What was the covariance between, say, a center forward and an outside-right? Did they complement each other or not? Insiders tell of phenomenally complex modeling being produced by Liverpool. The analysts concluded that Salah would combine well with a forward already at the club, Roberto Firmino.

Klopp initially wasn't keen on Salah. He preferred the German forward Julian Brandt. It took a while, but eventually the analysts persuaded him to buy the Egyptian. In 2019 Klopp and Salah won the Champions League trophy. A year later they added the club's first Premier League title since 1990.

Since the first edition of this book appeared, soccer's data revolution has progressed in leaps and bounds. To our minds it is the most interesting thing going on in the game today. And more than almost any other big club, Liverpool is committed to analytics. Its owner, John Henry, became a billionaire using analytics to trade on commodities markets. He bought the Boston Red Sox and employed data to help win four World Series. At Liverpool he introduced analytics from the start, hiring more people with scientific PhDs from serious universities than had ever worked in a single soccer club before.

The club's data analysts have gone beyond just studying players' statistics, and they are now trying to model soccer itself, much in the way that Google's research wing DeepMind built a computer program called AlphaZero to rethink chess from first principles. Very little of Liverpool's reimagining of soccer has come out. The club has no desire to share its secrets with outsiders, although it is keen to tell select journalists about its successes, such as the signings of Klopp and Salah.

Is Liverpool really the new frontier of data analytics in soccer? Can statistics win the game's biggest trophies, or at least help clubs overachieve? Have a few clubs succeeded in "doing a *Moneyball*": using data to find undervalued players and strategies? Is analytics cracking the codes of soccer?

A BRIEF HISTORY OF FOOTBALL STATS

Sports statistics were originally created not for teams or players but to entertain fans and sell newspapers. In the nineteenth century, newspapers filled pages with stats on every sport—soccer, baseball, football, cricket—as a means of fueling the endless debates among fans about who is the best, who would have been better, and who will be the next great thing. When asked, coaches and managers dismissed the numbers, asserting that their own gut feel for the game meant far more. Most sports clubs ignored data for as long as they felt they could.

Possibly the first person to recognize the potential of data to win soccer matches was Charles Reep, a wing commander in Britain's Royal Air Force. In *Inverting the Pyramid*, Jonathan Wilson recounts that Reep had become interested in the topic in the 1930s and began logging match events during the second half of a Swindon Town game in 1950. In that one half he recorded 147 attacks by Swindon. Extrapolating from this small sample, Reep calculated that 99.29 percent of attacks in soccer failed. He kept logging matches and gradually developed a theory that too much passing was a risky waste of time. Most goals came from very short moves, he said. The way to win, he concluded, was long balls forward.

Reep advised the strong Wolves team of the 1950s and in the early 1980s influenced Graham Taylor, the future England manager, and Charles Hughes, the English Football Association's future director of education and coaching. Reep encouraged both men to develop the long-ball thinking that would climax in England's failure to qualify for the World Cup of 1994.

There were two problems with Reep's analysis. First, his data was sketchy, barely accounting for the context in which passes were made—and context in sport is everything. A short pass from A to B can in one context be the key to opening up a game and in another a meaningless waste of effort. Second, Reep failed to recognize that strategies are mutually dependent: my best strategy in a game depends on what you do, and vice versa. The long-ball strategy proved easy to counter once teams knew to expect it. This basic concept from game theory is often ignored by soccer strategists.

Neil Lanham, a tidy-mustached English auctioneer, is a lesser-known innovator with an interesting story. He had gotten to know Reep in the Suffolk village in eastern England where both men lived, and in the 1960s, the early days of computing, he began logging games and creating a database. In 1984 Lanham persuaded Dave Bassett, the manager of Wimbledon FC, a team newly promoted to the third tier, to hire him on a "no promotion, no fee" basis. Within three seasons Wimbledon was in the top division, and in 1988 Bassett's men won the FA Cup. Lanham generated a lot more data than Reep: he logged by hand the outcome of one-third of a million possessions. As Bassett wrote in his autobiography, "Lanham was at all games analyzing and marking out possession—how it was won and lost and where. Players would get feedback in the middle of the week as to how good or bad the results were. Based on this information, which I had by Sunday evening, the training schedule for the week could be formulated."

Like Reep, Lanham concluded from his data that possession of the ball in the final third was the key to success—and the best way to get there was with long balls. Billing himself with the startlingly twenty-first-century title "soccer performance analyst," he went on to advise Sheffield United, Crystal Palace, and Cambridge United as they used long-ball tactics to climb the divisions. He also consulted for Taylor's England.

By the 1980s and 1990s, other pioneers of analytics were popping up in soccer, among them the vodka-sodden Ukrainian Valeri Lobanovsky, the Norwegian Marxist Egil Olsen, and the young French manager of late-1980s Monaco, Arsène Wenger. A keen mathematician, Wenger began using a computer program called Top Score, developed by a friend, which gave marks for every act performed during a game. "Most players who had very high scores went on to have successful careers," Wenger said later. However, these rudimentary schemes were held back by the limitations of data collection and technology.

That soon changed with the advent of cheap computing power and cable broadcasting of soccer. Suddenly, every game could be logged directly into a digital format and then analyzed. In 1996 Opta Consulting in London began collecting match data for the English Premier League. The management consultancy's main aim was to build its own brand by creating soccer rankings. The Premier League's sponsor, Carling, paid for the so-called Opta Index. Clubs and media received Excel reports with some basic statistics for free. In those early days, Stefan remembers visiting Opta's London HQ, located in a rather seedy tower block overlooking Waterloo station. The office consisted of an open space with endless banks of computer screens, not so different from the trading desks of the financial markets on the other side of the River Thames. The difference was that the workstations were not manned by well-paid traders but by soccer nuts who were willing to work long hours for low pay to fulfill their dream of watching sports for money. Their task was to log each game pass by pass, usually in teams of two or three in order to monitor mistakes. Burnout usually came after a year or two, but there was no shortage of recruits, and soon Opta was sending out the kinds of reports that Lanham had generated for Wimbledon, but with many more observations. Some clubs started to hire their own analysts to make sense of the data. Other companies soon set up following essentially the same plan as Opta, and not just for soccer.

This early, basic data simply counted how many passes, tackles, shots, interceptions, and so on that each player made per game. But it gradually emerged that these numbers could be misleading. A sideways shove into a teammate's feet isn't the same as a through-ball that puts your striker in front of the goalkeeper, yet each counted as one completed pass. Tackles, too, seemed a poor indicator. In 2001 Alex Ferguson of Manchester United suddenly sold his defender Jaap Stam to Lazio. The move surprised everyone. Some thought Ferguson was punishing the Dutchman for a silly autobiography he had just published. In truth, although Ferguson didn't say this publicly, the sale was prompted partly by match data. Studying the numbers, Ferguson had spotted that Stam was tackling less often than before. He presumed the defender, then twenty-nine, was declining. The sale was a milestone in soccer's history: a major transfer driven largely by stats. As Ferguson later admitted, it was also a mistake. Like many soccer men in the early days of match data, the Scot had looked at the wrong numbers. Stam wasn't in decline at all: he would go on to have several excellent years in Italy.

Similarly, there was the awkward case of the great Italian defender Paolo Maldini. "He made one tackle every two games," Mike Forde, former director of football at Chelsea, noted ruefully. It seems that Maldini positioned himself so well that he closed off his opponent's space and didn't need to tackle. That rather argued against judging defenders on their number of tackles. To this day, how to value a defender remains one of the mysteries of soccer.

The American statistician Nate Silver points out in his book *The Signal and the Noise* that as more data become available, we become more likely to use them to make mistaken decisions. Often, the masses of data seem to form a pattern that just isn't there. That's why you often see false positives for breast cancer in mammograms or false assessments of soccer players.

There was another problem with judging players on the numbers of their completed passes, tackles, shots, and so on. Players quickly learned to be de facto data analysts. This had good consequences and bad ones. On the one hand, giving players insight into data could help them do more useful things on the field. It also discouraged laziness. On the other hand, if you tell a player you will judge him largely on how many kilometers he runs, then you can be sure he will run a lot of kilometers, whether those runs help your team win or not.

The broader problem with the early data was that they mostly measured a player's interactions with the ball. But the average player had the ball for only a little more than a minute per match. What was he doing the rest of the time? A breakthrough came with the ability to use cameras located around the field to track each player's movements. At the end of the 1990s, Prozone was founded as a business to supply these data to clubs. Now clubs could have a dynamic picture of the game.

Wenger's reputation has been somewhat tarnished by his mediocre later years at Arsenal, but for more than a decade he set the standard for modern coaching. And he loved data. He once said that on the morning after a game he was like a junkie who needed his fix: he reached for the spreadsheets. He began using tracking stats to make counterintuitive team selections. Dennis Bergkamp, in his book *Stillness and Speed*, describes how the manager "used statistics on me" during the Dutchman's declining years as a player at Arsenal. Their conversations would go something like this:

BERGKAMP: Where in your statistics does it say that I changed the game with a killer pass?
WENGER: You run less in the last thirty minutes, and you're more at risk of getting injured, and your pace is dropping.

Above all, Wenger believed that data could give him an edge in the transfer market. In a game where, as we have shown, money usually buys success, analytics raised a manager's chance of spotting one of the rare players who had been undervalued by other clubs. Advances in video analysis made it possible to compile stats for players from around the world. Traditional scouts, who were limited by the number of games they could watch, began to lose out.

Wenger didn't think that data could solve every problem. Still, he would scan summary data of players produced by companies like Opta to search for potential diamonds. He spotted an unknown teenager at Olympique Marseille named Mathieu Flamini who was running fourteen kilometers a game. Alone, that stat wasn't enough. Did Flamini run in the right direction? Could he play soccer? Wenger went to look, established that he could, and signed him for peanuts.

Probably the biggest milestone in soccer analytics came from another sport entirely. In 2003 Michael Lewis published *Moneyball*. What the book appeared to prove was that a baseball team with limited financial resources could win by outsmarting its opponents. Specifically, the book claimed that the team of statisticians assembled by Billy Beane enabled the cash-strapped Oakland A's to perform better than many richer clubs. And Lewis's story turned out to be true. A couple of years after the book appeared, the economists Jahn Hakes and Skip Sauer demonstrated that Billy Beane was right in a peer-reviewed paper using replicable data.

When *Moneyball* came out, "I bought twenty copies and sent them out to all the Premier League managers," recalls Aidan Cooney, one of Opta's founders. He pauses and chuckles. "Didn't get one response." No wonder: most managers were former players who relied on their experience of actually having "been there" as a basis for their opinions. The typical manager lives with massive job insecurity. He wants to look like an expert (or even a messiah), a man without weaknesses, so if he isn't well versed in the subject of data, he will be tempted simply to reject it.

This manager might also have noticed that in other industries, lesser-educated working-class men like himself had been replaced by people with degrees or even by software programs. In American banks, for instance, Lewis told us, fat mortgage traders "who had high-school degrees from New Jersey and traded by their gut...are replaced by hairless wonders from MIT." To this day, some soccer managers remain suspicious of what is essentially a rival form of expertise that could put them out of a job.

Nonetheless, a few people in English soccer read Lewis's book and sat up. They began thinking about "doing a *Moneyball* of soccer": using stats to find new ways of valuing players.

It so happened that just as some soccer executives were getting interested in Billy Beane, he was getting interested in soccer. On a London vacation with his wife, he had fallen hard for the game. In 2011 Simon visited Beane in the Oakland Coliseum. They spoke in what looked like a junk room but in fact is the A's clubhouse. Beane could often be found sprawled out on a dilapidated sofa here watching European soccer matches while skeptical baseball players watched him. When Beane watches soccer, he sees a game full of emotion, and where there is emotion, he knows people will be making emotional decisions.

Soccer would follow baseball in turning into "more of a science," Beane predicted. "I always say, in a casino there's a reason guys who count cards get kicked out and guys who bet on gut feel don't." He agreed that data probably wouldn't transform soccer as they had baseball, but then they didn't need to. If using statistics in soccer gives you an edge, then all clubs will end up having to use statistics. He explained: "If somebody's right 30 percent of the time using gut feel, and you can find a way to be right 35 percent, you create a 5 percent arbitrage, and in sports that can make the difference between winning and losing."

Beane began making an impact in soccer. Around this time, Simon watched him and Wenger sit talking for hours, glued by mutual fascination, on a sofa at an analytics conference at Chelsea's Stamford Bridge stadium. Beane later became a successful minority owner of both AZ Alkmaar in the Netherlands and Barnsley in England. So far he has kept his day job with the A's.

In the 2011–2012 season, Arsenal's then head of business development, Hendrik Almstadt, persuaded Wenger to buy StatDNA, a sports analytics company based in Chicago that had been consulting the club. Almstadt argued that better data analytics could have helped Arsenal avoid bad signings such as Marouane Chamakh and South Korean Park Chu-Young. Wenger paid $4 million for StatDNA. The company's staff members began spending a lot of time at Arsenal's training ground. StatDNA produced stats tailored especially to the club, including some quite exotic data: for instance, the number of times a defender failed to spot an attacker running past him; the value of certain combinations of players; and each player's level of tiredness, measured by how long his foot was planted in the ground when he ran.

StatDNA didn't get everything right. On the upside, it encouraged Wenger to try to sign Gonzalo Higuain before the striker joined Napoli, but on the other hand, its metrics suggested that Real Sociedad's young French winger Antoine Griezmann would never set the world alight.

Above all, though, StatDNA used the new gold standard of soccer analytics: "expected goals," or xG, which predicts the chance of a given player generating a goal for or against his team in a given situation. The stat has its ancestry in baseball: the pathbreaking statistician George Lindsey, who with his dad in the early 1960s logged 27,000 events from 400 baseball games by hand and then identified the statistical concept of "run expectancy"—the expected production of a batter in a given state of the game.

The concept of expected goals is easy to understand. Shots are the business end of soccer: teams that take the most shots tend to win. A team's skill is in large part the capacity to engineer situations in which it can shoot. Teams can use xG to measure the ability of players to convert shots to goals. xG can be calculated by identifying the coordinates on the pitch of every shot taken (i.e., the angle of the shot and the distance from the goal) and then calculating the frequency with which these shots go in. The difference between a player's actual goals scored and xG then represents a measure of a player's ability.

There's a beautiful simplicity to xG: it really is a good way of ranking players. Of course, it is primarily focused on strikers, but because strikers are the most valuable players in soccer, this is less of a problem than it might seem. It is also a fairly flexible statistic. For example, you can rate the ability of entire teams by calculating their xG and xGA (expected goals against). The xG concept was later extended to concepts such as expected goal assists and expected saves for goalkeepers. It's a stat that insiders were using long before most outsiders had ever heard of it. That is why it was a milestone when Wenger once casually name-checked it in a press conference. By the 2020s, xG was such a familiar stat that even some less-evolved TV pundits had begun to use it.

The expected-value approach is not specific to soccer either. Expected goals in hockey are estimated in much the same way, expected yards is now a commonly used concept in football, and expected possession value is a statistic developed for basketball. These are signs that sports analytics may be transitioning from alchemy to science.

ISAAC NEWTON AND SOCCER NERDS

Isaac Newton was born in England on Christmas Day, 1642, and by the age of twenty-three had invented (or discovered) the differential calculus. He went on to contribute fundamental insights in the study of optics. Most important, he formulated the "laws" of physics that define the relationship among bodies, forces, and motion. In the process, he identified gravity. True, Einstein's relativity and Schrodinger's quantum mechanics have shown Newton's laws to be not quite so universal as was thought, but Newtonian physics fails only on an infinitesimally small or large scale. For most practical purposes, Newton was right.

Newton is often described as mathematician, physicist, and astronomer. One thing that is less well known is that he was an alchemist. In fact, he appears to have written more about alchemy—banned in his day—than about physics. Newton, like most alchemists, was searching for "the philosopher's stone": a material that could turn base metal into gold. This practice was connected with occult beliefs and secret societies.

Alchemy still has a bad name today, although some historians have recently pointed out that it produced quite a lot of insights. While alchemists searched for the philosopher's stone, they experimented with every imaginable combination of materials and in the process discovered many things that remain of practical value today, especially in metallurgy. Their insane quests laid the foundations of modern chemistry.

To cut to the chase: we think that a lot of the data analytics going on inside soccer clubs in the 2020s is like alchemy. More precisely, data analytics in sport is now in the alchemy phase of development. As with alchemy, there's a frantic quest, with very limited theoretical knowledge, aimed at profit for those engaged in it, which is why it's conducted in secrecy. The difference is that the motivation in soccer is winning the league rather than creating gold.

Take the example of Liverpool, which we started with. Liverpool may be experimenting with some interesting ideas. But it's impossible to say for sure because the club won't show its models to outsiders. Liverpool's data analysts aren't interested in opening themselves up to peer review because that would destroy the competitive edge they believe they have found. So the only thing outsiders can do is look at data that are available and see if there is any evidence of exceptional performance. We've already identified verifiable overachievers in soccer, such as Brian Clough or Alex Ferguson, by examining the relationship between wages and performance. By this metric, Liverpool does not yet have anything to show for its money. True, in 2020 the club won its first domestic title in thirty years, but this is more a reflection of its underperformance in the lean decades.

Liverpool spent 1.7 times the English Premier League (EPL) average over the decade 2011–2020 and achieved an average league position of 4.8. Chelsea and Manchester United averaged one league position higher while spending almost exactly twice the EPL average. And Manchester City—the league's standout team under Guardiola—won four titles while spending 2.2 times the EPL average. What the data show is simply that Liverpool spent a bit less and achieved a bit less than the three teams ahead of it. This isn't spectacular overperformance.

The wage data tell the same story if we look only at the five seasons through 2020–2021. In fact, if you had to guess which of England's top five teams was "doing a *Moneyball*," you'd say Tottenham, which achieved a comparable average league position to Liverpool's while spending barely above the EPL average. Some would argue that winning the title itself is such a big deal that these averages don't do the achievement justice. Maybe so, but in the season after winning the title Liverpool finished six wins behind City, well off the pace.

A counterargument that is sometimes heard coming from Liverpool is that the club outdoes its main English rivals in the transfer market. After John Henry bought Liverpool in 2010, he began instituting an analytics-driven transfer policy. Brendan Rodgers, manager from 2012 to 2015, was often reluctant to listen to the club's data analysts and sometimes took a fancy to players whose stats didn't look good. But Jürgen Klopp, who replaced him in 2015, worked more closely with the analysts and also tended to like players with good stats, so Liverpool's transfers became more data-driven. We saw in Chapter 2 that Liverpool's average net annual spending on transfers—i.e., the transfer fees paid minus fees received—was much higher than Tottenham's, similar to Arsenal's, lower than Chelsea's, and far lower than the two Manchester clubs'. In the last six years, taking transfer spending and wages together, Liverpool has been improving significantly, and has done far better than Arsenal, but looks rather similar to Chelsea. Based on these stats you'd say that John Henry's data-driven Liverpool has yet to prove that it has found a competitive advantage in the transfer market.

In any case, we are wary of attaching too much weight to each club's numbers because even over the course of a decade, just one or two transfers can make a big difference. In 2013 Liverpool bought the little-known twenty-year-old Philippe Coutinho from Inter Milan for a reported fee of just £8.5 million. He became the club's star player. In 2018 Liverpool sold him to Barcelona for a fee rising as high as £142 million, depending on certain bonuses being triggered. His sale was as well-timed as his purchase. Coutinho's game disintegrated in Catalonia. Looking at his arrival and departure, we can only say: Well done, Liverpool. Liverpool may yet usher in a new era of analytic dominance—who knows? But without stronger data to support the claim, we have to remain agnostic.

We don't believe that analytics is capable yet of winning trophies. Three of soccer's leading coaches of the 2010s—Guardiola, Mourinho, and Klopp himself—have little time for it. Probably the greatest tactical innovation in this century has been the tiki-taka, fast-passing, high-pressing style of Barcelona and the Spanish national team of the 2008–2012 years. Simon has written a whole book about Barcelona, and he noticed a dog that didn't bark: no one inside the club ever claimed that tiki taka emerged from analytics. The club's then coach, Guardiola, spent far more hours watching videos of opponents than studying numbers. La Masia, Barça's famed youth academy, didn't boast any MIT information scientists. In other words, world-beating innovation didn't seem to require analytics.

At the same time, we do think that another brand of data analytics is indeed transforming soccer. It's a rival model of research to Liverpool's closed-shop analytics: the open-source movement. These are open networks in which people share ideas and knowledge based on a common interest in making sense of the game. For centuries, science itself has been an open-source movement, with scientists around the world arguing about their theories and trying to tear holes in one another's models. It's the best way to discover truths: a crowd of experts testing ideas will generally end up knowing more than a small, secretive group.

To see soccer's open-source movement in action, take a look at the StatsBomb website, where you'll find data packages tailored for teams, media, and gambling. StatsBomb makes available some game data for free to enable users to calculate xG, encouraging the development of analysts in the wider community. Wyscout, one of the game's biggest suppliers of data, does charge for its data. It offers different packages tailored to the needs of teams, coaches, scouts, players, agents, referees, and journalists, and some of these packages are available at prices that many hobbyists can afford.

On GitHub or Kaggle, you will find large, freely available sports databases as well as code for analyzing the data using Python, R, or other open-source software. Often the data has been scraped from proprietary databases. And gambling sites such as Oddsportal or Football-Data .co.uk offer huge quantities of free data, hoping that this will encourage punters to bet on sports.

All these developments have brought about a thrilling democratization of data analytics. The ordinary fan no longer needs to rely on experts to process data and generate insights. The other big development of recent years has been the creation of user-friendly, powerful, open-source software packages. Anyone with a computer and access to the internet can now build their own predictive models.

In 2021 a team of researchers from the University of Michigan led by Stefan launched an online course on sports analytics on the Coursera platform. The course takes the learner step-by-step through the process of analyzing sports data. It goes through basic data visualization to regression analysis and machine-learning techniques, using data sets on a variety of sports, including soccer. Coursera courses can be followed for free; learners pay a fee only if they want a certificate to prove they have completed the course. And you don't need the proverbial "MIT PhD" in order to learn practical skills in analytics.

One of the Coursera modules teaches learners how to use Transfermarkt valuations of players to predict the results of games. The only data that go into the model are the ratio of the total player value for each team. The reliability of these forecasts is then compared with bookmakers' odds. If one could actually do better than the bookmaker odds, there would be fortunes to be made using the model. Sadly, that's not the case, but the model does produce results that are almost identical to the bookmaker odds. The purpose of the module is not to build the best model but to enable the learner to see how to build models so that they can set about building better ones.

Some of the people now learning about soccer analytics hope one day to work for a club. A few actually end up doing just that. Many clubs are struggling to get their heads around analytics and are remarkably open to unconventional applicants who know soccer, can manipulate data in spreadsheets, code it, and explain complex ideas to laypeople. In 2019 Stevie Grieve, head of analysis and opposition scouting at the Scottish club Dundee United, contacted Ashwin Raman and offered him a job as a scout. An everyday occurrence, you might think, except that Ashwin was a seventeen-year-old kid living in Bangalore, India. He had become interested in using data to analyze soccer after reading *Soccernomics* when he was eleven, before progressing to David Sumpter's book *Soccermatics*, StatsBomb, Analytics FC, and the online community of amateur scouts. Ashwin published a blog—something we recommend to any aspiring analyst wanting to show clubs their commitment. His capacity to absorb vast numbers of data points and express sensible ideas in plain English caught Dundee United's attention. With this came access to Wyscout and an even deeper global pool of players to analyze.

A *MONEYBALL* OF SOCCER IN WEST LONDON

Still, the application of open-source ideas will happen inside clubs, and it will mostly happen in secret because clubs don't want rivals to pinch their ideas. If we had to single out one club that's leading the way on analytics, it would be a much less glamorous outfit than Liverpool. For now, soccer's nearest equivalent to Billy Beane's Oakland A's is the little West London neighborhood club Brentford FC.

Like so many people, Matthew Benham gained his understanding of soccer analytics while working outside soccer. He used data to make a fortune as a professional sports bettor. In 2012 he took over the club that he had supported all his life. At that point, Brentford was a mid-table team in the third tier and had spent only one season in sixty years in England's top two divisions. It hadn't played in the very highest flight since before World War II. In 2021 the club entered the Premier League. In the process, the club generated only $130 million in revenue and spent $230 million on player wages. Almost three-quarters of this deficit ($72 million) was made up by profits on player trading. This is extraordinary by any standard—clubs seeking to move up the leagues usually have to become heavy net spenders, but Brentford managed to scale one of the most competitive league systems in all sports while at the same time trading players at a profit. At the same time, Benham sank a chunk of his own capital into the project: the 2021 financial statements records that he has so far loaned the club $83 million, which he may never get back.

One fall day a few months after the promotion to the Premier League, Stefan met Rasmus Ankersen, Brentford's director of football, in a backstreet café in London's oligarch neighborhood of South Kensington. As well as running Brentford, Ankersen and Benham are chairman and owner, respectively, of FC Midtjylland in Denmark, which they led to its first national title in 2015 and two more since. Clearly, Brentford and Midtjylland know something about player talent that bigger clubs don't.

Ankersen is painfully aware that talking about the ways you gained an edge is a good way to lose that edge. Nonetheless, he's given a few interviews—mostly in discreet media in languages other than English—in which he has explained how he and Benham work.

For instance, one of Midtjylland's mantras is "Distrust your eyes." Ankersen believes that sending a scout to watch a player could be a dangerous mistake. "If you base your opinion of a player on a few games you've attended, it will blur your vision," he told the journalist Michiel de Hoog. "It's a small sample. We believe it is more effective to see lots of matches on video."

Many of Ankersen and Benham's methods can be traced back to Benham's career in investment banking and sports betting. Success in this world is about evaluating probabilities and looking for cases where the odds are out of line with the true probability. Here are three methods Brentford uses to do that:

1. Take the road less traveled.

One lesson of modern finance theory is that "thin" markets—in which trades are less frequent—are often the sources of the largest inefficiencies. Together with Ed Wheatcroft and James Reade, Stefan has been investigating the efficiency of Transfermarkt values in forecasting results across twenty-two leagues. It turns out that their forecasts are extremely good in big leagues such as the Premier League or La Liga but are often less reliable in lower divisions such as England's League Two. Brentford searches more intensively for talent in lesser leagues, where a player's potential is sometimes overlooked.

2. Perfect techniques that others neglect.

Much of soccer has not proved susceptible to analytics modeling, precisely because the game has so many moving parts. Yes, many critics say, stats may well be useful in a stop-start sport like baseball. The pitcher pitches, the batter hits, and that event provides oodles of clear data for nerds to crunch. But isn't soccer too fluid of a game to measure?

The nerds do have answers to this question. For a start, good mathematicians can handle complex systems. Chelsea, for instance, employed a statistician who had a past in insurance modeling. Soccer—a game of twenty-two people played on a limited field with set rules—is not of unparalleled complexity. Marcus du Sautoy, math professor at Oxford University and soccer nut, says that players tend to move in fairly predictable patterns. It is simply not the case that data are useful in every single industry on Earth except soccer.

But there's another nerd retort that is core to Brentford's strategy: about one-third of goals don't come from fluid situations at all. They come from corners, free kicks, penalties, and throw-ins—stop-start set pieces that you can analyze much like a pitch in baseball. A set piece is one of those static situations in which it's not only possible to predict events but also to control them.

That makes it all the more shocking that most clubs waste set pieces, especially free kicks. Whenever a team gets a kick anywhere near the penalty area, the team's biggest name generally grabs the ball, makes a great show of placing it (probably the most exciting thing about free kicks is the choreography), then steps back, pauses, runs up, and whams the ball into the crowd. Taking free kicks is a superstar's perk, rather like the film star's trailer with his name on it in Hollywood. In the 2010–2011 season, write Anderson and Sally in *The Numbers Game*, the average team in the Premier League scored on just one of every thirty-five direct free kicks. Yet a free kick should be the perfect opportunity to pass. Your opponents have to retreat ten yards, and they need to put two or three people in the wall in case you shoot. That leaves large spaces to pass to runners in the penalty area—which is arguably what teams should usually do instead of shooting from free kicks.

The Benham group's biggest gains have been in set pieces. For a phase in 2015, Midtjylland scored nearly a goal a game from free kicks, the highest average in Europe. Four of Brentford's five set-piece coaches have been poached by Premier League clubs, which are slowly starting to cotton on. Even now, Brentford still reckons that other clubs underestimate the importance of set pieces and believes that this gives it a 0.5 goal per game advantage. Until everyone gets it, Brentford will have an edge.

3. Listen to the wisdom of the diversified crowd.

If a crowd can guess the weight of an ox to within one-tenth of 1 percent, it can also tell you who the right players to buy are. That's why Brentford looks for an advantage on fan forums. It's a simple idea: scouts have limited resources, video can tell you only so much, but the evidence of thousands of eyeballs on multiple games can get you close to the truth.

There is just one caveat. Crowds are excellent sources of information only so long as they contain a diversity of opinion. If everyone in the crowd believes exactly the same thing, then what you have is the opinion of a cult, not a crowd. Fortunately, soccer fans tend to come in all shapes and sizes, so their opinions tend to be reliably diverse. It might just be that the way forward for data analytics in the future is not so much to measure what happens on the field but to better capture the wisdom of the crowd in the stands.

More generally, Brentford is looking for ways to downgrade the manager's role in decision making—an inefficiency that hampers almost all other clubs.

At the time of writing, Ashwin Raman is taking a break from soccer to focus on college, but he hopes to work for a European club again one day. He and the open-source movement represent one possible future for soccer analytics; the closed-shop innovation at clubs like Liverpool is another. There will be countless exchanges between the two sides, but we know which one we're betting on to make the big breakthroughs.

11

THE ECONOMIST'S FEAR OF THE PENALTY KICK

Are Penalties Cosmically Unfair, or Only If You Are Nicolas Anelka?

A famous soccer manager stands up from the table. He's going to pretend he is Chelsea's captain, John Terry, about to take the crucial penalty against Manchester United in the Champions League final in Moscow in 2008.

The manager performs the part with schadenfreude; he is no friend of Chelsea. He adjusts his face into a mask of tension. He tells us what Terry is thinking: "If I score, we win the Champions League." And then, terrifyingly, "But first I have to score."

The manager begins pulling at the arm of his suit jacket: he is mimicking Terry pulling at his captain's armband. Terry is telling himself (the manager explains), "I am captain, I am strong, I will score."

Still pulling rhythmically at his suit, the manager looks up. He is eyeing an imaginary, grotesquely large Edwin van der Sar, who is guarding a goal a very long twelve yards away. Terry intends to hit the ball to van der Sar's left. We now know that a Basque economist told Chelsea that the Dutch keeper tended to dive right against right-footed kickers. Terry runs up—and here the manager, cackling, falls on his backside.

Van der Sar did indeed dive right, as the Basque economist had foreseen, but Terry slipped on the wet grass, and his shot into the left-hand corner missed by inches.

"This really is football," the manager concludes. A player hits the post, the ball goes out, and Chelsea's coach, Avram Grant, is sacked even though he is exactly the same manager as if the ball had gone in. By one estimate, Terry's penalty cost Chelsea $170 million.

The penalty kick is probably the single thing in soccer about which economists have the most to say. Penalties are often dismissed as a lottery; economists tell both kicker and goalkeeper exactly what to do. (Indeed, if only Nicolas Anelka had followed the economist's advice, Chelsea would have won the final.) And better yet, penalties may be the best way in the known world of understanding game theory.

RIGHT, LEFT, OR LET VAN DER SAR DECIDE FOR YOU? GAME THEORY IN BERLIN AND MOSCOW

The next question is how to take penalty kicks. Economists may have no idea when housing prices will crash, but they do know something about this one.

A surprising number of economists have thought hard about the humble penalty kick. Even Steve Levitt, author of *Freakonomics* and winner of perhaps the most important prize in economics (the Clark Medal, which some insiders think outranks the Nobel), once cowrote a paper on penalties. Probably only a trio of economists would have watched videos of 459 penalties taken in the French and Italian leagues. "Testing Mixed-Strategy Equilibria When Players Are Heterogeneous: The Case of Penalty Kicks in Soccer" is one of those you might have missed, but it always won Levitt handshakes from European economists. Here's an American who gets it, they must have thought. Pierre-André Chiappori, Steven Levitt, and Timothy Groseclose explain that they wrote the paper because "testing game theory in the real world may provide unique insights." Economists revere the penalty as a real-life example of game theory.

Game theory was developed in the 1940s by the likes of John von Neumann, a brilliant mathematician who also helped create the architecture of the modern computer. It is the study of what happens when people find themselves in situations exactly like a penalty taker facing a goalkeeper: when what I should do depends on what you do, and what you should do depends on what I do.

The American government used game theory extensively during the Cold War to plan its interactions with the Soviet Union and to try to predict Soviet moves. (It is said that game-theoretic advice was given during the Cuban missile crisis to consider situations such as "If we bomb Cuba, then the Russians will seize West Berlin, and then we'll have to attack Russian troops, and then they'll use nuclear bombs, and then....") Today economists use game theory all the time, particularly to plan government policies or analyze business strategy. Game theory even plays a big role in research on biology.

The key to game theory is the analysis of how the strategies of different actors interact. In a penalty kick, for instance, the kicker and the keeper must each choose a strategy: where to kick the ball and where to dive. But each person's strategy depends on what he thinks the other person will do.

Sometimes in game theory, what's best for the actors is if they both do the same thing—going to the same restaurant to meet for dinner, for instance. These kinds of situations are known as coordination or cooperative games. But the penalty kick is a noncooperative game: the actors succeed by achieving their objectives independently of others. In fact, the penalty is a "zero-sum game": any gain for one player is exactly offset by the loss to the other side (plus one goal for me is minus one goal for you).

The issue of game theory behind the penalty was best put in "The Longest Penalty Ever," a short story by the Argentine writer Osvaldo Soriano. A match in the Argentine provinces has to be abandoned seconds before time when a bent referee, who has just awarded a penalty, is knocked out by an irate player. The league court decides that the last twenty seconds of the game—the penalty kick, in effect—will be played the next Sunday. That gives everyone a week to prepare for the penalty.

At dinner a few nights before the penalty, Gato Díaz, the keeper who has to stop it, muses about the kicker:

> "Constante kicks to the right."
> "Always," said the president of the club.
> "But he knows that I know."
> "Then we're fucked."
> "Yeah, but I know that he knows," said el Gato.

"Then dive to the left and be ready," said someone at the table.

"No. He knows that I know that he knows," said Gato Díaz, and he got up to go to bed.

Game theorists try to work out strategies for players in different types of games and try to predict which strategy each player will pursue. Sometimes the prediction is easy. Consider the game in which each player has only two choices: either "develop a nuclear bomb" or "don't develop a nuclear bomb." To make a prediction, you have to know what the payoff is to each player depending on the game's outcome. Imagine that the players are India and Pakistan (but it could be Israel and Iran or any other pair of hostile nations). Initially, Pakistan does not know if India will or won't develop a bomb, so it figures:

IF INDIA HAS NO BOMB, THEN

a. We don't get a bomb: we can live alongside each other, but there will always be incidents.

b. We get a bomb: India will have to treat us with respect.

IF INDIA HAS A BOMB, THEN

c. We don't get a bomb: we can't resist anything India does.

d. We get a bomb: India will have to treat us with respect.

Plainly, if you are Pakistan, you will end up developing the bomb, whether India has the bomb or not. Likewise, India will choose the same strategy and will develop the bomb whether Pakistan does or doesn't. So the equilibrium of this game is for both nations to acquire a bomb. This is the gloomy logic of an arms race. The logic of soccer is much the same, and there are many examples of arms races in the sport, from inflation of players' wages to illegal doping.

PIECES OF PAPER IN STUTTGART, JOHANNESBURG, AND MILAN

The problem for experienced penalty takers and goalkeepers is that, over time, they build up track records. People come to spot any habits they might have—always shooting left or always diving right, for instance.

Levitt and his colleagues observed "one goalie in the sample who jumps left on all eight kicks that he faces (only two of eight kicks against him go to the left, suggesting that his proclivity for jumping left is not lost on the kickers)."

There have probably always been people in the game tracking the past behavior of kickers and keepers. Back in the 1970s a Dutch manager named Jan Reker began to build up an archive of index cards on thousands of players. One thing he noted was where the player hit his penalties—or at least the penalties that Reker happened to know about. The Dutch keeper Hans van Breukelen would often call Reker before an international match for a briefing.

Nobody paid much attention to this relationship until 1988. That May, Van Breukelen's PSV reached the European Cup final against Benfica. Before the match in Stuttgart, the keeper phoned Reker. Inevitably, the game went to a penalty shoot-out. At first, Reker's index cards didn't seem to be helping much—Benfica's first five penalties all went in—but Van Breukelen saved the sixth kick from Veloso, and PSV was the European champion. A month later, so was Holland. They were leading the USSR 2–0 in the final in Munich when a silly charge by Van Breukelen conceded a penalty. But using Reker's database, he saved Igor Belanov's weak kick.

The 2006 World Cup quarterfinal between Germany and Argentina in Berlin also went to penalties. Jens Lehmann, the German keeper, emerged with a crib sheet tucked into his sock. On a little page of hotel notepaper ("Schlosshotel, Grunewald," it said), the German keeper's trainer, Andreas Köpke, had jotted down the proclivities of some potential Argentine penalty takers:

1. Riquelme   left
2. Crespo   long run-up/right short run-up/left
3. Heinze   6 [his shirt number, presumably given for fear that Lehmann would not recognize him] left low
4. Ayala   2 [shirt number] waits long time, long run-up right
5. Messi   left
6. Aimar   16, waits a long time, left
7. Rodriquez   18, left

Apparently, the Germans had a database of thirteen thousand kicks. The crib sheet might just have tipped the balance. Of the seven Argentines on the list, only Ayala and Maxi Rodríguez actually took penalties. However, Ayala stuck exactly to Lehmann's plan: he took a long run-up, the keeper waited a long time, and when Ayala dutifully shot to Lehmann's right, the keeper saved. Rodríguez also did his best to oblige. He put the ball in Lehmann's left-hand corner as predicted, but hit it so well that the keeper couldn't reach.

By the time of Argentina's fourth penalty, Germany was leading 4–2. If Lehmann could save Esteban Cambiasso's kick, the Germans would maintain their record of never losing a penalty shoot-out in a World Cup. Lehmann consulted his crib sheet. Sönke Wortmann, the German film director, who was following the German team for a fly-on-the-wall documentary, reports what happened next: "Lehmann could find no indication on his note of how Cambiasso would shoot. And yet the piece of paper did its job, because Lehmann stood looking at it for a long time. Köpke had written it in pencil, the note was crumpled and the writing almost illegible."

Wortmann says that as Cambiasso prepared to take his kick, he must have been thinking, "What do they know?" The Germans knew nothing. But Cambiasso was psyched out nonetheless. Lehmann saved his shot, and afterward there was a massive brawl on the field.

Both Van Breukelen's and Lehmann's stories have been told before. What was not publicly known before we first wrote about it in *Soccernomics* is that Chelsea had received an excellent crib sheet before the Champions League final in Moscow in 2008.

In 1995 the Basque economist Ignacio Palacios-Huerta, who was then a graduate student at the University of Chicago, began recording the way penalties were taken. In the early years, this was quite an artisanal labor: his wife and mother would send him videotapes of Spanish soccer TV shows. His paper, "Professionals Play Minimax," was published in 2003.

One friend of Ignacio's who knew about his research was a professor of economics and mathematics at an Israeli university. It so happened that this man was also a friend of Avram Grant. When Grant's Chelsea reached the final in Moscow in 2008, the professor realized that Ignacio's research might help Grant. He put the two men in touch. Ignacio then sent Grant a report that made four points about Manchester United and penalties:

1. Van der Sar tended to dive to the kicker's "natural side" more often than most keepers did. This meant that when facing a right-footed kicker, van der Sar would usually dive to his own right and, when facing a left-footed kicker, to his own left. So Chelsea right-footed penalty takers would have a better chance if they shot to their "unnatural side," van der Sar's left.

2. Ignacio emphasized in his report that "the vast majority of the penalties that van der Sar stops are those kicked to a mid-height (say, between 1 and 1.5 meters), and hence that penalties against him should be kicked just on the ground or high up."

3. Cristiano Ronaldo was another special case. Ignacio wrote in the report, "Ronaldo often stops in the run-up to the ball. If he stops, he is likely (85 percent) to kick to the right-hand side of the goalkeeper." Ignacio added that Ronaldo seemed able to change his mind about where to put the ball at the very last instant. That meant it was crucial for the opposing keeper not to move early. When a keeper moved early, Ronaldo always scored.

4. The team that wins the toss before the shoot-out gets to choose whether to go first. But this is a no-brainer: it should always go first. Teams going first win on average 60 percent of the time, presumably because there is too much pressure on the team going second, which is always having to score to save the game. Many players—especially those who normally never take penalties—succumb to the stress. Ignacio explains: "Yes, they are hyper-professionals, but they are not professionals in shoot-outs. Shoot-outs happen very infrequently." Lots of players go their entire careers without ever taking a penalty in a shoot-out.

You find exactly the same pattern in chess. A chess match is typically played over six or ten games, but by two players who alternate the color of pieces from game to game. However, the player who has white in game one has a 60:40 chance of winning the entire match.

In soccer, few pundits even seem to be aware of the advantage of kicking first. When a game goes to a penalty shoot-out, many TV channels switch to a commercial break during the coin toss. The commentators rarely bother to mention who won it. Bookmakers don't shift their odds immediately after the toss is done—a mistake from which gamblers could benefit.

Usually, the team that wins the toss is smart enough to kick first, but not always. A month after Chelsea–Manchester United in Moscow, Italy's captain Gianluigi Buffon may have decided the outcome of Euro 2008 when he won the toss for a shoot-out against Spain but let the Spaniards shoot first. They won, and then won the tournament. (This didn't necessarily gladden the heart of the Basque Ignacio.)

Ignacio didn't know whether his research would be used by Chelsea in Moscow, but watching the shoot-out on TV, he was certain it was being used. Indeed, once you know the content of Ignacio's note, it's fascinating to study the shoot-out on YouTube. The Chelsea players followed his advice almost to the letter, as Grant confirmed to him years later—except for poor Anelka.

United's captain, Rio Ferdinand, won the toss and turned to the bench to ask what to do. Terry tried to influence him by offering to go first. Unsurprisingly, Ferdinand ignored him. United went first, meaning that they were now likely to win. Carlos Tevez scored from the first kick.

Michael Ballack hit Chelsea's first penalty high into the net to van der Sar's left. Juliano Belletti scored low to van der Sar's left. Ignacio had recommended that Chelsea's right-footed kickers choose that side. But at this early stage, he still couldn't be sure that Chelsea was being guided by his report. He told us later, "Interestingly, my wife had been quite skeptical about the whole thing as I was preparing the report for Coach Grant, not even interested in looking at it. But then the game went into extra time, and then into a penalty shoot-out. Well, still skeptical."

At this point, Cristiano Ronaldo stepped up to take his kick for United. Watching on TV, Ignacio told his wife the precise advice he had given Chelsea in his report: Chelsea's keeper shouldn't move early, and if Cristiano paused in his run-up, he would most probably hit the ball to the keeper's right. Cristiano did indeed pause in his run-up.

To Ignacio's delight, Chelsea's keeper, Petr Cech, stayed motionless—"not even blinking," in the Spanish soccer phrase. Then, when Cristiano duly shot to Cech's right as predicted, the keeper saved. Ignacio recalled later, "After that, I started to believe that they were following the advice quite closely." As for his wife, "I think she was a bit shocked."

What's astonishing—although it seems to have passed unnoticed at the time—is what happened after that. Chelsea's next four penalty takers, Frank Lampard, Ashley Cole, John Terry, and Salomon Kalou, all hit the ball to van der Sar's left, just as Ballack and Belletti had done. In other words, the first six Chelsea kicks went to the same corner.

Ashley Cole was the only one of the six who partly disregarded Ignacio's advice. Cole was left-footed, so when he hit the ball to van der Sar's left, he was shooting to his own "natural side"—the side that Ignacio had said van der Sar tended to choose. Indeed, the Dutchman chose correctly on Cole's kick, and very nearly saved the shot, but it was well struck, low (as Ignacio had recommended), and just wriggled out of the keeper's grip. But all Chelsea's right-footed penalty takers had obeyed Ignacio to the letter and kicked the ball to their "unnatural side," van der Sar's left.

So far, Ignacio's advice had worked very well. Much as the economist had predicted, van der Sar had dived to his natural side four times out of six. He hadn't saved a single penalty. Five of Chelsea's six kicks had gone in, while Terry's, as the whole world knows, flew out off the post with van der Sar in the wrong corner.

It was Anelka's turn to kick. On United's bench, Alex Ferguson was growing frustrated with his keeper. "As Anelka jogged to the penalty spot," Ferguson later recalled, "I was thinking—dive to your left. Edwin kept diving to the right."

But after six kicks, van der Sar, or someone else at Manchester United, had figured out that Chelsea was pursuing a strategy. The Dutchman had noticed that the team was putting all its kicks to his left.

As Anelka prepared to take Chelsea's seventh penalty, the gangling keeper, standing on the goal line, extended his arms to either side of him. Then, in what must have been a chilling moment for Anelka, the Dutchman pointed with his left hand to the left corner. "That's where you're all putting it, isn't it?" he seemed to be saying. (This is where books fall short as a medium. We urge you to watch the shoot-out on YouTube.)

Now Anelka had a terrible dilemma. This was game theory in its rawest form. United had come pretty close to divining Chelsea's strategy: Ignacio had indeed advised right-footed kickers like Anelka to put the ball to van der Sar's left side.

So Anelka knew that van der Sar knew that Anelka knew that van der Sar tended to dive right against right-footers. What was Anelka to do? He decided to avoid the left corner, where he had presumably planned to put the ball. Instead he kicked to van der Sar's right. That might have been fine, except that he hit the ball at mid-height—exactly the level that Ignacio had warned against. Watching the kick on TV, Ignacio was "very upset." Perhaps Anelka was at sea because van der Sar had pressured him to change his plans at the last moment. Van der Sar saved the shot. Ferguson said afterward, "That wasn't an accident, his penalty save. We knew exactly where certain players were putting the ball." Anelka's decision to ignore Ignacio's advice probably cost Chelsea the Champions League.

RANDOMIZATION: FRANCK RIBÉRY CRACKS GAME THEORY

Crib sheets like Lehmann's might just work on penalty shoot-outs. Many of the players who take kicks in a shoot-out aren't regular penalty takers. (After Gareth Southgate missed England's crucial kick in the semifinal against Germany at Euro '96, his mother said that the last time he'd taken a penalty was three years before, and he'd missed that one, too.) These inferior penalty takers are not skilled or steady-headed enough to be able to vary their strategy. Quite likely, they will just aim for their favorite corner, hoping that their lack of a track record means the other side won't know their preference.

However, that is not how a good penalty taker—his team's regular man—thinks.

Suppose that the good kicker always chose the same corner for his penalty (game theorists call this a "pure strategy"). It would be easy to oppose: if the kicker always kicks left, then the goalkeeper knows what to do. Pure strategies don't work for penalty taking. As Levitt and company found, "There are no kickers in our sample with at least four kicks who always kick in one direction." Take that, Jens Lehmann. According to the goalkeeper's crib sheet, Messi's penalties tended to go left. In fact, the mini-Argentine randomizes his spot kicks almost perfectly. "He can also change his mind at the very last instant," adds Ignacio. Sometimes Messi waits for the keeper to shift his weight very slightly to one side, then shoots to the other corner.

Even a more complicated pure strategy than always choosing the same corner does not work. For example, suppose that the kicker always shoots in the opposite corner to the one he chose last time. (Diego Forlán tended to do this.) Then a future opponent studying this player might discover the sequence—left, right, left, right, left, right—and with a bit of thought guess what comes next. The essence of good penalty taking is unpredictability: a good penalty taker will be one whose next penalty cannot be predicted with confidence from his history of penalty taking.

This is a particular kind of unpredictability. It does not mean that the kicker should go left half of the time and right half of the time. After all, most kickers have a natural side, and favoring that side gives them a higher chance of scoring. But even if you naturally shoot to the keeper's right, as most right-footed kickers do, sometimes you have to shoot to his left just to keep him honest. In fact, if a kicker knows his chances of scoring for either corner of the net (depending also on which way the goalkeeper dives), he can choose the proportion of kicks to his natural side that maximizes the probability of scoring. A right-footed kicker won't put 100 percent of his kicks to his natural right side because that would give the goalkeeper certainty. Even a small change, like kicking right only 99 percent of the time, would considerably raise the chances of scoring by creating uncertainty in the goalkeeper's mind.

Kicking to the left 50 percent of the time would leave the keeper very uncertain. However, it would also entail the kicker hitting many poor shots to his unnatural side. So the kicker does best by hitting somewhere over half his kicks to his natural right side.

Likewise, we can calculate the proportion of times a goalkeeper should dive left or right. (Note that we are assuming the goalkeeper cannot know which way the ball is going before he decides which way to dive.) Kickers and keepers who mix it up like this are pursuing what game theorists call "mixed strategies."

Mixed strategies are peculiar because they require the actor to incorporate randomness into decision making. Should I go to the pub or the cinema? A mixed strategy requires me to toss a coin, which sounds odd because one might expect that I prefer one to the other. With a mixed strategy, you let the coin make the decision for you.

Game theorists have wondered for years whether people in the real world follow mixed strategies. They have found in tests that people tend not to use mixed strategies even when it is profitable for them to do so. In fact, our behavior seems to fall short of mixed play in a very specific way: in most cases our sequence of choices is predictable because people tend to do the opposite of what they have done in the past. For instance, they choose first left, then right, then left, then right, left, right, left, right, confusing change with randomness. These guinea pigs would not make good penalty takers.

Eventually, game theorists began to test mixed strategies in the natural laboratory of penalty taking. Years before Ignacio Palacios-Huerta advised Chelsea, he collected a database of 1,417 penalties taken between 1995 and 2000. First he calculated the proportion of successful kicks based on whether the kicker went to his natural side (left or right). The success rate was 95 percent if the kicker went to his natural side and the goalkeeper went to the opposite side (the remaining 5 percent of kicks missed the goal). The success rate was 92 percent if the kicker went to his unnatural side and the goalkeeper went to his own natural side. Obviously, the kicker's success rates were lower if the keeper chose correctly: a scoring rate of 70 percent if both keeper and kicker went to the kicker's natural side and 58 percent if both went to the other side.

Using these figures, Ignacio calculated the optimal mixed-strategy choices for each player. To maximize the chance of scoring, an imaginary penalty taker would have to hit 61.5 percent of his kicks to his natural side and 38.5 percent to the other side. In reality, the penalty takers that Ignacio observed got pretty close to this: they hit 60 percent to their natural side and 40 percent the other way.

A keeper's best strategy (if he insists on diving rather than standing still) is to dive to the kicker's natural side 58 percent of the time and to the other side 42 percent of the time. The actual figures, Ignacio found, were scarily close: 57.7 percent and 42.3 percent. Levitt's team, using a different database of penalties, found that keepers went to the right 57 percent of the time. So it looks as if keepers as well as penalty takers really do follow mixed strategies.

But what we most want to know are the choices of individual kickers and goalkeepers, not the overall averages. Ignacio studied twenty-two kickers and twenty goalkeepers, each of whom was involved in more than thirty penalties in his database. Again, Ignacio calculated the success rates depending on the side the kicker and goalkeeper chose, and calculated the frequencies in each direction that would maximize the chances of success for kickers and keepers.

In real life the actual frequencies the players observed were indistinguishable from the best mixed-strategy choices in more than 95 percent of cases. We can say with a high degree of confidence that penalty takers and goalkeepers really do use mixed strategies. Levitt's paper found the same thing: except for the bizarre keeper who always dived left, almost all the other kickers and keepers played mixed strategies.

Finally, Ignacio tested the most important question of all: are soccer players capable of constructing a truly random sequence in their penalty-taking decisions, as the mixed-strategy theory requires? Careful statistical testing showed that indeed they are. In other words, it is impossible to predict which way a regular penalty taker will kick based on his history of kicks. Each time, he chooses his corner without any reference to what he did the last time.

Randomization of penalties is a completely logical theory that against all odds turns out to be true in practice. As long as the penalty taker is a pro, rather than some terrified Southgateian innocent roped in for a job that he doesn't understand, simple lists like Lehmann's are not much use.

All this shows the extraordinary amount of subconscious thought that goes into playing top-level soccer. Previous studies in game theory had shown that people could construct random sequences if the problem was first explained to them in some detail. Nobody is suggesting that soccer players have sat at home coming up with mixed-strategy equilibria. Rather, the best players intuitively grasp the truth of the theory and are able to execute it. That is what makes them good players.

For years, Franck Ribéry took penalties for Bayern Munich and France. Needless to say, the scar-faced little playmaker placed his kicks according to a randomized mixed strategy. But more than that, one of his former managers explains, even once Ribéry embarked on his jagged hither-and-thither run-up, he himself did not know which corner he would choose. When the born economist Arsène Wenger was told this, he gushed with admiration.

As good a player as Ribéry was, he was arguably even better as a game theorist.

THE ECONOMIST IN THE WORLD CUP FINAL

Ignacio Palacios-Huerta watched the World Cup of 2010 from his home in Spain's Basque country, in between bouts of child care. It baffled him, he told Simon over the phone during the tournament, that he probably knew more about the penalty takers there than did any team in South Africa. "I have nothing at stake," he reflected. "They have lots: the whole nation."

Four years on from 2006, some teams did have crib sheets more sophisticated than Lehmann's. One team in the quarterfinals told us it had an hour's film of penalties taken by players of the country it was due to face, plus a penalty database. That's why it was silly of England's coach Fabio Capello to announce his designated penalty takers before playing Germany. He potentially gave the opposition time to study their habits.

Still, Ignacio reckoned that even the smartest teams in South Africa probably just counted who shot how often to which corner. "I would be super-surprised if they do any kind of statistical test," he said. He himself runs two. The first: does a particular kicker follow a truly random strategy? If the kicker does randomize, then the direction he chooses for his next kick—right of the keeper, through the middle, or left—cannot be predicted from his previous kicks.

But Ignacio had detected patterns in several of the penalty takers at the World Cup. Before the World Cup, for instance, Argentina's Gonzalo Higuain had been kicking too often to the keeper's right. Germany's keeper Manuel Neuer had also been failing to randomize: too often in club games, Neuer had dived to the opposite corner from his previous dive, going first right, then left, then right, and so on.

Next, Ignacio tests the kicker's success rate with each strategy. The kicker should have an equally high scoring rate whether he shoots right, middle, or left. But going into the World Cup, both Argentina's Sergio Agüero and Germany's Miroslav Klose were scoring more often when shooting right of the keeper. That would logically encourage them to aim right if they had to take a kick in South Africa.

Only rarely does Ignacio find a kicker with a very skewed strategy, but England's Frank Lampard was such a man. For years Lampard had randomized his kicks beautifully. But in the 2009–2010 season, Ignacio noted, "He kicked 13 out of 15 times to the right of the goalkeeper—and the two lefts were in the same game when he had to retake the same penalty three times."

No wonder Lampard had developed a habit of missing penalties. Keepers were figuring him out. For instance, Portsmouth's David James had chosen the correct corner for Lampard's penalty for Chelsea in the FA Cup final held a month before the World Cup—perhaps with help from Ignacio, who had sent Portsmouth a briefing note before the game. As it happened, Lampard's shot went wide. Admittedly, Kevin-Prince Boateng missed his penalty for Portsmouth in the match, but then he had ignored Ignacio's advice to kick left of Petr Cech. It is probably harder for penalty takers than for goalkeepers to follow someone else's advice.

On the phone, Ignacio told Simon, "I don't think serious analysis of the data has arrived yet in soccer, but it's coming. I think the world will be a different place in a decade or so."

That phone call got Simon thinking. When Holland and Spain made the World Cup final, Simon, a lifelong fan of the Dutch, emailed an official he knew in Holland's camp. Would the Dutch be interested in a penalty analysis of the Spaniards provided by a specialist? The official said they would. So Ignacio began pulling all-nighters to draw up a report on his fellow countrymen ready for July 11, 2010. On the Sunday morning of the final, he emailed a PDF of his report to the Dutch camp. (True, Ignacio has a Spanish passport, but as a Basque he was perfectly happy to see Spain lose.) Soon we got an email back from the Dutch goalkeeping coach Ruud Hesp: "It's a report that we can use perfectly."

That chilly Johannesburg evening, we proponents of *Soccernomics* genuinely thought we might be within five minutes of deciding the World Cup final. In extra time at Soccer City, Holland and Spain were still tied 0–0. A penalty shoot-out loomed. Simon, sitting in the media stand, was barely watching the game anymore. Instead he was rereading Ignacio's PDF file on his laptop. Under the circumstances, it made compelling reading. For instance, Ignacio had predicted that Xavi and Andres Iniesta, as right-footed players who didn't usually take penalties, would probably hit their kicks to the right of the Dutch goalkeeper Maarten Stekelenburg. And Fernando Torres almost always kicked low. Against him, Stekelenburg would need to dive to the ground fast. It looked as if we might be about to help the Dutch win the World Cup. Alternatively, if our advice was wrong, we might be about to help them lose it. "I was super, super nervous," recalled Ignacio.

Just then, down on the field, Cesc Fabregas found Andres Iniesta unmarked as if in some childhood training session on the sunny fields of Barcelona's academy, the Masia. Iniesta fired home. Simon closed the PDF and began writing his match report.

Soccernomics hadn't won the World Cup, but soccer was changing. Over the last few years, penalty reports have become standard. Keepers at the most advanced big clubs now face penalties not as freewheeling gamblers, but with pretty precise instructions for what to do. In January 2017, for instance, when Chelsea's penalty taker Diego Costa stepped up to take his spot-kick, Liverpool's keeper Simon Mignolet had a plan. Liverpool's analysts—who always briefed him on all the opposition's set pieces—had told him that Costa usually kicked to the keeper's right, writes Murad Ahmed in the *Financial Times*. However, it was impossible to predict whether Costa would kick high or low. Liverpool's analysts had advised Mignolet to dive "in between," which would give him a chance whatever the height of the shot. Costa kicked low to Mignolet's right, and the keeper saved it. Analyses like these (never discussed at postmatch press conferences) increasingly decide soccer matches.

And that's especially true of Champions League finals, which often go to shoot-outs. In 2012 Chelsea played Bayern in the final. By then, the Londoners had enough in-house penalty knowledge not to need to call an outsider like Ignacio. Their keeper Petr Cech prepped for the match by watching a two-hour DVD containing every Bayern penalty since 2007, and he received an elaborate briefing from his club's sophisticated data team. On the night, Cech chose the correct corner for all six of Bayern's penalties (one during the game and five in the shoot-out). Chelsea won its first-ever Champions League.

But the spread of best practice was uneven. In 2016 the Champions League final in Milan's San Siro stadium between Real Madrid and its city rivals Atlético went to a penalty shoot-out. Atlético won the toss but then made a kindergarten error: it chose to shoot second. Why? Because in an earlier match in the tournament against PSV Eindhoven, Atlético had shot second and won. Ignacio emailed us: "Incredible to see this at this level!!!!!" Atléti had gambled its European title on a single event (victory over PSV), whereas Ignacio by then had eleven thousand events (penalties) in his database.

When Real Madrid's captain, Sergio Ramos, told his teammates that although he had lost the toss they would get to shoot first, they were incredulous. Real had the penalty smarts that Atlético so sadly lacked. Just like in the 2008 final in Moscow, almost none of the millions of people around the world watching the shoot-out spotted what was happening, but a couple of days later the Dutch soccer analyst Pieter Zwart posted a remarkable video on Facebook, titled "Did Real Madrid Know What Jan Oblak Was Going to Do?"[1] The video reveals that Atlético's keeper Oblak had a crucial tell, a giveaway: just before each penalty was taken he stepped toward the side where he was going to dive. The step helped him get to his chosen corner faster. The problem came when the opposition knew what he was doing—and Real clearly did. The players seemed to be working off a sophisticated penalty report. Four out of the five Real players ran up slowly, waited for Oblak to take his step, and then slotted the ball gently into the other corner. Data analysis won the Champions League. Soccer is getting smarter.

12

THE SUBURBAN NEWSAGENTS

City Sizes and Soccer Prizes

The scene: the VIP room at the Athens Olympic Stadium, a couple of hours before the 2007 Champions League final between Milan and Liverpool kicks off. Michel Platini and Franz Beckenbauer are being buttonholed every couple of yards by other middle-aged men in expensive suits. There is a crush at the buffet and another across the room, where a familiar silver cup with "big ears" stands on a dais. You line up, assume a conquering pose beside the Champions League trophy, and grin. Nice young ladies from UEFA slip the picture into a frame for you.

An Englishman watching the scene, a soccer official, confides that he first got this close to the cup thirty years ago. Where? In Bramcote, a suburb of Nottingham. One of Brian Clough's brothers ran the local post office-cum-newsagents, and Clough himself would sometimes pop in and serve customers or just stand behind the counter reading the papers. One Sunday morning when the future official went in with his grandfather, there was the European Cup, freshly won by Forest, plunked on top of a pile of Nottingham *Evening Posts*. Behind it stood Brian Clough, holding an open newspaper in front of his face. He neither moved nor spoke, but he knew the boy would remember the scene forever. The official recalls, "I was too young and shy to speak to the man, which I regret to this day."

It's odd to think of the game's biggest club trophy ending up in a place like Bramcote (population 7,318). Yet it's not that exceptional. The provincial towns Nottingham, Glasgow, Dortmund, Birmingham, and Rotterdam have all won European Cups, while London, Paris, Rome, Berlin, Istanbul, and Moscow never had until Chelsea finally got one in 2012. Nottingham still has more than all those first-rank metropoles put together. This points to an odd connection among city size, capital cities, and soccer success. Here's why London took so long to win the Champions League—and why Europe's biggest cities are now starting to pile up trophies.

GENERAL FRANCO'S TRANSISTOR RADIO: THE ERA OF TOTALITARIAN SOCCER

The best measure of success in club soccer is a simple list: the names of the clubs that have won the European Cup since the competition began in 1956. Study this list, and you'll see that the history of the European Cup breaks down into three periods.

The first, from 1956 through the late 1960s, is dominated by the capital cities of fascist regimes. Of the first eleven European Cups, eight were won by either Real Madrid (the favorite club of General Francisco Franco) or Benfica (from the capital of the Portuguese dictator Salazar). Seven of the losing teams in the first sixteen finals also came from fascist capitals: Real, Benfica, and, in 1971, Panathinaikos from the Athens of the colonels' regime.

But by the start of the 1970s, the dominance of fascist capitals was eroding. Fascist governments seldom outlast their leaders, and Portugal's had entered a twilight after Salazar died in 1970. Meanwhile, everyone was waiting for Franco to go, too.

Yet even after fascism disappeared, teams from Europe's remaining dictatorial capitals continued to thrive. Steaua Bucharest, run by a son of the Romanian dictator Nicolae Ceaușescu, won the cup in 1986. Red Star Belgrade triumphed in 1991 just as Yugoslavia was breaking into pieces. The same phenomenon was at work in the communist countries as in the fascist capitals before them. Dictators send resources to the capital because that is where they and their senior bureaucrats and soldiers and secret police officers live. So the dictators do up the main buildings, boost the local economy, and help the soccer club. That's totalitarian soccer.

A communist takeover of Britain could have done wonders for a capital team like Arsenal. Just look at the triumphs of Dynamo Berlin, founded in the former East Germany with the express purpose of keeping the league title in the capital. The club president until the Berlin Wall fell was Erich Mielke, feared octogenarian chief of the East German secret police, the Stasi. Mielke loved Dynamo. He made all the best East German players play for it. He also talked to referees, and Dynamo won a lot of matches with penalties in the ninety-fifth minute. Dynamo was popularly known as the *Elf Schweine*, the eleven pigs, but it did win the East German league title every year from 1979 to 1988. This was possibly Europe's most extreme case of politicians rigging the soccer market.

Dynamo never got far in the European Cup, but General Franco's local team did. The general made a point of catching Real Madrid's games on the radio, taking a transistor along with him if he was out partridge shooting, writes Jimmy Burns in *When Beckham Went to Spain*. It wasn't so much that Franco fixed referees or gave Real money. Rather, he helped the club indirectly by centralizing Spain's power and resources. And he believed that Real's European Cups helped him. Fernando María Castiella, foreign minister under Franco, called Real Madrid "the best embassy we have ever had."

DOWN AND OUT, PARIS AND LONDON: THE FAILURE OF DEMOCRATIC CAPITALS

Totalitarian capitals got off to a great start in the European Cup. But for the first forty-two years of the trophy's life, the democratic capitals of Europe never won it.

There is only one exception: Amsterdam is nominally the Dutch capital, and Ajax of that city has been European champion four times. However, Amsterdam really is only nominally the capital. The government, parliament, king's palace, and embassies are all in The Hague, a city that has often gone years at a stretch without having a team in the Dutch premier division. The Hague's only professional club, ADO, traditionally plays its games in front of a few thousand people, a large proportion of whom are nuts. Little happens on the field beyond the occasional smoke bomb or plague of rabbits. This is the curse of the democratic capital.

Instead of Western capitals, provincial Western European cities dominated the European Cup and Champions League. The rule of the provinces holds true even in the most obsessively centralized countries. Teams from five provincial British cities won the European Cup before London finally got one. Olympique Marseille won the cup in 1993, but as of 2022, Paris Saint-Germain never had. Porto has won it twice since Portugal went democratic, whereas the Lisbon clubs have been winless since 1962. Clubs from Milan and Turin have won a combined total of twelve trophies, but Roman clubs have won zero. The cup has gone to Munich and Hamburg but never to Bonn or Berlin. For many years, in fact, neither of those cities even had a team in the Bundesliga. Hertha Berlin, the only big club in the current capital, has not been champion of Germany since the Weimar Republic.

Capitals—especially London, Paris, and Moscow—tend to have the greatest concentrations of national resources. It's therefore striking how badly their clubs seem to have underperformed. We can speculate about why this is. But perhaps the main reason that teams from democratic capital cities weren't up to much for the first few decades of European cup soccer is psychological. In capital cities no soccer club can matter all that much. There was an instructive sight, sometime in the late 1990s, of a group of visiting fans from an English provincial town wandering down London's Baker Street yelling their club songs at passersby. In their minds they were shaming the Londoners, invading the city for a day, making all the noise. But the Londoners they were shouting at—many of them foreigners anyway—didn't care about or even understand the point they were making.

Capitals simply have less to prove than provincial cities. They have bigger sources of pride than their soccer teams. Londoners don't go around singing songs about their city, and they don't believe that a prize for Arsenal or Chelsea would enhance London's status. Roman Abramovich and David Dein helped bring trophies to Chelsea and Arsenal, but neither ever could have been voted mayor of London. Soccer mattered even less in Paris, where until quite recently it was possible to spend a lifetime without ever knowing that the sport existed. Paris Saint-Germain, whose ground is only just inside the city's Péripherique ring road, was hardly going to become the main focus of Parisian pride.

London, Paris, and Moscow don't need to win the Champions League. It is a different type of city where a soccer club can mean everything: the provincial industrial town. These are the places that have ousted the fascist capitals as rulers of European soccer.

DARK SATANIC MILLS: WHY FACTORY TOWNS BECAME SOCCER TOWNS

In 1878 a soccer club started up just by the newish railway line in Manchester. Because the players worked at the Newton Heath carriage works of the Lancashire and Yorkshire Railway Company, their team was called Newton Heath. They played in work clogs against other work teams.

Famously, Newton Heath became Manchester United. But what matters here is the club's origins, well recounted in Jim White's *Manchester United: The Biography*. White describes the L&YR's workers, "sucked in from all over the country to service the growing need for locomotives and carriages." Life in Manchester then was neither fun nor healthy: "In the middle of the nineteenth century the average male life expectancy in Little Ireland, the notorious part of Manchester…was as low as seventeen." This was still the same brutal Manchester where, a few decades before, Karl Marx's pal Friedrich Engels had run his father's factory, the industrial city so awful that it inspired communism.

Industrial Manchester had grown like no other city on Earth. In 1800 it had been a tranquil little place of eighty-four thousand inhabitants, so insignificant that as late as 1832, it did not even have a member of Parliament. It was the Industrial Revolution that changed everything. Workers poured in from English villages, from Ireland, from feeble economies everywhere. For instance, Simon's great-grandparents came to Manchester from Lithuania.

By 1900, all these newcomers had made Manchester the sixth-biggest city in Europe, with 1.25 million inhabitants, more than Moscow at the time. It was still a hard city. In the early twentieth century, Simon's great-grandparents emigrated on to much-healthier southern Africa, after two of their children had died in Manchester of scarlet fever.

Inevitably, most of the early "Mancunians" were rootless migrants. Unmoored in their new home, many of them embraced the local soccer clubs. Soccer must have given them something of the sense of the community that they had previously known in their villages.

The same thing happened in Britain's other new industrial cities: the migrants attached themselves to soccer clubs with a fervor unknown in more-established towns. When the English Football League was founded in 1888, six of the twelve founding members came from industrial Lancashire, and the other six were from the industrial Midlands. Montague Shearman wrote that year, "No words of ours can adequately describe the present popularity [of soccer] which, though great in the metropolis, is infinitely greater in the large provincial towns. . . . It is no rare thing in the north and midlands for 10,000 people to pay money to watch an ordinary club match, or for half as many again to assemble for a 'Cup Tie.'" It helped that workers in the textile industry in the Northwest began to get Saturdays off in the 1890s, a luxury that workers elsewhere in Britain did not enjoy.

By 1892, all twenty-eight English professional clubs were from the North or the Midlands. Soccer was as northern a game as rugby league. The champions in the Victorian era came from northern industrial towns such as Preston, Sheffield, or Sunderland, then still among the richest spots on Earth. When these places became too poor and small to support successful clubs, the league title merely migrated to larger northern cities.

The legacy of the Industrial Revolution still shapes English fandom. Today the combined population of Greater Merseyside, Greater Manchester, and Lancashire County is less than 5.5 million, or a little over 10 percent of the English population. Nonetheless, at the end of the 2020–2021 season, the top three teams in the Premier League table—the two Manchester teams and Liverpool—were all based in this region. Their advantage: more than a century of brand building. Manchester United became arguably the most popular club on Earth largely because Manchester had been the first industrial city on Earth. The club is only the biggest local soccer relic of that era. The forty-three professional clubs within ninety miles of Manchester probably represent the greatest soccer density in the world.

Almost all Europe's best traditional soccer cities have a profile like Manchester's. They were once new industrial centers that sucked in hapless villagers. The newcomers cast around for something to belong to and settled on soccer. Supporting a local club helped them make a place for themselves in the city. So clubs mattered more here, and grew bigger, than in capital cities or ancient cathedral towns with old-established hierarchies.

The best way to gauge a club's support nowadays (given that most fans don't come to the stadium on Saturday) is to tot up its social-media followers. The Deloitte Football Money League report ranked the biggest clubs at the start of 2021. At the top was Real Madrid with 251.5 million followers across all the main platforms, while Barça came second with 248 million. The top English club was Manchester United, with 140.8 million. Juventus (102.9 million) led in Italy, Paris Saint-Germain (89.6 million) in France, and Bayern Munich (87.1 million) in Germany.

These obviously aren't the total numbers of each club's fans. Many people follow multiple teams online, and lots change their allegiances depending on who just won the league or where Leo Messi is playing. However, the *Forbes* ranking does tell us something. Few would dispute that these five clubs are (at the moment, at least) the best supported in their respective countries. And there is something peculiar about this list: most of the biggest clubs are not in the biggest cities. They are in the formerly industrial ones. In only two of the five big European leagues— narrowly in Spain, and in France—does the most-followed club come from a capital city. That probably wasn't even true for most of the period before 2011, when a wing of the Qatari state took over PSG and stuffed the team with superstars. Remember that when the research company Sport+Markt surveyed European fandom in 2006, it found that France's most popular club was provincial Lyon.

Real Madrid is the king of European soccer, with thirteen European Cups, or Champions Leagues (through 2021), but it's the exception. All the other major powers are provincial industrial towns. If you take Barcelona, Manchester, Turin, and Munich, and add on Milan, Inter, and Hamburg, then large provincial cities won a combined twenty-seven out of fifty-nine European Cups from 1963 through 2021. The smaller industrial or port cities Liverpool, Glasgow, Nottingham, Birmingham, Marseille, Porto, Dortmund, Eindhoven, and Rotterdam have won an additional sixteen. And all these industrial cities have a story much like Manchester's, although their growth spurts happened later. Peasants arrived from the countryside, leaving all their roots behind. Needing something to belong to in their new cities, they chose soccer. That's why, in all these places, the soccer clubs arose soon after the factories.

In most of these cities the industrial migrants arrived in a whoosh in the late nineteenth century. Munich had 100,000 inhabitants in 1852 and five times as many by 1901. Barcelona's population trebled in the same period to 533,000. Turin, for centuries a quiet Piedmontese town, began acquiring factories in the 1870s. Milan surged with the new railways that followed Italian reunification.

Once the local merchants had grown wealthy and discovered English ways, they founded soccer clubs: Juventus in 1897, Barcelona and AC Milan two years later, Bayern in 1900. The clubs then grew with their cities. For instance, newly industrial Milan sucked in so many migrants that it could eventually support two of the three most popular teams in the country.

The second stage of the soccer boom in the Continent's industrial cities happened after World War II. The 1950s and 1960s were the years of Italy's "economic miracle," when flocks of poor southern Italian peasants took the "train of the sun" north. Many of these people ended up in Turin, making cars for Fiat. Historian Paul Ginsborg writes: "So great and persistent was the flow from the South, that by the end of the sixties Turin had become the third largest 'southern' city in Italy, after Naples and Palermo." The migrants found jobs, but not enough schools or hospitals or apartments. Often there was so little space that roommates had to take turns sleeping. Amid such dislocation, soccer mattered all the more. Goffredo Fofi, author of a study of southern immigration to Turin in the 1960s, said that "during a Juventus-Palermo match, there were many enthusiastic immigrant Sicilian fans whose sons, by now, like every respectable FIAT worker, backed the home team."

It's one of the flukes of history that this mass migration to Turin began soon after the Superga air disaster of 1949 had decimated the city's previous most popular team, Torino. The migrants arrived after Juve had established itself as the local top dog, and they helped make it a global top dog. For starters, they transmitted the passion to their relatives down south.

Barcelona experienced the same sort of growth spurt at about the same time as Turin. In the 1950s and 1960s, perhaps 1.5 million Spaniards moved to the Barcelona area. Entire villages in the country's interior were left almost empty. On wastelands outside Barcelona, self-built shantytowns sprang up—the sort of thing you might now see on the outskirts of Jakarta—packed with peasants who had left behind everything they knew. Many were illiterate. Hardly any spoke the local language, Catalan. A lot of them attached themselves to Barça. In Spain's new Manchester, it was the quickest way to belong.

The link between industry and soccer is almost universal across Europe. The largest crowds in Europe in the pre-pandemic 2018–2019 season were at Borussia Dortmund (average: 80,841), one of many clubs in the industrial German Ruhr region. In France, too, it is the industrial cities that have historically loved their clubs best. The country's few traditional hotbeds of soccer, other than the port of Marseille, are the mining towns of Lens and Saint-Étienne.

All these industrial towns were products of a particular era. In all of them the Industrial Revolution ended, often painfully. But along with the empty docks and factory buildings, the other legacy of industrialization was beloved soccer clubs. The quirk of a particular era gave Manchester United, Barcelona, Juventus, Bayern Munich, and the Milan clubs enough fans to dominate first their own countries and then Europe.

The universal principle holds in Turkey, too. The country's capital of soccer is not the capital city, Ankara, but the industrial powerhouse, Istanbul, which is home to all three of Turkey's most popular clubs: Galatasaray, Fenerbahce, and Besiktas.

It's true that Istanbul, like Saint Petersburg, was once the seat of government, but both cities lost that role more than ninety years ago, long before soccer amounted to anything in their countries. Even as late as 1950, Istanbul was a sleepy place with barely a million inhabitants. Then it became possibly the last big European city to experience an industrial revolution. Migrants were sucked in from all over Anatolia. Between 1980 and 1985 alone, Istanbul's population doubled. Today it is the largest metropolitan area in Europe, with 15 million inhabitants. The rootless peasants needed to find a sense of belonging in their new home, so they attached themselves to one or the other of the city's great clubs. Often, soccer provided them their strongest loyalties in Istanbul.

Admittedly, almost all cities in Europe have had some experience of industrialization. But very few have had as much as Manchester, Turin,

Milan, Istanbul, or Barcelona. These were the European cities with the most flux, the fewest long-standing hierarchies, the weakest ties between people and place. Here, there were emotional gaps to fill. This becomes obvious when we contrast the industrial cities with old towns that have a traditional upper-class streak. In England, Oxford, Cambridge, Cheltenham, Canterbury, York, and Bath (including its rural outskirts) are all decent-sized places, with somewhere between 100,000 and 175,000 inhabitants each. Many industrial towns of that size or even smaller—Middlesbrough, Reading, Ipswich, Blackburn, Watford, Burnley—have serious soccer traditions. Yet by the 2021–2022 season, Oxford, Cambridge, Bath, Canterbury, York, and Cheltenham had just three small teams in the English Football League between them: Cheltenham Town, which joined it only in 1999; Oxford United, which reentered the league after a spell in the semiprofessional "non-league" in 2010; and Cambridge United, which came back in 2014. In 2021–2022 all three teams were playing in the league's third tier. In ancient upmarket towns like these, with age-old hierarchies and few incoming peasants, people simply didn't need soccer clubs to root themselves.

Oxford's face to the world is the university. In industrial cities it is the soccer club. Barcelona, Marseille, and (most of the time) Newcastle are the pride of their cities, a symbolic two fingers up at the capital. When Barcelona wins something, the president of Catalonia traditionally hoists himself up on the balcony of his palace on the Plaça Sant Jaume and shouts at the crowds below, "Long live Barça, long live Catalonia!"

These provincial clubs have armies of fans, players who will bleed for the club, and backing from local plutocrats. Bernard Tapie put money into Olympique Marseille, the Agnelli family into Juventus, and Sir John Hall into Newcastle because they wanted to be kings of their towns. Local fans and sponsors invest in these clubs partly because they feel that civic pride is at stake. In the Middle Ages they would have built a cathedral instead.

Usually, provincial cities such as these have only one major club, which often becomes the only thing that many outsiders know about the place. For instance, there must be many Manchester United fans around the world who don't know that Manchester is a city in England. True, most provincial cities have two teams that compete for top-dog status:

United and City in Manchester, Inter and Milan in Milan, Torino and
Juventus in Turin, United and Wednesday in Sheffield, Celtic and Rangers in Glasgow, Forest and County in Nottingham, Everton and Liverpool FC in Liverpool, Bayern and 1860 in Munich, Barça and Espanyol
in Barcelona. Many of these rivalries have something to do with religion,
class, politics, or all three. But usually one team struggles. Manchester
City, Torino, and 1860 Munich have all spent long phases in the lower
divisions. City reached the top only after the arrival of a billionaire Arab
sheikh in 2008. Everton last won the league in 1987. FC Amsterdam
went bust. Midsize provincial cities are simply not big enough to sustain
two big clubs for long. Almost always, one club pulls ahead.

"THEY MOVED THE HIGHWAY": THE RISE AND FALL OF SMALL TOWNS

Provincial industrial towns began to dominate the European Cup in the
late 1960s. But their rule breaks down into two main periods. The first,
from 1970 to 1981, is the small-town era, when clubs from some very
modest places won the European Cup. Tables 12.1 and 12.2 show them,
with the populations not just of the cities themselves but also of their
entire metropolitan areas, including people in all the local suburbs.

Note that we are estimating the sizes of these places very generously,
going way beyond the city borders. The figure for Liverpool, for instance,
includes all of the local Merseyside region.

The rule of the small is even more striking when you consider some of the
losing teams in European Cup finals in this era. In a remarkable four-year

TABLE 12.1. European Cup winners

Club	Year(s) they won it	Size of total metropolitan area
Feyenoord Rotterdam	1970	1 million
Ajax Amsterdam	1971–1973	1 million
Bayern Munich	1974–1976	2.9 million
Liverpool	1977–1978 and 1981	1.4 million
Nottingham Forest	1979–1980	470,000

TABLE 12.2. Winning towns

Club	Size of town	Size of total metropolitan area
Saint-Étienne	175,000	320,000
Mönchengladbach	260,000	260,000
Bruges	115,000	270,000
Malmö	240,000	600,000

period from 1976 to 1979, the towns of Saint-Étienne, Mönchengladbach, Bruges, and Malmö all had teams in the final. Perhaps the emblematic small-town team of the seventies is Borussia Mönchengladbach, whose rise and fall encapsulates that of all these towns.

In the 1970s, "Gladbach" won five German titles and reached four European finals. The Bökelberg stadium, perched on a hill among the gardens of smart houses, saw the best years of Gunter Netzer, Rainer Bonhof, and Alan Simonsen. Fans drove in from neighboring Holland and Belgium, as well as from the town's British army barracks. Decades later, a German marketing company showed that the knee-jerk response of the country's fans to the word *counterattack* was still *Gladbach*.

It was a cozy little club: Berti Vogts spent his whole career here, and when Netzer later played in Zurich, he often used to drive up, sometimes to scout players for Spanish clubs but often just to eat sausages in the canteen.

Like midfielder David Cassidy, Gladbach would have done well to combust spontaneously at the end of the seventies. In 1980 the club lost its last UEFA Cup final to Eintracht Frankfurt, and the decades since have been disappointing. There was the spell in 1998, for instance, when it just couldn't stop getting thrashed. "We can only get better," announced Gladbach's coach, Friedel Rausch, just before his team lost 8–2 to Bayer Leverkusen. "I feel I can solve our problems," he said afterward. When Gladbach lost its next match 7–1 to Wolfsburg, Rausch was sacked. Gladbach spent time in Germany's second division and has never regained its former heights.

This upsets leftist, educated sixtysomethings all over Germany, who still dislike Bayern, revere the socialist Netzer, and on Saturday afternoons check the Gladbach result first. But there is nothing to be done. The glory days cannot come back because what did come in Gladbach was the modern era.

In the words of Norman Bates in Hitchcock's *Psycho*, "They moved the highway." In the seventies, Gladbach's coach, Hennes Weisweiler, was able to build a team of boys from the local towns. The part-Dutch Bonhof came from nearby Emmerich, Vogts was an orphan from Neuss-Buttgen, and Hacki Wimmer, who did Netzer's dirty work, spent decades after his playing career running his parents' stationery shop just down the road in Aachen.

These stars stayed at Gladbach for years because there was little more money to be earned anywhere else in soccer, because most rich clubs were allowed only a couple of foreign players at most, and because their own club could generally stop them from leaving. In short, there were market restraints. That's why Gladbach, Nottingham Forest, Bruges, and Saint-Étienne could thrive in the 1970s. Even then, big cities had more resources, but they had limited freedom, or limited desire, to use them.

The beginning of the end for small towns was the day in February 1979 when Trevor Francis became soccer's first "million-pound man." In fact, Clough agreed to a fee of only £999,999 (then about $2 million) to bring him from Birmingham to Forest, but there were taxes on top. Three months later, Francis headed the goal (against Malmö) that gave Forest the European Cup. But the swelling of the soccer economy that he embodied would eventually do in small clubs like Forest.

In the 1980s TV contracts grew, and Italy opened its borders to foreigners. Later, teams around Europe began renovating their stadiums, which allowed the ones with a lot of fans to make more money. After the European Court of Justice's "Bosman ruling" in 1995, big clubs could easily sign the best players from any country in the European Union. Around the same time, the clubs with the most fans began earning much more from their television rights. Big clubs everywhere got bigger. Bayern Munich, previously Gladbach's main rival, mushroomed into "FC Hollywood."

After that, clubs like Gladbach could no longer keep their best players. Lothar Matthäus made his debut for "Die Fohlen" at the end of the golden era, but when he was only twenty-three he graduated to Bayern.

The club's next great prospect, the local lad Sebastian Deisler, left Glad-bach for Hertha at age nineteen in 1999, as soon as he distantly began to resemble Netzer. Small towns couldn't afford the new soccer.

"THAT'S NOT COCAINE; IT'S SAFFRON": THE DEMISE OF THE CATHEDRAL CITIES

Wandering around Florence, you can still imagine it as the center of the universe. It's the effect of the great cathedral, the endless Michelangelos, and all the tourists paying $10 for an orange juice. A Medici ruler re-turning from the dead, as in one of Florence's umpteen paintings of the Day of Judgment, might feel that his city had won the battle of prestige among European city-states.

But he would be wrong. These days a midsize city in Europe derives its status less from its cathedral than from its soccer club. Here towns the size of Florence (six hundred thousand people in its metropolitan area) have slipped up.

Fiorentina's last flurry came in 1999, when it beat Arsenal in a Cham-pions League match at Wembley thanks to a goal by Gabriel Batistuta, with Giovanni Trapattoni sitting on the bench. In those days "Trap's" biggest problems were his players' insistence on busing the 150 yards from the locker room to the training ground and Brazilian Edmundo's ritual late return from the Rio Carnaval. But those days will never return. In the Champions League, the midsize cities are now finished.

Fiorentina's demise can be dated to the day in July 2001 that the Italian police raided the home of the team's owner, the Italian film baron Vittorio Cecchi Gori. What happened was exactly what should happen when police raid a film baron's home, as if Cecchi Gori had read up on Jackie Collins beforehand.

The police broke into his apartment in the Palazzo Borghese in Rome but then took ninety minutes to find him. This was because his bedroom door was concealed inside a mirrored wall. Only after the Filipina maid had pointed this out did they enter the bedroom to find Cecchi Gori asleep with his girlfriend, Valeria Marini, a sort of early prototype of Kim Kardashian, who calls herself a singer-actress but in fact can neither sing nor act.

The police told Cecchi Gori to open his safe. Donning his silk dress-ing gown, he did so. When the police remarked on the stash of cocaine stored inside, Cecchi Gori replied nonchalantly, "Cocaine? That's not cocaine; it's saffron!"

Meanwhile, his business empire was unraveling. It should be said that he acquired the empire only by inheritance from his father, Mario, who before dying in 1993 had warned his old business partner, Silvio Berlusconi, "Take care of Vittorio, he is so impulsive and naïve."

Vittorio's problem was that he wanted to be Berlusconi. He bought commercial TV channels (a failure), pumped fortunes into his soccer team (no titles), and dabbled in politics (getting no further than senator), but might have been OK had he not gotten caught up in a divorce expected to be so expensive that it alone could have funded Fiorentina for years. Cecchi Gori remained admirably upbeat even after all this, leaning out of the window of his Mercedes limousine on Rome's Via Veneto to shout "La dolce vita!" to friends. However, he ruined Fiorentina.

It was hard to work out which bit of Cecchi Gori's empire owed what to which, but it was clear that he had borrowed tens of millions of dollars from the club. After everything went wrong, he tried the traditional Italian remedy, putting his eighty-two-year-old mother in charge, but even she could not save Fiorentina. A fax from a Colombian bank offering to pay off the club's entire debt proved, amazingly, to be a forgery.

In 2002 Fiorentina went bankrupt, slipping into Italy's fourth division, where it had to visit Tuscan village teams whose players were mostly Fiorentina fans. Now it is back in Serie A, but the days of Trap, Batistuta, and "The Animal" Edmundo won't return. Florence is just too small now.

Florence is typical. Midsize European cities (between 150,000 and 1 million inhabitants) have all but dropped off the map of European soccer. They can no longer afford to compete with clubs from bigger places. In early 2004 it was the turn of Parma, whose owners, the dairy company Parmalat, turned out to have mislaid €10 billion (then $7.5 billion). Leeds United is the great English example. In Spain, Deportivo La Coruña, pride of a midsize Galician city, suddenly discovered in 2004 that its debt had hit the strictly notional figure of €178 million (then about $220 million). Valencia followed a few years later. These clubs fell short because they had hardly any supporters outside their own city walls. Other midsize cities—Glasgow, Rotterdam, Nottingham—have retreated with less fanfare, but they too must know they will never again produce a European champion.

The third period of the European Cup began in 1982 and started petering out only in the mid-2010s: rule by sturdy provincial city. There were still a few undersize winners: Porto and Liverpool twice each, and Eindhoven, Marseille, and Dortmund. However, these towns are not exactly small. Four of the five are agglomerations of 1.2 million inhabitants or more. Only Eindhoven has just 210,000 people and a metropolitan area—if you draw it very generously—of 750,000. In general, European champions are getting bigger. In modern times, the race has usually gone to the rich.

The swelling of the soccer economy—the bigger TV contracts, the new stadiums, the freer movement of players, and so on—favored the most popular clubs. For historical reasons, these tended to be the ones in big provincial cities. Their teams came to dominate the Champions League in a sort of endless loop. Every club that won the trophy from 1998 through 2011 had won it at least once before. Most had won it several times before. Are their fans growing blasé? When you have won the thing ten times, the buzz probably starts to fade.

The dominant clubs for almost all this period weren't from the megacities of Moscow, London, Paris, or Istanbul but from urban areas with about 2 million to 5 million inhabitants: Milan, Manchester, Munich, Madrid, and Barcelona. These cities are big enough to produce the required fan base yet provincial enough to generate a yearning for global recognition.

Strangely, one of these cities, Madrid, is a democratic capital. How could Real break the golden rule of the Champions League and win the trophy in 1998, 2000, 2002, 2014, 2016, 2017, and 2018? Because it had built its mammoth stadium, brand, and support in the days when Madrid was the capital of a dictatorship. Spain has gone democratic, but Real's players still enter the Santiago Bernabeu in those white "meringue" shirts as if it were 1955. The club's global standing is a relic of the fascist era.

GEORGE ZIPF COMES TO LONDON: THE DAWNING METROPOLITAN ERA

George Kingsley Zipf is an almost forgotten Harvard linguist. Born in 1902, he died in 1950, just as he was starting to make a name. Zipf is now known only for having formulated a law that explains almost everything.

Among other things, Zipf's Law told us in advance that London or Paris was eventually going to start challenging for Champions Leagues.

Consider the following: if you rank every American city by the size of its population, the difference in population between two consecutive cities is simply the ratio of their ranks. So if you compare cities number 1 and number 2, city 2 has half (or 1/2) the population of city 1. If you compare cities number 2 and number 3, city 3 has two-thirds (2/3) the population of city 2. City 100 has 99/100ths the population of city 99 and so on down the list. Statistically speaking, the fit of this relationship is almost as perfect as it is possible to be.

This is a particularly elegant example of Zipf's Law, which applies to a lot more than city sizes. For instance, it is also true for the frequency with which words are used in English. *The* is the most commonly used word in the language, *of* is second, so *of* is used about half (1/2) as often as *the*. All in all, Zipf's Law has been called possibly "the most accurate regularity in economics." (The Nobel Prize–winning economist Paul Krugman says, "Anyone who spends too much time thinking about Zipf's Law goes mad," but we hope that is a joke.)

Zipf's Law works for European cities, too, though not quite as neatly as for American ones. City sizes in most European countries are more closely bunched, so the second city is closer to the first city's size than in the United States, the third closer to the second, and so on.

Why might this be? Zipf's Law must have something to do with migration. People will always try to migrate to where the money is. In the United States, with its open markets and very high mobility of labor, they generally do. But in Europe, political and cultural barriers have curbed migration. That might explain why city sizes are more compressed there. Nonetheless, the academics Matthieu Cristelli, Michael Batty, and Luciano Pietronero have shown that "Zipf's Law holds approximately for the city sizes of each European country (France, Italy, Germany, Spain, etc.)." They add that the law "completely falls apart" if you rank them as cities within a single state (e.g., the European Union), but then that is no surprise—these cities grew big in their nation-states long before the EU was ever thought of.

For a long time, nobody could understand why Zipf's Law should hold for so many different phenomena. Now, though, economists and scientists are starting to generate models of growth in which the natural outcome of a process is distribution obeying Zipf's Law. The economist Xavier Gabaix of New York University has come up with an explanation for why Zipf's Law applies to city sizes. He says the law emerges when all cities grow at the same rate, regardless of their size and their history, but subject to random variation. This implies that common factors drive the growth of cities within a country and that the differences in growth are a result of a series of random events ("shocks," in the economic jargon), such as bombing during the war, which in principle could occur anywhere. A story this simple is enough to explain the city sizes that Zipf's Law predicts.

Two consequences of Zipf's Law are crucial to soccer. First, giants—whether giant cities, giant soccer clubs, or giants of any other kind—are rare. That is because becoming a giant requires a long sequence of positive shocks, like tossing a coin fifty times and coming up heads every time. It can happen, but it is rare. Second, once a city becomes a giant, it is unlikely to shrink into the middle ranks unless it experiences a long series of repeated misfortunes (fifty tails in a row). By contrast, small cities are unlikely ever to become giants. In other words, the hierarchy of cities, which has established itself over centuries, probably won't change much in the foreseeable future.

This "law of proportionate growth" has some other consequences. What's true for cities is also true for many other social phenomena. For example, if your kid is behind at school, don't worry: he or she will almost certainly catch up because all children tend to learn at the same rate, plus or minus a few shocks. Likewise, if you think your brilliant six-year-old soccer player is going to become another Messi or Ronaldo, don't. More likely the boy had a few positive shocks in his early years, which will cancel out. Messis and Ronaldos almost never happen. The distribution of talent is thus a bit like the distribution of city sizes: a few great talents stand out at the top, but as you go down the list, the differences become smaller and smaller.

This brings us back to European cities: there are only a few giants, chiefly Moscow, Istanbul, Paris, and London. You would expect these giant cities to produce the biggest clubs, yet they have won just two Champions Leagues between them—both for Chelsea. In 2012 it beat Bayern on penalties, and it repeated the trick against Manchester City in 2021. (This is one prediction we got right in the first edition of *Soccernomics* in 2009. We wrote then that "soon" Arsenal or Chelsea "could become the first London team to be champions of Europe.")

Significantly, both those trophies came in recent history. And soon the capitals might win more. Soccer is changing. It is becoming more of a free market: fascist dictators no longer interfere, and the best players can move between clubs almost at will. Inevitably, the best players are starting to move to the biggest markets, as happens in Major League Baseball. These biggest markets—the capital cities—have generally been doing better economically than the provinces. So you would expect dominance in European soccer to move, too: after rule by dictatorial capitals, midsize provincial towns, and big provincial cities, now London and Paris are starting to get in on the action at last, while Madrid has been expanding its dominance.

Paris is becoming a serious European competitor because it has more than twelve million inhabitants in its metropolitan region and only one top-division soccer club, Paris Saint-Germain, which was appallingly run for years before being taken over by Qataris who have converted oil into soccer players. And London has recently shown signs, for the first time ever, of matching the northern English soccer cities.

For the first few decades of English professional soccer, the North dominated. Only in 1931 did a club from the South of the country—Arsenal—first win the league. But the long decline of manufacturing hit the North's economy. That hit its soccer clubs, and from the early 1970s onward there were often more southern clubs than northern ones in England's top two divisions, as Figure 12.1 shows.

Yet throughout the twentieth century, the title still generally went north.

When Arsenal and Chelsea finished in the top two spots in the Premier League in 2004, it was the first time in history that two London teams had achieved that feat. In 2005 they did it again. No London team had ever reached the Champions League final before 2006. From 2006 through 2021 Arsenal and Spurs got there once each, and Chelsea won those two finals.

The rise of London clubs is exactly what you would expect in the city with the largest local economy in Europe. A soccer player can earn a

FIGURE 12.1. Share of teams in the top two divisions by region

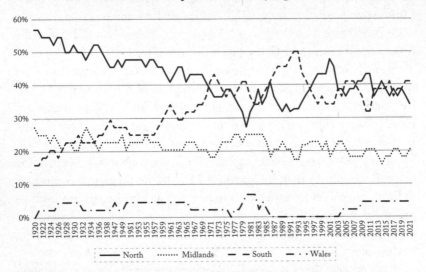

living here. The capital's clubs have been coining it. First, their customers can afford to pay the highest ticket prices in global soccer. In 2021–2022 Arsenal charged £891 ($1,220) for its cheapest season ticket, which was the highest rate in English (and probably in global) soccer.

So many Londoners are happy to fork out this kind of money that in 2006 Arsenal was able to open a new stadium with 60,000 seats and consistently sell it out. No club in London's history had drawn such a large regular crowd, but Arsenal's city rivals have since more or less matched it. West Ham moved into the converted Olympic Stadium in 2016, sold out the 57,000 seats, and intends to expand to 62,500. Spurs opened its new 62,850-seat stadium in 2019. The business advisory firm Deloitte ranked Arsenal, Chelsea, and Spurs among Europe's eleven richest clubs over the 2019–2020 season. PSG, another capital club, was seventh.

No other European city has more investors than London. When Roman Abramovich decided to buy a soccer club, it was always likely that he would end up owning Chelsea rather than, say, Bolton. The word is that he chose it because it was the nearest club to his house on Eaton Square. Yes, other rich foreigners have bought Liverpool, Manchester City, Blackburn, and Aston Villa, but London is still a touch more appealing to billionaires. Also, as the North's factories have closed, the region no longer produces many homegrown magnates like Sir John Hall at Newcastle or Jack Walker at Blackburn, who in the 1990s bankrolled their clubs to success.

Then there are London's other attractions. The best soccer players can now work wherever they want. Many of them—like many investment bankers and actors—choose London. Black and foreign players, in particular, like living in a multicultural capital. When Thierry Henry was spending his best years at Arsenal, he said, "I love this open, cosmopolitan city. Whatever your race, you never feel people's gaze on you." In a virtuous cycle, foreigners attract foreigners. The Frenchman Jacques Santini, Tottenham's manager for about five minutes, wanted to come to London because his son Sebastien already lived there—a classic example of chain migration.

The handful of the biggest provincial clubs—notably Manchester United, Liverpool, Bayern, and Juventus—have built up such strong brands that they will remain at the top of European soccer, chasing Real Madrid. However, the old elite's new challengers aren't other provincial clubs but teams from London and Paris, as well as Madrid's historical second team Atlético, which has gained a boost from its big chic new Wanda Metropolitano stadium. Even before the ground opened, Atlético reached the Champions League final in 2014 and 2016. In the ten finals from 2012 through 2021, six of the winners and four runners-up came from democratic capitals.

At last, being in a capital has become a strategic asset to a soccer club. Sports used to be practically the only bit of French and British life in which the provinces could humiliate the capitals. Now even that last pleasure has gone.

PART II
The Fans

Loyalty, Suicides, and Happiness

13

A FAN'S SUICIDE NOTES

Do People Jump Off Buildings When Their Teams Lose?

It is one of the eternal stories that are told about soccer: when Brazil gets knocked out of a World Cup, Brazilians jump off apartment blocks. It can happen even when Brazil wins. One writer at the World Cup in Sweden in 1958 claims to have seen a Brazilian fan kill himself out of "sheer joy" after his team's victory in the final. Janet Lever tells that story in *Soccer Madness*, her eye-opening study of Brazilian soccer culture published way back in 1983, when nobody (and certainly not female American social scientists) wrote books about soccer. Lever continues:

> Of course, Brazilians are not the only fans to kill themselves for their teams. In the 1966 World Cup a West German fatally shot himself when his television set broke down during the final game between his country and England. Nor have Americans escaped some bizarre ends. An often cited case is the Denver man who wrote a suicide note—"I have been a Broncos fan since the Broncos were first organized and I can't stand their fumbling anymore"—and then shot himself.

> Then there was the Bangladeshi woman who reportedly hanged herself after Cameroon lost to England in the World Cup of 1990. "The elimination of Cameroon also means the end of my life," said her suicide

note. In fact, if the *Hindu* newspaper in India is right, Bangladeshis have a terrible proclivity for soccer suicides. After Diego Maradona was thrown out of the World Cup of 1994 for using ephedrine, "about a hundred fans in Bangladesh committed suicide," said an article in the *Hindu* in 2006. (It would be fascinating to know the newspaper's source.)

By now, the notion that soccer prompts suicide has become a truism. It is often cited to show the grip of the game over its devotees and as one reason (along with heart attacks on sofas during televised matches) the average World Cup causes more deaths than goals.

We found that there is indeed an intimate connection between suicide and soccer. However, the connection is the opposite of what is commonly believed. It's not the case that fans jump off buildings when their teams lose. (Indeed, after Brazil's 1–7 defeat to Germany in Belo Horizonte in 2014, the international media could find only one fan of Brazil who was moved to commit suicide: a teenage Nepalese schoolgirl who lived nearly ten thousand miles away.) Working with a crack team of Greek epidemiologists, we have found evidence that rather than prompting suicide, soccer stops thousands of people from killing themselves. The game seems to be a lifesaver.

More than 700,000 people die by suicide each year, estimated the World Health Organization (WHO) in 2019. In the US that year, the total age-adjusted suicide rate was 13.9 per 100,000 people, which represented a rise of 32 percent since 1999. This meant that the country experienced nearly two-and-a-half times as many suicides as homicides. Contrary to what is sometimes said, overall suicide rates do not appear to have risen during the COVID-19 pandemic, but then they were already terrifyingly high as they were. Globally, there were nearly fourteen times more suicides than deaths in armed conflict in 2019. And the reported figures for suicides are probably understatements. The German University Hamburg-Eppendorf, which runs a therapy center for people at risk of suicide, has explained: "There may be a significant share of unrecognized suicides among the death types labeled 'traffic accidents,' 'drugs,' and 'causes of death unknown.'"

The suicide risk varies depending on who in the world you are. If you are an elderly, alcoholic, clinically depressed, divorced Lithuanian man, be very afraid, but suicide rates are relatively low in Latin America, leaving aside for the moment the issue of World Cups. Globally, women attempt suicide more often than men do, but most "successful" suicides are males. In the US, for instance, the suicide rate among males in 2019 was 3.7 times higher than among females. For reasons that nobody quite understands, suicide peaks in spring when daylight hours are longest. In the Northern Hemisphere, that means May and June.

The question of why people commit suicide has preoccupied sociologists since sociology began. In 1897 Émile Durkheim, descendant of a long line of French rabbis, published his study *Suicide*. It wasn't just the first serious sociological study of suicide; it was one of the first serious sociological studies of almost anything. Drawing on copious statistics, Durkheim showed that when people lost their connection to wider society because of a sudden change—divorce, the death of a partner, a financial crisis—they sometimes killed themselves. He concluded that this particular form of suicide "results from man's activities lacking regulation and his consequent sufferings."

A few decades later, sociologists began to wonder whether man's sufferings might possibly include the results of sports matches. The numbers of suicides this caused might be significant: after all, most suicides are men, and sports gives meaning to many men's lives. Frank Trovato, a sociology professor at the University of Alberta in Canada, was among the first to investigate the suicide-sports nexus. He found that when the Montreal Canadiens ice hockey team—once described as the national team of French Canada—got knocked out of the playoffs early between 1951 and 1992, Quebecois males aged fifteen to thirty-four became more likely to kill themselves. Robert Fernquist, a sociologist at the University of Central Missouri, went further. He studied thirty American metropolitan areas with professional sports teams from 1971 to 1990 and showed that fewer suicides occurred in cities whose teams made the playoffs more often. Routinely reaching the playoffs could reduce suicides by about twenty each year in a metropolitan area the size of Boston or Atlanta, said Fernquist. These saved lives were the converse of the mythical Brazilians throwing themselves off apartment blocks.

Later, Fernquist investigated another link between sports and suicide: he looked at the suicide rate in American cities after a local sports team moved to another town. It turned out that some of the fans abandoned by their team killed themselves. This happened in New York in 1957 when the Brooklyn Dodgers and New York Giants baseball teams left, in Cleveland in 1995–1996 when the Browns football team moved to Baltimore, and in Houston in 1997–1998 when the Oilers football team departed. In each case the suicide rate was 10 percent to 14 percent higher in the two months around the team's departure than in the same months of the previous year. Each move probably helped prompt a handful of suicides. As Fernquist wrote, "The sudden change brought about due to the geographic relocations of pro sports teams does appear to, at least for a short time, make highly identified fans drastically change the way they view the normative order in society." Clearly, none of these people killed themselves just because they lost their team. Rather, they were very troubled individuals for whom this sporting disappointment was too much to bear.

Perhaps the most famous case of a man who found he could not live without sports was the Gonzo author Hunter S. Thompson. He shot himself in February 2005, four days after writing a note in black marker with the title "Football Season Is Over":

No More Games. No More Bombs. No More Walking. No More Fun. No More Swimming. 67. That is 17 years past 50. 17 more than I needed or wanted. Boring...

Thompson, an occasional sportswriter, loved football. One night during the presidential campaign of 1968, he took a limousine journey through New Hampshire with his least-favorite person, the Republican candidate Richard Nixon, and they talked football nonstop in the backseat. "It was a very weird trip," Thompson wrote later, "probably one of the weirdest things I've ever done, and especially weird because both Nixon and I enjoyed it." The reminiscence, in *Fear and Loathing on the Campaign Trail '72*, segues into an ominous musing on suicide, as a Nixon aide snatches away the cigarette Thompson is smoking over the fuel tank of the candidate's plane. Thompson tells the aide, "You people are lucky I'm a sane, responsible journalist; otherwise I might have hurled my flaming Zippo into the fuel tank."

"Not you," the aide replies. "Egomaniacs don't do that kind of thing. You wouldn't do anything you couldn't live to write about, would you?"

"You're probably right," says Thompson. As it later turned out, he was wrong. His ashes were fired from a cannon in Aspen, Colorado.

So much for suicides and North American sports. We know much less about the connection between suicides and European soccer. In one of the very few European studies done so far, Mark Steels, a psychiatrist at the University Hospital in Nottingham, asked whether Nottingham Forest's worst defeats prompted local suicides. He looked at admissions for deliberate self-poisoning to his hospital's accident and emergency department on two bad days for Forest: after the team's defeats in the FA Cup final of 1991 and the FA Cup quarterfinal of 1992. He found that both games were followed by an increase in self-poisonings. After the cup final, the rise was statistically significant, meaning that it was unlikely to have happened by chance. Steels concluded that "a sudden disappointment experienced through an entire community may prove one stress too many for some vulnerable members of this community."

All this is fascinating but inconclusive. For starters, the sample sizes of all these studies are pretty small. How many people are admitted to a Nottingham hospital for self-poisoning after a soccer match? (Answer: ten in the twelve hours after the 1991 cup final, nine after the 1992 quarterfinal.) How many people kill themselves in Cleveland in any given month? The other problem is that almost all these researchers pursued what you might call the Brazilian apartment-building hypothesis: that when people suffer a sporting disappointment, they kill themselves. Mostly these are studies of the dogs that barked: people who did commit suicide.

But what if the relationship between suicide and sports is deeper than that? If sports give meaning to fans' lives, if they make them feel part of a larger family of fans of their team, if fans really do eat and sleep soccer as in a Coca-Cola ad, then perhaps sports might stop some of these fans from killing themselves. We wanted to find out whether there were dogs that didn't bark: people who didn't commit suicide because sports kept them going.

It so happens that we have a case study. Frederick Exley was a fan of the New York Giants football team whose life alternated between incarcerations in mental hospitals and equally unhappy periods spent in the bosom of his family. In 1968 Exley published what he called "a fictional memoir," *A Fan's Notes*, one of the best books ever written about sports. Nick Hornby gave *Fever Pitch* the subtitle "A Fan's Life" in part as a tribute to Exley.

The Exley depicted in *A Fan's Notes* is a classic suicide risk. He is an alcoholic loner separated from his wife. He has disastrous relationships with women, alienates his friends, and spends months at a time lying in bed or on a sofa at his mother's or aunt's house. For a while his only friend is his dog, Christie III, whom he dresses in a miniature blue sweatshirt like his own and teaches to stand up like a human. "Like most Americans," Exley writes, "I had led a numbingly chaste and uncommitted existence in which one forms neither sympathies nor antipathies of any enduring consequence."

Only one thing in life provides him with any community: the New York Giants. While living in New York City, he stands on the terrace during every home game with a group of Brooklyn men: "an Italian bread-truck driver, an Irish patrolman, a fat garage mechanic, two or three burly longshoremen, and some others whose occupations I forget.... And they liked me."

When the Giants are not playing, Exley spends much of his time drinking alone. But when a game is on, he watches—depending on the stage of his life—with his Brooklyn group, with other people in bars, or with his stepfather at home. Exley is the stepfather's eternal houseguest from Hell, but "things were never better between us than on autumn Sunday afternoons.... After a time, hardly noticeable at first, he caught something of my enthusiasm for the beauty and permanent character of staying with someone through victory and defeat and came round to the Giants." Fittingly, the stepfather dies just before a Giants game: "Seated on the edge of the davenport watching the starting line-ups being introduced, he closed his eyes, slid silently to the floor, and died painlessly of a coronary occlusion."

Inevitably, at one point in the memoir Exley contemplates suicide. He has convinced himself he has lung cancer. Determined to avoid the suffering his father went through, he decides to kill himself instead. Drinking with strangers in bars, he gets into the habit of working "the conversation round to suicide" and soliciting their views on how best to do it. The strangers are happy to oblige: "Such was the clinical and speculative enthusiasm for the subject—'Now, if I was gonna knock myself off...'—that I came to see suicide occupying a greater piece of the American consciousness than I had theretofore imagined."

Only one thing keeps Exley going. The Giants are "a life-giving, an exalting force." He is "unable to conceive what [his] life would have been without football to cushion the knocks." When he is drunk, unemployed, and loveless in Chicago, he writes: "Though I had completely disregarded football my first year in that happy city, during the autumn of 1956, after losing my job, I once again found that it was the only thing that gave me comfort." At some point or other in life, we have all known how that feels.

The real-life Frederick Exley lived to the age of sixty-three, dying in 1992 after suffering a stroke alone in his apartment. He might never have gotten that old without the Giants.

There may be a great many Exleys around. The viewing figures we saw earlier in this book suggest that sport is the most important communal activity in many people's lives. About a third of Americans watch the Super Bowl. However, European soccer is even more popular. In the Netherlands, possibly the European country that follows its national team most eagerly, three-quarters of the population have watched Holland's biggest soccer games. In many European countries, World Cups may now be the greatest shared events of any kind. To cap it all, World Cups mostly take place in June, the peak month for suicides in the Northern Hemisphere. How many Exleys have been saved from jumping off apartment buildings by international soccer tournaments, the world's biggest sporting events?

This is not just a rhetorical question. A study of soccer tournaments and suicide would bring together both an incomparably compelling communal event and a sample the size of several countries. So we set about finding the data.

We needed suicide statistics per month over several years for as many European countries as possible. These figures do not seem to be published anywhere. Luckily, we found out that the Greek epidemiologists Eleni Petridou and Fotis Papadopoulos had laboriously gotten hold of these data by writing to the statistical offices of several countries. A statistician who works with Petridou and Papadopoulos, Nick Dessypris, went through the numbers for us. He found that in almost every country for which he had numbers, fewer people kill themselves while the national team is playing in a World Cup or a European Championship. Dessypris said the declines were "statistically significant"—unlikely to be a result of chance.

Let's take Germany, the biggest country in our study and one that always qualifies for big tournaments. Petridou and Papadopoulos had obtained monthly suicide data for Germany from 1991 through 1997. A horrifying total of ninety thousand people in Germany officially killed themselves in this period. The peak months for suicides were March through June.

But when Germany was playing in a soccer tournament—as it did in the Junes of 1992, 1994, and 1996—fewer people died. In the average June with soccer, there were 787 male and 329 female suicides in Germany. But rather more people killed themselves in the Junes of 1991, 1993, 1995, and 1997, when Germany was not playing soccer. In those soccer-free Junes, there was an average of 817 male and 343 female suicides, or thirty more dead men and fourteen more dead women than in the average June with a big tournament. For both German men and women, the June with the fewest suicides in our seven-year sample was 1996, the month that Germany won Euro '96.

We found the same trend for ten of the twelve countries we studied. In Junes when the country was playing in a soccer tournament, there were fewer suicides. These declines are particularly remarkable given how much alcohol is consumed during soccer tournaments, because drinking would normally be expected to help prompt suicides. Only in the Netherlands and Switzerland did soccer tournaments not seem to save lives; these two countries saw very slight increases in the suicide rate during tournaments. In the other countries, the lifesaving effect of soccer was sometimes spectacular. Our data for Norway, for instance, run from 1988 through 1995. The soccer-mad country played in only one tournament in that period, the World Cup of 1994. The average for the seven Junes when Norway was not playing soccer was fifty-five suicides. But in June 1994 there were only thirty-six Norwegian suicides, by far the lowest figure for all eight Junes in our data set. Or take Denmark, for which we have suicide tallies from 1973 through 1996, the longest period for any country. In June 1992 the Danes won the European Championship. That month there were fifty-four male suicides, the fewest for any June since 1978, and twenty-eight female suicides, the joint lowest (with 1991) since the data set began.

We have tried to make some very rough estimates of how many lives these tournaments saved in each country. "Lives saved" represents the decline in deaths during the average June when a country's national team is playing in a World Cup or European Championship compared with the average June when the team isn't playing. Table 13.1 shows the tally. The figures are negative for the Netherlands and Switzerland because more people killed themselves when their teams were playing than when there was no soccer.

The next question is what happens after a team is knocked out. Do all the people who had been saved from suicide by soccer then fall into a void and jump off apartment buildings? If so, you would expect a rise in suicides in the period after the tournament.

TABLE 13.1. Lives saved from suicide during World Cup or European Championship compared with the average June

	Male lives saved	Female lives saved
Austria	9	–3
Czech Republic	14	6
Denmark	4	4
France	59	8
Germany	30	14
Greece	0	5
Ireland	2	1
Netherlands	–5	0
Norway[a]	[19 lives saved spread across both genders]	
Spain	4	1
Sweden	4	15
Switzerland	–1	–2

[a] *The data for Norway were not broken down by gender.*

However, we found that in ten of our twelve countries, suicides declined for the entire year when the national team played in a big tournament. Only in the Netherlands did suicides rise in the year when the team played; in Spain the difference was negligible. But in the other ten countries, even after the team got knocked out and the euphoria ended, there was no compensating rise in suicide. On the contrary: it seems that the uniting effect of the tournament lasted for a while afterward, continuing to depress the suicide rate. For each of these ten countries, more lives were saved on average over the entire year than in June alone. Table 13.2 contains our very rough estimates for lives saved over the entire year when the national team plays in a tournament ("lives saved" represents the decline in deaths during a "soccer" year compared with the average year). Very roughly, the typical soccer tournament in this period appears to have helped save several hundred Europeans from suicide.

We couldn't find any monthly suicide data for any of the British nations. However, the only two previous studies on this topic that we know of in Britain suggest that the lifesaving effect works there, too.

"Parasuicide" is a suicidal gesture in which the aim is not death but rather self-harm, a cry for help. One example of parasuicide is taking

TABLE 13.2. Lives saved by gender in "soccer" years

	Male lives saved	Female lives saved
Austria	46	15
Czech Republic	55	12
Denmark	37	47
France	95	82
Germany	61	39
Greece	9	13
Ireland	19	–10
Netherlands	–10	–1
Norway	[92 lives saved spread across both genders]	
Spain	2	–3
Sweden	44	16
Switzerland	20	2

a not-quite-lethal overdose. George Masterton, a psychiatrist in Edinburgh, and his coauthor J. A. Strachan studied Scottish parasuicides during and immediately after the World Cups of 1974, 1978, 1982, and 1986. Each time, Scotland had qualified for the tournament. Each time, Masterton and Strachan found a fall in parasuicide for both genders during the tournament that "has been sustained for at least eight weeks after the last game." The Scottish case is a pretty strong piece of evidence against the apartment-building theory of soccer suicides because if there was ever an excuse for soccer fans to try to kill themselves, it was Scotland's disastrous performance at the World Cup of 1978. (The team's fantasist manager, Ally McLeod, had boasted beforehand that the Scots would leave with a "medal of some sort.")

Later, Masterton and Anthony J. Mander studied the numbers of people who came to the Royal Edinburgh Hospital with psychiatric emergencies during and after the World Cups of 1978, 1982, and 1986. The researchers found "reductions in all illness categories during and afterwards (with the exception of alcoholism during)." The decline in emergencies applied to both genders and was more marked after each World Cup than during it. For instance, there was a 56 percent fall in admissions of male neurotics in the weeks after a tournament. The authors then tried to explain what was going on here: "There are few outlets which permit a wide and acceptable expression of Scottish nationhood—sport is perhaps the most powerful, and [soccer] is the national game.... We would speculate that such a common interest and endeavor, fused with a surge of nationalism, might enhance social cohesion in the manner proposed by Durkheim to explain the decreased suicide rates that accompany times of war."

"Social cohesion" is the key phrase here. This is the benefit that almost all fans—potential suicides and the rest of us—get from fandom. Winning or losing is not the point. You can get social cohesion even from losing. Very often, a nation will bond over a defeat in a big soccer game. People sob in public, perform postmortems in the office the next morning, hunt for scapegoats together. For Brazilians, for instance, their 1–7 defeat in 2014 was a shared national moment at least as memorable as victory in Yokohama in 2002. It is not the case that losing matches makes significant numbers of people so unhappy that they jump off apartment buildings. In the US, fans of longtime losers like the Chicago Cubs and the Boston Red Sox baseball teams (Boston became frequent winners again only from 2004 onward, and the Cubs won their first World Series in 108 years in 2016) did not kill themselves more than other people, says Thomas Joiner, author of *Why People Die by Suicide*, whose own father died by suicide.

Joiner's article "On Buckeyes, Gators, Super Bowl Sunday, and the Miracle on Ice" makes a strong case that it's not the winning that counts but the taking part—the shared experience. It is true that he found fewer suicides in Columbus, Ohio, and Gainesville, Florida, in the years when the local college football teams did well. But Joiner argues that this is because fans of winning teams "pull together" more: they wear the team shirt more often, watch games together in bars, talk about the team, and so on, much as happens in a European country while the national team is playing in a World Cup. The "pulling together" saves people from suicide, not the winning. Proof of this is that Joiner found fewer suicides in the US on Super Bowl Sundays than on other Sundays at that time of year, even though few of the Americans who watch the Super Bowl are passionate supporters of either team. What they get from the day's parties is a sense of belonging.

That is the lifesaver. In Europe today there may be nothing that brings a society together like a World Cup with your team in it. For once, almost everyone in the country is watching the same TV programs and talking about them at work the next day, just as Europeans used to do thirty years ago before they got cable TV and the internet. Part of the point of watching a World Cup is that almost everyone else is watching, too. Isolated people—the types at most risk of suicide—are suddenly welcomed into the national conversation. They are given social cohesion. All this helps explain why big soccer tournaments seem to save so many female lives in Europe, even though relatively few women either commit suicide or (before about 2000 at least) watch soccer. The "pulling together" during a big soccer tournament is so universal that it drags many women along in a way that club soccer does not.

Other than sports, only war and catastrophe can create this sort of national unity. Most strikingly, in the week after John F. Kennedy's murder in 1963—a time of American sadness but also of "pulling together"—not one suicide was reported in twenty-nine cities studied. Likewise, in the US in the days after the September 11, 2001, attacks, another phase of national "pulling together," the number of calls to the 1-800-SUICIDE hotline halved to about three hundred a day, "an all-time low," writes Joiner. And in Britain in 1997, suicides declined after Princess Diana died.

Joiner speculates that "pulling together" through sports may particularly suit "individuals who have poor interpersonal skills (often characteristic of severely depressed or suicidal persons)." You don't have to be charming to be a fan among fans.

The rowdy communal emotion invested in soccer tournaments helps deter suicide. But precisely the same emotion can also encourage crime. The number of victims of assault (mostly young men) admitted to English hospital emergency departments rose 38 percent on England's match days during the 2010 World Cup, according to a study by Liverpool John Moores University. And World Cups also seem to encourage men (mostly) to beat their partners (both women and men).

Domestic violence accounted for about a fifth of violent crime in the US from 2003 to 2012, according to interviews with crime victims. However, domestic violence is often an invisible crime, carried out behind closed doors and rarely reported to the police.

World Cups combine several risk factors for women in relationships with men. Sports, alcohol, and "hegemonic masculinity" make up an awful "holy trinity" for domestic violence, write Damien Williams and Fergus Neville of Scotland's University of St. Andrews. Men watching their national teams often drink themselves into a state of aggressive arousal. And this usually happens on hot summer nights, when violent crimes of all kinds tend to increase.

Big club games can also cause mayhem in family homes. After Scotland's "Old Firm" derbies between Celtic and Rangers, domestic violence in Glasgow rises by an average of 36 percent—comparable to "the Christmas holiday effect," report economists Alex Dickson, Colin Jennings, and Gary Koop. But a World Cup rolls the effect out globally. We don't have statistics for every participating country (many don't measure domestic violence, and some don't even forbid it), but there are several recent studies looking at the case of England.

Stuart Kirby, Brian Francis, and Rosalie O'Flaherty analyzed domestic abuse reported to the police in Northwest England during the World Cups of 2002, 2006, and 2010. They found that the risk of abuse on match days rose 26 percent if England won or tied, and by 38 percent if the team lost: "The final day of the tournament for the England team in both 2006 and 2010 exhibited the highest level of reported incidents for the entire month." There was a smaller rise the day after the game, too, which probably reflects assaults after midnight. Practitioners working to combat domestic violence are well aware of the problem.

So although it's nice to know that soccer seems to deter some suicides, the evidence on domestic abuse is extremely disturbing. What can be done? Well, knowing about the link between sports and domestic violence helps. Just as sports organizations have accepted that they have a role to play in combating racism, they also need to acknowledge their role in promoting the emotions that can provoke abuse. And there are signs that they do know. Super Bowls now routinely feature public-service announcements on domestic violence. Women who have been assaulted get a number to call, and their partners may think twice before hitting them.

In England, too, at recent World Cups, police and charities have tried to raise awareness. One video made by the charity Tender shows a woman with two black eyes staring at the TV in horror after England is eliminated. She knows she is about to be assaulted. But more must be done. To those who argue that sports can't be blamed for society's problems, we say that sports claim a special place in society, and that means they have special responsibilities. Here is an unambiguous relationship between sports and a specific social problem. People who organize sporting events and profit from the extraordinary commitment of fans need to show that these events are a force for good. Sports are like an addiction—and when it comes to addictive and potentially dangerous activities, society has to choose between two positions. Either we encourage socially responsible consumption (e.g., alcohol and cigarettes) or we ban the thing (various narcotics). We think that sports should go for social responsibility.

14

HAPPINESS

Why Hosting a World Cup Is Good for You

You don't often see people consciously building a white elephant, but that's what was happening in Brasilia in 2012. Smack in downtown, on the main avenue of Brazil's tropical capital, workers were finishing off a stadium for seventy thousand people. The Estadio Nacional was one of twelve stadiums built for the World Cup in 2014. Yet even before the World Cup ended, it was redundant. Brasilia's tin-pot clubs seldom draw a thousand spectators. A few months after the tournament, it was already being used as chiefly a bus depot, and before COVID-19 closed stadiums, local clubs were allowed to play there rent-free. Nor has Taylor Swift been spotted flying into this city in the middle of nowhere to fill the Nacional. Brasilia probably ought to have torn down the stadium after the last World Cup game and saved itself about $200,000 a month in upkeep costs. Other host cities such as Manaus, Cuiabá, and Natal should have done likewise.

That useless Brasilia stadium cost $900 million, three times more than budgeted, largely because of alleged fraud, making it the most expensive stadium in football's history at the time, after London's new Wembley. It's this kind of waste that brought Brazilians onto the streets in 2013, demonstrating against their country's hosting of the World Cup and the Rio Olympics of 2016. "We have world-class stadiums—now we need a country to go around them," read one protester's banner. "A teacher is worth more than Neymar," said another. Worldwide, from Boston to the International Olympic Committee's headquarters in Lausanne, Switzerland, people are reaching the same conclusion: hosting sports events doesn't make you rich. A truth long known to economists is finally sinking in with the general public. That doesn't happen often.

Whenever a country prepares to host a World Cup or an Olympics, its politicians prophesy an "economic bonanza." They invoke hordes of shopaholic visitors, the free advertising of host cities to the world's TV viewers, and the long-term benefits of all the roads and stadiums that will get built, meanwhile intoning the holy word *sustainability*. No wonder that for decades, countries competed to host these events. The bidding to stage the World Cups of 2018 and 2022 was the most cutthroat ever. If only the bidding countries were to grasp the real benefit to being a host: hosting doesn't make you rich, but it does make you happier. The US, Canada, and Mexico will probably benefit from hosting the World Cup in 2026, but emotionally rather than financially.

The 1989 movie *Field of Dreams* is a sentimental redemption story starring Kevin Costner as an Iowa farmer. Growing up the son of a baseball fanatic, the farmer had dreamed of being a baseball star. As an adult, he hears a voice telling him to build a baseball diamond on his cornfield. "If you build it, he will come" is the film's catchphrase. The moral: building stadiums where they do not currently exist is uplifting and good for you. This originally American idea later spread to soccer around the world.

There is in the US a small industry of "consultants" who exist to provide an economic rationale for "If you build it, he will come." In almost any city in the US at almost any time, someone is scheming to build a spanking new sports stadium. The big prize for most American cities is to host a major league team, ideally a National Football League (NFL) franchise, but if that can't be had, then baseball, basketball, or, if nothing else is going, ice hockey. North American cities frequently fall over themselves trying to attract a Major League Soccer franchise. Hosting an American sports franchise has a lot in common with hosting a World Cup. Both the franchise and the World Cup are mobile beasts. Their owners are generally willing to move to whichever city or country offers them the best deal. In the US, owners of sports teams usually demand that the host city's taxpayers pony up for a stadium, with lucrative parking lots thrown in. All this is then handed over to the franchise owner, who also gets to keep the money he makes from selling tickets. About seventy new major league stadiums and arenas were built in the US in the twenty years before the financial crisis of 2008. The total cost: $20 billion, about half of which came from the public. In New Orleans, for instance, the taxpayers paid for the Superdome but not for better levees.

In one typical case in 1989, seventy investors, including one George W. Bush, son of America's then president, George H. W. Bush, paid $83 million for the Texas Rangers baseball club. The Bush group wanted a bigger stadium. Strangely for a phalanx of right-wing millionaires, it decided that local taxpayers should finance it. And the new owners threatened to move the Rangers elsewhere if that didn't happen. The people of the local town of Arlington duly voted to increase the local sales tax by half a percent, raising the $191 million needed for the ballpark.

George W. became the Rangers' managing director. Mostly this just meant being the official face of the club. He would sit in the stands during games handing out baseball cards with pictures of himself. When he ran for governor of Texas in 1994, he constantly cited his experience in baseball. There wasn't much else on his CV. He was duly elected, and he decorated his Austin office with 250 signed baseballs.

In 1998 the Bush group sold the Rangers to Tom Hicks (the man who later briefly became co-owner of Liverpool FC) for $250 million. Most of the value was in the stadium that the taxpayers had built. Bush personally netted $14.9 million. He admitted, "When it is all said and done, I will have made more money than I ever dreamed I would make." Meanwhile, he was already beginning to parlay his governorship into a bigger political prize.

So the trick for American club owners is to persuade the taxpayer to cough up for stadiums. This is where economists come in handy. Economists like to say that people respond to incentives. Well, economists certainly respond to incentives. Anyone hoping to persuade taxpayers to pay for a stadium in the US commissioned an economist to write an "economic impact" study. By a strange coincidence, these studies always showed that the stadium would make taxpayers rich. (An excellent book that describes this racket is the aptly titled *Field of Schemes*, by Neil deMause and Joanna Cagan; the authors also run a website by the same name detailing the latest scams.)

The argument typically went as follows: building the stadium would create jobs first for construction workers and later for people who worked in it. Fans would flock in from all around ("If you build it, he will come"), and they would spend money. New businesses would spring up to serve them. As the area around the stadium became populated, more people would want to live there, and even more businesses (and jobs) would spring up. "The building of publicly funded stadiums has become a substitute for anything resembling an urban policy," notes Dave Zirin in his *People's History of Sports in the United States*.

The "economic impact" study then typically clothed this model with some big numbers. If you put your mind to it, you could think up a total in benefits that ran into the billions, whatever currency you happened to be working in. Best of all, no one would ever be able to prove that number wrong. Suppose you promise that a stadium will bring a city economic benefits of $2 billion over ten years. If the city's income (hard to measure in the first place) rises by only $1 billion over the decade, then, of course, it was something completely different (the world economy, say) that restricted the income growth. You could prove the original estimates wrong only if you could estimate how much economic growth there would have been had the stadium never been built—but this "counterfactual" figure is unknowable, precisely because it is a counterfactual. The same economists soon branched out into writing studies that justified ever-more-extravagant spending on the Olympics.

It would have seemed rude to derail this industry with anything so inconvenient as the truth. But then along came Rob Baade. The quiet, courteous academic seemed an unlikely figure to be taking on the stadium lobby. After all, he is a former top-class athlete himself: at college, Baade captained the Wisconsin basketball team. When the white coach seemed antagonistic to the majority of Black players, Baade found himself championing players against coach in what he describes as one of the most difficult years of his life.

Afterward, he wanted to do graduate work in public finance, a branch of economics that usually involves many equations and few words. But he also wanted to coach basketball and to apply something of what he had learned while on the Wisconsin team. A colleague told him about a job at Lake Forest College, an idyllic little place just outside Chicago. To the dismay of some of his purist professors, he went to Lake Forest on a temporary appointment and ended up coaching there for eighteen years, while also rising to full professor of economics. He was a good coach, too: the year before he arrived, the team had not won a single game, but within four years they were winning 85 percent of their games.

When you start out as an academic, you try to write papers that will grab your colleagues' attention. Baade used his own background to enter the economics of sports, then still almost virgin terrain. At a seminar in New York, he presented a paper titled "The Sports Tax." Journalists from the *New York Times* and the *Wall Street Journal* happened to be in the audience, and they zeroed in on what had been almost a throwaway line in his talk: public investment in stadiums does not provide a good return for taxpayers. As a coach himself, Baade might have been expected to join the stadium boosters. Had he done so, he could have earned himself good money in consulting. Instead, he went into opposition.

The Heartland Institute, a conservative think tank, asked him to write up his thoughts. There have never been many issues in American political life where the Right joined with an intellectual liberal like Baade, but the paper he published in 1987 laid out the problem clearly: "Contrary to the claims of city officials, this study has found that sports and stadiums frequently had no significant positive impact on a city's economy and, in a regional context, may actually contribute to a reduction in a sports-minded city's share of regional income."

Baade had asked the awkward questions that stadium boosters always ignored. For instance, where would all the construction workers for the new stadium come from? Wouldn't they have jobs already, and therefore wouldn't a shortage arise somewhere else? Worse still, as competition for their skills intensified, wouldn't costs rise?

Once you start thinking of people as having alternatives rather than just standing around waiting for stadiums to arrive, the economics begin to look less appealing. For every dollar going in, there is probably a dollar going out somewhere else. In particular, if a city has to balance its budget, then spending more on stadiums must mean spending less on hospitals and schools. These lost jobs have to be counted against the stadium's benefits. And if the city doesn't balance its budget, isn't it storing up future burdens for taxpayers, who will have to forgo something, someday?

That is bad enough, but what if the stadium doesn't produce the promised benefits? After all, most stadiums are used for only a few hours a week, and barely at all in the off-season. Even allowing for the occasional rock concert (and there is a limit to how many times the Rolling Stones can play in your town), most of the time the neighborhood around the stadium will be deserted. Not many people want to live in a place like that. The neighborhoods around the old Yankee Stadium or Shea Stadium never became desirable, for instance.

Nor did Baade believe that a stadium would draw in much spending from outside the city. Most out-of-town fans would buy a hot dog and beer, watch the game, and leave—hardly an economic bonanza. A mall, or a cineplex, or even a hospital would generate more local spending.

Around the end of the 1980s, other economists began asking these awkward questions. However, Baade went one better. To show that the boosters' numbers didn't add up, he generated some numbers of his own. Perhaps he couldn't measure the counterfactual, but he could get close by comparing economic growth in cities that had major league teams with those that didn't. After all, he reasoned, if the boosters were right, then over time cities with stadiums must do better than cities without stadiums.

Baade examined data such as income per head and the numbers of new businesses and jobs created in various cities. The more he looked, the less difference he found between the economic profiles of cities with and without stadiums. All this spending was evidently producing no benefit.

Gradually, people took notice. Other economists started to replicate Baade's findings and found new ways to test the proposition that stadiums create wealth. "Antistadium movements" began in many American cities.

In the mid-1990s Baade was asked to testify before Congress. On the day of his testimony, Congress was also holding hearings on the Clinton Whitewater affair and on military intervention in Bosnia, but when the stadium hearings started, the other chambers emptied. One of the people in the room was Paul Tagliabue, commissioner of the NFL and someone all the members of Congress wanted to be seen with. Powerful people like Tagliabue were getting quite irritated by Baade's inconvenient facts.

Academic freedom is a cherished value of American universities, but as Baade was starting to realize, so is making money. He recalls an old guy coming up to him after one meeting and saying, "You might be right, professor, but if I were you I would watch my back. You're getting in the way of a whole lotta commercial projects." A university seldom likes seeing its employees upset local politicians and businesspeople. Lake Forest College always supported Baade, but at times it would have been convenient for the institution had he thought differently.

He kept on telling the truth regardless. Among economists, often not the sportiest of types, he developed a special credibility as a former athlete. This sometimes came in handy, such as when a questioner in a public debate asked, "No disrespect, professor, but what does an economist like you know about athletics?"

Eventually, Baade descended on soccer. He and Victor Matheson conducted a study of the impact of hosting the World Cup of 1994 in the US. They looked for evidence of faster economic growth in the host cities, and as usual they found nothing. Yet by now, the old bogus American arguments for hosting sports had spread to other countries.

The raising and dashing of hopes of an economic bonanza became as integral a part of a modern soccer tournament as the raising and dashing of hopes that England would win it. A few months after England hosted Euro '96, for instance, a report by a body called Tourism Research & Marketing said that fewer than 100,000 overseas fans had visited England for the tournament, against a forecast—admittedly plucked out of thin air by the English Football Association—of 250,000. Nor had the visitors spent much. Euro '96 generated about $155 million in direct income for Britain. This was peanuts compared with the $20 billion spent by all overseas visitors to the country in 1996. Meanwhile, a study by Liverpool University and the city council found that the 30,000 visitors to Liverpool during Euro '96 spent only $1.56 million among them. How many jobs had that created? Thirty, all of them temporary.

A few years later, Japanese and Korean government officials were predicting that the World Cup of 2002 could boost their economies by a staggering $26 billion and $9 billion, respectively. Of course, after the event there was little sign of any such boost, and indeed some evidence that tourists had stayed away for fear of soccer hooligans. Big sports tournaments attract some visitors and deter many others. Greek tourism officials estimated in late 2004 that there'd been a 10 percent fall in tourist arrivals during that year's Athens Olympics, as vacationers choosing summer destinations steered clear of the frenzy. Nor did the twenty-two venues built for the Athens Games generate an economic bonanza. Many of them now lie abandoned, sometimes under piles of garbage, while the canoe and kayaking venue has effectively vanished: it dried up. This is a waste that Greece could not afford.

After a couple of decades, the weight of this research finally began to stack up. It was becoming obvious that even if you build it, he won't necessarily come. The boosters' claims of economic benefits were growing muted. The estimates produced for the World Cup in Germany in 2006 were altogether more sober. Even a study sponsored by the German soccer federation suggested a mere $2 billion in new benefits. (Similarly in London, estimates of the likely economic benefits from the 2012 Olympics were kept studiously vague.)

Perhaps the best estimate we have of how much visitors to soccer tournaments actually spend was done at the German World Cup. This was the biggest media event in history at the time, a month-long party (except for the boring soccer), yet even here the hosts didn't make much money.

A team of economists, led by Holger Preuss from the University of Mainz, decided to work out how much "new" money that visitors to the World Cup actually spent. In the old days, when boosters estimated economic bonanzas, they simply multiplied the number of seats in stadiums by some imaginary spending number (counting meals, hotels, and transportation, as well as tickets) to produce an enormous hypothetical sum.

The problem with this method, as serious economists pointed out, is that not every visitor to an event really injects extra spending into the economy. Preuss's team surveyed a large sample of visitors to the World Cup and found that only about one-fifth were foreigners who had traveled to Germany specifically for the soccer. More than half the "visitors" were in fact Germans. For the most part these Germans would have been in Germany anyway, and had there been no World Cup they presumably would have spent their money on other forms of entertainment (such as going to movies or restaurants). If they spent money at the World Cup, they spent less elsewhere in the German economy, which largely offset any economic benefit from the soccer. Of course, some Germans who might otherwise have been spending their money on Spanish vacations stayed home for the soccer. However, their spending was probably offset by other Germans who went abroad precisely to avoid the madness of the World Cup.

The remaining foreign visitors to the World Cup—about a quarter of all visitors—were either "time switchers," who would have come to Germany anyway at some point and simply timed their visit to coincide with the World Cup, or foreigners who would have been in Germany during the World Cup anyway and just decided to go along and see what all the fuss was about. Preuss's team called this last category "casuals."

"Time switchers" and "casuals" would have added little to spending because even without the World Cup, they would have spent their money in Germany. Preuss's team asked respondents detailed questions about their spending plans. They concluded that the World Cup generated spending by visitors of €2.8 billion (equivalent to $3.5 billion in 2006). That was negligible beside the Kardashian-esque €1 trillion-plus ($1.3 trillion) spent annually by consumers in Germany. It was also much less than the German state spent preparing for the tournament. Remarkably, more than a third of that visitor income came from people who never got inside a stadium but merely watched the games on big screens in public places. In short, even the World Cup was barely a hiccup in the German economy.

Study after study shows the same thing: hosting sports tournaments doesn't increase the number of tourists or full-time jobs, or the total economic growth. Added to all this are the host's costs. If the economic benefits of putting on these tournaments are muted, the expenses seldom are. Economists Brad Humphreys and Szymon Prokopowicz made some rough estimates of the costs to Poland of hosting just half of Euro 2012. Poland needed to lay on a lot more than just new stadiums, airports, and hotels for fans. UEFA requires, for its own officials and guests, the use of one entire five-star hotel within a forty-five-minute drive of every stadium. The teams need an additional sixteen hotels, most of them five-star. The referees have to be in five-star hotels near the stadiums. The doctors who perform the doping controls need five-stars "in the countryside." Much of the cost of these hotels came courtesy of the Polish government. Poland also had to put up surveillance cameras all over its stadiums and towns.

In all, Humphreys and Prokopowicz estimated that the country would have to spend about $10 billion on Euro 2012. With hindsight, this looks like a serious underestimate. True, some of the infrastructure that Poland bought still has its uses after the tournament. However, much of it doesn't: the things you need for a soccer tournament—a massive new stadium, roads to that stadium, an airport in a sleepy town—are never quite the same as the things you need for daily life. This has costs. After the tournament, the annual education budget in one Polish host city, Poznan, had to be cut by 20 million Polish zlotys (about $7 million)—which just happened to be the cost of the "fan zone" that Poznan built for the Euro, reports local anthropologist Małgorzata Zofia Kowalska.

Almost all the research points in one direction: hosting doesn't create an economic bonanza. Yet South Africa went into its World Cup in 2010 promising its citizens an economic bonanza. In a sense the country had to. When about a third of your population lives on less than $2 a day, the government can hardly say it's blowing billions on a month of fun. It has to argue that the soccer will benefit the poor. You then end up with people like Irvin Khoza, who chaired the tournament's local organizing committee, saying things such as "The 2010 World Cup will change the face of the country. It may prove a pivotal point in our development as a young democracy."

The South African ruling class put this message across so energetically that when the country was named host in 2004, crowds celebrating in the township of Soweto shouted, "The money is coming!" Half the people you met in South Africa in the years before the tournament had a scheme for 2010: buying apartments just to rent them out during the tournament, selling sausage and maize pudding outside stadiums, corralling peasant women to weave beaded flags in the colors of all the participating teams. Much of South African conversation was about such schemes, and in newspaper profiles, when a celebrity described what he was working on, he would often add, "The key thing is to be ready for 2010." The year had become a magic number.

As 2010 approached, the tournament's expected costs inevitably soared. South Africa had initially promised a cheap World Cup. All the stadiums put together, it had said in 2004, would cost only about $170 million. When we spoke to a FIFA official at the time, he seemed to presume that South Africa would stage the tournament in its existing stadiums, although he did worry that some of them didn't have roofs. Sponsors didn't like getting wet, he noted. But in the end, with FIFA pushing for perfection, and every local power broker in South Africa wanting their own "world-class" stadium, the bill for stadiums ended up at about ten times that initial estimate. This embarrassing overrun may be why copies of South Africa's original bid book were "disappeared."

Some of the South African organizers ended their journey in 2010 feeling rather chastened. For a start, the expected hordes of foreign visitors never showed up. In 2009 the management consultancy Grant Thornton—a serial producer of upbeat economic forecasts about the World Cup—was predicting 483,000 foreign visitors for the tournament. (Earlier forecasts had been even sunnier.) A retrospective study based on official South African statistics, coauthored by Stefan with the economists Thomas Peeters and Victor Matheson, estimates that the number of additional visitors in June and July 2010 was only 220,000, less than half of Grant Thornton's prediction. Given that tourist arrivals from countries outside of Africa averaged about 2 million per year, this represented a boost to tourism, but not a big one. Nor did the economy as a whole see much benefit. As John Saker, chief operating officer of KPMG Africa, said, "The big boost didn't happen."

Predictably, most of the stadiums that South Africa built for the tournament are now white elephants. The country never had any need for them. The larger hosting cities—Cape Town, Johannesburg, Durban, and Pretoria—have for decades possessed large, very decent rugby grounds that can serve the modest needs of local soccer, too. Johannesburg also had the original Soccer City, a stadium rightly touted as the best in Africa when South Africa was bidding for the World Cup.

Very few domestic games outside the Johannesburg region draw more than about ten thousand spectators. Provincial towns such as Nelspruit, Polokwane, and Port Elizabeth now have World Cup stadiums but no teams capable of filling them. Cape Town ought to pull down its stadium and find better uses for that prime piece of land overlooking the Atlantic Ocean.

BRAZIL 2014: THE HYPE NEVER CEASES

You would have thought that people would learn from the shame of the South African World Cup, from the way FIFA bullied a developing country to build unnecessary stadiums fancy enough for sponsors, while a few miles away people lived in corrugated-iron shacks. In 2009 a senior European soccer official mused to us about putting pressure on FIFA to let Brazil host a cheaper World Cup. It could be done, this man said, if a few powerful soccer federations—Germany, France, the US, England, and some others—argued that Brazil needn't build the most expensive stadiums on Earth, just some good solid ones that wouldn't turn into white elephants the day the circus left town.

No such luck, however. Brazil 2014 became a rerun of South Africa 2010. In 2010 the respected Brazilian think tank Fundação Getulio Vargas had predicted that public spending on the tournament (or "investment," as officials like to call it) would total 12.8 billion Brazilian reals (about $5.4 billion in 2014); actual public spending ended up almost exactly double that, at 25.6 billion reals ($10.8 billion), according to the government's own "Transparency Portal" in October 2014.

Sports tournaments almost always cost more than forecast. When researchers at the Saïd Business School in Oxford analyzed thirty Summer and Winter Olympics in 2016, they found that none came in within their initial budget. The cost overrun isn't simply bad luck. To the contrary, it's intentional, says Christopher Gaffney of New York University. If you are a construction company or a chamber of commerce that has initiated a city's Olympic bid, you want cost estimates to start off low so as to get taxpayers and the government on board. But once everyone is committed to the bid, you then want costs to soar because higher spending generally means higher profits for suppliers. And forcing up spending is easy. The construction companies know that the stadiums must be ready by the opening ceremony. This means they can charge almost whatever they like to build them; the government will pay.

No wonder that the construction of stadiums so often hits delays. This allows the construction companies to tell the government, "Oops, this is costing more than we thought. Give us more cash, or we won't finish on time, and you'll look stupid in front of the world."

The Brazilian World Cup was a wonderful thing if you happen to own a construction business, not so wonderful if you pay taxes in Brazil or if you were hoping the government would do something about all the terrible Brazilian roads that don't lead to soccer stadiums.

By the time the last party animals had flown home, there was little sign of any economic boost to Brazil. True, the World Cup had attracted an unexpectedly large number of foreign visitors, about a million. However, a lot of the visitors had driven up for just a couple of days from Argentina, Chile, or Uruguay, and many saved money in comparatively expensive Brazil by bringing their own food, living in their cars, and showering on Rio's beaches. According to the Brazilian Central Bank, tourists spent about $1.6 billion in Brazil during the World Cup, or 60 percent more than during the equivalent period in 2013. However, in the same period, Brazilians themselves spent much more abroad: $4.4 billion. In fact, July 2014 was the most spendthrift month for Brazilians abroad since 1947. In short, many of them seem to have left the country to escape the World Cup.

Indeed, the World Cup coincided with the start of Brazil's longest recession since the 1930s. That rather undermined claims that it would boost the economy. The impoverished country then had to fork out another $4.6 billion (predictably, 51 percent over budget) to host the Rio Olympics, according to the Oxford study.

Even if the new stadiums made Brazilian clubs a tiny bit richer, this didn't make Brazil as a whole richer. Rather, the Brazilian World Cup is best understood as a series of financial transfers: from women to men (who probably had more fun, given that more males like soccer), from Brazilian taxpayers to FIFA and the world's soccer fans, and from taxpayers to Brazilian soccer clubs and construction companies. Possibly, Brazilian society desired these transfers. Still, we have to be clear that this is what happened: a transfer of wealth from Brazil as a whole to various interest groups inside and outside the country. This is not an economic bonanza. Brazil sacrificed a little bit of its future to host the World Cup.

Ah, say the boosters, but the biggest economic benefits from these events are long-term and intangible. Think of all the billions of people seeing the host country on TV every night. Orlando Silva Junior, Brazil's then sports minister, told us (before he regrettably had to resign over a corruption scandal) that the 2014 World Cup would promote Brazil's image in the world. Well, maybe. First of all, as the American sports economist Andrew Zimbalist says, "Brazil is hardly a secret as an international tourist destination." Rio was already the most visited city in the Southern Hemi-sphere before the two tournaments, he notes. And for years in advance of Brazil's World Cup, foreign media coverage highlighted the country's crime and traffic jams. Some of that bad publicity probably stuck.

PLEASE, WILL YOU HOST OUR TOURNAMENT?

In just the last few years, much of the world has come around to the *Soccernomics* view of hosting. The realization is dawning that hosting doesn't make you rich. We wish we could claim the slightest bit of credit for this turnaround.

It's possible to date the peak in global appetites for hosting quite precisely, to the afternoon of December 2, 2010, when the twenty-two mostly elderly men on FIFA's executive committee gathered in Zurich to choose Russia as host country for the World Cup in 2018 and Qatar for 2022. Among the disappointed bidders were the US, England, and Australia. The shift of power from the West to the Gulf countries and Russia had manifested itself in FIFA before it became obvious in geopolitics.

We soon learned that the Zurich votes were rigged. The exposure began one day in 2011, when the FBI tapped the New Yorker Chuck Blazer on the shoulder as he trundled his mobility scooter down East 56th Street, on his way to yet another luxury restaurant. Blazer had been executive vice president of the United States Soccer Federation, and then general secretary of Concacaf, the confederation that governs soccer in North and Central America and the Caribbean. He was a man of extraordinary appetites. Weighing in at 450 pounds, he lived on an entire floor in Trump Tower in New York, with one apartment exclusively for his cats. But as the FBI had worked out, Blazer financed this grand life by taking bribes—typically 10 percent of any deal. Soon after that tap on the shoulder, he was back on FIFA's luxury-hotel circuit, but now as an FBI informer wearing a wire in a key fob.

Blazer struck a plea deal with the government, and in 2013 he admit-ted, in a secret session of a New York court, "I and others on the FIFA executive committee agreed to accept bribes in conjunction with the se-lection of South Africa as the host nation for the 2010 World Cup." He said he had also helped his crony in Concacaf, the Trinidadian Jack

Warner, pocket a bribe to vote for Morocco to host in 1998, although in the end that tournament went to France. Blazer died disgraced in 2017. His fall is a reminder that corruption—in soccer and elsewhere—doesn't only happen in developing countries. The US, much as it likes to pose as the global policeman, is often a culprit, too.

Armed with Blazer's information, the FBI rolled up much of the senior leadership of FIFA. At dawn on May 27, 2015, Swiss police, working with the FBI, raided Zurich's five-star Baur au Lac hotel and arrested seven senior international soccer officials. "Some of them were led out of back doors into waiting cars, and shielded from photographers by thoughtful hotel staff holding Baur au Lac bed sheets in front of them," writes David Conn in *The Fall of the House of FIFA.* One FBI official spoke of "the World Cup of fraud." Blatter resigned as FIFA's president in June 2015, only four days after being unanimously reelected. The pressure from media, the FBI, and officials in Switzerland (fed up with being embarrassed by FIFA) had become unbearable. In November 2021 Swiss prosecutors indicted Blatter and Michel Platini, former head of UEFA, for an unrelated fraud.

Many of Blatter's and Platini's cronies went down with them. As of November 2021, sixteen of the twenty-two Exco members who had voted that day in 2010 had been suspended, charged, or sentenced to prison for corruption. And much of this crookery related to the choices of World Cup hosts. In fact, for many inside FIFA, bribes seem to have been the point of choosing a host—a tradition that probably goes back to the mists of time. (Brazil in 2014 was the rare host that didn't have to use bribery, simply because there were no other bidders.) The Exco members who allegedly took bribes to vote for a particular host didn't necessarily do what they had promised, but that is the risk every bribe payer runs.

It appears that Qatar, too, sprinkled money and favors on some officials (something the Qataris deny). But so did the Western bidders—they just took care to sprinkle legally. England's bid, for instance, paid various sums into Warner's pet projects. He knew nobody was going to monitor how he spent the money. Still, even if almost everybody cheated, that doesn't make it right.

As of 2022, the FBI and Swiss police continue to investigate wrongdoing inside FIFA. However, FIFA has barely reformed, Qatar and Russia kept their World Cups, and Western countries seem powerless to force change.

Most of the heat is now off FIFA itself. Almost no journalists cover the organization full-time. Sure, the federation has found sponsors harder to come by lately, what with all the scandals and two straight World Cups being scheduled in unsexy nondemocracies. But that won't bother FIFA much because it's still a low-cost monopoly producer of World Cups.

FIFA does have a problem, though: ever fewer countries want to host these tournaments. When the US, Canada, and Mexico put together their united bid to host the 2026 World Cup, the only competitor they faced was perennial losing bidder Morocco. And the three host countries won't have to spend billions building white-elephant stadiums: almost the entire tournament will be played on existing grounds. Had they needed to spend serious money, we're guessing they probably wouldn't have bid.

People everywhere are cottoning on to the truth that hosting doesn't bring wealth. International sporting bodies have grown afraid of angering taxpayers in host countries the way FIFA did in South Africa and Brazil. That's partly why the IOC gave the 2020 Olympics to Tokyo: the megacity could better afford to stage the Games than its poorer rivals Istanbul and Madrid. In soccer, UEFA went one step further: it didn't choose a host at all for Euro 2020. The burden would have been too great, explained UEFA's then general secretary Gianni Infantino (who is now president of FIFA). Instead, eleven countries shared the hosting.

Several European cities bidding for the 2022 Winter Olympics pulled out before the vote. The Games were awarded to Beijing, which has no snow, but, crucially, has no referenda either. For the 2024 Summer Games, Boston, the original American candidate, dropped its bid after failing to get enough local support. In the end, the only two cities that still wanted to host were Paris and Los Angeles. The IOC gave 2024 to Paris, but immediately locked in LA for 2028, and then chose Brisbane, Australia, without any rival bid for 2032, perhaps fearful that nobody else would want this event. Hosting is finally going out of fashion.

HAPPINESS IS A WORLD CUP

Most people now agree with Rob Baade: hosting doesn't make you rich. But it can make you happy.

In recent years, social scientists have learned a lot about happiness. Their best source in Europe is the Eurobarometer research program, which is funded by the European Commission. Each year it asks approximately a thousand citizens from each European country how happy they are. To quote the exact question: "On the whole, are you very satisfied, fairly satisfied, not very satisfied, or not at all satisfied with the life you lead?"

The survey has been conducted for more than forty years. By now, some insights have accumulated. Perhaps the most interesting is that the simple fact of having lots of money doesn't in itself make you happy. "There is a paradox at the heart of our lives" is how Richard Layard opens his book *Happiness: Lessons from a New Science*, one of a flood of recent works on the subject. "Most people want more income and strive for it. Yet as Western societies have got richer, their people have become no happier." Layard says that in the US, Britain, and Japan, people have gotten no happier in the past fifty years even as average incomes have more than doubled.

Most theorists of happiness argue that we do become happier during economic recoveries while incomes are rising. "That's also because growth is full of promise," says Claudia Senik, professor at the Paris School of Economics. However, it's not clear that high but stagnant incomes boost happiness in developed countries. It seems that we humans adapt quickly to our environment. The things we once thought of as luxuries soon become necessities (although, by the same token, our sense of well-being would quickly adapt to losing half our income). What we care about is not so much our absolute wealth but our rung on the ladder. The richest people in developed countries are on average happier than middling and poorer people—chiefly, it seems, because they compare themselves with the middling and poorer people.

Only in countries where per capita income is below about $15,000—countries such as Brazil, the Philippines, and India—has more money indisputably brought greater national happiness. As Layard writes, "The reason is clear—extra income is really valuable when it lifts people away from sheer physical poverty."

Some other truths emerge from the European data. Scandinavians are very happy; Eastern Europeans are not. The Irish both north and south of the border are surprisingly happy. Age, sex, and social status matter, too. In the European Union at least, according to Eurobarometer's figures, the average person's happiness tends to peak before the age of twenty-five. (This is a controversial issue. Many economic studies find that happiness increases with age, but the psychology literature finds no relationship between age and happiness.) Women seem to be happier than men, which might help explain their much lower rates of suicide. The more educated people are, the happier they tend to be. Married people are generally happier than unmarried ones. What happens around you in society also matters: when unemployment or inflation rises, people tend to grow unhappier. Mentally ill people tend to be very unhappy. Spending time with friends and family makes people happy.

And, we discovered, so does hosting soccer tournaments. Staging a World Cup won't make you rich, but it does tend to cheer you up.

The day before the World Cup final of 2006, Simon visited the street where he used to live in Berlin. Fifteen years before, the Hohenfriedberg-strasse had been a dull-brown place with toilets on the stairwells and potentially fatal ancient coal ovens in every apartment. Nobody ever spoke to anyone else. This time he had to check the street sign to make sure it was the same place. Flags were flying from every house—German flags made in China, but also the flags of many other nations—and children were playing everywhere even though they had supposedly gone extinct in Germany. The World Cup seemed to have made a usually gloomy nation happy.

This is typical. Georgios Kavetsos and Stefan (with a lot of help from Robert MacCulloch, guru of happiness research) took the European Commission's happiness data for twelve Western European countries from 1974 to 2004 and checked whether the data correlated at all with sports tournaments. The obvious first question was whether people became happier when their national team did well. It turned out that they didn't: there was no visible correlation. Then they looked at hosting and happiness, and here they found a link. After a country hosts a soccer tournament, its inhabitants report increased happiness.

In their research they replicated existing studies of happiness using all the measures that researchers normally consider (income, age, marital status, and so on), and then they tested whether living in a host country made a difference as well. Their data on happiness covered eight separate hosts of tournaments: Italy and France for the World Cups of 1990 and 1998, and for the European championships Italy (1980), France (1984),

West Germany (1988), England (1996), and Belgium and the Nether-lands (2000). In all but one of these eight host countries, there was a sig-nificant uptick in self-reported happiness just after the tournament. The only exception was the UK, where happiness fell slightly just after Euro '96, but then we all know that the UK is not England.

Georgios and Stefan are pretty sure that these results cannot be as-cribed to coincidence. For one thing, their analysis controlled for many potentially confounding factors (such as age, gender, employment, and marital status). But one piece of evidence that they found particularly con-vincing had to do with a peculiarity of the study. Generally, Eurobarom-eter reports the results in annual format, but in fact the data is a product of two surveys, one in the spring and one in the fall, and researchers can separate these observations in the raw data. It was very clear in the data that the jump in happiness in host nations came from people surveyed in the fall (just after the soccer tournament) and not in spring (before).

Interestingly, this chimes with what Arthur Hopcraft, the late British soccer writer, observed when England hosted the World Cup in 1966. He wrote two years later,

> The competition released in our country a communal exuberance which I think astonished ourselves more than our visitors. It gave us a chance to spruce up a lot, to lighten the leaden character of the grounds where the matches were played, to throw off much of our inhibition of behavior, particularly in the provinces, so that we became a gay, almost reckless people in our own streets, which is commonly only how we conduct ourselves when we put on our raffia hats in other countries' holiday resorts. Except in the celebrations that greeted the end of the Second World War, I have never seen England look as unashamedly delighted by life as it did during the World Cup.

Because the Eurobarometer also includes data on incomes, it's pos-sible to work out how far the increase in happiness associated with a soccer tournament compares with an increase in income. The monetary equivalent of the jump in happiness was quite large. Citizens of wealthy countries like the Netherlands or France would need to make hundreds of euros more a month to experience a similar leap. The effect can also be likened to an unexpected increase in income that takes someone from the bottom half of the income distribution to the middle of the top half. It's not quite winning the lottery, but very satisfying nonetheless. If you calculate this for an entire nation, then the leap in happiness from hosting can easily be worth a few billion euros.

In general, older men in host countries gained the most extra happiness, presumably because many of them were sitting in front of their television sets with little else to do. Lesser-educated people gained more happiness than better-educated ones. Of all the subgroups we studied, only one (a significant one) did not get any happier: women.

For World Cups, the gain in happiness was quite persistent: even two and four years after the tournament, every subgroup we looked at was still happier than before the tournament. European championships, though, lifted happiness only briefly. George and Stefan found no impact on happiness in the host country a year after the Euro.

But if people gain a lot of happiness after hosting a tournament, they seem to lose a little happiness in the run-up. The ritual fuss over whether the stadiums will be ready, whether hooligans or terrorists will invade their country, and whether their team will be made to look ridiculous appears to cause stress. Six years and four years before hosting a tournament, many of the subgroups studied showed a decline in happiness.

The London Olympics also seem to have boosted British happiness. The UK's Office for National Statistics (ONS) registered a small rise in self-reported "life satisfaction" from 2011–2012 to 2012–2013, despite the economic crisis. Of the 165,000 British adults polled, 77 percent rated their life satisfaction at 7 or more out of 10—up a touch from 75.9 percent in 2011–2012. The ONS commented that the Olympics and the Queen's Diamond Jubilee may have "influenced people's assessment of their...well-being." Stefan participated in a study with seven other researchers[1] using a panel of 26,000 respondents who were residents of London, Berlin, and Paris in 2011, 2012, and 2013, and asked the simple happiness question. They wanted to see if Londoners' happiness increased during the Olympics, if it increased compared with the same time in the previous/following year, and if it increased relative to changes in Berlin and Paris. What they found was remarkable: a clear and significant jump in happiness on the day of the opening ceremony, sustained throughout the games until the closing ceremony, after which happiness fell back to exactly where it would have been without the Olympics.

All of this begs a question. If countries want to host soccer tournaments (and American cities want to host major league teams) as part of their pursuit of happiness, why don't they just say so? Surely they must sense that people enjoy hosting. Why bother clothing their arguments in bogus economics?

The answer is that few politicians try to speak the language of happiness. Instead, they talk mostly about money. Anything that serves only to make people happy is often derided with the contemptuous phrase "feelgood factor," as if politics should be above such trivialities. Most politicians simply assume that the real business of government is to make people richer. And so, when politicians argue for hosting tournaments, they typically use the language of money. It is almost the only vocabulary they have. As the British economist John Kay, looking back on the London Olympics, remarked, "A curious puritanism requires politicians to pretend activities intended to make us feel good about ourselves are justified by their contribution to 'the economy.' The Olympiad was a good party, which cost the British population about £200 [then about $320] per head."

On occasion, politicians in rich countries have pointed out that there is more to happiness than money alone. Robert F. Kennedy remarked in March 1968, three months before he was murdered, that the gross domestic product "measures everything...except that which makes life worthwhile." For a few years before the economic crisis hit in 2008, some European politicians did begin talking less about money and more about happiness. In Britain in 2006, for instance, the Conservative leader David Cameron tried to introduce the acronym "GWB"—"general wellbeing"—to counter the decades-old "GDP" for "gross domestic product." He said, "Improving our society's sense of well-being is, I believe, the central political challenge of our times.... Politics in Britain has too often sounded as though it was just about economic growth." Instead, Cameron wanted politics "to recognize the value of relationships with family, friends, and the world around us."

Like most European politicians, Cameron dropped the happiness talk after the 2008 economic crisis. Regardless, it seems that soccer tournaments create exactly the sort of relationships he had been talking about: people gathered together in pubs and living rooms, a whole country suddenly caring about the same event. A World Cup is the sort of common project that otherwise barely exists in modern societies. We've seen that the mere fact of following a team in the World Cup deters some very isolated people from committing suicide. If playing in a tournament creates social cohesion, hosting one creates even more. The inhabitants of the host country—especially the men—come to feel more connected to everyone else around them. Moreover, hosting can boost a population's self-esteem.

In the end, the best reason for hosting a World Cup is that it's fun. Brazil's government ought to have been honest and said, "It'll cost us money, we'll have less left over for schools and roads and poor people, but we all love soccer and it should be a fun month, so it'll be worth it." Then Brazilians could have a clearheaded debate about the true pros and cons of hosting. It's reasonable enough to want to throw the world's biggest party. But you generally don't throw a party to make money. You do it because it makes you happy.

Hosting makes even politicians happy. Most of a politician's work is frustrating. You try to get money to build, say, roads, but other politicians stop you. Even when you get the money, it's hard to build the roads because people pop up to object. It's the same with housing or foreign policy or recycling: being a politician is an endless, tedious struggle with your enemies.

But it isn't when you want to host a sports tournament. Suddenly, everyone gets on board. While London was bidding for the Olympics, the rower Steve Redgrave pulled an Olympic gold medal out of his pocket during a meeting at the House of Commons, and MPs of all parties began drooling over him. Even going to war doesn't create that sort of unanimous sentiment anymore.

Ken Livingstone wrote when he was mayor of London, "Crucially, the Olympics will also bring much-needed new facilities: an Olympic-size swimming pool in a city that has just two Olympic pools to Berlin's 19, and a warm-up track that would be turned over to community use."

But plainly, arguments like these are just excuses. If you want to regenerate a poor neighborhood, regenerate it. Build nice houses and a train line. If you want an Olympic pool and a warm-up track, build them. You could build pools and tracks all across London, and it would still be cheaper than hosting the Olympics. The only good reason to host an Olympics is that it makes people happy. The politicians behind London's bid did not say so, but they did sense that the voters would reward them for winning the Games. The 8.7 million Londoners, in particular, had the highest incomes in the European Union at the time, so they would have needed to receive a fortune in tax rebates to buy the happiness that the Olympics seems to have brought them.

Many might rightly argue that even a rich country like Britain has better things on which to spend money. But the likely gain in happiness from the Olympics does mean the politicians are canny to give the people bread and circuses. In wealthy countries such as Britain, the math of hosting and happiness probably stacks up.

It's much less probable that Brazil got its money's worth in happiness from hosting the World Cup. Brazil is still very much a sub-$15,000 country, where putting more money in people's pockets would have made them happier. And like South Africa, it's among the most economically unequal countries on Earth. Both countries have a first-world sector of the economy with the money and skills to host a World Cup—but also a third-world sector that desperately needs the fruits of the money and skills. Millions of Brazilians are still stuck in life-diminishing poverty. Some of them were pushed out of slums to make way for the World Cup. The American satirical newspaper *The Onion* got it about right with the headline "World Cup Stadium's Walls Reinforced with 10,000 Homeless Brazilians." Many people in Brazil were left wondering how many homes with running water could have been built for the cost of their new stadiums. We already know that the World Cup didn't make Brazilians richer. It also probably wasn't an efficient way to make them happier.

15

FOOTBALL VERSUS FOOTBALL

A Tale of Two Empires

When Nelson Mandela was a teenager in the Transkei region of South Africa, he was sent to a mock British boarding school. The Clarkebury Institute taught Black students but was of course run by a white man, the Reverend C. Harris. "The school itself consisted of a cluster of two dozen or so graceful, colonial-style buildings," Mandela recalled in his autobiography, *Long Walk to Freedom*. "It was the first place I'd lived in that was western, not African, and I felt I was entering a new world whose rules were not yet clear to me."

Like the Victorian British schools that it imitated, Clarkebury aimed to turn its pupils into Christian gentlemen. A gentleman, to Victorian Britons, was someone with posh manners who spoke English and played British games. As Mandela described his school days, "I participated in sports and games as often as I could, but my performances were no more than mediocre. . . . We played lawn tennis with home-made wooden rackets and soccer with bare feet on a field of dust."

He had encountered the British Empire. The British colonial officers, merchants, and sailors who went around the world in the nineteenth century didn't merely aim to exploit the natives. They also tried to teach them British values. They succeeded spectacularly with Mandela, who at an earlier school had acquired a new first name (Admiral Nelson was a British naval hero) and eventually became the epitome of the courtly British gentleman. However, his story is exemplary of millions of people around the world, both in Britain's official colonies and in the "informal empire," the countries where the Brits supposedly didn't rule.

From about 1917 to 1947 the British gradually stopped running the world and handed over the keys to the Americans. But the American empire was much less ambitious. It barely spread Americanism. Football, the American empire's most popular sport, still hardly exists outside its home country. In fact, when American troops in Afghanistan wanted to woo natives, they were reduced to handing out soccer balls. (The exercise failed: Allah's name was found to be printed on a ball, a blasphemy for an object designed for kicking.)

At this point, let's agree to call the global game "soccer" and the American game "football." Many people, both in America and in Europe, imagine that "soccer" is an American term invented in the late twentieth century to distinguish it from gridiron football. Indeed, anti-American Europeans often frown on the use of the word. They consider it a mark of American imperialism. Even some American soccer fans seem embarrassed by the word. This is a silly position. As best we know, the word *soccer* was coined at Oxford University sometime in the 1890s, and it remained a common name for the game in Britain until the 1970s. Its declining usage in Britain seems to coincide with the rise of the North American Soccer League in the 1970s. Somewhat absurdly, it appears that the more the Americans use the word, the less the British do.

It's actually possible to show this little bit of linguistic snobbery on a chart. To do this we engaged the help of Antoinette Renouf, emeritus professor of English language and linguistics at the UK's Birmingham City University. Antoinette is a "corpus" linguist, which means that she trawls electronic "text collections" to study how language is used. Corpora come in all sizes and shapes, but she works mainly on a corpus derived from two British national newspapers, the *Guardian* and the *Independent*, which she has been building with successive software research teams since 1984. So far, her corpus contains approximately 1.3 billion words of running text. We can see from the corpus how word usage changes over time. Antoinette generated two charts for us, one showing the frequency of use of the word *football*, the other of *soccer*, from 1984 to 2011.

Back in 1984, the word *football* appeared about fifty times per million words used, and *soccer* appeared about ten times per million. The year

1984 is close to the nadir of the game in England: the time of hooligans, collapsing stadiums, and cheap tickets. Since then, English soccer's renaissance has brought millions of new fans and billions of dollars into the game. The game became a talking point in all walks of life, from politics to fashion. As result, the frequency of use of the word *football* rose steadily through the year 2000 to about two hundred times per million, where it has stabilized for the last decade or so.

By contrast, the relative use of the word *soccer* didn't increase between 1984 and 2008 but remained at around ten times per million words. Since then, its usage has actually fallen to about five times per million. Another way to express this is as follows: in 1984, about 17 percent of references to the English game (*football* or *soccer*) employed the word *soccer*, but by 2011, only about 2 percent did. In the space of thirty years, *soccer* has become a bad word among the British, probably for the simple reason that they found out that Americans were using it. Having consulted numerous linguists on the question, we believe this to be a unique example of "linguistic exile": the deliberate banishing to another country of a formerly acceptable word, making it a very interesting cultural phenomenon. In 2018 Stefan wrote a short book on the subject with Silke-Maria Weineck, a professor of comparative literature, titled *It's Football, Not Soccer (and Vice Versa)*. However, we will use the word *soccer* for the round-ball-kicking game and *football* for the oval-ball-throwing-with-helmets game, and readers will know what we mean.

What follows is a tale of two games and two empires. Soccer spread around the world, whereas football did not, largely because Victorian Britons were instinctive colonialists, whereas today's Americans are not. This is a tale of two very different types of empire: the British (which contrary to popular opinion still exists) and the American (which contrary to popular opinion may never have existed). And as the Britons continue their colonizing work in soccer, they are creating a new breed of global sports fan.

GENTLEMEN WITH LEATHER BALLS

In 1884 a nine-year-old boy named Charles Miller embarked on the SS *Elbe* in Brazil and set off for England. Miller's father had emigrated from Britain to Brazil to work as an engineer for the São Paulo Railway Company. Now Charles was making the return journey to enroll at an English boarding school. Like Mandela at Clarkebury, Miller at Banister Court School learned games. "Just as a schoolboy, in the Garden of Childhood, listens to the teacher, so I, fascinated, saw my first game of Association Football," he later wrote.

In 1894 Miller returned to Brazil with a leather ball and a set of rules in his luggage. He set up the first Brazilian soccer league. He also introduced rugby to Brazil, though with rather less success. He died in 1953, having lived long enough to see Brazil host the World Cup of 1950 and reach the final.

Miller's story was typical of soccer pioneers in many countries. First, he was posh, or at least posh enough to go to boarding school. (Contrary to myth, it wasn't on the whole British sailors who gave the world soccer. The upper classes had considerably more soft power.) Second, Miller was typical in that he spread soccer to a country that wasn't a British colony. In the colonies, places like Australia and India, British schoolteachers and administrators mostly taught the natives cricket and rugby. Soccer did best in the informal empire, the noncolonies: most of Europe, Latin America, and parts of Asia. Here it probably benefited from not being seen as a colonial ruler's game. Brits in the informal empire were supposedly just businesspeople, even if in practice their commercial clout gave the British prime minister vast influence over many unlikely countries.

From about 1850 until World War I, Britain was the sole economic superpower. As late as 1914, Britons still owned about 42 percent of all the world's foreign investment. The British expats who inhabited the informal empire represented the empire's economic might. The men tended to work in the railways (like Miller's father), as businessmen (like the Charnock brothers, who set up Russia's first soccer club, the future Dynamo Moscow, for their mill employees outside Moscow), or as schoolteachers (like Alexander Watson Hutton, the Scottish teacher who in the early 1880s introduced soccer in Argentina).

These people had only soft power: the wealth and prestige of the British gentleman. That was enough to spread their games. Men like Hutton taught foreigners to see sports as a British upper-class and hence aspirational product. If you were a young man like Mandela who wanted to become a British gentleman, one of the things you did was play soccer. That's why the game's early adopters in the informal empire tended to be rich people who had contact with British gentlemen. For instance, Pim Mulier, who introduced a panoply of sports to the Netherlands, first encountered soccer as a five-year-old at a Dutch boarding school that had some British pupils. In 1879, when Mulier was fourteen, he founded the first Dutch soccer club.

By the 1930s, when Mandela went to Clarkebury, the British Empire had already begun to fade. However, many of the empire's global networks outlived the loss of the colonies. The most important survivor would be the English language, even if it sustained its global reach largely thanks to the Americans. English gave people around the world an easy connection with Britain. As Steven Stark, an American soccer fan, former speechwriter for Jimmy Carter, and a teacher of English rhetoric, asks, "Isn't the best thing the Premiership has going for it is that it's in English? I mean, if everyone in France spoke English and everyone in England spoke French, we'd all be following the French league. In an international economy, English trumps the competition."

Many people in former British colonies grew up absorbing British soccer from British media outlets that had also outlived the empire. Peter Draper, when he was marketing director of Manchester United, noted that English soccer had been televised for decades in many Asian countries. That built loyalty. Real Madrid, Draper told us, "didn't have the platform. Spanish television is nowhere in Asia. Best team of the 1950s? Sorry, didn't see them in Asia."

Mike Abrahams is a gangster turned intellectual who grew up in a poor, nonwhite Cape Flats township outside Cape Town. As a child, he used to sit in the local library reading British boys' magazines like *Shoot* and *Tiger*. He admits that classic British soccer cartoons like *Billy's Magic Boots* shaped him.

Abrahams was a leftist who identified with only one product of white capitalist imperialist Britain: soccer: "People in the Cape follow English football very seriously. One of my friends, his first child's name is Shankly [after Bill Shankly, the former Liverpool manager]. And this is an activist! You can say England is a bitch on Friday night, and on Saturday afternoon you go to a sports pub to watch English soccer."

People are always complaining that American culture has conquered the world. In fact, British culture probably remains more dominant. This fading midsize island has kept a bizarre grip on the global imagination. It's not only their sports that the Brits have exported. The world's six best-selling novels of the past hundred years are all British: four Harry

Potters, one Agatha Christie, and one J. R. R. Tolkien. The world's best-selling band ever is the Beatles. And the sports league with the biggest global impact is surely the Premier League. England has produced few great soccer players, yet on an average Saturday people in San Francisco and Shanghai gather in bars for the kickoff at Goodison Park rather than for anything from Germany.

They certainly aren't watching the NFL. In fact, the United States has rarely even aspired to vast cultural reach. The Americans fought wars, but mostly tried to avoid creating long-term colonies, notes the British philosopher John Gray. In Vietnam and Iraq, for instance, the aim was to "go in, do the job, get out." Unlike Britons, Americans generally didn't want to be in the business of empire. We know an American lawyer who spent a few months working for the British government during the occupation of Iraq. In the "Green Zone" in Baghdad he noticed a difference between the way Brits and Americans worked. When American officials wanted an Iraqi to do something, the lawyer said, they would generally call the person into the Green Zone and, if necessary, "bawl him out." Sometimes this strategy worked. Sometimes it didn't. But the Americans summoned Iraqis only when something needed fixing. British officials worked differently, said the lawyer. They were always inviting Iraqis in, for parties or just for chats, even when there was nothing in particular to discuss. This was exactly how the British had operated both in their colonies and in their "informal empire": they made long-term contacts. The Reverend Harris at Clarkebury Institute may not entirely have known it, but in effect he was a British agent charged with teaching Mandela Britishness.

By contrast, few American Harrises ever taught baseball or football to budding foreign rulers. There have been a handful of prominent American colonialists, but they are so rare as to stand out. Douglas MacArthur ruled Japan for years. Hollywood makes its blockbusters chiefly for the global market. And in sports, David Stern spent precisely thirty years as NBA commissioner working to interest foreigners in basketball. But most American sporting moguls, like most American producers in general, have been satisfied with their giant domestic market. Baseball's last great overseas tour was in 1913–1914, after which Americans barely even tried to spread baseball or football abroad until the 1990s.

The American empire's favorite games have been no good at cultural imperialism. It's a story told in one statistic: Super Bowl XLIV in 2010 briefly became the most popular TV program in American history, with 106.5 million domestic viewers, yet the media agency Futures Sport & Entertainment estimates that only 4 million people outside North America watched it.

WHILE AMERICA SLEPT: HOW SOCCER INVADED THE US

After the British Victorians spread their games, sports experienced a century of relative stability. The Indians played cricket, the US resisted soccer, and the isolated city of Melbourne favored Australian Rules football, which barely existed even in some other parts of Australia. But from the 1980s, new TV channels—free, cable, and satellite—began mushrooming almost everywhere. They took up the burden of carrying sports around the world. After Britain's Channel Four was created in 1982, for instance, it began broadcasting NFL games. They were a hit. Suddenly, there were people in Norwich or Manchester who called themselves 49ers fans. William "the Refrigerator" Perry, the supersized Chicago Bears lineman, became a cult hero in Britain. Alistair Kirkwood, the NFL's former UK managing director, fondly recalls that for a year or two in the 1980s, the Super Bowl had higher ratings in Britain than the beloved soccer program "Match of the Day" on the same weekend.

It didn't last. English soccer cleaned up its stadiums, kicked out most of its hooligans, sold its rights to Rupert Murdoch's Sky Television, and revived. Eventually, Channel Four dropped the NFL.

Meanwhile, across the ocean, soccer was slowly infecting American life. Even though the US already had four big team sports and seemed to have no need of another, in the 1970s the game came from almost nowhere to conquer American childhoods. It turned out there was a gap in the American sports market after all. The most popular sport in the US, football, was too dangerous, too male, and too expensive for mass participation. Fitting out a kid with all the necessary equipment for football costs around $300 to $400, a significant expense, especially if the child quickly decides that he doesn't like being beaten up. Today, probably fewer than a million people in the world play tackle football, compared with hundreds of millions who play at least some soccer.

Victorian British men had conceived of soccer as a "man's game." But Americans saw that it was a unisex sport, safe for girls as well as boys.

So soccer in the US became an unlikely beneficiary of feminism. It did almost as well out of another post-1960s social trend: Mexican immigration. The estimated sixty million people of Hispanic origin now living in the US (up more than threefold since 1980) outnumber the population of Spain.

The upshot is that more American children under twelve play soccer than baseball, football, and ice hockey put together. Contrary to popular opinion, soccer in America has been a success. According to a 2018 survey by Nielsen, 32 percent of the US population is either "interested" or "very interested" in soccer. The figure rises to more than 50 percent in the all-important 18–34 age demographic. The US has a strong soccer culture that is set to grow healthily in the coming decades. It's just different from any other country's soccer culture. In particular, it doesn't require a strong domestic men's professional league.

Major League Soccer is not American soccer. It's just a tiny piece of the mosaic. The combination of kids' soccer, college soccer, women's soccer, indoor soccer, Mexican, English, and Spanish soccer, the Champions League, and the World Cup dwarfs MLS. The most-watched soccer game in US history was the women's national team's victory over Japan in the World Cup final in 2015, which drew 27 million American viewers. The US men's biggest domestic audience was the 24.7 million people who saw them draw 2–2 with Portugal in a group-stage match of the 2014 World Cup. This was a bigger audience than the deciding Game Seven of the 2014 World Series, which was played in prime time. The Portugal game kicked off at 5:00 p.m. Eastern time, or 2:00 p.m. Pacific time. It would have drawn even more viewers had it kicked off in prime time (8:00 to 10:00 p.m. Eastern time). The US had the world's fourth-highest total audience figures for that World Cup, behind only Brazil, Germany, and China, says Futures Sport & Entertainment.

But you can't build a soccer culture on World Cups alone. American soccer people often fret over the MLS's marginality. As novelist Dave Eggers has noted, "Newspaper coverage of the games usually is found in the nether regions of the sports section, near the car ads and the biathlon roundups." MLS has now passed the legal drinking age in America (twenty-one), but it's metaphorically still holed up in its parents' basement, unable to stand on its own two feet. Born in 1996 to a proud

FIFA and US Soccer Federation (USSF), it was already a late developer, considering it had been meant to launch before the 1994 World Cup. It started out with ten teams, increased to twelve in 1998, and cut back to ten again in 2002 after a period of heavy financial losses. Then, like a teenager experiencing a growth spurt, it rose from fifteen teams in 2009 to twenty-eight in 2022, and plans to reach thirty well before its thirtieth birthday. In 2019, the year before the pandemic started, it announced total attendance of 8.7 million for the season, which would make it the sixth-most-popular soccer league in the world.

However, MLS remains an awkward youth, occasionally brilliant but still betraying its immaturity. The "attendance" measure in fact refers to tickets distributed. Most leagues give some tickets away, but there are claims that the MLS is exceptionally generous (e.g., in local supermarket promotions). Judge for yourself by taking a look at the Twitter account @EmptySeatsMLS.

A far bigger problem is that television viewing figures remain abysmal. Some TV ratings for MLS games "are in the realm of—or, in some cases, actually below—tractor pulls, skateboarding competitions, and bass fishing tournaments," writes Andrei Markovits, political science professor at the University of Michigan. Ratings for soccer in the US are complex, given the proliferation of channels catering to Hispanic and English-language audiences and the fact that many MLS teams have local as well as national broadcast contracts. However, ratings data are available. Here's a snapshot for the week of November 16 to 22, 2021, courtesy of livesoccertv.com. The most-watched games in the US were Liverpool-Arsenal (EPL, 877,000), Washington Spirit–Chicago Red Stars (National Women's Soccer League final, 525,000), and Cruz-Azul–Monterrey (Liga MX, 512,000). The highest-rated MLS game of the week ranked only sixth, and this at the beginning of the MLS playoffs, supposedly the pinnacle of the season. To put it another way, only 13 percent of the TV viewership for soccer in the US was for MLS.

That makes it very hard for the league to become world class. In 2021 MLS was spending around $13 million on players' salaries per team—compared with roughly $150 million in the EPL in 2019. MLS's spending was somewhere between Switzerland ($13.6 million per team) and Scotland ($10.9 million per team), the eleventh and twelfth highest spenders in Europe. MLS salaries in 2021 started at a modest $63,547 a year, with one-third of players making less than $100,000. Without a bigger broadcast contract, MLS cannot afford to put players on the field who will raise quality to the levels of the best European leagues.

So why, then, one might ask, were MLS teams valued at $550 million on average in 2021? That's a higher valuation than almost any European club outside of the continent's top twenty. The Seattle Sounders, valued at over $700 million, is considered more valuable than historic clubs such as Everton, AC Milan, and Ajax. The most credible explanation is the demographic one. It might even be as simple as the FIFA video game, which has made a generation of American kids soccer-curious. If soccer fandom grows in the US, there will be room enough for MLS alongside EPL, Liga MX, and all the rest. But viewership remains the key. With more viewers, broadcasters would pay more, enabling the teams to spend more on better players. The 2014–2022 broadcast contract worked out at something in the region of $2.5 million per team per year. As we write, MLS is hopeful of achieving a significant improvement with the next contract. Doubling the value per team seems achievable. That could raise MLS to the buying power of the Belgian Jupiler Pro League—a league that doesn't have much of a following outside of, well, Belgium. None of this is to say that MLS could not one day become a great league, just that it still has a long way to go.

But MLS is not the be-all-end-all of American soccer. The game has thrived as a pastime for wealthy kids in part precisely because there is no big soccer in the US. Many soccer moms and dads are glad that soccer is not a big professional American sport like basketball or football. Like a lot of other Americans, they are wary of big-time male American sports, whose stars tend to do lousy and unethical things like shooting their limousine drivers. Many white suburban parents see soccer as an innocent game, free of certain aspects of modern America: not violent, not drenched in money, and (reassuringly to closet or overt racists) not very Black. A large number of MLS players are white college boys. Meanwhile, soccer has penetrated most branches of the American entertainment industry, with "soccer moms" being touted as pivotal voters in presidential elections, and the *Ted Lasso* TV series notching 509 million views for its first twenty episodes.

Another piece of the American soccer mosaic, the domestic women's game, may finally be acquiring a league worthy of its national team. The NWSL, founded in 2013, is the third women's professional soccer league to be created in the US this millennium, and its beginnings were comparable with those of the previous failed leagues: a good first year followed by a struggle to maintain momentum. It seemed to languish in a media landscape managed primarily by men, but it did have a powerful weapon: the quality of female American players. The national team's triumphs in the 2015 and 2019 World Cups significantly boosted attendance in subsequent league seasons. But for years, the NWSL failed to build television viewership. Unable to sustain a long-term broadcast contract, games attracted TV audiences of less than 100,000. Only after the 2019 World Cup did the tide seem to turn. In March 2020 the league announced a three-year deal for broadcast coverage on CBS. This was the first time the network had agreed to show American professional league soccer since 1976, when Pelé was still playing in the old NASL. And then COVID-19 hit. With all sports leagues suspended, NWSL seized the opportunity to create a competition—the NWSL Challenge Cup—to be played inside a COVID bubble. In July 2020 it was the only American professional sports league on TV. Suddenly, women's professional soccer could draw audiences of 400,000—similar to and often more than that of the MLS. Some of those new viewers stuck with the league even after sports returned to a more normal schedule in 2021. Strong TV ratings culminated in an audience of more than half a million for the NWSL's championship game.

Yet another example of America's soccer diversity is the rise of clubs like Detroit City FC. Founded in 2011 by five Detroit residents who wanted to bring soccer back to the city, the club quickly gained a cult following despite playing on a high school field on which the ball did not so much bobble as alternately disappear into craters and then erupt randomly in any direction. In 2015 the club raised $750,000 to get a lease on six-thousand-seat Keyworth Stadium. Going to a game nowadays is a remarkable experience. The soccer used to be so-so but has improved significantly in recent years, and in 2022 the club is entering the professional second-tier USL Championship. The fans are already first tier, led by the Northern Guard, an informal group of two thousand or so singing, dancing, flare-toting Detroit crazies. Their performance is something to behold (to get an idea, look up "Detroit City Tetris" online). These people have managed to create a sense of community, in contrast with the more corporate major league sports. In Detroit, a city so often the subject of hard-luck stories, this is a refreshing tale. And Detroit isn't alone. Teams like Cincinnati FC and Atlanta FC have grown fast, and the MLS clubs of the Pacific Northwest—the Portland Timbers, Seattle Sounders, and Vancouver Whitecaps—have successfully cultivated a local identity. Traveling around many bits of the US, you get the sense of a vibrant soccer culture.

We shouldn't exaggerate this. Most soccer-playing American kids probably still prefer to watch the NBA or NFL. But professional soccer is gaining ground. A Gallup poll in January 2018 found that 7 percent of American adults named soccer their favorite sport to watch—the game's highest number ever, and only 2 percentage points behind baseball.

ANY GIVEN SUNDAY: IS THE NFL REALLY SO EQUAL?

When it comes to what Americans call football, it's clear that the NFL is still doing something right. Table 15.1 shows the average attendance rates of the most-watched leagues of all the world's ball games.

TABLE 15.1. Attendances in the world's largest sports leagues

	Average attendance per game	Regular season attendance
1. National Football League (2019)	66,515	16.9 million
2. German soccer, Bundesliga (2018–19)	43,449	13.3 million
3. English Premier League (2018–19)	38,168	14.5 million
4. Australian Football League (2019)	36,317	7.5 million
5. Major League Baseball (2016)	28,343	68.5 million

1 (source: http://www.espn.com/nfl/attendance/_/year/2019)

2 (source: https://www.worldfootball.net/attendance/bundesliga-2018-2019/1/)

3 (source: https://www.worldfootball.net/attendance/eng-premier-league-2018-2019/1/)

4 (source: https://www.footywire.com/afl/footy/attendances?year=2019&t=A&h=A&s=T)

5 (source: https://www.espn.com/mlb/attendance/_/year/2019)

The NFL comes out on top as measured by attendance per game, but MLB is way ahead in terms of attendance for the whole season. Aussie Rules clearly dominates in terms of attendance per capita (i.e., attendance divided by the country's population), but the Premier League is not far behind, with a rate of 26 percent for the season, compared with 5 percent for the NFL (and just 16 percent for the much-feted Bundesliga).

But measured by the number of fans inside the stadium for any given game, no other professional league on Earth can begin to rival the NFL. When people try to explain the NFL's popularity, they often mention its famous slogan: "On any given Sunday any team in our league can beat any other team." This is a boast that the Premier League would never dare make. English soccer looks horribly unbalanced, with a few rich teams almost always dominating at the top, whereas the NFL claims to be a league of equals.

Indeed, the NFL is often called "the socialist league." Its clubs share TV income equally, and 40 percent of each game's gate receipts goes to the visiting team. This aspiration to equality is a general American sporting trait. Clubs in American baseball, basketball, and the MLS also share far more of their income than European soccer does. Take the ubiquitous New York Yankees baseball cap. Outside of New York, the Yankees receive only one-thirtieth of the profit on each cap sold, the same as every other team in baseball. By contrast, Manchester United wouldn't dream of giving Brentford or Crystal Palace a cut of its shirt profits.

Many in European soccer, and particularly in England, have come to envy the NFL. English fans often complain that their sport is getting boring because the big clubs win everything. A handful of clubs—chiefly Liverpool, Chelsea, and Manchester City—dominate the Premier League and increasingly the Champions League.

As early as 2008, Andy Burnham, Britain's then culture secretary, warned that although the Premier League was "the world's most successful domestic sporting competition," it risked becoming "too predictable." He added, "I keep referring to the NFL, which has equal sharing.... In the US, the most free-market country in the world, they understand that equal distribution of money creates genuine competition."

Some others in Europe seemed to agree. People who think like this tend to accept two truisms: the NFL is much more equal than European soccer, and sports fans like equality. Unfortunately, neither of these truisms is true. First, the NFL isn't nearly as balanced as it pretends. Second, we have data to show that, overall, fans prefer unbalanced leagues.

At first glance, you could be forgiven for believing that the NFL is really much more equal than the Premier League. In the decade through 2021, eight different teams won the Super Bowl. In the same period, only five teams won the Premier League, including the extraordinary case of Leicester in 2016. On any given Sunday (or Saturday lunchtime, Tuesday night, whenever), Burnley or Watford can beat Chelsea, but the fact is that they usually don't.

But is the NFL much more equal than the Premier League? Does it have a more even distribution of wins? Measuring the level of equality in both leagues is tricky, first because there are almost no ties in the NFL and second because the NFL's regular season consists of just sixteen games, whereas the Premier League's season has thirty-eight. In any given season, a weak English team has many more chances to get lucky.

Happily, there is a way to allow for these differences so that we can compare the two leagues. We will do this by dreaming up another league, a totally equal one in which every team always has an equal chance of winning any given game. This equal league would be a league of coin flips. Obviously, in the coin-flip league, each team would be expected to win an average of 50 percent of its games. Even so, the outcome of any sixteen- or thirty-eight-game sequence would produce some random inequalities. Hardly any team in the coin-flip league would win exactly half its games. Rather, the win percentages for the season would be randomly dispersed around 50 percent. The question then is, which looks more like the totally equal coin-flip league, the NFL or the Premier League?

To work this out, we must calculate how random the dispersion of wins is in each of our three leagues. The measure of dispersion is commonly called the standard deviation. Let's calculate standard deviation for the coin-flip league and then for the NFL and the Premier League. (And please feel free to skip the next few paragraphs if you aren't interested in the math.)

To calculate the standard deviation of win percentages for any league, we first take the difference between each team's win percentage and 50 percent (the difference will be positive when the team has a winning season, negative for a losing season). Then we square the difference, to make sure pluses and minuses don't cancel out. Next we add up the difference for all teams in the league and take the square root. That gives a number that is comparable with the average win percentage.

Now we are ready to find the figure we want: the standard deviation, or dispersion of win percentages. If our average win percentage is fifty, a standard deviation of one would mean that most teams are close to the average. If the standard deviation was twenty, it would mean that there is quite a lot of dispersion. In coin-tossing leagues, we know what the standard deviation should be: close to half of the reciprocal of the square root of the number of games played. This is easy to calculate. If you play sixteen games, the square root is four, the reciprocal is one-quarter, and half of that is one-eighth, or 12.5 percent.

That is what the standard deviation of win percentage in the NFL would be if on any given Sunday any team in the league really had a fifty-fifty chance of beating its opponent. Well, the NFL is not a coin-tossing league. In the decade from 2011 through 2020, the standard deviation of win-loss records has fluctuated between 18 percent and 21 percent, and has averaged 19.5 percent. That's well above the 12.5 percent of the coin-tossing league.

The Premier League is only slightly less equal than the NFL. If the Premier League were a coin-tossing league, the expected standard deviation would be just over 8 percent. In fact, in the decade from 2011–2012 through 2020–2021, the Premier League's standard deviation averaged 15.2 percent. So it's not a coin-tossing league, either, but the difference is not much greater than for the NFL. To put it another way, the NFL has a standard deviation about 56 percent larger than a coin-tossing league, while the English Premier League's is about 87 percent larger than a coin-tossing league. This is a difference, but in the scale of things not a very big one. Moreover, there's a lot more variation from year to year in the Premier League ratio, and in some seasons (2011, for instance) it actually looks more balanced than the NFL on this measure.

You might object that even if there isn't a huge difference in the statistical balance of the NFL and Premier League, the identities of the dominant teams and doormats change each season in the NFL but not in the Premier League. After all, each season the worst NFL team gets the first draft pick, a very large human being who is in fact a device for bouncing back. Sudden reversals of fortune are much more likely in the NFL. In 2011 the Indianapolis Colts, having been dominant for a decade, endured a season with only two wins after their star quarterback Peyton Manning was injured. This dismal record was rewarded with first pick of the 2012 draft. They chose the Stanford graduate Andrew Luck, thought to be one of the best quarterback prospects to come out of college in recent years. This allowed them to start winning again the following season. As the distinguished "Chicago school" economists Sherwin Rosen and Allen Sanderson pointed out, the Premier League punishes failure, but the NFL rewards it.

But for all the NFL's efforts, the identities of winners and losers are pretty stable in both leagues. The best team in the NFL, the New England Patriots, won 74 percent of its regular-season games from 2011 through 2020. The Green Bay Packers and Seattle Seahawks each won 66 percent in that period, and the Pittsburgh Steelers 64 percent. Well, in the same decade in the Premier League, Manchester City won 76 percent, Liverpool and Manchester United 68 percent, and Chelsea 67 percent (treating ties as half a win). In other words, in both the EPL and NFL one team has been dominant for a decade and three other teams in each league have approached dominance. It's hard to say on that basis which league is more balanced.

Likewise, there are as many losers in the NFL as in the Premier League. From 2011 through 2020, the Jacksonville Jaguars achieved a pitiful win percentage of 27.5 percent. Over the same number of seasons, only one team in the EPL was worse (Huddersfield Town), but there's a difference. Calamitous teams in the Premier League get relegated— Huddersfield narrowly survived its first season and was relegated the next—whereas the Jaguars sustained their peculiar brand of misery for a decade.

So the NFL isn't much more equal than the Premier League. It just looks like it is. It manages to appear more equal thanks largely to randomization devices which ensure that the best team doesn't always win the Super Bowl: the small number of regular-season games and the playoffs. Both these devices ensure that no NFL team is likely to dominate for years like Manchester United did in the Ferguson era. However, this randomization comes at the expense of justice. Fans often feel that the best team in the NFL did not win the Super Bowl. In fact, the NFL looks a lot like the Champions League, where the knockout rounds add a random element that often ambushes the best team.

This disposes of our first truism: the claim that the NFL is much more equal than the Premier League. What about the second one: the notion that sports fans, like French revolutionaries, desire equality?

If fans want all teams to be equal, then they will shun games in which results are predictable. If so, more of them will watch games whose outcomes are very uncertain. How to test whether fans really behave like that? Researchers have tried to gauge expected outcomes of games either by using prematch betting odds or the form of both teams over the previous half-dozen games. Studies of soccer, mostly in England, show mixed results. Some studies find that more-balanced games attract more fans. Others find the reverse.

The British economists David Forrest of Salford Business School and Robert Simmons of Lancaster University have done some of the best work in this field. They found that a balanced English game could sometimes increase attendance. However, they also carried out a simulation to show that if the English leagues became more balanced, they would attract fewer fans. That is because a balanced league, in which all teams are equally good, would turn into an almost interminable procession of home wins. By contrast, in real existing soccer, some of the most balanced games occur when a weak team plays at home against a strong team (Southampton versus Manchester United, for instance).

Forrest and Simmons found that the people who care most about competitive balance are television viewers. The spectators at the grounds tend to be the hard core: they simply want to see their team. However, most TV viewers are "floating voters." When the outcome of a game seems too predictable, they switch off. The two economists found that the closer a televised English soccer game was expected to be (measured by the form of both teams going into the game), the higher the viewing figures on Sky TV in Britain. Still, the size of this effect was modest. Forrest and Simmons said that even if the Premier League were perfectly balanced (in the sense that each team had an equal probability of winning each game), TV audiences would rise by only 6 percent. That would be a small effect for such a revolutionary change.

A moment's thought suggests why some unequal games might be very attractive. Most fans in the stadium are fans of the home team, so they do not really want a balanced outcome. Often, the most-attractive games involve strong home teams playing weak visiting teams (Manchester United versus Southampton, again), in which case the home team typically has a lot of supporters who enjoy watching their heroes score a lot of goals, or they are games between weak home teams and strong away teams (Southampton versus Manchester United), in which local fans come to see the visiting stars.

Furthermore, big teams have more fans than small ones, so if Manchester United beats Southampton, more people are happy than if Southampton wins. Also, fans are surprisingly good at losing. Psychological studies show that they are skilled at transferring blame: "We played well, but the referee was garbage." This means that fans will often stick with a team even if it always loses. It also explains why, the morning after their team gets knocked out of the World Cup, people don't sink into depression but instead get on with their lives.

Last, dominant teams create a special interest of their own. In the era of Manchester United's dominance under Ferguson, millions of people supported the club, and millions of others despised it. In a way, both groups were following United. The club was the star of English soccer's soap opera. Everyone else dreamed of beating it. Much of the meaning of supporting a smaller club like West Ham, for instance, derived from disliking Manchester United. Kevin Keegan, when he was chasing the title as manager of Newcastle in 1996, thrillingly captured that national sentiment with his famous "I will love it if we beat them! Love it!" monologue. (United beat him instead.) Ferguson's big bad United made the Premier League more fun.

Another way of looking at competitive balance is to view the league as a whole, rather than match by match. Do more spectators come when the title race is exciting than when one team runs away with it?

It turns out that a thrilling title race does little to improve attendance. English fans will watch their teams play in the league even when they don't have a hope of winning it (or else dozens of English clubs would not exist).

It is true that a game has to be significant to draw fans, but that significance need not have anything to do with winning the title. A study by

Stephen Dobson and John Goddard showed that when a match matters more either for winning the league or for avoiding relegation to a lower league, then attendance tends to rise. In every soccer league in Europe the bottom few teams are "relegated" at the end of the season to a lower tier. The worst three teams in the Premier League, for instance, drop to the Championship. It's as if the cellar teams in Major League Baseball got exiled to Triple A. Relegation is brutal, but the device has a genius to it. The annual English relegation battle boosts fans' interest to the point that teams at the bottom often outdraw teams at the top as the season comes to an end. The NFL, too, could do with a system of relegation. It could replace losers with rising teams. This would be in the fans' interest, but not in the owners'.

Fans need a reason to care. Most matches in the Premier League are significant for something or other, even if it's only qualifying for European competition. Given that games can be significant in many different ways, it is unclear why a more balanced Premier League would create more significance.

There is also a third way of looking at balance: the long term. Does the dominance of the same teams year in, year out, turn fans off?

Let's compare a long period with dominance in English soccer with a long period without dominance: the fairly equal era that ran from 1949 to 1968, and the "unfair" era of the Premier League from 1993 to 2012.

In the first, "equal" twenty-year period, eleven different teams won the English league. The most frequent champion, Manchester United, won five titles in the period. The second period was far more predictable: only five teams won the title, with United taking it thirteen times. Yet during the first "equal" period, total annual attendance in the top division fell from an all-time high of eighteen million in 1949 to only fifteen million in 1968 (and even that figure got a temporary boost from England winning the World Cup in 1966). During the second, "unequal" period, total attendance rose from below ten million to more than thirteen million, even though tickets became much more expensive and people had many more choices of how to spend their free time.

Anyone who dismisses the Premier League as "one of the most boring leagues in the world" (in Keegan's words), a closed shop that shuts out smaller clubs from the lower divisions, has to explain why so many people now watch all levels of English league football. In the 2009–2010 season, in the pits of recession, more than thirty million spectators paid to see professional games in England, "a level not seen since well before the introduction of all seated stadia [in the early 1990s]," commented Dan Jones of Deloitte's Sports Business Group. The Premier League pulled fans even though, as Keegan noted, everyone knew the top finishers in advance. Yet more than half of those thirty-million-plus spectators watched the Football League, the three divisions below the Premier League. In fact, the Football League that season drew its biggest crowds in fifty years. The clubs in the Championship, the second tier of English soccer, have supposedly been doomed to irrelevance by Manchester City and can only dream of one day clinging on at the bottom of the Premier League, yet their division in 2018–2019 was the third-best-attended league in Europe, ranked by total number of spectators: more than Italy's Serie A and more than Spain's top division.

The Premier League's inequality coexists with rising crowds, revenues, and global interest, not least from North American businessmen schooled in American major league sports: notably, the Glazer family at United itself, Stan Kroenke at Arsenal, and John Henry at Liverpool. These people do not seem too worried about competitive balance in English soccer.

Some of English soccer's critics have not digested these facts. When we pointed out to Michel Platini at UEFA's headquarters on Lake Geneva in 2008 that English stadiums are full nowadays, he replied, "Not all. They're full at the teams that win." This argument is often made but flawed nonetheless. Whenever rows of empty seats appear at the grounds of struggling teams, it is back-page news and regarded as ominous for the Premier League as a whole. But it's a constant of soccer history that some fans desert disappointing teams in small towns (especially during a recession), whereas others flock to exciting ones. Tottenham, Arsenal, Manchester United, and other clubs have built bigger stadiums and filled them. Some clubs, such as Liverpool and Manchester City, have expanded capacity. West Ham has enjoyed the windfall of a brand-new Olympic stadium.

Not every English team has gained spectators since 1992–1993, but most have. All twenty clubs in the Premier League in 2018–2019 had a higher average attendance than in 1992–1993. If the team had been in the Premier League in 1992, the average increase was 98 percent; if it had risen from a lower division, the attendance more than doubled. Half of the teams that were in the Premier League in 1992–1993 but not in 2018–2019 had higher attendance. Of the seventy-eight clubs present in the four top divisions in both seasons, sixty-four had higher attendance. The rising English tide lifted almost all boats.

Admittedly, today's large crowds don't in themselves prove that dominance attracts fans. After all, many other things have changed in England since the more equal 1949–1968 period. Crucially, the country's stadiums have improved. However, the rising attendance rates do make it hard to believe that dominance in itself significantly undermines interest. Indeed, pretty much every soccer league in Europe exhibits more dominance than the American major leagues, yet fans still go.

WHY DAVID BEAT GOLIATH

Strangely, it was the British fanzine *When Saturday Comes* (WSC) that best expressed the joys of an unbalanced league. WSC is, in large part, the journal of small clubs. It publishes moving and funny pieces by fans of minnows like Crewe or Swansea. Few of its readers have much sympathy with Manchester United (though some, inevitably, are United fans). Many of WSC's writers have argued for a fairer league. Yet in 2008, Ian Plenderleith, a contributor living outside Washington, DC, argued in WSC that America's MLS, in which "all teams started equal, with the same squad size, and the same amount of money to spread among its players' wages," was boring. The reason: "No truly memorable teams have the space to develop." The "MLS is crying out for a couple of big, successful teams," Plenderleith admitted. "Teams you can hate. Dynasties you really, really want to beat. Right now, as LA Galaxy coach Bruce Arena once memorably said: 'It's a crapshoot.'"

In short, the MLS lacks one of the joys of an unbalanced league: the David versus Goliath match. And one reason that fans enjoy those encounters is, surprisingly often, given their respective budgets, the Davids win. The economist Jack Hirshleifer called this phenomenon "the paradox of power." Imagine, he said, that there are two tribes, one large, one small. Each can devote its efforts to just two activities, farming and fighting. Each tribe produces its own food through farming and steals the other tribe's food through fighting. Which tribe will devote a larger share of its efforts to fighting?

The answer is the small tribe. The best way to understand this is to imagine that the small tribe is very small indeed. It would then have to devote almost all its limited resources to either fighting or farming. If it chose farming, it would be vulnerable to attack. Everything it produced could be stolen. On the other hand, if the tribe devoted all its resources to fighting, it would have at least a chance of stealing some resources. So Hirshleifer concludes—and proves with a mathematical model—that smaller competitors will tend to devote a greater share of resources to competitive activities.

He found many real-world examples of the paradox of power. He liked citing Vietnam's defeat of the US, but one might also add to the list the Afghan resistance to the Soviet Union in the 1980s and the US in this century, the Dutch resistance to the Spanish in the sixteenth century, or the American resistance to the British in the Revolutionary War. In these cases the little guy actually defeated the big guy. In many other cases the little guy was eventually defeated, but at much greater cost than might have been expected based on physical resources (the Spartans at Thermopylae, the Afrikaners in the Boer War, the Texans at the Alamo).

In soccer, as in war, the underdog tends to try harder. Big teams fight more big battles, so each big contest weighs slightly less heavily than it does for their smaller rivals. Little teams understand that they may have few opportunities to compete at the highest level, so they give it everything. They therefore probably win more often than you would predict based on ability alone.

NOTHING WORSE THAN NEW MONEY

Fans enjoy unbalanced modern soccer. Yet the complaints about its imbalance continue. The curious thing is that these complaints are relatively new, a product of the past fifteen or so years. Contrary to popular opinion, soccer was unbalanced in the past, too, but before the 1990s fewer people protested.

It is a fantasy that Europe was ever a very balanced soccer continent. In smaller countries, clubs from the capital have tended to rule. The Italian league was always dominated by Juventus, Milan, and Inter, and the Spanish league by Barcelona and Real Madrid. By the 1980s, Bayern Munich controlled the Bundesliga, and in the postwar era, English soccer has mostly been dominated by Manchester United, Arsenal, and Liverpool. United's thirteen titles in the twenty seasons through 2013 may sound boring, but Liverpool won ten in twenty between 1969 and 1988. Almost all other clubs are so firmly excluded from power that even very big Newcastle has not won the title since 1927. The imbalance in England, as in all European leagues, was reinforced by the European Cup (now the Champions League), which handed the dominant teams more money.

The old European Cup was seldom much fairer than the Champions League is now. We saw earlier in the book that only between 1970 and 1981 did clubs from modest-size towns regularly win the trophy. Usually, the cup went to the biggest provincial cities, or to Madrid. Even Platini admitted to us, "For forty years it's been the biggest clubs that won the Champions League; when I played, too. With or without homegrown players, it was Real Madrid, Liverpool, Manchester, Juventus who won. English clubs won the cup ten times in a row, I think. No? In the 1980s."

Oh, dear. Platini won't be spending his retirement (after that ban from soccer for taking Blatter's bribe) winning pub quizzes. In fact, English clubs won six straight European Cups from 1977 through 1982. But his point stands: inequality in European soccer is nothing new.

Platini smiled, thinking again of that English dominance in the 1980s: "It's funny. There were no great debates then, saying, 'We have to change everything.' Today it's the money that makes the difference."

That is precisely the point. Today's inequality in soccer bothers people not because it is unprecedented but because it is more driven by money than it used to be. In the old days, a middling soccer team could suddenly enjoy years of dominance if it happened to hire an excellent manager who signed excellent players. That's what happened in the 1970s to Liverpool under Bill Shankly and to Nottingham Forest under Brian Clough. Today, a middling team can suddenly enjoy years of dominance if it happens to be bought by a billionaire who hires an excellent manager who signs excellent players. That is what happened to Chelsea under Abramovich. So inequality in soccer, in addition to not being boring, is not even new. All that's new is the money.

Many people feel that inequality becomes unfair when it is bought with money. It disgusts them that Chelsea (or the New York Yankees) can sign the best players simply because it is a rich club. This is a moral argument. It's a form of idealistic egalitarianism, which says that all teams should have more or less equal resources. This stance may be morally right (we cannot judge), but it is not a practical political agenda, and it probably doesn't reflect what most soccer fans want. Spectators vote with their feet. It's certainly not the case that millions of them are abandoning the Premier League because the money offends them. Based on the evidence of what they go to watch, they want to see the best players competing against one another. Many people find the big clubs evil. Not many seem to find them boring.

COUCH POTATOES AND THE STRUGGLE FOR WORLD DOMINATION

Not long ago, there was very little money in soccer. By the 1970s, most Western Europeans had acquired TV sets (except in Spain, where in 1970 only 28 percent of households had one). However, they hardly ever used those TVs for watching soccer. Europe's state broadcasters of the day barely screened the game. In most countries it wasn't possible to watch regular league competition, week in, week out, in the way that American viewers could watch baseball or gridiron football. European sponsors weren't very interested in soccer, so almost the only people putting money into the sport were the ones showing up on the weekend at their local club's run-down stadium. In 1974 the total income of all of European professional soccer was probably a bit over $200 million. That made it a slightly bigger business than American Major League Baseball ($153 million) or the National Football League ($172 million), but it was a little amoeba compared to Hollywood. In 1974 total box-office receipts for the movie industry in the US alone were $1.9 billion. In 1980 the average NFL team still had nearly as much income each year as all the clubs in the English top division put together.

Today, things are different. There is an economic momentum behind sports as a whole. Once upon a time, athletes wanted to be seen with movie stars, but now the roles have reversed. And European soccer has become preeminent in global sports. It now generates more money than football (NFL and college) combined (see Table 15.2).

You could quibble with these numbers. If you add in high school football, there's probably a few billion more on the US side. The NFL remains the largest single league by revenue, with a largish lead over the English Premier League, but the gap is shrinking. In 2019–2020 the average Premier League team earned about £125 million a year from TV, equaling around $160 million, while its NFL counterpart received about $255 million in shared broadcast revenue. This is fairly impressive given that England has about 275 million fewer inhabitants than the US. And before long the English might even pull ahead as they finally start making big money out of the global market. One day we might see English soccer club owners buying NFL teams.

American sports have been trying to fight back. Sometime in the early 2000s, when Paul Tagliabue was NFL commissioner, he told the team owners something like this: "You have to ask yourself, 'Do you want a potential fan base of 400 million or 4 billion in twenty or thirty years?'" His point was that if they wanted 4 billion, they'd have to find them abroad.

Ever since then, the American and British empires have been locked in sporting combat. The NFL's game in London has become an annual ritual.

The market in sports fans has become more global. This means that a century-old model of fandom—the man who supports the hometown

TABLE 15.2. Estimates of industry sales

Industry	Annual revenue in billions of dollars (2019)
European soccer	32.7
US collegiate sports (mainly football and basketball)	18.9
National Football League	16
Hollywood (US) and Canada box office receipts	11.4

team he inherited from his father—is collapsing. The new globalized sports fan might almost equally well be a woman, and she may happily snub her local domestic league. If you live in London and you like football, you probably support an NFL team rather than some bunch of no-hopers playing on a converted rugby field a few miles from your house. Similarly, if you live in the US and like soccer, you are more likely to support Manchester United than your local MLS or NWSL team, which in any case may be hundreds of miles from your house. Even in Argentina, with its great historic soccer clubs, people increasingly watch the English Premier League on TV. That's all the more true in the US, China, and Japan, countries whose soccer fans mostly came of age during the second wave of sporting globalization.

These people want to see the real thing. Global fans want global leagues. For most of them, that means the NBA, the NFL, or the Premier League. It was therefore wrong to imagine that David Beckham could save American soccer by joining LA Galaxy in 2007. The cliché was that his task was to "put soccer on the map" in America. In fact, this was impossible because soccer was already "on the map" in America. American soccer may not be very big, but it's alive and well and lying on the sofa watching either (a) LigaMX on Univision Deportes (if you're Hispanic) or (b) Liverpool on Peacock.

The Premier League is going to spread ever further, and the NFL will try to. This struggle won't be fought to the death. There is room for them both. "I personally don't know anybody who follows only one sport and nothing else," Kirkwood, the NFL's then UK managing director, told us years ago. "I don't think it's as competitive as it looks. We don't have a vision of being a top-three sport in Britain. If you go into a big enough market, you can carve a niche. So you can be an Arsenal fan and a New York Giants fan."

Some Arsenal fans have probably become Giants fans, but we suspect that a lot more Giants fans are becoming Arsenal fans. Long after the sun set on the British Empire, it is achieving a posthumous victory in sports.

16

ARE SOCCER FANS POLYGAMISTS?

A Critique of the Nick Hornby Model of Fandom

Just this one afternoon started the whole thing off—there was no prolonged courtship....In a desperate and percipient attempt to stop the inevitable, Dad quickly took me to Spurs to see Jimmy Greaves score four against Sunderland in a 5–1 win, but the damage had been done, and the six goals and all the great players left me cold: I'd already fallen for the team that beat Stoke 1–0 from a penalty rebound.

—Nick Hornby in *Fever Pitch* (1992), on the
origin of his lifelong love of Arsenal

Fever Pitch is a wonderful memoir, the most influential soccer book ever written, and an important source for our image of the soccer fan. The "Fan," as most Britons in particular have come to think of him, is a creature tied for life to the club he first "fell for" as a child. Hornby says that his love of Arsenal has lasted "longer than any relationship I have made of my own free will." But is Hornby's "Fan" found much in real life? Or are most British soccer supporters much less loyal than the world imagines them to be?

Let's start with Hornby's version because it is the accepted story of the British Fan (and a story that is told to greater or lesser degree in most countries with a long soccer tradition). As far as life allows, the Horn-byesque Fan sees all of his club's home games. (It's accepted even in the rhetoric of fandom that traveling to away games is best left to unmarried men under the age of twenty-five.) No matter how bad his team gets, the Fan cannot abandon it. When Hornby watched the Arsenal of the late 1960s with his dad, the team's incompetence shamed him, but he could not leave: "I was chained to Arsenal and my dad was chained to me, and there was no way out for any of us."

Chained is a very Hornbyesque word for a Fan's feelings for his club. Often, the Fan uses metaphors from drugs (*hooked*) or romantic love (*relationship, fell for*). Indeed, some adult Englishmen who would hardly dare tell their wives that they love them will happily appear in public singing of their love for a club or for a player who would snub them in a nightclub if they ever managed to sneak past his entourage.

No wonder the Fan's loyalty to his club is sometimes described as a bond stronger than marriage. Rick Parry, chief executive of the Premier League in the 1990s, recited the then dominant cliché about fandom: "You can change your job, you can change your wife, but you can't change your soccer team.... You can move from one end of the country to another, but you never, ever lose your allegiance to your first team. That's what English soccer is all about. It's about fierce loyalty, about dedication." (The Argentine variant: "You can change your wife—but your club and your mother, never.") Recently, soccer officials trying to emphasize the strength of club brands have modified the cliché: you can change your gender, the officials say, but not your club.

Ideally, the Hornbyesque Fan supports his local team (even if Hornby did not). This gives the Fan roots, a sense of belonging. In a wonderful essay on fandom in the highbrow journal *Prospect*, Gideon Rachman quotes an archetypal declaration of faith from a Carlisle Fan named Charles Burgess, who wrote in the *Guardian* that "there never was any choice. My dad...took me down to Brunton Park to watch the derby match against Workington Town just after Christmas 41 years ago—I was hooked and have been ever since.... My support has been about who we are and where we are from."

In his day job, Rachman is a commentator on international politics in the *Financial Times*, but his essay in *Prospect* is a key text in the British debate about fandom. It is the anti–*Fever Pitch*. In it, Rachman outs himself as a "fair-weather fan, an allegiance-switcher," who at different times in his life has supported Chelsea, QPR, and Spurs. So casual are his allegiances that he registered with FIFA for the World Cup of 2006 as an Ivory Coast supporter, figuring that he wouldn't face as much competition for tickets. He got into every round including the final. He went to the World Cup in South Africa as a registered Paraguay fan.

Rachman treats the passions of Hornbyesque Fans as slightly bizarre. After all, in England a Fan's choice of team is largely random. Few clubs have particular religious or class affiliations, and few English people have an attachment dating back generations to any particular location. Some children become Fans of their local team, however terrible it might be, but if you live in a rural part of England like Cornwall, you may have no local team, whereas if you live in London or around Manchester, you will have many. As Rachman asks, "Why devote a huge amount of emotion to favoring one part of west London over another?"

Nonetheless, the Hornbyesque Fan is a widely admired figure in Britain, at least among men. Whereas *fanatic* is usually a pejorative word, a Fan is someone who has roots somewhere. As we will argue later, this respect is connected to the quirks of British history: in Britain, roots of any kind are in short supply.

However, our first question is this: How true is the Hornby model of fandom? Does it really describe the way most British fans feel about their clubs?

THE CHINESE SERIAL FAN

Very little is known about sports fans who are not hooligans. The academics D. L. Wann and M. A. Hamlet estimated in 1995 that only 4 percent of research on sports concentrated on the spectator.

So we start our quest into the nature of fandom with only one or two fairly safe premises. One is that foreign fans of English clubs, at least, are not all monogamous in their devotion. Rowan Simons explains in *Bamboo Goalposts*, his book about Chinese soccer, that many Chinese fans support "a number of rival teams at the same time" and are always changing their favorite club. Simons adds, "So dominant is the serial supporter in China that it is quite rare to find a fan with a real unflinching loyalty to one team."

The market researchers Sport+Markt found polling data to back up Simons's claim. Sport+Markt noted that since the late 1990s, hordes of new fans around the world—including many women—have come to soccer without long-standing loyalties. A lot of these people appear to be "serial supporters" who probably support Manchester United and Liverpool, or Real Madrid and Barcelona, simultaneously. No wonder that clubs like United or Real keep changing their guesses as to how many fans they have worldwide. Table 16.1 presents a few of United's estimates from the past few years.

None of these estimates are necessarily wrong. There may well be 659 million people on Earth who have feelings for Manchester United. However, few of these "fans" are likely to be lifelong Hornbyesque devotees. Jose Angel Sanchez, now director general of Real Madrid, a club with its own share of foreign serial supporters, thought that many of these serial fans might eventually evolve into Hornbys. He told us in 2003, "We used to say that the chances of changing your team is less than changing your partner or even your sex. But the way that people enter soccer in Asia is different: they enter through the stars. But this will not stay this way, in my opinion." Well, perhaps.

Surely, British fans are a lot more loyal than those fickle Chinese supporters, right? Unfortunately, polling suggests otherwise. In 2008 Sport+Markt found that Chelsea had 2.4 million "fans" in Britain. Again according to Sport+Markt, that represented a rise of 523 percent in the five years since Roman Abramovich had bought the club. Yet even that figure of 2.4 million represented a swift decline: in 2006, when, no

TABLE 16.1. Fan estimates for Manchester United

Year	Estimated fans	Source
2003	75 million	Mori
2007	About 90 million	Manchester United
2008	333 million (including 139 million "core fans")	TNS Sport
2012	659 million	Kantar

doubt coincidentally, Chelsea had just won the league twice running, Sport+Markt credited the club with a mammoth 3.8 million British fans.

Again, we are not saying that Sport+Markt's figures were wrong. Rather, its premise was. To serial supporters, the question "Which is your preferred soccer club?" does not make sense. It presumes that everyone who likes soccer is a one-club Hornbyesque Fan. Instead, researchers should be asking, "Which are your preferred soccer clubs?" After all, a very large proportion of people who like soccer are polygamous consumers. One of the authors of this book, Stefan, as a Saturday-morning coach of grade-school children, saw the color of the shirts switch from red to blue and back again depending on who last won the league. It's likely that fantasy soccer leagues encourage this behavior: you can easily end up rooting for the players in your fantasy team, no matter which clubs they play for. Newly rising clubs (such as Chelsea in the early 2000s) are particularly prone to attracting short-term fans, a Sport+Markt executive told us. Clubs like Liverpool or Manchester United, with more long-standing brands, tend to have more loyal long-term supporters, he added. In fact, the likes of Manchester United are likely to have both far more Hornbys and far more casual fans than other clubs. But detractors of United tend to seize upon the hordes of casual fans and don't mention the Hornbys.

Hornby himself recognized the prevalence of casual fans in soccer. Many of the people who pop up briefly in the pages of *Fever Pitch* enjoy the game but are not wedded to a particular club. Hornby calls this type the "sod-that-for-a-lark floating punter" and speaks of it with admiration: "I would like to be one of those people who treat their local team like their local restaurant, and thus withdraw their patronage if they are being served up noxious rubbish."

SPECTATORS: THE HARD CORE

We know there are, broadly speaking, two types of soccer fan: the Hornbys and the sod-that-for-a-lark floating punters. We know that the sod-that-for-a-lark people are heavily represented among foreign fans of clubs like United and even seem to be pretty common in Britain. By 2006, if we can believe Sport+Markt's figures, about 90 percent of Chelsea's British fans were people who had not supported them in 2003. No doubt, clubs like Hartlepool have a higher percentage of devoted Hornbys among their fans, but then clubs like Hartlepool don't have many fans full stop.

One might carp that the sod-that-for-a-lark lot are mostly just armchair fans and that "real" fans tend to be Hornbys. However, it would be wrong to dismiss armchair fans as irrelevant. The overwhelming majority of soccer fans in Britain are armchair fans, in the sense that they hardly ever go to games. According to a survey by the market researcher Kantar Media in 2016, about 36 percent of Britons describe themselves as soccer fans. Yet average weekly attendance figures of all professional clubs in England and Scotland equal only about 3 percent of the population. In other words, most of the country's soccer fans rarely or never enter soccer stadiums.

In 1997 Fletcher Research, in one of the first serious market analyses of English soccer, found that only about 5 percent of supporters of Premier League clubs attend even one match in an average season. If only a small minority of soccer fans get to the stadium at all, even fewer see every single home game for years on end, as Hornby did.

Most soccer fans are armchair supporters. If we want to unearth the Hornbys, we need to concentrate on the elite of fans who actually go to games: the spectators.

We know that in the Premier League, at least, most spectators now watch every home game that their club plays. Often they have to: at the most successful clubs, only season-ticket holders can get seats. Many of these regular spectators may be sod-that-for-a-lark punters at heart who have been enticed by ticketing policies to show up every week. However, it's among this group of week-in and week-out spectators that we must look for the small hard core of lifelong Hornbys in English soccer. At moments of high emotion, the TV cameras like to zoom in on spectators in the stands—heads in hands, or hugging their friends—as if these people incarnated the feelings of the club's millions of supporters. They don't. Rather, they are the exceptions, the fanatical few who bother to go to games. Some of these spectators presumably support their club "through thick and thin," watching them unto eternity like Hornby does.

At least, that is the theory. But we studied attendance numbers in English soccer over the past sixty years and found that even among the actual spectators, a startlingly high proportion appeared to be sod-that-for-a-lark types.

Nobody seems to have tried before to calculate how many British fans are Hornbys. Yet the figures required to make some sort of estimate do exist. That marvelous website www.european-football-statistics.co.uk has statistics on attendance rates and league performance for all clubs in the top four divisions of English soccer since 1947. Using these data, we can find out (a) the annual mortality rate of soccer spectators—that is, how many of the people who watched last season don't come back the next?—and (b) the sensitivity of new spectators to the success of teams. Do most newcomers flock to Chelsea when it wins the league?

Our model is based on some fundamental truths of soccer fandom. Generally speaking, teams cannot have very loyal Hornbyesque Fans (that is, a low mortality rate) and at the same time be capable of attracting large numbers of new spectators when they are successful. If most of the crowd consisted of Hornbys who never gave up their seats, then when a team did well, there would be no room in the stadium for all the new fans who wanted to watch them. So floating supporters can get tickets only if the mortality rate of the existing spectators is high enough.

Previous studies have shown that a club's attendance tends to rise and fall with its league position. (The rare exceptions include Newcastle, Sunderland, and the Manchester City of the late 1990s, when bad results failed to deter spectators.) In our data for the sixty-one-year period from 1947 through 2008, there were 4,454 changes in clubs' final league position. The average club moves six or seven league positions a year. In 64 percent of the cases where the club rose in the league, its home crowd increased, too. In 74 percent of the "down" years, home attendance fell. This means that 69 percent of all cases confirmed the simple hypothesis that fans respond to performance. Simply put: there is a market in soccer spectators. The few academics who study fandom—most of them in the US—explain the fans' motives through the psychological phenomenon of "BIRGing," or "basking in reflected glory."

To account for the ebb and flow of English soccer fans, we have constructed a very simple model. It consists of two elements that are logically connected to each other. First, there are the "new fans" coming into the game. New fans are estimated as the difference between the total attendance for the season and the number of loyal fans left over from the previous season. We divide new fans into two groups: the BIRGers, who come to watch the team depending on its success, and those who come for reasons we can't explain. We will treat these reasons as random factors, although each person probably had a good reason to come to the game at the time—a friend invited them, a partner left them, or some such.

The second element of our model is the "loyal fans": those who came back from the previous season. Loyal fans are estimated as the difference between the total attendance for the season and the new fans entering the game. Of course, the difference between the loyal fans plus the new fans and last season's attendance is the "lost fans." We can think of these lost fans as falling into two groups as well: the BIRGers who were lost to the club because its performance declined and those who were lost for other reasons that we cannot measure (got back together with partner, took up DIY, or whatever).

So,

Total fans = loyal fans from last year
+ fans sensitive to winning
+ random fans

In our model we estimate the shares of loyal fans and fans sensitive to winning by minimizing the number of random fans. We minimize random fans precisely because we think that most fans go for a reason: either loyalty or BIRGing. Randomness surely plays a relatively small role.

Now, we are not claiming that we can identify new fans, loyal fans, and lost fans individually. However, we can identify these categories in a statistical sense, as groups. We know how many people are in each group even if we do not know their names.

Our model produces two results. First, it gives us an estimate of the BIRGers: the fraction of new fans that a team can expect to attract as a result of the position it achieves in the league. Looking at the annual changes in attendance figures, we found that spectators are only mildly sensitive to a team's performance. Our estimates implied that the club that won the Premier League would attract 2.5 percent of all new spectators entering the league the next season (presuming there was space in the club's stadium). However, a team that finished at the bottom of the Premier League, or at the top of the Championship (English soccer's second tier), does almost as well: it attracts 2 percent of all the league's new spectators. Teams in the middle of the four divisions (that is, those ranked around forty-sixth in England) would attract 1 percent of all new spectators, whereas teams at the very bottom of the fourth tier would attract almost nobody. In short, while new spectators do like success, the vast majority of them are not simple BIRGers, glory hunters. Judging by the ebb and flow of crowds over the sixty-one years through 2008, most people seem to go to a plausible club playing near their home.

That is the profile of the newcomers. But how much of last year's crowd do they replace? What is the mortality rate of the existing spectators?

We know how many spectators each club lost or gained, season by season, for sixty-one years. We also know how many spectators the league as a whole lost or gained. That means that for every club, we can calculate the average percentage of spectators at a given game one season who would not attend that same fixture the next season. And the percentage that fits the data best: 50. Yes, on average in the postwar era, half of all spectators in English soccer did not take their seats again for the equivalent match the next season.

Let's be clear about what exactly we are saying. Imagine that Bristol City plays Preston one season, in front of 15,000 spectators. The next season, for the same fixture, even if there are again 15,000 spectators, half of them would typically be people who had not seen the previous year's match. Of last year's crowd, 7,500 would be gone. Now, many of those 7,500 people might well see other games in the new season. Many of the "newcomers" might be people who had seen Bristol City–Preston two years before, or ten years before, but had then gone missing at that fixture for a while. However, the point still stands: at any given match in England, half the spectators would be new compared with the same match the season before.

Here's an example of how the model works (for the sake of simplicity, we have rounded up all numbers):

Bristol City finished the 2006–2007 season in second place in League One, the English third tier. The team's total attendance that season was 295,000. Note that that doesn't mean 295,000 different people. Rather,

295,000 tickets were sold for all of City's matches combined. Most fans would have attended multiple matches. The total attendance for all four divisions was 29.5 million.

The next season,

(a) The total attendance for all four divisions rose by 400,000, to 29.9 million.

(b) Bristol City came in fourth in the championship—a rise of twenty-two places.

So to calculate Bristol City's expected attendance in 2007–2008, we estimate its number of loyal "returning" fans and of new fans:

(c) Loyal fans are 50 percent of the previous season's total: 148,000.

(d) New fans are calculated by estimating Bristol City's share (based on league performance) of new fans of the entire league.

(e) We predict 15.1 million new spectators for English soccer as a whole. That equals this year's total attendance (29.9 million) minus loyal fans from last year (50 percent of 29.5 million = 14.8 million) = 15.1 million.

(f) Given that Bristol City finished twenty-fourth out of ninety-two clubs, we estimate its share of all new fans in the country at 1.7 percent. Its number of new fans should therefore equal .017 × 15.1 million = 257,000.

(g) So Bristol City's loyal + new spectators = 148,000 + 257,000 = 405,000.

(h) Bristol City's actual number for 2007–2008 was 374,000, so our model overestimated their support by 31,000, or 8 percent.

Obviously, the model does not work perfectly for every club. At big clubs, such as Arsenal or Manchester United, there is very little flux in the stands. Their stadiums are pretty much always full, and total attendance is therefore always the same. Most of their spectators are season-ticket holders who see every game. These people generally renew their season tickets each year because they know that if they don't, their seats will be snapped up by others and they might never get back into the stadium again.

However, taking all ninety-two clubs together, the estimate that fits the data best is that 50 percent of the fans who saw a game last season do not see it again the next season. To quote one analysis of the English game, "One Third Division club in the London area, for example, has an estimated 'hard core' support of about 10,000; this rises to 20,000 according to the team's success and the standing of the visiting team." These words were written in 1951 in an economic study of soccer published by the London-based Political and Economic Planning think tank. They remain a good summary of English fandom as a whole since the war.

The discovery that half of all spectators—supposedly the hardest of hard-core Fans—are not there when the same fixture rolls around the next season conflicts with the Hornby version of loyal one-club fandom. Yet this estimate is our best explanation of the churn we see in attendance numbers. Even a club like Leeds, noted for its devoted fans—while stuck in League One, it drew significantly larger crowds than Juventus—saw attendance fall from a peak of 755,000 in the 2001–2002 season to only 479,000 in 2006–2007.

Nor is this high mortality rate a new phenomenon. Our sixty-one years of attendance data suggest that habits of English spectators have changed little over the years. There has always been a hard core of Hornbys, but it seems it has also always been the case that the majority of people who go to English soccer matches go only once in a while and are often quite fluid about whom they choose to watch. And given that spectators are the fans who commit the most time and money to the game, their devotion is in most cases really rather limited. The long-term devoted spectator of the kind that Hornby described in *Fever Pitch*, far from being typical, is a rare species. Committed one-club lifelong fandom is a beautiful theory—or, as Gandhi supposedly said of Western civilization, "It would be a good idea." The reality is that in English soccer, the loyal Hornbys are a small shoal in an ocean of casual Rachmans. England may be a nation of fans, but it's scarcely a nation of Hornbys.

CALL YOURSELVES "LOYAL SUPPORTERS"

In 1996 Alan Tapp, a professor of marketing at Bristol Business School, started to develop a relationship with a struggling club in the Premier

League. Over the next four years he met the club's executives, got to see the data they had on their supporters, and assembled a team of researchers who conducted hundreds of interviews with the club's fans. Tapp eventually published two papers about his work in academic marketing journals. Together they add up to a rare, marvelous study of how the spectators of one club actually behave. Tapp titled his second paper, published in 2004, "The Loyalty of Soccer Fans—We'll Support You Evermore?" with a very pregnant question mark. What he found was that fans talk loyal but don't always act it.

The club that Tapp and his colleague Jeff Clowes studied—based in a Midlands town that is quite easy to identify—was not very good. It wasn't the sort of outfit to attract many BIRGing glory hunters. Most of the club's spectators lived locally. In a survey in 1998, a massive 87 percent of them agreed slightly or strongly with the phrase "I would describe myself as a loyal supporter."

Well, they would say that, wouldn't they? Tapp cautioned that many of those 87 percent might have been engaging in "socially desirable responding." After all, almost nobody in English soccer calls himself a "sod-that-for-a-lark floating punter." That would be socially taboo. Most fans told Tapp and Clowes that they regarded sod-that-for-a-lark types as "pariahs." As Rick Parry said, English fans pride themselves on their loyalty.

Yet when Tapp studied how these spectators behaved, he found a peculiar lack of loyalty. To start with the most basic fact: the club's average crowd during the four-year period of study slipped from about 24,000 to just 16,000. The average across the period was about 21,000, which broke down as follows:

- About 8,000 season-ticket holders
- Another 8,000 places typically filled from a group of 15,000 or so regular attendees
- And 5,000 spectators who came from "a 'revolving door' of perhaps 20,000 'casual fans'"

Tapp came up with three labels for the different groups: "fanatics," "committed casuals," and "carefree casuals."

The "fanatics," or Hornbys, were mostly season-ticket holders. Tapp said that some of these people were veritable "'soccer extremists' who had commitment to the sport and the club that is arguably unparalleled in other business or leisure sectors." There was the man who, when asked by Tapp's team what he would save if there were a fire in his house, replied, "Oh, my [match] programs and tapes. No question. And my wife and kids, of course." Many of the fanatics came from the local area and had supported the club since childhood.

But even some of the fanatics were less fanatical than they claimed to be. Tapp found that each season, on average, 1,000 of the 8,000 season-ticket holders did not renew their seats and were replaced by new people. "Even at the fanatic end, the loyalty bucket had significant leaks," he remarked.

The team was playing badly. In one season, a mere 2 percent of fans proclaimed themselves "very satisfied" with performances. However, it was not the bad soccer that was driving them away. When Tapp's team asked people why they were letting their season tickets lapse, the lapsers usually talked about their lives away from the stadium. Fans were much more likely to give up their season tickets if they had children under age five or if they described their lives as "complicated."

So it wasn't that the lapsers felt less loyal to the team than the people who kept going year in, year out. They were simply at different stages in life. Some regular fans admitted that at one point in life "they had simply lost interest, often in their late teens and early 20s." Others had been "triggered" by a son or daughter to return to the stadium. Older people, whose lives were presumably more stable, were the most likely to renew their season tickets. Tapp surmised that they "have simply settled into some form of auto-repurchase." In other words, showing up to the stadium every year is not a good marker of loyalty. Rather, it is a good marker of age.

At the far end of the scale from the "fanatics" were the "carefree casuals." Few of the carefree casuals claimed to be "loyal supporters." They were "soccer fans" rather than "club fans," they preferred to see a good game rather than a victory for their team, and they treated soccer as just one of several possible activities on a Saturday. Tapp noted, "Being club supporters is not part of their self-image."

Many of the "carefree casuals" sometimes went to watch other teams. Tapp reckoned that it is probable that some regulars at Derby County, for instance, also occasionally show up at Derby's rival Nottingham Forest, even if this flies in the face of everything we are always told about English soccer fans.

Tapp added that these people are mostly not "brand switchers," who switch from supporting one club to supporting another. Very few people love Derby one year, Forest the next, and Carlisle the year after. Rather, these adulterous spectators are engaging in what marketing experts call "repertoire buying": they purchase different brands at different times. In normal consumer markets in almost every country, "repertoire buyers" are thought to outnumber both "brand-loyal" and "price buyers." In soccer, too, repertoire buyers seem to be fairly common. Tapp said, "Repertoire fans took a lot of pleasure from a multiplicity of aspects of the game itself, while single club fanatics were less interested in soccer, more devoted to the club as an entity."

Tapp's middle group of spectators at the Midlands club was made up of "committed casuals." These people didn't go to every match, but they did tend to describe themselves as "loyal supporters." They rarely watched other clubs and were more interested than the "carefree casuals" in seeing their team win. However, they too treated soccer as just one option for their Saturday. Tapp said they "perhaps have their soccer support in perspective with the rest of their lives."

In short, through close-up study very rare in English soccer, he had gotten past the cliché of "We'll support you evermore." Instead, he found the same thing that we did: there are some Hornbys in British soccer, but even among the self-proclaimed "loyal supporters" of an inglorious club they are outnumbered by casual fans who can take it or leave it. Tapp ended by cautioning sports marketers that for all the rhetoric of undying love pervading English soccer, fans' "loyalty cannot be relied upon." He urged marketers to "look under the surface of supporter loyalty," where they will find "loyalty patterns quite similar to, say, supermarket goods sectors."

HORNBYS, CLIENTS, SPECTATORS, AND OTHERS

It turns out that few British soccer fans are either Hornbys or BIRGing glory hunters. Rather, most have a shifting relationship with the club or clubs they support. Of the 50 percent of spectators who do not show up for the same fixture from one season to the next, the largest group may well continue to be monogamous fans of that club. They just don't watch every game, or can't afford to go anymore, or are busy raising children, or have moved to another part of the country, or simply care less than they used to. The object of their love might not have changed, but the intensity has. Many of them may once have been a Hornby, who fell for a team as an eight-year-old when their father took them to their first game. However, by the time they are twenty-eight or eighty-eight, they are no longer the same fans. For many people, fandom is not a static condition but a process.

Alex Ferguson, the legendary Manchester United manager, understood this. In the mid-1970s he managed the Scottish club St Mirren, which played in Paisley, a town that by Ferguson's account had displayed "years of apathy towards football." He began campaigning to engage people who were only mildly interested in the club:

> An electrician at the ground, Freddie Douglas, had the idea that he and I should go round the town in his van and address the potential supporters through a loudspeaker. I was gaining a reputation for innovative management but to me it was simply a case of being willing to try anything that might make the club more successful. . . . I have to confess that Freddie did most of the hailing, but I was good at waving.

Some lapsed fans will have lost interest in soccer altogether. Others still might be shifting their allegiances to another club or clubs because they have moved to a new town, started to follow the team their kids support, or fallen for better soccer elsewhere. Rachman, for example, explains in his *Prospect* essay that he stopped supporting Chelsea "because they were a terrible team, followed by violent cretins."

Instead, he made a two-and-a-half-mile journey within West London and became a QPR fan. In the rhetoric of English soccer, the choice facing the supporter is often presented as stark: either he sticks with his local team or he becomes a BIRGing glory hunter. However, reality is more nuanced. England is so densely stuffed with professional soccer clubs—forty-three within ninety miles of Manchester, as we saw—that many people can find a new local side without going to the trouble of moving house.

Then there is the dirty secret, as we've mentioned, that many fans support more than one team. If you live in Plymouth, say, you might support Plymouth Argyle, Chelsea, and Barcelona, and have a fondness for a half-dozen other clubs, even though if Plymouth ever makes the FA Cup final, you will travel to Wembley decked out as a "lifelong Plymouth fan." Hornby himself, in *Fever Pitch*, supports Cambridge United as well as Arsenal. In fact, whereas the usual analogy for soccer fandom is idealized monogamous marriage, a better one might be music fandom. People are fans of the Arctic Monkeys, or Radiohead, or Tame Impala, but they generally like more than one band at the same time and are capable of moving on when their heroes fade.

As so often, it was Arsène Wenger who put this best. In 2009 he gave Arsenal's website a nontraditional account of how he thought fandom worked:

> Soccer has different types of people coming to the game. You have the client, who is the guy who pays one time to go to a big game and wants to be entertained. Then you have the spectator, who is the guy who comes to watch soccer. These two categories are between 40 and 60 [years old]. Then you have two other categories. The first is the supporter of the club. He supports his club and goes to as many games as he can. Then you have the fan. The fan is a guy between 15 and 25 years old who gives all his money to his club.

Obviously, Wenger's four categories are not exact. Here and there they even conflict with those of Tapp and Clowes, who found that many fans lose interest between fifteen and twenty-five. But Wenger agrees with the other observers that there are several different categories of spectator, of varying emotional intensity, and that people move between these categories depending largely on their stage in life. Ties in soccer fandom are much looser than the rhetoric of "We'll support you evermore" suggests. In that regard, they resemble the ties of real existing marriage in Britain today. People still get married promising "till death do us part," but in 2019 there were 107,599 divorces in England and Wales, more than four times as many as in 1960, even though the number of marriages has plummeted. In 2019 only just over half of all adults in England and Wales (50.4 percent) were either married or in a civil partnership. The typical English marriage lasts a bit more than twelve years. A lifelong monogamous marriage has become almost as rare as a lifelong monogamous love of a soccer club.

THE INAUTHENTIC NATION

Against all evidence, the stereotype persists that the typical British soccer fan is a full-on Hornby. No wonder it does, because the tiny percentage of fans who are Hornbys dominate the national conversation about fandom. After all, they are the people who are most motivated to join the conversation. For them, following soccer is not just a hobby but an identity. Also, they make up a disproportionately large share of the soccer economy—"the most valuable customers," Tapp calls them—so clubs and media listen to them more than to the sod-that-for-a-lark punters. And the Hornbys have a compelling story to tell. Most of the best stories are about love, and these are people who proclaim their love in public every week.

Yet there is a deeper reason that the Hornby account of fandom has been so easily accepted in Britain. That is because it tells a story of roots, of belonging—a lifelong love of the club that your father or grandfather supported before you—in a country that is unusually rootless. In transient Britain, the story of the rooted Fan is especially seductive.

Britain was the first country on Earth where peasants left their native villages to go to work in rootless industrial cities. It was among the first countries where the churches began to empty; a tie that helps root people all over the world has long been extraordinarily weak among native Britons.

Britons have continued to move around a lot, both within their country and abroad. About 4.9 million of them live outside Britain, a larger number than for any other country in the European Union, estimated the United Nations in 2015. (This may surprise some of the Brits who voted for Brexit because they were fed up with immigration.) Probably only India and China have produced diasporas that are as large and as widely spread, says the British government.

It is hard for people this transitory to build up deep ties of any kind, even to soccer clubs. Admittedly, Tapp and Clowes found that many of the "fanatical" supporters of the club they studied had spent their lives in the local town. But it was the club's "casual" fans, who "had often moved to the area as adults," who were more typical of British migratory patterns. For instance, Tapp and Clowes identified one group whom they called "professional wanderers": "people (mainly managers/professionals) who have held jobs in a number of different places who tended to strike up (weakly held) allegiances with local teams, which they retain when they next move." Like most Britons, the professional wanderers were too rootless to become Hornbyesque Fans. None of the casual fans interviewed by Tapp and Clowes "felt a close part of the local community, in contrast to the fanatics."

And Britons have suffered yet another uprooting: as well as leaving their place of birth, many of them have left their class of birth, too. This upheaval began on a large scale in the 1960s. As the economy grew and more Britons stayed on at school and went to university, a mostly working-class nation turned into a mostly middle-class one. For many people this was a deeply felt change. Their fathers had been factory workers, and now they were managers/professionals, with the different set of experiences and attitudes that this entails. They lost touch with their roots. Naturally, many of them began to worry about their authenticity deficits.

In the 1990s British soccer went upscale. The price of tickets jumped. In the food stands outside the stadiums, the proverbial middle-class quiches replaced the proverbial working-class pies. All these changes prompted endless laments for a lost cloth-capped proletarian culture from people who themselves somewhere along the way had ceased to be cloth-capped proletarians. They yearned to be authentic.

All this makes the true Fan a particularly appealing character to Britons. He is the British version of a blood-and-soil myth. Unlike so many actual Britons, the Fan has roots. Generations may pass, and blue collars turn to white, but he still supports his "local" team in what is supposed to be the "workingman's game." Lots of Britons who aren't Hornbyesque Fans would like to be. The Fan is more than just a compelling character. He is a British national fantasy.

PART III
Countries

---

*Rich and Poor, Tom Thumb, England, Spain, Palestine,
and the Champions of the Future*

17

THE CURSE OF POVERTY

Why Poor Countries Are Poor at Sports

When Didier Drogba was five, his parents put him on a plane in the Ivory Coast and sent him to live with an uncle in France. The six-hour flight, alone with his favorite toy, passed in a blur of tears and tissues.

About a decade later, Drogba's father lost his job at a bank in the Ivory Coast, and the family moved to a suburb of Paris, where they were reunited with their exiled son. Eight Drogbas ended up living in an apartment of a bit over 100 square feet. "A very large wardrobe, really," Drogba recalled in his autobiography. "Hard. Very hard. Even enough to drive you crazy." The apartment was cold, and his younger brothers were so noisy he couldn't concentrate on his schoolwork. "Luckily, my father had allowed me to start playing soccer again."

There is a myth that poor people are somehow best equipped to make it as sports stars, that sports are their "only escape route from poverty." The poor are supposedly figuratively "hungrier" than the rich. And the evidence that poor people excel at sports really does seem to be in front of our eyes. France since the 1990s has generally fielded a majority of non-white players, drawn from the poor suburbs of the big cities; England's team also tends to be heavily working-class and immigrant (as we'll discuss); and few Brazilian internationals are sons of corporate lawyers. Most of the world's best soccer players started life poor: South Americans like Diego Maradona, who as a toddler almost drowned in a local cesspit;

Africans like Samuel Eto'o, who appears to support hundreds of people back home; or European immigrants like Zlatan Ibrahimovic and Zinedine Zidane, who grew up in some of the toughest neighborhoods on the Continent. Drogba's childhood was only slightly more Dickensian than most. The origins of American basketball players and football players are mostly lowly, too. You would think that the best preparation for sporting greatness was a poor childhood.

But this isn't the case. The facts show that the world's poor people and poor countries are worse at sports than rich ones. It is true that poorer immigrants in rich countries often excel at sports, but the reasons for that have nothing to do with "hunger."

Let's look at poor countries first. The vast majority of countries on Earth are excluded from sporting success simply because they are poor. This becomes apparent in a simple exercise to discover which countries are the world's best at sports, and which are best for their size.

To find the best countries, we combined the historical results from many major international sporting events: the Summer and Winter Olympics, world cups in several sports, and the most popular individual sports. For some sports the data go back more than a century—for others, only a couple of decades. For all sports, we took November 2021 as the end point.

Our methodology is not perfect. We started with the men's world cups in biggish sports that have seldom or never been featured at the Olympics. We ranked the top five countries in these sports, based first on the number of world titles they have won and, in case of ties, on finishes in the final four. We gave the best country in each sport five points, the second four, the third three, the fourth two, and the fifth one. There is no need to read the rankings for every sport, but following are the detailed points tallies for those who are interested.

Rugby union and cricket are barely played in the US but are major sports in the former British empire and beyond:

Rugby Union

New Zealand	5
Australia	4
South Africa	3

England	2
France	1

Cricket

Australia	5
India	4
West Indies	3
England	2
Sri Lanka	1

Basketball is an Olympic event. However, as the world's second-most-popular team game, it deserves additional input in this quest. We therefore added the results of the basketball world cup for both genders:

Men's Basketball

US	5
Yugoslavia/Serbia and Montenegro	4
USSR	3
Brazil	2
Spain	1

Women's Basketball

US	5
USSR	4
Australia	3
Brazil	2
Russia	1

Baseball was trickier. Historically, the US dominates the sport. However, it traditionally sent amateurs or minor leaguers to the men's world cup—now superseded by the World Baseball Classic. The US ranks only second all-time in the two tournaments combined. But we used our judgment to rank it as the world's best country in baseball, producing this ranking:

US	5
Cuba	4
Venezuela	3

Dominican Republic	2
Colombia	1

Favoring the US in baseball did not affect the outcome of our quest.

The only women's world cup we counted was soccer. Women's soccer is an Olympic event, too, but far more widely played than most other women's team games, so it seemed to merit more input. The rankings for women's soccer:

US	5
Germany	4
Norway	3
Japan	2
Sweden	1

We also assessed popular individual sports that have seldom or never been represented in the Olympics. We rewarded countries for triumphs by their citizens. In tennis we counted men's and women's Grand Slam tournaments—tennis being a rare sport in that it is played widely by women. We used only results from the "Open era" starting in 1968, when tennis became very competitive:

Men's Tennis

US	5
Spain	4
Sweden	3
Switzerland	2
Australia and Serbia	1 each

Women's Tennis

US	5
Germany/West Germany	4
Australia	3
Belgium	2
Yugoslavia/Serbia	1

In golf we used the results of the men's majors:

US	5
Britain (including all four home countries and Jersey)	4
South Africa	3
Australia	2
Spain	1

In cycling we counted victories by citizens of each country in the Tour de France, a more prestigious event than the world championship. We didn't count doped winners, such as Lance Armstrong, who were later stripped of their titles:

France	5
Belgium	4
Spain	3
Italy	2
Britain	1

In auto racing we chose the most prestigious competition, Formula 1, thus discriminating against the US, which prefers its own races. Again, we counted world championships by citizenship. The rankings:

Britain	5
Germany	4
Brazil	3
Argentina	2
Finland, Australia, Austria, France	1 each

We did not include the world cups of popular sports such as volleyball and ice hockey because these are long-standing Olympic sports, so we will assess them through their role in the Olympics' all-time medals table. Boxing was too hard to assess because there are various rival "world championships." We also excluded the athletics world cup. Athletics is copiously represented at the Olympics, and for most of the history of its world cup, the entrants have been entire continents rather than single countries.

Clearly, the Summer and Winter Games deserve to carry more weight in our quest than any single world cup. The Summer Olympics of 2020 featured thirty-three sports. Many of these, such as archery or canoeing, are played by very few people. Still, because of the event's profusion of sports and its prestige, we gave the Summer Games ten times the weighting of world cups in single sports. So we gave the top country in the all-time medals table fifty points rather than five points for a single world cup. (We used the most common global method of ranking countries by gold medals and counting silvers and bronzes only in case of ties.) Because the whole planet competes in the Olympics—unlike, say, in baseball or cricket—we rewarded the top ten rather than five countries in the all-time medals table. The rankings:

US	50
USSR/Russia	40
Great Britain	30
China	20
France	10
Italy	8
Germany	6
Hungary	4
Australia	2
East Germany	1

We gave the Winter Olympics three times the weighting of a world cup. Because few countries play winter sports, we rewarded only the top five in the all-time medals table:

Norway	15 points
USSR/Russia	12
US	9
Germany (including West Germany)	6
Canada	3

Finally, the men's soccer world cup. Soccer is an Olympic sport, but it is also the planet's most popular game. We gave its men's world cup six

times the weighting of world cups in other sports and rewarded the top
ten countries in the all-time points table. The rankings:

Brazil	30
Germany	24
Italy	18
Argentina	12
France	6
England	5
Spain	4
Netherlands	3
Uruguay	2
Sweden	1

We then totaled up all the points. Here are our top twenty-three sporting
countries on Earth:

US	94
USSR/Russia	60
Great Britain (including England)	49
Germany (including West Germany)	48
Brazil	37
Italy	28
France	23
Australia	21
China	20
Norway	18
Argentina	14
Spain	13
Yugoslavia/Serbia and Montenegro, Belgium, South Africa	6
Sweden and New Zealand	5
Hungary, India, Cuba	4
Netherlands, Canada, West Indies, Venezuela	3

The winner, the US, deserves particular praise given that we omitted two of its favorite sports—gridiron football and NASCAR—because

almost nobody else plays them. Germany, in fourth place, would have come second if we had credited the united country with East Germany's Olympic medals (and forgotten all the male growth hormones that went into winning them). The USSR/Russia, which did come second, can be slightly less pleased with itself because it won most of its points when it was still a multinational empire.

Australia, in eighth place, did brilliantly given that we ignored its prowess at its very own version of football, "Aussie Rules." Brazil was the best developing country by a very long way, and not just thanks to soccer. It has also diversified successfully into basketball and Formula 1 auto racing. India (1.2 billion inhabitants, four points for cricket) was the biggest flop per capita, while China is at least rising—when we first calculated this table in 2006, it didn't score a single point. The Arab world combined is still on zero points.

But which country is world champion per capita? To find out, we worked out how many points each country scored per million inhabitants (taking their population figures for 2021). That produced this top ten of overachievers:

Norway	3.33
New Zealand	0.98
Australia	0.82
Britain (including England)	0.73
United Germany (excluding the GDR's Olympic medals)	0.58
Uruguay	0.58
West Indies (or the nations that together supply almost all West Indian cricketers, namely Jamaica, Trinidad and Tobago, Guyana, Barbados, and Antigua and Barbuda)	0.58
Belgium	0.52
Sweden	0.48
Italy	0.47

Heia Norge. Norway's lead as the world's best sporting country per capita is so large that it would most probably have won our sporting Tom Thumb trophy even with a different scoring system. This is a country where, at a state kindergarten in suburban Oslo in mid-afternoon, among the throng of mothers picking up their toddlers someone pointed out to us an anonymous mom who happened to be an Olympic gold medal-ist in cross-country skiing. Norway won more points in our competition than all of Africa, or China and India put together. We could even have omitted the Winter Olympics—almost a Norwegian fiefdom—and the country still would have finished in the top ten of our efficiency table.

But the most important lesson of our rankings is that wealth is a sig-nificant contributor to national sporting success. Critics might argue that we have omitted important sports, weighted the sports we include in-appropriately, or otherwise find fault. No doubt that different methods would produce different results. But we are convinced that any reason-able ranking of national sporting achievement will inevitably be highly correlated with national wealth. Tellingly, our efficiency table for sports bears a striking resemblance to another global ranking: the United Na-tions' human development index (UNHDI). This measures life expec-tancy, literacy, education, and living standards to rank the countries of the world according to their well-being. So sporting success seems to correlate not only with wealth but also with well-being. Guess which country topped the UN's rankings for human development in 2020? *Heia Norge*, again.

Germany, Sweden, and Australia also made the top nine for human development as well as sports. The only somewhat less wealthy nations that sneaked into our sporting top ten were Uruguay and the West In-dian nations. But generally the most developed countries also tend to be best at sports.

The case of Norway shows why. It's Norwegian government policy that every farmer, every fisherman, no matter where he lives in the coun-try, has the right to play sports. And Norway will spend what it takes to achieve that. Just as supermarkets have sprouted all over Britain, there are all-weather sports grounds everywhere in Norway. Even in the unlikeliest corners of the country there's generally one around the corner from your house. Usually the locker rooms are warm, and the coaches have acquired some sort of diploma. A kid can play and train on a proper team for about $150 a year, really not much for most Norwegians. Almost everyone in the country plays something. Knut Helland, a professor at Bergen Uni-versity who has written a book on Norwegian sports and media, told us that Norway had the biggest ski race in the world, with about thirteen thousand participants. "I'm taking part in it myself," he added. People all over the world might want to play sports, but to make that possible requires money and organization that poor countries don't have. Money buys sporting trophies.

In soccer, the best example is probably Iceland (fourth in the UNHDI rankings). When the land of fish, volcanoes, and endless winters qualified for Euro 2016, its population of 330,000 made it the smallest country ever to reach a Euro or a World Cup. Qualification, as it turned out, was only the start of it. Many of us will long remember the Icelandic TV commentator "Gummi Ben" ascending into hysteria—"Never, ever, have I felt as good!"—as he narrated his team's last-minute winning goal against Austria. Next, Iceland beat England to reach the quarterfinals and then made the 2018 World Cup, where it held Argentina to a tie.

Like Norway, Iceland is a social democracy whose government does its best to give all inhabitants the chance to play sports. It's also a cold country, with long winters, which Icelanders tend to spend hunkered down inside, either working hard or drinking hard while they wait for the summer partying season. What to do while hibernating? Vidar Halldórsson, an Icelandic sports sociologist, says: "We grew up watching English football on TV, from the 1970s. The only TV station in Iceland showed English games once a week, on Saturdays (not live, but a week later). They were the only professional sports we saw." In a survey of Icelandic men in 2003, Halldórsson found that 88 percent could name a favorite English soccer team. Aron Jóhansson (who was raised in Iceland but became an American international) recalls boys fighting in the streets of Reykjavik over English soccer results. "That passion was very deep," he says. It's a passion that arguably reached its apogee in 2006 when the billionaire Björgólfur Guðmundsson—then Iceland's second-richest man after his son, Björgólfur Thor—bought West Ham United. After the financial crisis struck Iceland in 2008, *Forbes* revalued Guðmundsson's estimated net worth from $1.1 billion to zero. In 2009 he was declared bankrupt. Still, no doubt the passion remained.

In the twentieth century, Icelanders watched English soccer but didn't have much opportunity to play or watch their own. Iceland's league runs from May to September—"the shortest football season in the world," the country's soccer federation proudly calls it. But around 2000, Iceland began building an all-weather soccer infrastructure that may be unparalleled on Earth. More than 110 Icelandic schools got artificial mini-fields, and there are now seven heated indoor halls with full-sized soccer grounds. Nowadays, Icelanders can play all year round, whether they belong to a club or not.

Playing soccer is now a part of life in Iceland, especially in the villages. Nearly a quarter of the country's registered soccer players are girls under eighteen years old. Even six-year-old kids are trained by qualified paid soccer coaches. As the Dutch journalist Michiel de Hoog notes, this distinguishes Iceland from pretty much every other country on Earth, where most child players are coached (or just yelled at) by somebody's mom or dad. And Icelandic kids usually play other sports besides.

Sport in Iceland is something you do very seriously, for fun, while continuing real life on the side. There can't be many countries where the national team's goalkeeper is also a professional filmmaker. Hannes Thor Halldórsson actually shot the commercial for Icelandair that featured his own team. "It was weird," he told *Sports Illustrated*. "I had to act in the commercial as well, so I was directing the commercial in the national kit and boots." Meanwhile, Iceland's legendary handball captain, Olafur Stefansson, seemed to regard himself primarily as an existentialist philosopher. When we asked him during the London Olympics what a handball gold would mean for the little country, he replied that he was unable to answer: "You have so many different realities. The game is—what is it? A simulacrum of life itself, maybe in simplified terms."

In Beijing in 2008, Stefansson's team had beaten Spain in the Olympic semifinal. During that game, "there was not a single transaction made on the Icelandic stock exchange," says the sociologist Halldórsson. Stefansson's men ended up with silver. No country that small had ever won an Olympic medal in a team sport.

Broad access to sports is much less common in poor countries. The money that FIFA supposedly spends to build soccer fields for kids in these places is often wasted. Over the years, the corrupt Trinidadian soccer boss Jack Warner received at least $26 million from FIFA to build the Dr João Havelange Center of Excellence in his home country, on land that later turned out to belong to him. But the center didn't actually host much soccer because Warner preferred to put on profitable "weddings, dinners, shows," writes David Conn in *The Fall of the House of FIFA*. This helps explain why in January 2022, Trinidad and Tobago stood 100th in the FIFA rankings, thirty-eight places below Iceland.

After we published the first edition of *Soccernomics*, Christopher Anderson, then still a political scientist at Cornell University before his brief stint as managing director of Coventry City, riposted that we placed undue weight on wealth. In his paper "Do Democracies Win More?" Anderson analyzed all soccer World Cups from 1950 through 2006. The key to winning wasn't so much wealth, he argued, as democracy.

Quite possibly. But wealth and democracy tend to correlate very closely. Almost all rich countries (leaving aside a few oil states in the Middle East) are democracies. That makes it tricky to separate the effects of wealth from the effects of democracy. Anderson might well be right that democracy contributes more to winning soccer games (although in making our case, we were looking at many sports rather than just soccer). Perhaps the average quality of schooling in different countries—if you could measure it perfectly—would be an even better predictor of success in soccer. After all, schooling is a pretty good gauge of how well a country channels resources to its people. If you're good at providing schools for everyone, as most democracies are, then you are probably also good at providing soccer fields and coaches for everyone. It's impossible to say whether Norway is good at sports because it's rich, because it's a democracy, or because it's highly educated. Being rich and democratic and well educated and good at sports usually seems to be part of the same thing.

However you measure it, poor countries are generally poorer at sports. It's no coincidence that China won nothing at sports before its economy took off and that it has been climbing the Olympic medals table ever since. Most African countries barely even try to compete in any sports other than soccer and a few running events—the cheapest sports to become good at. And the best place to find out why the world's poor do worse than the world's rich is South Africa, where some very poor and very rich neighborhoods are almost side by side, separated only by a highway or a golf course.

South Africa is the one African country to score any points at all in our sporting table. Yet it owes almost all those points to a group that makes up just 8 percent of the country's inhabitants: white people.

Only about 4.7 million of the 59 million South Africans are white. Nonetheless, whites accounted for fourteen of the fifteen players in the

Springbok rugby team that won the world cup in 1995 and thirteen of the fifteen who won it in 2007, as well as all five South African golfers who have won majors and most of the country's best cricketers. If we treated white South Africa as a separate country, then its six sporting points would have put it in second place in the world in our sporting efficiency table. That is entirely predictable. South African whites were nurtured under apartheid on almost all the resources of the country. In 2021 their average incomes were still about four times higher than those of Black South Africans.

The national teams of South African whites remain world class in their respective sports. Nonwhite South Africa's national team does less well. In January 2022 the Bafana Bafana soccer team, sometimes known at home as the "Banana Banana," was 68th in FIFA's rankings.

Here are five vignettes to explain why the largely poor Black population of South Africa—just like most poor nations—fails at sport.

YOU ARE WHAT YOU EAT: JOHANNESBURG

Steven Pienaar, the South African midfielder who had a long career in the English Premier League, has the frame of a prepubescent boy. There's hardly a European soccer player as reedy as he is. But in South African soccer his body type is common. Frank Eulberg, a German who was once very briefly assistant coach of the Kaizer Chiefs, South Africa's best team, says that when he arrived at the club, sixteen of the players were shorter than five foot nine. "I sometimes thought, 'Frank, you're in the land of the dwarves.'"

Most likely, Pienaar was reedy because he grew up malnourished and without much access to doctors. He was born in a poor township in 1982, the apogee of apartheid, when almost all money and health care went to whites. Growing tall is not just a matter of what you eat. When children become ill, their growth is interrupted, and because poor children tend to get ill more often than rich ones, they usually end up shorter.

Most of the players who represented South Africa in 2010 were born in nonwhite townships in the 1980s. So the ghost of apartheid bugged the Bafana at their own World Cup. One reason that South Africans are so bad at soccer is that most of them didn't get enough good food.

Apartheid, based on the bogus ideology that races are different, ended up creating white, Black, and Indian South Africans who really look like separate peoples. The whites on average tower over the Blacks. No wonder the cricket and rugby teams are so much better than the Bafana. "Well, they have their moments," laughs Demitri Constantinou.

Constantinou directs the Centre for Exercise Science and Sports Medicine at Wits University in Johannesburg. When we met, he was running a project with the South African Football Association (SAFA) to help develop young soccer players. Constantinou's team tested the health of all the players selected for SAFA's program. In a Woolworths tearoom in one of Johannesburg's posh northern suburbs, among white ladies having afternoon tea, he said, "The biggest issue was nutrition." Was malnutrition one reason that African teams perform poorly at World Cups? "I think yes. And I think it has been overlooked as a possible cause."

Hardly any male players in the top level of international soccer were shorter than about five foot eight, Constantinou noted. "There is a minimum height." If a large proportion of your male population was below that height, you were picking your team from a reduced pool.

A BEAST INTO A TOOTHPICK: CAPE TOWN

George Dearnaley is a big, ruddy white man who looks like a rugby player, but in fact he was once the Bafana's promising young center forward. Dearnaley never got beyond promising because when he was in his early twenties, his knee went. He didn't mind much. He spoke a bit of Zulu and had studied literature and journalism at college in Toledo, Ohio, so he joined the soccer magazine *Kick Off.* He became its publisher as well as the author of an excellent column.

Over an English breakfast in a Cape Town greasy spoon near the *Kick Off* offices, Dearnaley reflected on the Amazulu team in Durban, where his career peaked. Seven of his teammates from the Amazulu side of 1992 were dead fifteen years later, out of a squad of about twenty-four. Dearnaley said, "One guy died when his house exploded, so that was probably a taxi war or something. But the rest must have been AIDS. One player, a Durban newspaper said he was bewitched. A six-foot-four beast of a man, who was suddenly whittled down to a toothpick."

Constantinou says it's quite possible that a fifth of the Bafana's potential pool of players for 2010 carried the HIV virus. Not many people now remember Emmanuel "Scara" Ngobese, once a South African "dribbling wizard," who died at age twenty-eight in a Johannesburg hospital on May 11, 2010, a month before the World Cup kicked off. His cause of death was given as "tuberculosis." Scara won the league with the Kaizer Chiefs in 2005 and once played for the Bafana. How many South Africans who could have played in 2010 were dead instead? Thankfully, most South Africans with HIV now finally get treatment, but still many of them won't be fit enough to maximize their athletic potential.

THE DARK SIDE OF THE MOON: SANDTON, JUST OUTSIDE JOHANNESBURG

It was quite a step for Danny Jordaan to organize a World Cup because until he was thirty-eight he had never even seen one. The chief executive officer of the FIFA World Cup 2010 grew up a million miles from the world's best soccer. Being in South Africa under apartheid was not quite like being on the Moon, or being in North Korea, but it was almost as isolated. South Africa was the last industrialized country to get television, in 1976, because the white government was afraid of the device. Even after that, hardly any Black people had TV sets, and FIFA did not allow its World Cup to be broadcast in the apartheid state. So the first time Jordaan saw a World Cup on television was in 1990.

The country's isolation continued even after that. As far as most South Africans were concerned, international soccer might still as well have been happening on Mars. As Jordaan told us, "South Africans played on their own. We thought we were so smart. That's why when we played our first competitive match against Zimbabwe [in 1992], every South African knew we were going to hammer Zimbabwe. But Zimbabwe had this little player called Peter Ndlovu. Nobody knew Peter Ndlovu. By halftime it was 3–0 for them. That was the first entry into international soccer. That really shook this country."

As late as 1998, when South Africa entered its first World Cup, large swaths of the population assumed that the Bafana would win it. After all, everyone knew that their native style of "piano and shoeshine"— essentially, doing tricks on the ball while standing around—was just like Brazilian soccer but better. The Bafana did not win the World Cup.

Black South Africa was isolated twice over: first by sanctions, then by poverty. However, isolation—a distance from the networks of the world's best soccer—is the fate of most poor countries. Their citizens can't easily travel to Spain or Germany and see how soccer is played there, let alone talk to the best coaches. Some can't even see foreign soccer on television because they don't have television sets. And only a couple of the very best players in these countries ever make it to the best leagues in the world.

One reason poor countries do badly in sports—and one reason they are poor—is that they tend to be less "networked," less connected to other countries, than rich ones. It is hard for them just to find out the latest best practice on how to play a sport.

Playing for national teams in Africa hardly lifts the isolation. Most poor, isolated African countries compete only against other poor, isolated African countries. At most, they might encounter the world's best once every four years at a World Cup. No wonder they have little idea of what top-class soccer is like.

"THE ORGANIZERS. IT'S THE BIGGEST PROBLEM": LONDON

For mysterious reasons, in 2006 someone decided that the Bafana should play their annual charity match, the Nelson Mandela Challenge, not in the magnificent 78,000-seat FNB Stadium just outside Johannesburg but more than five thousand miles away at Brentford's Griffin Park in West London.

On a gray November London afternoon the day before the game, the Bafana were in their gray-colored three-star hotel on the outskirts of Heathrow Airport. In the lobby were flight crews, traveling salespeople, and cheery men in green-and-yellow tracksuits hanging with their entourage: the Bafana Bafana. The Bafana's opponents, the Egyptians, who were also staying in the hotel, had congregated in the bar. Apparently, Egypt was furious. It had been promised a five-star hotel and a match fee that had yet to materialize.

Pitso Mosimane, the Bafana's caretaker manager—a big, bald, bullet-headed man—was also hanging around the lobby. Mosimane complained that African coaches never got jobs in Europe. He gestured toward the bar: "The coach of Egypt, who won the African Cup of Nations. Don't you think he could at least coach a team in the English first division?" Then Mosimane went off for a prematch practice at Griffin Park.

Minutes later he was back at the table. "That was quick," someone remarked. "No, we didn't train!" Mosimane said. Nobody had bothered telling Brentford the Bafana were coming, so the field wasn't ready for them. Now they would have to play the African champions without having trained on the field. "And I'm carrying players who play for Blackburn Rovers and Borussia Dortmund, and you know? We're laughing about it." Mosimane jerked a thumb toward four men in suits drinking at the next table: "The organizers. It is the biggest problem. This wouldn't happen with any other national team."

He was wrong. Organizational mishaps are always happening to national teams from poor countries. On most sub-Saharan African national teams that make it to a World Cup, players and officials have a ritual dispute over pay about a week before the tournament. During the 2014 World Cup, quarrels between officials and unpaid players unsettled the Nigerian, Cameroonian, and Ghanaian camps. Ghana's president finally sent $3 million to Brazil on a chartered plane—surely a cash transfer would have been easier?—and Brazilian TV showed defender John Boye kissing his pile of notes. Eventually Moses Armah, an official of the country's football federation, confirmed that he had decked Sulley Muntari after the midfielder had slapped him in the face twice. Muntari and Kevin-Prince Boateng were expelled from the squad. And Ghana, remember, is one of Africa's healthiest democracies and strongest teams, one that came within inches of the semifinal in 2010. Clearly, FIFA needs to move to a system of sidestepping potentially corrupt national officials and paying players directly at World Cups. But that alone wouldn't solve Africa's soccer problems.

To win at sports, you need to find, develop, and nurture talent. Doing that requires money, know-how, and some kind of administrative infrastructure. Few African countries have enough of any.

"COLOURED" BEATS "BLACK": THE CAPE FLATS

If you stand on Table Mountain at night and look down at Cape Town, you will see a city of lights. Next to the lights are the railway tracks. And on the far side of the tracks are "Black spots": nonwhite townships without lights. These are the rainy, murderous Cape Flats, where most of South Africa's best soccer players grew up.

Benni McCarthy—South Africa's record goal scorer—comes from the Cape Flats. So does the man just behind him in the scoring charts, Shaun Bartlett. So does Benni's old friend Quinton Fortune, for years a loyal reserve at Manchester United.

The key point here is that according to the racial classifications of apartheid, still tacitly used by most South Africans today, none of these players is "Black." They are known as "Coloured": a group of generally lighter-skinned people, mostly derived from the lighter African tribes of the Cape, although some descend from Asian slaves and mixed white-Black liaisons. Less than 10 percent of South Africans are "Coloured," whereas about three-quarters are Black. However, Coloureds often make up as much as half of the Bafana team. This density of Coloured talent is a legacy of apartheid.

Under apartheid, so-called Coloureds were slightly better off than so-called Blacks. They had more to eat and more opportunities to organize themselves. In the Coloured Cape Flats, for instance, there were amateur soccer clubs with proper coaches like you might find in Europe. Not so in Black townships, where a boys' team would typically be run by a local gangster or the shebeen owner, who seldom bothered much with training.

To the irritation of many Black South Africans, the Bafana have been a largely Coloured team for much of their history since 1992. The Blacks are simply too poor to compete within their own country, let alone with Europeans. Even in soccer, the simplest game, the poor are excluded by malnutrition, disease, and disorganization. Poor people in poor countries do worse at sports.

That leaves one thing unexplained: why is it that so many of the best European soccer players of recent times—Zidane, Drogba (officially an Ivorian but raised in France), Ibrahimovic, Rooney, Cristiano Ronaldo, and Paul Pogba—come from the poorest neighborhoods in Europe?

It cannot be that boys from poor neighborhoods have an unquenchable hunger to succeed. If that were so, they would do better at school and in jobs outside soccer. There must be something about their childhoods that makes them particularly well suited to soccer. That reason is practice.

Malcolm Gladwell, in his book *Outliers: The Story of Success*, popularized the "10,000-hour rule." This is a notion from psychology which says that to achieve expertise in any field, you need at least ten thousand hours of practice. "In study after study, of composers, basketball players, fiction writers, ice-skaters, concert pianists, chess players, master criminals," says neurologist Daniel Levitin in *Outliers*, "this number comes up again and again. Ten thousand hours is equivalent to roughly three hours a day, or 20 hours a week, of practice over 10 years....No one has yet found a case in which true world-class expertise was accomplished in less time."

The 10,000-hour rule has since been questioned by academics in various fields. Indeed, it may not apply in very physical sports like running or jumping, where somebody with the perfect genes can become world class without much training. However, in a highly skill-based sport like soccer, Gladwell's essential point is correct: practice makes perfect. "Soccer is a very technical sport that unfortunately takes a ridiculous time to become good," says Tom Byer, an American who has advised China's education ministry on soccer. "So how do you get to 10,000 hours?"

In soccer it is the poorest European boys who are most likely to hit that number. They tend to live in small apartments, which forces them to spend time outdoors. There they meet a ready supply of local boys equally eager to get out of their apartments and play soccer. Their parents are less likely than middle-class parents to force them to waste precious time doing homework. (In China, where most families have just one child, the intense pressure on the kid to do well at school helps explain the country's underachievement in soccer, says Byer.)

Poorer children also have less money for other leisure pursuits, which pushes them toward kicking a ball. A constant in players' ghosted autobiographies is the monomaniacal childhood spent playing nonstop soccer and, in a classic story, sleeping with a ball. Here, for instance, is Nourdin Boukhari, a Dutch-Moroccan soccer player who grew up in an immigrant neighborhood of Rotterdam, recalling his childhood for a Dutch magazine:

> I grew up in a family of eight children....There was no chance of pocket money....I lived more on the street than at home....And look at Robin van Persie, Mounir El Hamdaoui and Said Boutahar. And I'm forgetting Youssef El-Akchaoui. [Like the other players Boukhari mentions, El-Akchaoui became a professional soccer player.] Those

boys and I played on the street in Rotterdam together. We never forget where we came from and that we used to have nothing except for one thing: the ball....

What we have in common is that we were on the street every minute playing soccer, day and night. We were always busy, games, juggling, shooting at the crossbar. The ball was everything for me, for us. We'd meet on squares.

By the time these boys were fifteen, they were much better players than suburban kids. That's probably still more true in Latin America, where poor kids have even fewer options than in Europe and therefore play more soccer. This may help explain why the world's most skillful players tend to be Latin Americans. The importance of practice also explains why Black men raised in the poorest American neighborhoods are overrepresented in basketball and football.

But it would be misleading to say these European soccer players grew up "poor." By global standards, they were rich. Even in Cristiano Ronaldo's Madeira, Ibrahimovic's Rosengård, or Pogba's Roissy-en-Brie, children generally got enough to eat and decent medical care. It is true that Cristiano Ronaldo grew up in a house so small that they kept the washing machine on the roof, but in Black South Africa that washing machine would have marked the family as rich. Besides the 10,000-hour rule, there is another rule that explains sporting success: the $15,000 rule. That's the minimum average income per person that a country needs to win anything. There is only one way around this: be Brazil.

18

CORE BEATS PERIPHERY

Why Little Western Europe Rules International Soccer

When we published the first edition of *Soccernomics*, in 2009, Western Europe was the dominant soccer region. (By "Western Europe" we mean the half of the continent that was west of the communist bloc during the Cold War.) Although the region has only about 400 million inhabitants, or 5 percent of the world's population, only once at the World Cup of 2006 did one of its teams lose to a team from elsewhere: Switzerland's insanely dull loss on penalties to Ukraine, a match that was the nadir of ten thousand years of human civilization. Big countries outside the region, such as Mexico, Japan, the US, and Poland, could not match little Western European countries such as Portugal, Holland, or Sweden. If you understood the geographical rule of that World Cup, you could sit in the stands for almost every match before the quarterfinals confident of the outcome. All four semifinalists—Italy, France, Germany, and Portugal—came from Western Europe.

At the time we thought the region's dominance was unsustainable. We expected rising powers to catch up with and outstrip Western Europe and South America in soccer, just as economic and political power was also moving away from the West. That explains the subtitle of that first edition of our book: "Why the US, Japan, Australia, Turkey—and Even Iraq—Are Destined to Become the Kings of the World's Most Popular Sport."

TABLE 18.1. World Cup dominance of European countries, 2006–2018

World Cup	Winner	Runner-up	Third
2006	Italy	France	Germany
2010	Spain	Holland	Germany
2014	Germany	Argentina	Holland
2018	France	Croatia	Belgium

Well, we were wrong. So far, at least, there's no sign of any of those countries becoming kings. To the contrary: heading into the World Cup in Qatar, Western Europe looks more dominant than ever. Since 2006, teams from the region have won four straight World Cups, something no continent had managed before. Two of those trophies were won outside Europe, something no European team had managed before. Better, continental Europeans (including Croatia, just on the other side of the old Iron Curtain) hogged eleven of the twelve places on the podium in this period, as shown in Table 18.1.

Notice the region's depth: seven different European countries have made it into the top three. All teams will inevitably fail sometimes, as Italy and Spain did at the 2014 World Cup, and Germany in 2018, but there is always a neighbor coming through. From 2006 through 2018, the other 95 percent of humanity produced just one team that could match the best Europeans: Leo Messi's Argentina in 2014.

So how did Western Europe become unbeatable? And why has the rest of the world failed to catch up? Which countries might yet do it, and what would they need to take that final step?

SOCCER AND THE POWER OF NETWORKS

When the internet arrived, many pundits predicted the decline of the city. After all, why live in a small apartment in Brooklyn when you could set up your laptop in an old farmhouse beside a lake?

The prediction turned out to be wrong. Cities have continued their growth of the past two hundred years, which is why apartments in Brooklyn became so expensive. Meanwhile, the countryside has turned into something of a desert, inhabited by farmers and old people and used by the rest of us mostly for hiking. It turns out that many people still want to live in dirty, overcrowded, overpriced cities, even after the rise of remote working. And the reason they do is the social networks. To be rural is to be isolated. Networks give you contacts. Someone you meet at a party or at your kids' playground can give you a job or an idea. Just as the brain works by building new connections between huge bundles of neurons, with each connection producing a new thought, so we as individuals need to find ourselves in the center of the bundle to make more connections.

Networks are key to the latest thinking about economic development. Better networks are one reason why some countries are richer than others. As it happens, networks also help explain why the best soccer is played in continental Western Europe.

Once upon a time, the center of soccer's knowledge network was Britain. From the first official soccer international in 1872 until at least World War I, and perhaps even until England's first home defeat against foreign opposition (a largely forgotten 0–2 against Ireland in 1949, which came before the famous 3–6 against Hungary in 1953), you could argue that England was the dominant soccer nation. It exported coaching know-how to the world. The English expatriate manager became such a legendary figure that to this day in Spain and Italy a head coach is known as a "mister."

Many English people clung to their belief in England's supremacy long after it had ceased to be true. The astonishment each time England didn't win the World Cup ended only with the team's abject failures in the 1970s.

The gradual British decline in soccer echoes the decline in Britain's economic status. The country went from supreme economic power under Queen Victoria to having its hand held by the International Monetary Fund in the late 1970s. Admittedly, in soccer as in economics, most observers exaggerated Britain's slide. The country's position in the top-ten largest economies was never much in doubt. But in soccer it became clear by 1970 that dominance had shifted just across the Channel.

Western Europe excels at soccer for the same fundamental reason that it had the scientific revolution in the sixteenth and seventeenth centuries and was for centuries the world's richest region. Its secret is what the historian Norman Davies calls its "user-friendly climate." Western Europe is mild and rainy. Because of that, the land is fertile. This allows hundreds of millions of people to inhabit a small territory. Moreover, as Malise Ruthven, the scholar of Islam, has pointed out, Europe has "a higher ratio of coast to landmass than any other continent or subcontinent, and a coastline some 23,000 miles long—equivalent to the circumference of the globe." No wonder Europeans were the first people to sail the world. Geography has always helped them exchange ideas, inside their continent and beyond. In short, they are networked.

From the World Cup in Germany, you could have flown in two and a half hours to any one of about 20 countries containing roughly 300 million people in total. That is the densest network on Earth. There was nothing like that in Japan at the World Cup of 2002: the only foreign capital you could have reached within that time from Tokyo was Seoul. South Africa, host in 2010, was even more isolated. And there's just one foreign capital within two hours flight of Brazil's biggest city, São Paulo: Asunción in Paraguay. Qatar's capital, Doha, host in 2022, was until recently blockaded by its neighbors.

Admittedly, the southern tip of South America has its own fruitful soccer network. Uruguay and Argentina, in particular, have benefited from their long exchange. Their capitals, Montevideo and Buenos Aires, respectively, are separated only by an easy boat ride, and in 1901 the two countries met in the first international match ever played outside the British Isles and North America (Canada and the US had already played each other twice by then).

Brazil has been playing against both its neighbors for over a century, too. It's no wonder that this is the only region outside Western Europe to have won World Cups. No wonder, either, that every winning country borders another winning country (if you count England and France, separated by twenty miles and a lot of seawater, as bordering each other). If you want to be the best, it helps to be in a good neighborhood.

But the Western European neighborhood is unique. For centuries now, the Continent's interconnected peoples have exchanged ideas fast. The scientific revolution could happen in Western Europe because its scientists were near one another, networking, holding a dialogue in their shared language: Latin. Copernicus, Polish son of a German merchant, wrote that the Earth circled the Sun. Galileo in Florence read Copernicus and confirmed his findings through a telescope. The English philosopher Francis Bacon described their "scientific method": deductions based on data. Southern England at the time was very much a part of the European network. As the late British historian Tony Judt noted, cross-Channel ferries have been sailing between the English port of Dover and the French port of Calais for nearly nine hundred years. Even in the Bronze Age, boats went back and forth between the two coasts pretty much daily.

A typical product of that European network was the lens grinder, a crucial new machine in the development of the microscope in the early 1660s. Robert Hooke in London invented a new grinder, which made lenses so accurate that Hooke could publish a detailed engraving of a louse attached to a human hair. But meanwhile Sir Robert Moray, a Scot in London who knew what Hooke was up to, was sending letters in French about the new grinder to the Dutch scientist Christiaan Huygens. Thanks to Moray, Huygens had previously gotten hold of details of Hooke's balance-spring watch.

Moray and Huygens "sometimes wrote to each other several times a week," writes the historian Lisa Jardine. Their letters crossed the Channel in days, or about as quickly as mail does now. At the same time, the French astronomer Adrien Auzout in Paris was getting copies of some of their letters. So Hooke's breakthroughs were being spread to his European competitors almost instantly.

All this irritated Hooke. But the proximity of many thinkers in Western Europe created an intellectual ferment. That is why so many of the great scientific discoveries were made there. These discoveries then helped make the region rich.

Centuries later, soccer spread the same way. In the nineteenth century, the game infected Western Europe first because there it had the shortest distances to travel. Later, the proximity of so many peoples brought the region two world wars. After 1945, Western Europeans decided they could live crammed together only under a sort of single government: the European Union. Borders opened, and the region became the most integrated in the history of the world.

Again, the best ideas spread fastest there, just as they had in the scientific revolution. The region's soccer benefited. One of the first men who carried tactical ideas around Europe was the Hungarian-Jewish

Holocaust survivor Béla Guttmann, possibly soccer's leading coach in the 1950s and 1960s. "In the course of my long career I have been to a lot of countries and have also worked in some of them," said Guttmann, who coached everywhere from the Netherlands to Uruguay (but mostly in Europe). "If I saw anything good in soccer, I stole it immediately and kept it for myself. After a while, I mixed myself a cocktail from these stolen delicacies."

The tradition continued with Arrigo Sacchi. His father was a shoe manufacturer in Ravenna, Italy, and the young Sacchi used to accompany him on business trips. He saw a lot of games in Germany, Switzerland, France, and the Netherlands. "It opened my mind," he later said. As manager of AC Milan in the 1980s, he imported a version of Dutch soccer that revolutionized the Italian game.

Another great European networker was Arsène Wenger. While growing up in a village in the French Alsace, near the German border, he used to watch the legendary German soccer program *Die Sportschau* on Saturday afternoons. He became a fan of Borussia Mönchengladbach and generally absorbed German soccer. Later, Wenger took a French coaching course and came to admire Dutch "total football." In other words, he was taking in influences from all the countries around him. It was easy because they were so close. More recently, Pep Guardiola has borrowed from Cruyff, Sacchi, and Capello, as well as from Spanish-speaking Latin Americans such as Marcelo Bielsa. Intriguingly, Guardiola uses the same "theft" metaphor that Guttmann did: "Ideas belong to everyone and I have stolen as many as I could."

Ideas spread even more quickly in European soccer than in other economic sectors because soccer is the most integrated part of the Continent's economy. Only about 3 percent of all Western Europeans live in a different European Union country because few companies bother hiring bus drivers or office administrators from neighboring countries. In some professions, language barriers stop workers from moving abroad. But many soccer players do find work abroad, largely because television advertises their wares to employers across Europe. So most of the EU's best players have gathered in the biggest European leagues and meet one another on weekday nights in the Champions League. This competition is the European single market come to life, a dense network of talent. There's always much debate about the superiority of one soccer model over another—the Bundesliga versus the Premier League versus the Spanish league and Italy's Serie A—but the real point is the intensity of competition inside Europe, on the field and in the boardroom. That forces the big clubs to strive constantly for improvements.

The teams in the Champions League can draw talent from anywhere in the world. Nonetheless, an overwhelming majority of their players are Western European. With the world's best players and coaches packed together, the world's best soccer is constantly being refined there. That's what the German coach Joachim Löw explained at the press conference after his team won the final in Rio in 2014. Immaculate as ever and speaking despite the circumstances in his usual thoughtful manner, he reminded us how the Germans rebuilt their football after hitting a low in the early 2000s. They learned passing from the Dutch and Spaniards, speed of play from the English Premier League, and minority recruitment from the French. Their leading club, Bayern, imported as head coach first the leading Dutch thinker on football, Louis van Gaal, and then the leading Spaniard, Guardiola. Löw had also sent his assistant to chat with the coach of the Swiss handball team, which had developed the tactic of playing without a goalkeeper—an idea Löw himself had toyed with. In soccer you always have to keep innovating even when you are the best.

"Stealing" ideas paid off in Brazil in 2014. The best European countries had developed a game in which there are no specialists anymore: no nonpassing man-markers or big center forwards or ankle-biting midfielders who drop every ball at the feet of a skilled playmaker. Rather, in the better teams, especially Germany, every player looked like a passing, high-pressing midfielder—even the German keeper Manuel Neuer. Lionel Messi completed 242 passes at the World Cup; Neuer completed 244. His team completed 3,754 in total, one more than Spain in 2010, and the most for any team at any World Cup since 1966 (we simply don't know passing totals before then). Spain's tiki taka wasn't dead. It had just been updated—first by Germany and later, at Euro 2020, by Italy.

Western European soccer is a passing game played by athletes. Rarely does anyone dribble or keep the ball for a second. You pass instantly. It's not the beautiful game—dribbles are prettier—but it works best. All good teams everywhere in the world now play this way. Chris Anderson and David Sally showed in their book *The Numbers Game* how statistically alike the top European leagues are. Whether in the English Premier League, Serie A, the Bundesliga, or Spain's premier division, the average team completed similar numbers of passes per game, of similar lengths, and had comparable numbers of shots and corners. In all four leagues the average game produces somewhere between two-and-a-half and three goals. The differences between these nations "are cosmetic, shallow," the authors conclude. "If it was not for the shirts, you would not be able to tell them apart." All four leagues are producing Western European soccer. Even the Brazilians cannot compete with the Europeans because Brazil is excluded from the knowledge networks of Western Europe. In recent years it hasn't even tried to pass at a European pace. The 1–7 loss to Germany in 2014 was a one-off, but Brazil's decline is a long-term phenomenon.

Western Europe has discovered the secret of soccer. More precisely, a core group of Western European countries has—namely, five of the six nations that in 1957 founded the European Economic Community, ancestor of the European Union. (We'll leave out the sixth founding nation, the hopeless minnow Luxembourg.) Germany, France, Italy, the Netherlands, and Belgium don't all play in exactly the same style. But they all adhere to the basic tenets of rapid collectivized Western European soccer. Here are some results from the period 1968–2006:

- The core five countries won twelve European championships and World Cups between them.
- The countries at the corners of Europe—the Brits, the Iberians, the Balkans, the former Soviet bloc, and Scandinavian nations north of the Baltic Sea—between them won one: Greece's European Championship of 2004, delivered by a German coach.
- Europe's only other trophies in this period went to Denmark and Czechoslovakia. Denmark enjoys an utterly permeable border with the five core countries. Czechoslovakia was the exception, the only Eastern European country to win anything in this period.

Countries separated from the core of the EU—by great distance, by poverty, or by closed borders under dictatorships—often underperform in soccer. That's why large European countries like Russia and (contrary to our 2009 prediction) Turkey remain poor at the sport. The countries at great distance—and it can be a distance of the mind rather than geographical distance—are often out of touch with core European soccer tactics. Our point is not that "Europe" leads the world; it's that continental Western Europe does.

Again, this is explained by theories of networks. If you are on the periphery, like the Turks or Russians, it's harder to make new connections because you have to travel farther. Worse, those not on the periphery see you as only a second-best connection. You are the end of the line, not the gateway to a new set of links. As a result, the people on the periphery become more and more isolated and insular. The Ukrainian manager Valeri Lobanovsky was a soccer genius, but during the days of the Soviet Union he was so isolated that when a Dutch journalist came to interview him in the mid-1980s, Lobanovsky pumped him for information about Holland's players.

Spain had the same problem when it was cut off from the rest of the continent under General Franco's dictatorship, from 1939 through 1975. "Europe ends at the Pyrenees" was the saying in those days. Jimmy Burns, the Anglo-Spanish writer born in Madrid in 1953, recalls in *When Beckham Went to Spain*:

> Spain was virtually a closed economy. I spent part of my childhood between England and Spain, smuggling things from London to Madrid, never the other way round—clothes, gramophone records, books and magazines. While England seemed to be very much part of the world, Spain even to my young eyes struck me as something of a world of its own, where kids of my age all seemed to be taught by either priests or nuns.

The cosmopolitan Real Madrid of Burns's childhood, studded with imported stars such as Alfredo di Stefano (from Argentina), Ferenc Puskás (Hungary), and Raymond Kopa (France), was very much the exception in Franco's Spain. Few foreigners wanted to join lesser clubs in this poor country, and those who tried to come were often blocked. For most of the 1960s, Spain officially let in only foreign players of Spanish descent. In fact, many Latin American players invented Spanish ancestors to get in—one Argentine claimed his father had come from "Celta," which isn't a town at all but the name of the club in Vigo—but even these imports didn't transform Spanish soccer. There weren't many of them, and they mostly weren't very good. Nor did Spanish players of the Franco era go abroad to learn new tricks. During that period, Spain did almost nothing in international tournaments.

1990 TO 2002: THE LAST CONVERTS

Soccer seems to have a quality that enables it eventually to conquer every known society. However, for a century after Victorian Britons began spreading the game, Asia and North America remained almost immune. Contrary to myth, soccer took a long time to become a global game. What people called the "World Cup" should until the 1980s have been called "the Euro–Latin American Duopoly." Although most people on the planet lived in Asia, the continent's only representative at the World Cup of 1978 was Iran. Even in 1990 the British Isles had more teams at the World Cup (three) than all of Asia combined (two). Many Asian countries still barely knew about soccer. When that year's World Cup final was shown on Japanese television, there was a surprising studio guest: baseball player Sadaharu Oh. "Mr. Oh," he was asked during the match, "what is the difference between sliding in baseball and in soccer?" In Australia, too, soccer then was still marginal. Johnny Warren, an Australian international and later TV commentator on the game, called his memoirs *Sheilas, Wogs, and Poofters* because, according to Australian myth in the last century, women, immigrants, and gays were the three core elements of the national soccer public.

But by 1990, the so-called third wave of globalization was underway. Increased world trade, cable television, and finally the internet brought soccer to new territories. Roberto Fontanarrosa, the late Argentinian cartoonist, novelist, and soccer nut, said, "If TV were only an invention to broadcast soccer, it would be justified."

Suddenly, the Chinese, Japanese, Americans, and many urban Indians could see soccer's magic. Soccer by now had the prestige of being the world's biggest sport, and everyone wanted a piece of its fans' passion.

Soccer is often mocked for its low scores, but precisely because goals are so scarce the release of joy when they come is greater than in other sports. When the former goalkeeper Osama bin Laden visited London in 1994, he watched four Arsenal matches, bought souvenirs for his sons in the club shop, and remarked that he had never seen as much passion as among soccer supporters.

Just then, soccer was capturing the last holdouts. On May 15, 1993, Japan's J-League kicked off. The next year China acquired a national professional league, and in 1996 the US and India followed. A therapist we met at a soccer debate in San Francisco nicely described the game's impact on new converts. When she'd first seen a World Cup on TV, her reaction was, "Why didn't anybody ever tell me about this?" She hadn't stopped watching soccer since.

FROM THE BACK CORNER TO THE WORLD

From the 1990s, these new countries began to hire European coaches who could quickly teach them the latest in soccer. Perhaps the archetypal one was the Dutchman Guus Hiddink. His journey tells the story of how soccer knowledge spread around the world—yet didn't spread deeply enough.

Born in 1946, Hiddink grew up close to what was just becoming the epicenter of global soccer knowledge. He is the son of a village schoolteacher and Resistance hero from a small town in the Achterhoek, or "Back Corner," about five miles from the German border. The Back Corner is wooded and quiet, one of the few empty bits of the Netherlands, and on visits home from stints coaching in Seoul or Moscow, Hiddink enjoyed tooling along its back roads on his Harley-Davidson Fat Boy. "Pom-pom-pom-pom-pom." He puffs out his cheeks to mimic the motor's roar.

He grew up milking cows, plowing behind two horses, and dreaming of becoming a farmer. But Dutch farms were already dying, and he became a soccer coach instead. At nineteen he took an assistant's job at the Back Corner's semiprofessional club, De Graafschap, where his father had played before him. He then made an unusual career move: from coach to player. The head coach, seeing that his young assistant could kick a ball, stuck him in the team and thus launched a sixteen-year playing career.

The handsome, round-faced, wavy-haired playmaker was too lazy and slow for the top, yet he was present at a golden age. The Dutch 1970s shaped Hiddink. Johan Cruyff's national team, playing what foreigners called "total football," a new kind of game in which players constantly swapped positions and thought for themselves, reached two World Cup finals. Dutch clubs won four European Cups. Off the field, Dutch players of Hiddink's generation answered foreign journalists' questions with sophisticated discourses in several languages. For a keen observer like Hiddink, the players' constant squabbles provided object lessons in how to keep stars just about functioning within a collective.

Dutch soccer's renown at the time helped even a second-rate player like Hiddink find work abroad, with the Washington Diplomats and the San Jose Earthquakes. "I was Best's roommate," says Hiddink, enjoying the quirky American word, and he mimics himself fielding phone calls from Best's groupies: "George is not here. George is sleeping."

By the turn of the millennium, Hiddink was an obvious candidate for export. He had won the European Cup with PSV Eindhoven, had managed clubs in Turkey and Spain, and had taken Holland to the World Cup semifinal in 1998. After passing fifty, he felt his ambition beginning to wane. Never a workaholic to start with, the boy from the Back Corner had by now proven himself. He had met with triumph and disaster and treated those two impostors just the same. He had gone from villager to cosmopolitan. He had fallen in love with golf. Soccer was becoming just a hobby.

He took a break and in 2001 popped up in his first missionary posting, as manager of South Korea. As part of the globalization of soccer, the country was due to cohost the 2002 World Cup with Japan. South Korea had played in several World Cups before but had never won a single match, and in 1998 it had lost 5–0 to Hiddink's Holland.

When Hiddink landed in Seoul, history was beginning to work in his favor. Like many emerging nations, the South Koreans were getting bigger. Thanks to increased wealth, the average height of a South Korean man had risen from five foot four in the 1930s to about five foot eight by 2002. That meant a bigger pool of men with the physique required to play international soccer. In an interview during a Korean training camp in the Back Corner, a year before the World Cup, Hiddink told us he'd caught Koreans using their smallness as an excuse in soccer. He added, "But I won't allow that. I won't let them say beforehand, 'They're a bit bigger and broader; we're small and sad.' And gradually I notice that some of our players are big, too, and know how to look after themselves." The "height effect" was also quietly lifting many other emerging soccer countries, from Japan to Turkey.

But the Koreans had other problems. The Dutch psychological quirk was squabbling. The Korean disease, as Hiddink soon discovered, was hierarchy. In Korean soccer the older the player, the higher his status. A thirty-one-year-old veteran international was so respected that he could coast. At meals, the group of older players would sit down at the table first, and the youngest last.

Whereas Dutch players talked too much, Koreans were practically mute. "Slavishness is a big word," Hiddink said that day in the Back Corner, "but they do have something like, 'If the commander says it, we'll follow it blindly.' They are used to thinking, 'I'm a soldier. I'll do what's asked of me.' And you have to go a step further if you want to make a team really mature. You need people who can and will take the team in their hands." Hiddink wanted autonomous-thinking "Dutch" players: a center-half who at a certain point in the game sees he should push into midfield, a striker who drops back a few yards. He was teaching the Koreans the Dutch variant of the continental European style.

At the 2002 World Cup, the Koreans played with a fervor rarely seen in soccer. Helped by bizarre refereeing decisions, the country from soccer's periphery reached the semifinal. It remains the only team from outside Europe and South America to reach that stage in a World Cup since 1934.

Korea had craved global recognition, and Hiddink achieved it. Korean cities planned statues in his honor, and a caricature of his face appeared on Korean stamps. Hiddink's autobiography appeared in a Korean print run of half a million, despite having to compete with an estimated sixteen Hiddink biographies. In the Back Corner, Korean tour buses made pilgrimages to the Hiddink ancestral home. Soon after the World Cup, the man himself dropped by to visit his octogenarian parents. "Well, it wasn't bad," admitted his father. "Coffee?"

The Hiddink story is only one among many. When we first wrote about the value of soccer networks back in 2009, there was little empirical evidence to prove it one way or the other. That evidence is now starting to appear. In a paper first published in 2019, Thomas Peeters, Brian Mills, Enrico Pennings, and Hojung Sung analyzed the performance of men's national soccer teams and the identity of the manager for the period 1980–2015. They found that, in general, hiring a foreign coach didn't help the national team but that it did make a positive difference if the coach came from a country that was more successful in international competition than the destination country. Moreover, the effect was enhanced when there was a smaller cultural distance (measured using characteristics widely employed in sociology) between the origin country and destination country of the manager. Given the dominance and cultural homogeneity of Western Europe, this is evidence that supports our network theory.

2002 TO 2004: THE PERIPHERY STARTS BEATING THE CORE

At that World Cup of 2002, other peripheral soccer countries were emerging, too. Japan reached the second round, the US got to the quarters, and Korea was conquered in the match for third place by Turkey, which hadn't even played in a World Cup since 1954.

Several other countries also began to jettison their traditional soccer culture. Most countries on the fringes of Europe had dysfunctional indigenous playing styles. The ones on the southern fringe—Greece, Turkey, Portugal—favored pointless dribbling, whereas the British and Scandinavians played kick-and-rush. Eventually, they accepted that these styles didn't work. They came to the realization that every marginal country should, that there is only one way to play good soccer: combine traditional Italian defending with German work ethic and Dutch passing. This is the European style. ("Industrial soccer," some Turks sulkily call it.) In soccer, national styles don't work. You have to have all the different elements. You cannot win international matches playing traditional British or Turkish soccer. You need to play the continental European way.

Nobody did better out of abandoning their roots and adopting continental European soccer than Turkey's friends across the water, the Greeks. The Greek national team had traditionally played terrible soccer in front of a couple thousand spectators. But in 2002 it gave up on the

Greek style and imported a vast chunk of experience in the person of an aging German manager, Otto Rehhagel.

The Rhinelander was the prototypical postwar West German collectivist. He had grown up a healthy drive across the border from Hiddink, amid the ruins of postwar western Germany. An apprentice housepainter and bone-hard defender, Rehhagel was brought up on the "German virtues" of hard work and discipline. As a coach in Germany for decades, he aimed to sign only collectivist European-type players whose personalities had been vetted by his wife over dinner in the Rehhagel home. Everywhere he tried to build an organization. Sacked as manager of Arminia Bielefeld, he sighed, "At least thanks to me there is now a toilet at the training ground." On later visits to Bielefeld with other clubs, he always inquired about his toilet.

Rehhagel rooted out Greece's cult of the soloist, introduced core European soccer, and took the team to Euro 2004 in Portugal. As Angelos Charisteas, the reserve at Werder Bremen who would become the highest scorer of Euro 2004, eulogized, "We have a German coach, he has a German mentality, and we play like a German team." Greece had made the journey from Lilliputian dribblers to boring European soccer thanks to German coaching.

Rehhagel himself called it "learning from European soccer." At the time, becoming "European"—code for becoming organized—was the aspiration of many marginal European countries. Just as these countries were joining the European Union, they were absorbing European soccer. The final of Euro 2004 pitted Greece against another recently marginal country. The Greeks beat the Portuguese 1–0 thanks to a header from Charisteas, who soon afterward would be a reserve again at Ajax Amsterdam. It turned out that with merely half-decent players, a good continental European coach, and time to prepare, almost any marginal country could do well. But with hindsight, the 2002–2004 period was probably the periphery's peak to date.

2005 AND 2006: EVEN AUSTRALIA

In the new climate of the early 2000s, the best continental European coaches could pick their jobs. Hiddink received many offers to take teams to the World Cup of 2006, but he chose the most marginal country of all: Australia.

In 1974, while Hiddink was still absorbing total soccer in the Back Corner, Australia had qualified for its first World Cup as Asia's sole representative. The Socceroos of the day were part-timers, and some had to give up their jobs to go to Germany. The German press was particularly interested in the milkman-cum-defender Manfred Schaefer, who had been born in Hitler's Reich in 1943 and came to Australia as a child refugee after the war. At one point in the tournament, West Germany's striker Gerd Müller asked him if he really was an amateur. Well, Schaefer proudly replied, he had earned $4,600 by qualifying for the World Cup. "That's what I earn a week," said Müller.

The Australians achieved one tie in three matches at the World Cup. "However," writes Matthew Hall in his excellent book about Australian soccer, *The Away Game*, "their thongs, super-tight Aussie Rules–style shorts and marsupial mascots endeared them to the German public."

In the next thirty years, soccer sank so low in Australia that the country's soccer federation was sometimes reduced to filming its own matches and giving them to TV channels for free. Australian club soccer was punctuated by weird vendettas between Balkan ethnic groups. Only in 1997, during the new wave of globalization, were the Socceroos of 1974 publicly honored in their own country.

Then, in 2005, Hiddink landed with a mission to teach European soccer. First he gathered the Australian team in a training camp in his native Back Corner. He spent the first training session watching his new charges fly into each other like kamikaze pilots. "You don't have to chase these guys up," he remarked. After a half hour he stopped the game. When the players' cries of "Come on, Emmo!" "Hold the ball, Johnno!" "Let's go!" and the streams of "fucking" had finally faded, Hiddink asked them to shout only when a teammate was in trouble and needed coaching. That would improve everyone's vision of play, he said. The game resumed in near silence. It was Australia's first baby step toward continental European soccer.

Just as he had with the Koreans, Hiddink was turning the Australians into Dutch soccer players. That meant giving them the intellectual discipline needed for the World Cup. The Australian way was to train hard, play hard, but then relax with late-night beers in the hotel bar. Hiddink wanted the players thinking on their own about their jobs. Working hard wasn't enough. Hiddink was teaching them to think like their European peers. The Socceroos tended to run to wherever the ball was. Hiddink forbade them from entering certain zones. In European soccer, doing the right things is better than doing a lot of things.

Before taking over, he had watched the Confederations Cup of 2005, where the Socceroos had lost all three of their games and conceded ten goals. Hiddink noticed that all four Australian defenders would often stay back to mark a single forward. That left them short elsewhere on the field. No semiprofessional Western European team would be so naive.

It was striking how quickly the Socceroos learned the basics of European soccer. In November 2005, only a couple of months after Hiddink had started part-time work with them (he was also coaching PSV at the other end of the globe), they beat Uruguay in a playoff to qualify for the World Cup. Suddenly the *Melbourne Herald Sun* found itself wondering whether "Aussie Rules" football could remain dominant in Australia's southern states. Already, more Australian children played soccer than Aussie Rules and both rugby codes combined.

The newspaper's worries appeared justified when, just before the World Cup of 2006, an Australia-Greece soccer exhibition game drew 95,000 people to the Melbourne Cricket Ground. In no city in Europe or Latin America could such a matchup have drawn such a crowd. Australia had also just become approximately the last country on Earth to acquire a national professional soccer league.

And then Hiddink led the Socceroos to the second round of the World Cup of 2006. Great crowds of Australians set their alarm clocks to watch at unearthly hours. A century from now, Aussie Rules might exist only at subsidized folklore festivals.

THE YEARS 2006 TO 2009: HIDDINK TO GHIDDINK IN A MOSCOW HOTEL SUITE

After Australia, Hiddink could have had almost any job in soccer. He decided to spread his continental European know-how to Russia.

Russia had always been removed from the best Western European soccer know-how. The country didn't have much of a tradition. The excellent Soviet side of the 1980s had been mostly Ukrainian. But now, after communism, Russia's door to the West had opened slightly. There was potential here.

When Hiddink took the job, the Russian economy was moving the right way. In the decade from 1998, Russian income per capita nearly doubled (before it fell again). The country's new oil money bought Hiddink's brain. (Oil in general has become one of the dominant financial forces in modern soccer.)

As in Korea, Hiddink's job was to force his players to be free. Traditionally, Russian soccer players had the "I only work here" demeanor of *Homo sovieticus*. They feared their coaches as much as they feared the mafiosi who stole their jeeps. They shoved safe sideways passes into each other's feet because that way nobody could ever shout at them. There was *zaorganizovannost*, over-organization.

Ghiddink, as the Russians call him, joked with his players, relaxing them. As a "punishment" in training, a player might have a ball kicked at his backside while the rest of the squad stood around laughing.

As he had in Korea, Hiddink practically ordered his players to think for themselves, to give riskier passes, to move into new positions without his telling them to. As Marc Bennetts, author of *Soccer Dynamo: Modern Russia and the People's Game*, said, "It's as if he's beaten the Marxism-Leninism out of them." At Euro 2008, Russia's hammering of Ghiddink's native Holland was the ultimate triumph of a marginal country over a core one. It also provided the almost unprecedented sight of Russian soccer players having fun. They swapped positions and dribbled, knowing that if they lost the ball no one would scream at them. After the game, their best player, Andrei Arshavin, muttered something about "a wise Dutch coach" and cried.

Russia lost in the semis of Euro 2008 to another former marginal country, Spain. The Spaniards went on to win the tournament, then the World Cup of 2010, and finally Euro 2012.

MADE IN AMSTERDAM: THE EUROPEAN NETWORK REACHES SPAIN

What saved Spain's soccer was the country's opening to Europe and the world from the 1970s onward. For decades the dictator General Franco had closed off the country, but by the early 1970s he was dying and his grip was waning. In 1973, just after Spain reopened its borders to foreign soccer players, FC Barcelona imported the great Dutchman Johan

Cruyff. It is possible to draw a direct line between his arrival in Barcelona and Spain's victory in Johannesburg thirty-seven years later.

Signing Cruyff had not been easy. Franco's regime often obstructed Spanish companies from making foreign payments, and Barcelona ended up having to register the player as a piece of agricultural machinery. In another mark of the isolationist climate of the time, an elderly Barça director lamented to the club's secretary, Armand Carabén, "A Dutchman in the Nou Camp! What's the world coming to? This is pure madness. A man from the land of butter comes to the land of olive oil. Does nobody understand that even if he plays nicely, his stomach will be a mess within four days?"

But Cruyff was more than just stomach and legs. Possibly more than any other great player, he was brain, too. He was a philosopher of soccer, and the most important thing about soccer, for Cruyff, was the pass. He could (and often did) spend hours talking about the pass. You never passed into a teammate's feet, he lectured, but always a meter in front of him, to keep the pace in the game. While the first man was passing to the second man, the third man already had to be in motion ready to receive the second man's pass. Cruyff talked people silly about the pass.

In the early 1970s he and Barcelona's Dutch manager, Rinus Michels, introduced Spaniards to a form of Dutch "total football." The two men had arrived at just the right time. Besides opening to the world, Spain was then beginning its long economic rise.

Cruyff played his last game for Barcelona in 1978, but Spain would hear from him again. As coach of Barça from 1988 through 1996, he brought his ideas on soccer back to Catalonia. Barcelona began building a style based on knowledge transfer from Amsterdam. From the late 1990s Spain, too, began adopting this made-in-Amsterdam game. They began passing the ball up and down like little men filling in a crossword puzzle at top speed. Whenever they went 1–0 up, they simply made sure that the opponent never got the ball again.

Spain became a great soccer nation because it shook off isolation and joined European knowledge networks. This might sound like too neat a theory—the sort of thing you get when you let academics loose on something as mysterious and intuitive as soccer. But the facts seem to match our idea. Let's look at Spain's results, decade by decade.

We'll take the 1920s as an illustration of what Table 18.2 shows. Spain won twenty-three of its thirty-two matches in the decade, or 72 percent. It also tied four games. If we count a tie as worth half a win, then Spain's total winning percentage for the decade was 78 percent. The figure in the last column for each decade is the most telling one. It provides the best measure of Spain's success decade by decade.

The table demonstrates how closely Spain's soccer success tracks the country's integration with Europe. In the 1920s Spain performed very well. But civil war broke out in 1936, and in 1939 Franco took power and shut off the country. From the 1930s through the 1980s, Spain's winning percentage hovered around a disappointing 60 percent. The team was winning about half its games and drawing another quarter. Victory in the European Championship of 1964 was an anomaly. The broader story was that a poor, shut-off Spain was struggling to access the world's best soccer know-how. In these sorry decades, di Stefano, the Argentinian turned Colombian turned Spanish international, summed up Spain's soccer history in a phrase: "We played like never before, and lost like always."

But in 1986 Spain joined the European Union—a sort of formal entry into European networks. Soon after, the Spanish national team improved sharply. We have seen that a country's success at soccer correlates with its wealth. And Spain from the 1980s was growing richer fast. In the 1960s and 1970s, its income per capita had been stuck at about 60 percent of

TABLE 18.2. The rise of Spain

Decade	Played	Won	Tied	Lost	Wpc	Wpc (counting a tie as half a win)
1920s	32	23	4	5	0.72	0.78
1930s	25	13	5	7	0.52	0.62
1940s	19	8	6	5	0.42	0.58
1950s	44	20	13	11	0.45	0.6
1960s	60	28	13	19	0.47	0.58
1970s	59	29	18	12	0.49	0.64
1980s	103	49	28	26	0.48	0.61
1990s	98	57	26	15	0.58	0.71
2000s	128	91	25	12	0.71	0.81
2010s	132	93	21	18	0.78	0.78

the average of the core fifteen member nations of the EU. In the 1980s and 1990s, Spain began to catch up. The Barcelona Olympics of 1992 nicely captured the rise: the Games showcased a "new Spain," and a young Spanish soccer team guided by Cruyff's chosen disciple, the twenty-one-year-old Pep Guardiola, won gold.

Spain's resources continued to improve. Since the country joined the EU, and despite its terrible sufferings since the 2008 economic crisis, its average income has risen to about three-quarters of the core EU's average. Its population has grown to 47 million. Spain has also become fully networked in Europe. Its best soccer players now experience the Champions League every season. A richer, more populous, more experienced, and more networked post-Franco Spain became first a serious contender and then finally the best team on Earth.

In the 1990s, Spain's win percentage (still treating ties as worth half a win) shot up to over 70 percent. In the 2000s, it was over 80 percent, with Spain losing just 12 percent of its games. From 2000 through 2009, the country won 71 percent of its matches outright, a long-term performance about as good as any other national team's since international soccer took off in the 1930s. Brazil never managed it. Even the all-conquering Italy of the 1930s won just 70 percent of its games in that decade. In 2010 the Spaniards sealed their rise by winning the World Cup final against their mentor country, the Netherlands.

THE 2010S AND BEYOND: THE PERIPHERY STALLS

It seemed at the time that the rise of the periphery was threatening soccer's traditional order. We thought that other, bigger, richer countries around the world would "do a Spain" or a Korea: copy the leading Western European teams and then beat them at their own game. Hence the subtitle of that first edition of *Soccernomics*. But it hasn't happened. Spain aside, the soccer powers of a generation ago are mostly still the powers of today.

Until the late 1990s, the cliché in soccer was that an African country would "soon" win the World Cup. Everyone said it, from Pelé to the 1950s England manager Walter Winterbottom. But it turned out not to be true. Nor can the richer Asian countries compete with the world's best. Look at Figure 18.1, which shows how the "new" continents have performed against established Europe and South America since 1950.

FIGURE 18.1. Cumulative win percentages since 1950 of the Asian (AFC), African (CAF), and Central/North American (CONCACAF) teams against the European (UEFA) and South American (CONMEBOL) teams (including both competitive and exhibition games)

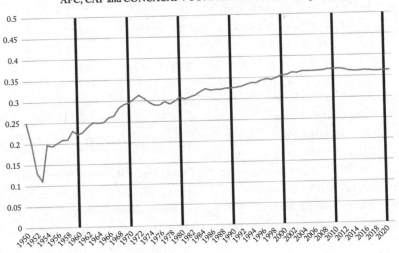

AFC, CAF and CONCACAF v CONMEBOL and UEFA win percentage

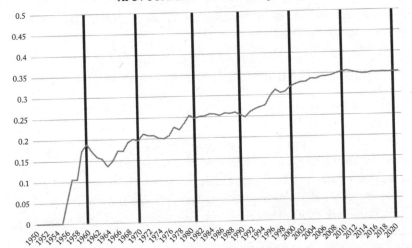

AFC v CONMEBOL and UEFA win percentage

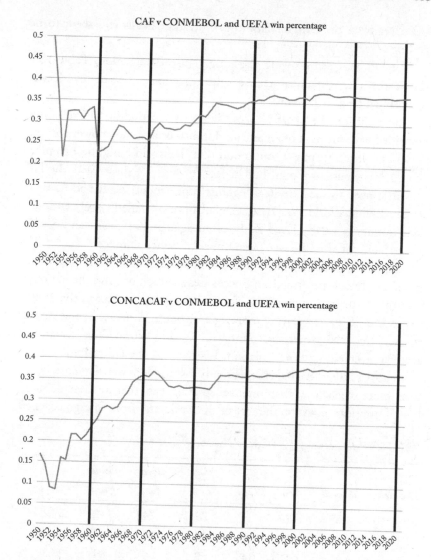

The charts allot more space to decades in which more matches were played. What we see is that all the emerging continents initially improve but then stall. The Africans reach their peak in about 1990 before plateauing. (With hindsight, Cameroon's thrilling run to the World Cup quarterfinals in 1990 was the end of Africa's rise, not the start of it, as most people thought at the time.) The North and Central Americans stalled early in the new millennium. Only the Asians still seem to be getting very slightly better.

The US has been showing alarming signs of stagnation. Table 18.3 shows the men's national team's win percentage, decade by decade (counting a tie as half a win).

The nadir for "Team USA" was the postwar period up to 1960. This coincided with the peak of American dominance as a superpower and the American dream. It might sound odd that the world's mightiest country was such a mouse at soccer, but in fact for most of these years the US felt little need to measure itself against other countries. It had its own games. Before World War II, an American team staffed largely with recent immigrants had played fairly often against Europeans and South Americans, but after the war the number of games slumped.

The table shows that from the 1970s, the US grew more interested in soccer. The North American Soccer League took off, and the national team began playing more often. Things kept getting better in the 1980s (when the US started playing more against South Americans) and stayed stable in the 1990s, when the country returned to World Cups. American soccer was emerging from isolation. It's not that the US started scoring more goals; rather, it gradually learned to concede fewer. Defense is always more mechanical than offense, so it appears that in these decades the US was learning from the rest of the world and from foreign coaches

TABLE 18.3. Win percentage for US men's national team

Decade	Played	Won	Tied	Lost	Goals for	Goals against	Wpc
pre-1950	39	13	3	23	74	141	37.2%
1950s	18	4	0	14	31	69	22.2%
1960s	17	4	4	9	26	44	35.3%
1970s	48	9	9	30	30	102	28.1%
1980s	53	19	17	17	52	55	51.9%
1990s	195	72	50	73	247	219	49.7%
2000s	168	95	31	42	288	148	65.8%
2010s	153	77	30	46	254	172	60.1%

such as Bora Milutinovic. Yet when we calculated the world's worst underachieving nations for the period 1980–2001 (more on this later), the US still made our bottom ten. Given the country's fabulous wealth and enormous population, it "should" have scored nearly three-quarters of a goal more per game than it did. Its win percentage in those twenty-one years (counting ties as half a win) was just 52 percent.

In the 2000s the US's win percentage jumped to 66 percent, double what it had been before 1960. Admittedly, that statistic flattered the country. The Americans were playing fewer internationals against the strong teams from Europe and South America. In the decade through 2010, for the first time since the 1970s the US played the majority of its games against North and Central American teams. That isn't the way to learn global cutting-edge best practice. Then, from 2011 through 2020, the team's win percentage fell to 60 percent; performance began declining well before the remarkable American failure to qualify for World Cup 2018. The US has never regained its peak FIFA ranking of eighth place in 2005. It spent much of the 2010s in the range of twenties through thirties. There is currently much optimism about a clutch of rising stars, notably Christian Pulisic, but it is as if the US started the 2020s from the same place it found itself twenty years before.

In short, there is a common pattern for soccer's developing nations: for a while they catch up, but then they stall before reaching the top. Why?

Almost exactly the same question has long been asked about developing countries in a different context: national income. Is the gap between rich and poor countries narrowing or expanding? This research is often associated with the pioneering work of Robert Barro (of Harvard) and Pep Guardiola's friend Xavier Sala-i-Martin (of Columbia University, and the treasurer of FC Barcelona from 2004 to 2010). They reasoned that it's easier for a poor country like Vietnam to grow its economy than it is for a rich one like the US. That's because much of what Vietnam has to do in the early stages is simply copy: if it imports the kinds of computers and other machines that are already being used in the US, then its offices and factories will quickly become more productive.

By contrast, if the US wants to grow, it has to do new things, which is more difficult. Investors, knowing that, will be keener to invest their capital in Vietnam than in the US. All things being equal, Vietnam's economy will then grow faster than the US's. That's catch-up—at least for countries going from poverty to middle income.

There are possibly only two topics in this world about which we can gather data for every country over an extended period. Luckily, those topics happen to be national income and national soccer teams' results. When a country becomes independent, it joins the UN, sets up a central bank, collects taxes, and starts reporting national income accounts. It also joins FIFA to create a national soccer team. And if we want to study convergence, arguably soccer data are best, for we know the score of every international game ever played, whereas measuring national income is notoriously unreliable.

So what do the data tell us? On national income, there is evidence for the convergence of incomes across many parts of the world, notably Europe, Asia, and North America. Certainly before the pandemic, poor countries were closing the gap between their living standards and those of rich countries. The bad news is that the global economic picture is extremely patchy. For much of the 1980s, 1990s, and 2000s, African countries in particular actually fell further behind the developed world. War, political instability, climate change, underinvestment in health and education, and bad infrastructure held them back.

The picture for soccer convergence is different. Stefan, together with Melanie Krause from the University of Hamburg, looked for convergence in two statistics: average goal difference and average win percentage (counting draws as half a win) from 1950 through 2014, averaged over four-year World Cup cycles.

The main finding: if your national team started off underperforming, it was likely to get better, regardless of when and where you were in the world. Standards across the world have slowly converged for many years. The poorest countries have improved fastest. FIFA deserves some credit for this. Just by staging World Cups in all age ranges and running a regulated international transfer market, it has helped the weak catch up. Of course, FIFA could have done so much more if only it had put all the billions it earned from World Cups into building facilities in poor countries.

Catch-up seems to be simpler in soccer than in macroeconomics. A developing country can improve its soccer just by copying the training and tactics used in the best countries. That's easier when much of the know-how you need is broadcast worldwide every evening on TV. Migrant coaches like Hiddink help do the copying. By contrast, copying whole economic systems is much harder and requires extraordinary coordination.

It probably also matters that so many people care deeply about their national soccer teams' results and that outcomes are highly visible. Meeting a clear target is often much simpler than meeting a complex one. A bad economy can always be blamed on someone else, but the national soccer team is more accountable.

And whereas governments can nationalize or steal foreign investments, they can't easily steal the returns on the skills of soccer players. If a country's soccer is dysfunctional, the best players will simply go abroad and learn new skills there.

So why do developing soccer nations stall before entirely catching up with the best countries? Melanie and Stefan have scoured the wider convergence literature for an explanation, and they think they have found the culprit: the middle-income trap. The idea is that convergence from a low level of income is relatively simple: invest, invest, invest. As we've said, you just need to import or copy capital (machines) from more advanced countries. Capital makes people more productive. Almost regardless of the wider economic system, this prescription will work.

However, it works only up to a point. Once a certain minimum of catch-up has been achieved, you need to become innovative. The greatest wealth ultimately goes to innovators (in today's world, think Apple, Google, Amazon, Facebook, and Tesla). A nation's mind-set therefore needs to change as national income increases. We see this today in many Asian countries where governments are encouraging individualism in order to promote more-innovative economies. But it's a hard shift to make.

The same applies in soccer. Teams from Asia, North America, and Africa have in recent decades managed to replicate some of the basic patterns of play developed in Europe and South America. In particular, the weak have gotten fit and learned to defend. They no longer lose 10–0. Yet they now appear caught in soccer's equivalent of the middle-income trap. They play organized soccer, but the exciting new tactics (think of Italian and German forward pressing) still come from Western Europe.

Who might eventually catch up with the best? Our outside bets for future kings of the world are three large, relatively well-off countries that are now taking soccer seriously: the US, Japan, and China.

As we write, the US remains the poor little rich boy of men's soccer, but more than any other non-European country it has the means to get to the top. In the last twenty-five years it has regularly reached the last sixteen of World Cups, and it has the most registered young soccer players of any nation.

Japan, for its part, has drawn up a plan to host the World Cup again by 2050 and win it. Both countries already dominate women's soccer: Japan won the World Cup in 2011 and the US in 2015 and 2019. In the women's game, where no country has much experience, big, rich nations win.

However, as we've seen, both nations are stagnating in men's soccer. More than twenty years after they set up national competitions, neither the J-League nor MLS looks capable of nurturing world-class players. In fact, the best advice we can give any aspiring star from either country is simple: move to Western Europe fast. The US and Japan have come far since the 1990s, but the final step to excellence is often the hardest one.

China is a different story. It hasn't come far at all yet. As of 2022, the country of 1.3 billion people has still only ever qualified for that single World Cup in 2002 and is a humiliating seventy-fourth in the FIFA rankings, one spot behind the Cape Verde Islands.

But soccer-mad president-for-life Xi Jinping is trying to turn around the Chinese game. Historically, very few Chinese kids were ever given the chance to play sports, which were seen as a "distraction" from the serious business of learning. Travel around Shanghai or Beijing, and you would scarcely see a ball being kicked anywhere. Then, in 2014, China's State Council issued "Document No. 46," outlining a policy to build sports into a $770 billion industry by 2025. Xi had made soccer a national priority. He set China the goal of becoming a "football power" that would host and win the World Cup before 2050. China began hiring foreign coaches to train thousands of Chinese soccer teachers. In theory, if not quite yet in practice, soccer became compulsory in schools. The number of soccer fields in the country rose about sixfold, to about one for every twenty thousand people by 2021. And as more Chinese parents get into soccer themselves, they will start kicking balls with their kids in the crucial under-six age group.

Over time, all this might pay off. A country the size of China cannot easily continue to perform so badly. We expect that it will soon routinely start to qualify for World Cups. Still, we are skeptical about the potential for a soccer system imposed from the top to create world-beating teams. There is a difference between producing an Olympic swimming champion—which is all about physiology, biomechanics, and workaholic training—and nurturing thinking, autonomous, joyous soccer players. We suspect that soccer is a little too individualistic to succumb to the iron will of five-year plans.

Something else will help the biggest non-European countries. The expansion of the World Cup to forty-eight teams in 2026 will make the competition more random. In the group phase, teams will play just two matches each, so a lucky win will be enough to reach the second round. If teams are tied, there will be penalty shoot-outs—another randomizer. Then there will be five straight knockout rounds, one more than in the current system. The upshot will be a competition in which chance plays a bigger role, much as with the playoff stages of the NFL. That should favor plausible outsiders, such as the US (especially playing at home in 2026), Japan, and soon probably China.

In the long term, Western Europe's dominance still looks unsustainable. When the whole world is playing soccer and watching the best games on TV every night, a region with 5 percent of the planet's population surely can't keep winning forever. But then we called catch-up once before, and we were wrong. The safest thing to say is that it will happen one day, but we're no longer specifying in which century.

19

WHY ENGLAND STILL LOSES— BUT NOWADAYS ONLY JUST

The original version of this chapter, published in our first *Soccernomics* edition in 2009, was called "Why England Loses." In fact, in Britain the book itself was called *Why England Lose*. (In British grammar all collective nouns are plural. For instance, "The jury have returned.") Going into the 2010 World Cup, English people often asked us: "Aren't you worried about your title? What if England win?" We weren't very worried. Later we changed the British title anyway, to *Soccernomics*, because it turned out (amazingly) that few English people wanted to buy a book called *Why England Lose*.

At the time, England's journeys to major tournaments had become a kind of ritual of national failure. The English would take an emotional roller coaster from great expectations—"I think we will win it," said England's coach Sven Goran Eriksson a month before the World Cup 2006—to communal bafflement when the team crashed out early, generally on penalties. England's failure to win anything since the holy year of 1966 became a cause of much embarrassment for British expatriates in bars on the Spanish coast. The London media also felt almost perpetually let down by the players. England was "known as perennial underachievers on the world stage," according to the tabloid the *Sun*; its history "has been a landscape sculpted from valleys of underachievement," said the *Independent*. The former England captain Terry Butcher grumbled in the *Sunday Mirror* in 2006 that "historical underachievement has somehow conspired to make England feel even more important." When we first wrote this chapter, our mission was to try to explain why England lost.

But with the years, two things changed. First, after about 2010, English expectations collapsed. To adapt T. S. Eliot, humankind can take only so much reality. The endless disappointments seem to have finally persuaded England's fans and media to shed the fantasy of manifest destiny. Perhaps helped by a general decline in national status, they had begun to realize they were just another country, not destined to rule the world. In 2014, when the pollsters Yougov surveyed nineteen participating countries before the World Cup, the most pessimistic fans (jointly with Costa Ricans) were the English: only 4 percent expected to win in Brazil. (The most optimistic supporters, incidentally, were Brazilians, 64 percent of whom expected victory.) At last, the English were becoming realistic. (The 2016 vote for Brexit—to leave the European Union and "go it alone"—was in part a last-ditch attempt by the older generation to hang on to the idea of national exceptionalism.)

Then a second, more surprising change occurred: England started to win. In 2018 the team reached the World Cup semifinal. Three years later, at the delayed Euro 2020, it reached its first final of any major tournament since 1966 and lost to Italy only on penalties. So this revised chapter now asks two questions: Why does England lose? But also, why has it recently begun to win?

In trying to explain why England loses, we hear strange echoes from the arena of development economics. The central question in that field is "Why are some countries less productive than others?" Some of the reasons why England loses would sound familiar to any development economist. So would the most popular incorrect explanation for their defeats. Here's our attempt to explain England's eliminations—first by dismissing the false explanation, then by setting out the correct ones.

BRITISH JOBS FOR BRITISH WORKERS? WHY THERE ARE TOO MANY ENGLISHMEN IN THE PREMIER LEAGUE

When pundits gathered to explain England's defeats, their favorite scapegoat for many years was imports: the hundreds of foreigners who play in the Premier League. Here is England's midfielder Steven Gerrard speaking before England lost at home to Croatia and failed to qualify for Euro

2008: "I think there is a risk of too many foreign players coming over, which would affect our national team eventually if it's not already. It is important we keep producing players."

After all, if our boys can barely even get a game in their own league, how can they hope to mature into internationals? Following England's defeat to Croatia, Sepp Blatter (FIFA's president), Alex Ferguson (Manchester United's manager), and Michel Platini (UEFA's president) all made versions of Gerrard's argument.

These men were effectively blaming imports for the English lack of skills. They reasoned that England's own workers weren't getting a chance because they were being displaced by foreign ones. Exactly the same argument is often made in development economics. Why are some countries not very productive? Partly because their inhabitants don't have enough skills. The best place to learn skills—such as making toothpaste, teaching math, or playing soccer—is on the job. To learn how to make toothpaste, you have to actually make it, not just take a class to learn how to make it. But if you are always importing toothpaste, you will never learn.

This is why there is a long history of development economists (and nationalist politicians) calling for "import substitution." Ban or tax certain imports so that the country can learn to make the stuff itself. Import substitution has worked for a few countries. After World War II, Japan managed to teach itself, almost from scratch, how to make all sorts of high-quality cars and electrical gadgets.

The idea of import substitution in the Premier League has an emotional appeal to many English fans. Some Britons complain about feeling overrun by immigrants, and few spots in the country are more foreign than a Premier League field on match day. All told, Englishmen accounted for only 37 percent of the minutes played by individual players in the Premier League in the 2007–2008 season before Croatia's night at Wembley. A decade later, that figure was almost exactly the same. To some degree, English soccer was ceasing to exist.

Imagine for a moment that English clubs had agreed to discriminate against players from other European countries. Had that happened, the people who complain about imports would probably have ended up disappointed. If inferior English players were handed places in Premier League teams, they would have little incentive to improve. This is a classic problem with import substitution: it protects bad producers. What then tends to happen is that short-term protection becomes long-term protection.

But in fact, Gerrard's entire premise was wrong. If people in soccer understood numbers better, they would have grasped that the problem of the English team was not that there were too few Englishmen playing in the Premier League.

You could argue that English players accounted for "only" about 37 percent of minutes in the Premier League. Or you could argue that they accounted for a massive 37 percent of minutes. That works out to over seventy Englishmen per match day—more than any other nationality in one of the world's best leagues. The Portuguese, Croatians, and Uruguayans dream of accounting for 37 percent of minutes in the Premier League, or indeed in any big league. If you have more than seventy Englishmen playing regularly at that level, it should be enough to make up a decent squad of twenty-two.

In other words, English players get a lot of regular experience in top-level club soccer. If we lump together the world's three toughest leagues—the Premier League, Spain's Primera División, and Germany's Bundesliga—then only German, Spanish, and possibly Brazilian national players participate in more-demanding club soccer. But certainly English players get far more experience in top-level soccer than, say, Croatians or Uruguayans do.

The experience of competing against the best foreign players every week has probably helped English internationals to improve. Englishmen have had to get better just to stay in their club teams. They now learn about international soccer every week.

Lo and behold, since the Premier League has become more international, England's performances have improved. The switch from a mostly British league to a mostly foreign one can be dated to 1995, the year of the "Bosman ruling" that allowed players from European Union countries to play anywhere in the EU. Let's compare England's performances in the era of a British league, from 1968 through 1992, with its performances from 1998 through 2018. (We have consciously excluded the World Cup of 1966, Euro 1996, and Euro 2020, which were anomalous events given that England was playing at home.) In that first "British" period, England reached one World Cup semifinal, in 1990. However, that was the exception. In the years when England had a "national" league, it reached the quarterfinals of major tournaments only four times in thirteen attempts.

By contrast, in the subsequent "international" period, it reached five quarterfinals in just eleven attempts. The figures suggest that, if anything, the international league has been good for the England team.

In any case, English fans want to see foreign players. Platini, when he was running UEFA, wondered whether Liverpudlians could identify with a Liverpool team full of foreigners. Well, they seem to manage. Judging by the Premiership's record crowds despite its record ticket prices, fans still identify enough. England can have the world's best league or it can have an English league, but it can't have both. Given the choice, fans seem to prefer the world's best. In that sense, they are typical consumers. When you try to eliminate imports, then, at least at first, consumers have to put up with worse products. They generally don't like that.

Once England began to win, from 2018, you strangely heard a lot less about the Premier League hurting the team. The false argument has finally (we hope) been buried.

SHOULD DO BETTER: IS ENGLAND WORSE THAN IT OUGHT TO BE?

That England underachieves was long taken for granted in Britain. But does it really? Or is it just that the English expect too much? To answer this, we first need to work out how well England should do, given its resources.

Before we are accused of looking for excuses, let's consider what is and isn't possible. A five-year-old can't win the hundred-meter finals at the Olympics, and neither can a seventy-year-old. You aren't going to have a career in the NBA if you are only five feet tall, and you'll never ride the winner in the Kentucky Derby if you are six foot eight. It is very unlikely that you will have a career in show jumping if your parents earn less than $50,000 per year, you probably won't win a boxing match if you've never had any training as a boxer, and you won't have a shot at being world chess champion unless you can persuade a team of grand masters to act as your seconds. Genetics are beyond our control; training depends partly on our own effort but also partly on the resources that other people give us.

What is true for the individual is also true for the nation. During his tenure an England soccer manager cannot easily (a) increase the size of the population from which he will have to draw the talent, (b) increase the national income to ensure a significant increase in the financial resources devoted to developing soccer, or (c) increase the accumulated experience of the national team by very much. (England has played about a thousand games since 1872 and currently plays around a dozen a year, so each extra game doesn't add much to the history.)

But in any international match, these three factors—the size of the nation's population, the size of the national income, and the country's experience in international soccer—hugely affect the outcome. It's unfair to expect Jamaica, say, to perform as well as much larger, more experienced, and richer Germany. It is fairer to assess how well each country should perform given its experience, income, and population, and then measure that expected performance against reality. Countries like Jamaica or Luxembourg will never win a World Cup. The only measure of performance that makes any sense for them is one based on how effectively they use their limited resources. The same exercise makes sense for England, too, if only as a check on jingoistic hysteria. Does England really underperform, given what it has to work with?

In absolute terms, England is about tenth in the world. That was the country's average position in the FIFA rankings from 1993 through 2021. England's highest ranking in this period was fourth, and its lowest was twenty-first, but most of the time England moved in a fairly narrow band between fifth and fifteenth place. Although England wasn't winning the all-important games, the fact is that it ranked only a notch below the world's best teams.

But we want to know how well England does in relative terms—not relative to the media's expectations but relative to English resources. Might it be that England performs about as well as it should, given the country's experience, population, and income?

To work this out, we need to know the soccer results for all the national teams in the world. Luckily, we have them. In fact, there are now a number of databases easily available online. In the first edition of *Soccernomics* we used a database assembled by Russell Gerrard, a mathematics professor at Cass Business School in London. By day, Gerrard worries about mathematical ways to represent the management problems of pension funds. For example, one of his papers is snappily titled "Mean-Variance Optimization Problems for the Accumulation Phase in a Defined Benefit Plan." It concerns, among other things, Lévy diffusion financial markets, the Hamilton-Jacobi-Bellman equation, and the Feynman-Kac representation. As you might expect, Gerrard has been meticulous in accumulating the soccer data, which took him seven years of his life. His database runs from 1872 through 2001 and includes 22,130 games.

In the last couple of editions we updated Gerrard's database using results compiled by Christian Muck on his website Länderspielausgabe, which he very kindly put on spreadsheet for us. Christian also leads a dual life; by day he is a Scrum Master and software developer for an insurance company in Luxembourg, and by night he runs his database. He started out in 2000 helping collect some data for a computer game and then began creating HTML pages of results because no searchable databases existed at the time.

For the current version we turned to Mart Jürisoo, a data scientist who works for a telecom company in Estonia. Mart's data are freely available on Kaggle, which is an online open-source community of data scientists and machine-learning practitioners who publish data sets and code. Among other things, Mart has published a data set of men's "International football results from 1872 to 2021," which he scraped from the internet. Mart's data are interesting because they include results for non-FIFA international teams. This raises an interesting point about international data. Soccer results are among the most reliable international statistics available, as results are seldom a matter of dispute or recording error, but there are some discrepancies when it comes to which games are acknowledged. This means that different sources may produce slightly different results, particularly when you go back in time. We found some small differences when comparing the Gerrard/Muck and Jürisoo data sets, but nothing that caused us concern.

THE JÜRISOO DATABASE

At the end of this book, we will crunch the Jürisoo data to discover which is the best soccer country on Earth and which punches most above its weight. But here, let's limit ourselves to a sneak preview of where

England stands. The distant past is of limited relevance. Let's therefore concentrate on recent history, from 2000 through 2019. England played 237 games in this period. It won 58 percent of them and tied 23 percent, for a "win percentage" of 70 percent (remember that for these purposes we treat a tie as half a win). That is near the top end of the country's historical range.

We want to see how much of a team's success, match by match, can be explained by population, wealth, and experience. However, for this purpose win percentage is not the best measure of success because any two wins are not the same. We all know that the 1–5 away win against Germany in 2001 is not the same as a drab 1–0 against Luxembourg.

Instead, we chose goal difference as our measure because for any match we expect that the greater the difference between the two teams' populations, wealth, and experience, the greater the disparity will be in scores. (Of course, a positive goal difference tends to be highly correlated with winning.) England ranked 8th out of 181 countries in terms of goal difference per game in the 2000–2019 era, which is almost exactly in line with its average FIFA ranking.

We then analyzed the Jürisoo database of international matches using the technique of multiple regression. Quite simply, multiple regression is a mathematical formula (first identified by the mathematician Carl Friedrich Gauss in 1801) for finding the closest statistical fit between one thing—in this case, success of the national team—and any other collection of things—here, experience, population, and income per head. The idea is beautifully simple. The problem used to be the endless amount of computation required to find the closest fit. Fortunately, modern computers have reduced this process to the press of a button (just look up "regression" on your spreadsheet package).

For each international match, you simply input the population, the income per head, and the team experience of the two nations at that date, and in split seconds you get a readout telling you how sensitive (on average) each team's performance is to each factor. We also take into account home advantage for each match.

Collecting the data is usually the toughest part. Happily, we have the Penn World Tables, which provide the best data on historical national income statistics going back to 1950 and are the authoritative source for international economic comparisons. (They can be downloaded online.[1])

The measure of national income typically used is gross domestic product (GDP). This is the total value of all goods and services bought and sold within an economy. (It includes imports and exports but excludes income from assets owned overseas and profits repatriated to foreign countries.) To measure the economic resources available to each person, we divide GDP by population. Admittedly, there are all sorts of finicky issues involved in making comparisons across countries and across time, not to mention worries about measurement error and statistical reliability. Nonetheless, these data are the best we've got.

We have used the Penn data for the populations and national incomes of 184 countries. We will unveil our findings about the other 183 countries in the next few chapters. Here, we'll focus just on England and its supposed underperformance.

In the first few editions of *Soccernomics* we used data from 1980–2001 to estimate performance, but for the present edition we have rerun the entire exercise using international results over the period 2000–2019.

How good is our model? Well, if it could predict the outcome of individual games, there would be no point in watching soccer. It's one of the most random of sports, with lots of victories for underdogs, which is one reason why it's so entertaining. To get a feel for how our model works game by game, consider England's performance at the World Cup 2014. England lost 2–1 to both Italy and Uruguay, drew 0–0 with Costa Rica, and flew home in disgrace. Our model suggests that the team definitely underperformed. Given England's resources, it should have lost to Italy but beaten smaller, poorer, less-experienced Costa Rica. Over the three games, the model predicted a goal difference of +1.1 for England rather than the actual outcome of –2. Still, it's worth noting that the model expected close results: in none of the three games was the predicted margin larger than a single goal.

Importantly, our model is considerably more accurate *on average*, measured over the long term. Over the 212 England games in our database where we had figures for GDP and population, the team scored 194 goals more than its opponents. Our model "predicted" England's goal difference at +162, which was 32 goals fewer than the actual number. That's an average error of only one goal every seven games. And this is fairly typical for the data: we got very close for most countries. Rather than thinking of this as a forecasting model, think of it as a reasonably accurate way of summarizing recent history. Our model is good at characterizing a country's long-term record. It's less good at predicting any individual match.

One thing that has changed since we first ran this exercise is the rising significance of home advantage. Our estimates for the 1980–2001 era suggested that home field represented an advantage of around two-thirds of a goal. In the period 2000–2019 it became worth nearly an entire goal per game.

The next most important variable we identify is experience, which we measure by the number of games a country has played in its history. Having twice the international experience of your opponent is worth 0.45 goals per game (or about four to five goals per ten games). Income and population size are less important. Having double the income per person of the opposing country is worth just 0.08 goals per game, or an extra goal every twelve games. Having double the population of your opponent is worth very little: roughly one goal every thirty-three games.

In other words, being large and rich helps a country win matches, but having a long soccer history helps a lot more. This is why the Portuguese and Croats win more than huge but inexperienced China and India. The importance of experience is not good news for the US.

But for now, we are interested only in England. Are its resources so outstanding that it should do better than merely ranking around eighth or tenth in the world? First, let's look at experience. In 2020 England recorded its thousandth international, making it one of the most experienced nations in international soccer, which is not surprising given that it was the first to start, along with Scotland, in 1872. According to the Jürisoo data, only Sweden had played more games by 2021 (1,036). However, England's much-vaunted history is not worth much against the other leading soccer nations because most of them have now accumulated similar amounts of experience. Brazil, Uruguay, France, Italy, and the Netherlands had all played more than eight hundred internationals by 2021, as had Germany and Russia if we include their pre-1990 incarnations.

When it comes to our second variable, national income, England scores high, too. It is usually one of the richest of the serious soccer countries. Where England falls short is in size. What often seems to go unnoticed is that England's population of 56 million puts it at a disadvantage compared with the countries it likes to measure itself against in soccer. Germany is much bigger, with 83 million inhabitants, and France has 67 million. England is catching up with an aging Italy, whose population has stagnated over the years at 60 million, which must reduce the country's long-term soccer potential. But among the leading European nations, England is ahead of only Spain (47 million). So in soccer terms, England is an experienced, rich, but medium-sized competitor.

A PERFECTLY DECENT TEAM

Any mathematician would say that it's absurd to expect England to win the World Cup.

England wins just over two-thirds of its matches. To be precise, from the end of the 1998 World Cup to the end of the 2018 World Cup, England played 235, won 133, tied 57, and lost 45. If we treat a tie as half a win, this translates into a winning percentage of 68.7 percent. If we then break this down into five four-year World Cup cycles, England's winning percentage was only 60 percent in the 1998–2002 cycle but since then has ranged between 67 and 74 percent. In other words, its performance for most of recent history has been fairly constant. As of 2021, the country's cumulative all-time winning percentage was just under 69 percent.

Yes, these statistics conceal some ghastly mishaps as well as some highs, but the statistics tell us that the difference between anguish and euphoria is a few percentage points.

On the face of it, winning two-thirds of the time is not too shabby in a two-horse race. Of course, some countries do even better. Brazil's winning percentage is about 75 percent. But against most teams, England is the deserved favorite.

The problem comes when we try to translate this achievement into lifting trophies. To win, say, the World Cup in Qatar, a team needs to get through the group stage and then win the four games of the knockout stage—so let's say six wins out of seven games played. If the probability of winning each game is 69 percent, then the probability of winning six games in a row is little better than 10 percent. In fact, in the knockout stage, against the best teams on Earth, England's chances of winning each game would be somewhere below 69 percent, so its total shot at the pot would be under 10 percent. This means a team like England is not likely to win many tournaments, and it doesn't. It could very feasibly win one, but that would require better timing (fewer wins in friendlies and more in World Cup semis), some penalty-taking skills, and ideally a few million more inhabitants.

Contrary to ancient English opinion, the obvious statistical truth is that England is not an exceptional soccer country that ought to be ruling the world. The "thirty years of hurt," rhapsodized in the quasi-official fan anthem "Three Lions," shouldn't be a mystery. England simply should not expect to be world-beaters. As so often, the former England defender Jamie Carragher gets it right: "The psychology of our international game is wrong. England ought to be embracing the idea of being the underdog on the world stage.... We should be reveling in the image of the plucky outsider trying to unbalance the superpowers of Argentina and Brazil, while matching the French, Germans, and Italians."

TIREDNESS: THE CHEAP-BATTERY PROBLEM

Still, there are things that England could be doing better already—some national weaknesses that highly professional managers and players ought to be able to erase. And the first one is England's traditional decline after halftime.

In every World Cup ever played, most goals were scored in the second halves of matches. That is natural: in the second half, players tire, teams start chasing goals, and gaps open up on the field. But England is the exception. Its scoring record is very unusual. Overall, in England's eleven big tournaments from 1998 through 2021, it scored a slight majority of its goals—forty-one out of seventy-two—in the *first* half. But the team's record in crucial games is much starker: in the matches in which it was eliminated from tournaments between 1992 and 2021, it scored twelve of its fourteen goals before halftime and six of those twelve in the opening five minutes. (Think of Luke Shaw's strike in the second minute of the Euro 2020 final.) In other words, England performs like a cheap battery.

The typical pattern (recall the 2–1 defeat by Brazil in Shizuoka in 2002) is for the English to get an early goal and then re-create the

British army's retreat from Dunkirk in 1940, spending much of the game with their backs to the wall in their own penalty area before inevitably conceding.

We don't believe this is because English players, worn out by the Premier League, start tournaments more tired than other teams. The theory that the "terrible toll" of "a long, hard season" is hurting England in summer tournaments sounds plausible; the problem is that this theory isn't backed up by data.

Stefan and Guy Wilkinson went looking for evidence that overburdened players lose more matches. They studied rest days per player, rest days per team, and distance traveled to away games for every Premier League season from 1992–1993 to 2012–2013. But in a database of more than ten thousand matches, they found no link between number of games played and a club's results. It seems that squads are big enough and coaches have become sufficiently versed in rotation since the 1990s that nobody loses club games, at least, just because they are tired. "Scheduling is not the problem it is often made out to be by managers and the media," the paper concludes. "If a team loses on the weekend after playing a midweek game a manager might complain that his players are tired but these excuses rarely appear if the team wins."

It is true, according to Prozone stats, that the Premier League has more high-tempo attacks than other leagues. On the other hand, Prozone also shows that the league features fewer counterattacks—and those tend to be particularly exhausting because they force both forwards and defenders to cover lots of space quickly.

Nor do English players go into international tournaments with an unusually high number of games in their legs. Sure, players in other leagues get a winter break—but that means they have to cram more of those extra games into the spring, so they should be more tired than the English come June. It may even be that players who have appeared in more games have an advantage: perhaps experience outweighs exhaustion.

Rather, to explain England's tiredness, we would focus on what happens during the tournaments themselves. England has long played a particular brand of soccer: high tempo, low possession. That's exhausting, especially in blazing summer heat (it was over 100 degrees in Shizuoka) during knockout rounds against the leading European and Latin

American teams, which rarely give away the ball. The Euro 2020 final against Italy was a case study, bar the chilly weather. If you're chasing opponents all afternoon, you probably won't score many after halftime. So the problem isn't that the English arrive at the tournament tired. It's that they exhaust themselves in the course of each game.

UNLUCKY LOSERS

The most prosaic reason why England loses is plain bad luck.

England over the last fifty years has often been close enough to the world's best sides that it could have lucked into winning a tournament. A better penalty here, a stronger goalkeeper's stomach there, Darren Anderton's shot rolling home in extra time against Germany at Euro '96 instead of hitting the post, and it all could have been different. What we see here is partly the enormous role of luck in history. We tend to think with hindsight that a team that won a particular tournament was somehow always going to do well and a team that lost was doomed to do so. The winner's victory comes to seem inevitable. This is a common flaw in the writing of any kind of history.

In fact, inevitable victories hardly ever happen in soccer tournaments. Perhaps the only recent case was Brazil at the World Cup of 2002. Just how dominant the country was dawned on a leading European club manager a few months after the final. This manager was trying to sign Brazil's goalkeeper, Marcos. After all, Marcos was a world champion. Marcos visited the club and did some physical tests, in which he didn't perform particularly well. Never mind, thought the manager, the guy won the World Cup. So he offered Marcos a contract. At two o'clock the next morning, the manager was awakened at home by a phone call. It was Marcos's agent.

The agent said, "I'm sorry, but Marcos won't sign for you."

The sleepy manager said, "All right, but why not?"

Then the agent confessed. A couple of years before the World Cup, Marcos had broken his wrist. It had never healed properly. But his old club manager, Luiz Felipe Scolari, became manager of Brazil and put Marcos on the team. Suddenly, Marcos was going to a World Cup. Every day at the tournament, the agent explained, Marcos was in pain. He could barely even train. In matches he could barely catch a ball. Every day, Marcos told himself, "I really must tell Scolari about my wrist." But he could never quite bring himself to. So he went on, day after day, until he found that he had won the World Cup. Brazil was so superior that it won the World Cup with a crocked goalkeeper.

However, such dominance is very rare. Normally, the differences between teams in the final stages of a World Cup are tiny. The difference between an English team being considered legendary or a failure is two to three games, each generally decided by a single goal, over two years. After all, the difference between making a World Cup and spending the summer on the beach can be just a point. Sometimes it's a point that you lost by hitting the post. Sometimes it's a point garnered by a rival in a match you didn't even play in.

Once you're at the World Cup, the difference between going home ignominiously in the first round and making the semifinals is often a matter of a few inches here or there on a couple of shots. The greatest prize in the sport hinges on just several moments. Jonathan Wilson puts it well in *Anatomy of England*: "One moment can shape a game, and one game can shape a tournament, and one tournament can shape a career. Football is not always fair." Wilson points out "one of the major problems of international football: that there is so little of it huge conclusions are drawn from individual games." As Arsène Wenger once noted, European championships are over in about three weeks, and any team in a league can be top of the table after three weeks.

In those short tournaments, England has probably been unluckier than most. Over lunch in London in 2013, the FA's then chairman Greg Dyke, who had spent a lot of time asking people in the game why England lose, told Simon: "There's another argument. The guy who owns Brentford [the club that Dyke supports] is Matthew Benham, right? He's very rich. He's made all his money gambling on football. He employs top-quality graduates, maths graduates. All they do is study football around the world. He does everything on statistics. Everything is on probabilities. He says the single biggest factor why England haven't done well is because they've been unlucky."

Luck is particularly important in World Cups, Simon interjected.

"And also," said Dyke, "the number of times you're knocked out on penalties."

Of the ten tournaments for which England had qualified from 1990 until our conversation, it had exited six on penalties. It happened again at Euro 2020.

Dyke continued: "[Benham] says you can alter the chances of winning or losing on penalties, but not by a lot. So if the luck had gone the other way, his argument is that we'd have won one or two of those and we wouldn't be sitting here having this conversation."

Yet there we were, having this conversation.

EXCLUSION: HOW ENGLISH SOCCER DRIVES OUT THE EDUCATED CLASSES

The bigger the talent pool you recruit from, the more new ideas are likely to bubble up. That's why large networks like Silicon Valley or the City of London, which draw talent from around the world, are so creative. So is the Premier League. But when you limit your talent pool, you limit the development of skills, and that's what English soccer has done.

The problem is the exclusion of talent that happens even before the best English players reach the Premier League. The Englishmen who make it to the top are drawn very largely from one single and shrinking social group: the traditional working class. The country's more-educated classes are mostly barred from professional soccer. That holds back the national team.

There are many ways to classify which social class someone was born into, but one good indicator is the profession of that person's father. Joe Boyle, with some help from Dan Kuper, researched for us the jobs of the fathers of England players at the World Cups of 1998, 2002, and 2006. Boyle ignored jobs that the fathers might have been handed after their sons' rise to stardom. As much as possible, he tried to establish what the father did while the son was growing up. Using players' autobiographies and newspaper profiles, he came up with the list in Table 19.1. It doesn't include every player (asked, for instance, what Wayne Bridge's dad did for a living, we threw up our hands in despair), but most are here. Another caveat: some of the dads on the list were absent while their boys were growing up.

Many of these job descriptions are imprecise. What exactly did Rob Lee's dad do at the shipping company, for instance? Still, it's possible to

TABLE 19.1. Employment of World Cup fathers

Player	Father's job
Tony Adams	Roofer
Darren Anderton	Ran moving company—later a taxi driver
David Batty	Sanitation worker
David Beckham	Heating engineer
Sol Campbell	Railway worker
Jamie Carragher	Pub landlord
Ashley Cole	None given, but Cole's autobiography describes "a grounded working-class upbringing in east London"
Joe Cole	Fruit and vegetable trader
Peter Crouch	Creative director at international advertising agency
Stewart Downing	Painter and decorator on oil rigs
Kieron Dyer	Manager of Caribbean social club
Rio Ferdinand	Tailor
Robbie Fowler	Laborer—later worked night shift at railway maintenance depot
Steven Gerrard	Laborer (bricklaying, paving, and so on)
Emile Heskey	Security worker at nightclub
Paul Ince	Railway worker
David James	Artist who runs gallery in Jamaica
Jermaine Jenas	Soccer coach in the United States
Frank Lampard	Soccer player
Rob Lee	"Involved in a shipping company"
Graeme Le Saux	Ran fruit and vegetable stall
Steve McManaman	Printer
Paul Merson	Coal worker
Danny Mills	Coach in Norwich City's youth academy
Michael Owen	Soccer player
Wayne Rooney	Laborer, mainly on building sites; often unemployed
Paul Scholes	Gas-pipe fitter

Player	Father's job
David Seaman	Garage mechanic—later ran sandwich shop, then worked at steelworks
Alan Shearer	Sheet-metal worker
Teddy Sheringham	Policeman
Gareth Southgate	Worked for IBM
John Terry	Forklift-truck operator
Darius Vassell	Factory worker
Theo Walcott	Royal Air Force administrator—later joined services company working for British Gas

break down the list of thirty-four players into a few categories. Eighteen players, or more than half the total, were sons of skilled or unskilled manual laborers: Vassell, Terry, Shearer, Seaman, Scholes, Rooney, Merson, McManaman, Ince, Heskey, Gerrard, Fowler, Adams, Batty, Beckham, Campbell, Ferdinand, and Downing. Ashley Cole with his "working-class upbringing" by a single mother is probably best assigned to this category, too. Four players (Jenas, Lampard, Mills, and Owen) had fathers who worked in soccer. Le Saux and Joe Cole were both sons of fruit and vegetable traders. Anderton's dad ran a moving company, which seems to have failed, before becoming a cab driver. Sheringham's father was a police officer. Carragher's and Dyer's dads ran a pub and a social club, respectively. That leaves only five players out of thirty-four— Crouch, James, Lee, Southgate, and Walcott—whose fathers seem to have worked in professions that required them to have had an education beyond the age of sixteen. If we define class by education, then only 15 percent of England players of recent years had "middle-class" origins.

The male population as a whole was much better educated. Of British men between ages thirty-five and fifty-four in 1996—the generation of most of these players' fathers—a little more than half had qualifications above the most basic level, according to the British Household Panel Study.

English soccer's reliance on an overwhelmingly working-class talent pool was only moderately damaging in the past, when most English people were working-class. In the late 1980s, 70 percent of Britons still left school at the age of sixteen, often for manual jobs. But by then, the growth of the upper middle classes had already begun. In fact, upper-middle-class values began to permeate the country, a process that sociologists call "embourgeoisement." It happened on what used to be the soccer terraces, which because of high ticket prices are now slightly more upper middle class than even the country at large.

By 2020, 91 percent of sixteen- and seventeen-year-olds in the UK were in education or doing apprenticeships, a record high. A year later, 37 percent of British eighteen-year-olds were due to start full-time undergraduate degrees, also a record. More and more, Britain is an upper-middle-class nation. Yet English soccer continues to recruit overwhelmingly from the traditional working classes. When we looked at the socioeconomic origins of England's squad at Euro 2020, they were much the same as in 2006. There was a group of players with roots in the construction industry: Kyle Walker and Jordan Pickford are sons of builders, Jack Grealish's dad was a plasterer, and Kieran Trippier's a bricklayer. Then there are the security professions: Jude Bellingham's and Jordan Henderson's fathers were policemen, and Jadon Sancho's a security guard. Harry Kane, whose dad ran a garage, also comes from a blue-collar home.

Reece James, Mason Mount, and Tyrone Mings are all sons of soccer coaches. Raheem Sterling, Marcus Rashford, and Kalvin Phillips were raised by poor single mothers. The only players we could identify whose dads had white-collar jobs were Harry Maguire (whose father worked his way up to regional manager at the Co-operative Insurance Society) and John Stones (whose dad was an administrator at the government's then Department of Health and Social Security). But even those jobs wouldn't have required a university education.

In short, British soccer continues to exclude an ever-growing swath of the population. That must be a brake on the England team. Britons from higher social classes still run up against a particular obstacle: what you might call the "anti-education requirement."

Most British soccer players still leave school at sixteen, or at the latest eighteen. The belief persists that only thus can they concentrate fully on the game. The argument that many great foreign players—Tostao, Socrates, Osvaldo Ardiles, Jorge Valdano, Slaven Bilic, Josep Guardiola, Andres Iniesta,

Fernando Redondo, Kaká, Juan Mata, and Vincent Kompany—finished school or even attended university is ignored. In 2017 four of Athletic Bilbao's squad alone had college degrees. By contrast, when Sunderland's Duncan Watmore graduated from Newcastle University with a first-class degree in economics in 2015, he was discussed in the media as a near miracle. There is no top-level English equivalent of the Italian defender Giorgio Chiellini (son of an orthopedic surgeon and the vice president of a Norwegian navigation company), who completed an MBA in 2017.

Once again, Germany leads the way in making professional soccer classless. Of the twenty-four players in the German squad that won the World Cup in 2014, thirteen had finished the highest stream in the country's school system, the Gymnasium. That wasn't a coincidence. Germany's soccer academies had about the same proportion of Gymnasium students, about 55 percent—slightly more than the country's population as a whole. To cap it off, the scorer of the German goal in the final against Argentina, Mario Götze, is the son of a professor of data technology at the Technical University of Dortmund. German soccer "has, it seems, become thoroughly middle class," writes Raphael Honigstein in *Das Reboot*. British soccer has not. Indeed, many British coaches and players remain suspicious of educated people.

English soccer has historically been unwelcoming to upper-middle-class teenagers. For instance, Stuart Ford, who at seventeen played for England Schools, gave up on becoming a professional because he got tired of listening to rants from uneducated coaches. He always felt like an outsider. He recalled, "I was often goaded about my posh school or my gross misunderstanding of street fashion. That was just from the management." Instead, he became a Hollywood lawyer. Later, as a senior executive at a Hollywood studio, he was one of the people behind an unsuccessful bid to buy Liverpool FC.

Or there was the youth trainee at Oldham Athletic whose teammates hounded him and called him an intellectual snob after he walked into the club one day carrying a copy of the midmarket newspaper the *Daily Mail*. He told us years later, "Aside from the clubwide piss-taking, I had Deep Heat rubbed into the lining of my slips. I took so much verbal (and physical) abuse that month that I often wonder what would have happened had it been the *Financial Times*."

One of the few remotely upper-middle-class Englishmen to have made the national team in recent decades is Graeme Le Saux. He has a fairly posh accent, reads the upmarket *Guardian* newspaper, and when he joined Chelsea looked forward to exploring London's galleries and museums. Naturally, throughout his career in soccer, Le Saux was abused by his fellow professionals. So far, so typical. What's curious is the particular slant the abuse took. The heterosexual Le Saux was branded "gay." Liverpool's Robbie Fowler once pretended to offer him his backside on the field during a game. Le Saux has said that during another match, David Beckham called him a "poof" (derogatory British slang for gay), although a spokesperson for Beckham denied the allegation.

Some of the foreign players in the Premier League must view these goings-on with dismay. Erik Thorstvedt, Tottenham's Norwegian goalkeeper of the 1990s, recalls bread rolls being chucked at his head when he opened a broadsheet newspaper on the team bus.

Many English upper-middle-class athletes drift to cricket or rugby instead. Often, this represents a direct loss to soccer. For most people, sporting talent is fairly transferable until they reach their late teens. Many English soccer players, like Gary Neville and Gary Lineker, were gifted cricketers, too. Some well-known rugby players took up rugby only as teenagers, when they realized they weren't going to make it in soccer. And in the past, several paragons represented England in more than one sport. Only a few sports demand very specific qualities that can't be transferred: it's hard to go from being a jockey to being a basketball player, for instance. But English soccer competes with other ball games for talent, and it scares away the educated.

This is particularly sad because there is growing evidence that sporting talent and academic talent are linked. The best athletes have fast mental reactions, and those reactions, if properly honed, could make for high intellects.

Interestingly, some people inside English soccer have become aware of the game's class discrimination. Daniel Hargreaves, who in 2013 was working for Everton's academy with the remit to make sure that its decisions were based on evidence (the sort of job that didn't exist in English soccer a few years earlier), spotted the club's tendency to scout mainly in working-class neighborhoods. "Traditionally we have core areas where we think we find players," he said. "But there's a growing middle class;

there are more green spaces in the middle-class areas." Has Everton operated an unintentional bias against the middle classes? "I think evidence would suggest that's the case."

This class bias helps explain why even though the academies of English clubs are the richest in the world, England hasn't produced many outstanding players. Instead of trying to exclude foreigners from English soccer, it would be smart to include more middle-class and upper-middle-class English people. If England's players were drawn from all segments of society, then the national team might maximize its potential.

I'VE GOT TO ADMIT IT'S GETTING BETTER, A LITTLE BETTER ALL THE TIME

So those are four reasons why England isn't beating the world. First, it's just a midsize, moderately rich country without superior soccer experience. Second, its national teams tend to play like cheap batteries. Third, it's had bad luck, and fourth, the English male professional game excludes almost the entire population outside the working class.

But having said all that, England in this century has taken a step toward being world-beaters. How did that happen? Well, what preceded the improvement in soccer was the whole country moving closer to the knowledge networks of core continental Europe.

Britain entered an era of extreme separation from Europe on Sunday, September 3, 1939, when the country's borders closed on the outbreak of World War II. In soccer that isolation deepened when English clubs were banned from European competitions after the Heysel disaster of 1985. Over time, foreign countries stopped hiring British coaches and players. As a result, the British become more and more isolated and insular. They lost what modest network they had.

But between 1990 and 1994, British isolation began to break down: English clubs were readmitted to European competitions, new laws enforced free movement of labor and capital within the EU, and Eurostar trains and budget airlines connected Britain to the Continent. London turned into a global city. English became the global language. Southern England, at least, became part of core Europe again, just as it had been during the scientific revolution.

The embrace of internationalism from the early 1990s meant, for a while, the end of English soccer managers managing England or the best English clubs. You wouldn't appoint a Frenchman to manage your baseball team because the French don't have a history of thinking hard about baseball. And you wouldn't appoint an Englishman to manage your soccer team because the English don't have a history of thinking hard about soccer. No English manager has won the Premier League since its creation in 1992. Finally, in 2000, fed up with the endless failures of the traditional British style of kick-and-rush, the England team hired a Swedish manager with long experience in Italian soccer, Sven Goran Eriksson.

At this, the conservative *Daily Mail* newspaper lamented, in a wonderful statement of English exceptionalism, "The mother country of soccer, birthplace of the greatest game, has finally gone from the cradle to the shame."

But the decision paid off. Eriksson until 2006, and later the Italian Fabio Capello from 2008 to 2012, raised England's winning percentage, even if the team still didn't win any tournaments. The improvement wasn't because Eriksson and Capello had a "golden generation" of players to work with. Many of the same men who played well for the foreign duo performed abysmally for the English managers Steve McClaren and Kevin Keegan. It's painful to imagine how well England might have done if the FA had stopped discriminating against foreigners decades earlier.

It may sound odd that a foreign passport can make such a difference in a coach. After all, England's players these days have a wealth of foreign experience of their own. They play with, for, and against foreigners at their clubs every week. Michael Owen, the first England international to play his entire professional career after the border-opening Bosman ruling of 1995, told us that he had grown up a "European" rather than a purely English footballer. Surely, players like him no longer need foreign managers.

Why they do was best demonstrated that miserable night at Wembley against Croatia in 2007. A team of Englishmen managed by an Englishman played like caricatures of Englishmen. Gerrard in particular was a remarkable sight, charging around in the rain at top pace, hitting impossibly ambitious passes, constantly losing the ball. He played like a headless chicken, or like an English footballer circa 1988.

For Liverpool, Gerrard usually played like a European sophisticate. He had mastered the international, globalized style of top-class modern football. The problem against Croatia was that there wasn't a foreigner on the field or the bench to check him. When things began going badly, he shed that cosmopolitan skin and returned to childhood. He and all the other England players had grown up until about the age of twenty playing an only slightly diluted version of English football. That's why England still needed a foreign manager to correct its players' flaws.

Other peripheral countries, from Greece to the US, began following the English path and hired foreign coaches from the core of Europe. Importing know-how helps remedy the problem of isolation, which makes it odd that in 2006 England did an about-face and appointed the Englishman McClaren, who at that point had never even worked abroad. The English Football Association didn't realize that England, as a recovering isolationist, still needed foreign help.

By hiring Capello to succeed McClaren, England accepted the need for continental European know-how. Capello was like one of the overpaid consultants so common in development economics, flying in on business class to tell the natives what to do. His job was to teach the English some of the virtues of Western European soccer, such as not exhausting yourself before halftime. In much the same period, British cycling, cricket, and athletics became world class by stealing foreign ideas (and possibly with the help of a few steroids). In tennis in 2013, Andy Murray became the first male Briton to win Wimbledon since 1936, largely because as a teenager he had taken himself off to an academy in Barcelona. (If only some English soccer players had made the same move.)

But the English (as opposed to British) vote for Brexit in 2016 expressed a widespread desire for a bit more isolation. That desire had already become visible in soccer. Since 2012, England has been hiring English managers again. Roy Hodgson had at least spent decades coaching abroad and spoke fluent Swedish and Italian. But Sam Allardyce—appointed one month after the Brexit vote—was a much more old-school Englishman. As it happened, he lasted only one match in charge before being forced out by a corruption scandal. England then appointed the almost untried Gareth Southgate, who proved to be a spiritual European, aiming to learn from the best Continental teams and dismissing any notion of English exceptionalism. Early in Euro 2020, rather than talking up England's chances, he pointed out: "We've only won one knockout match in a European Championship as a country."

Moreover, Southgate's players are products of the "European" era of English soccer. Even more than Michael Owen in the 1990s, English footballers of today have grown up with the Continental emphasis on the pass rather than the old British obsession with physique. Little ballplayers like Raheem Sterling, Phil Foden, and Bukayo Saka could have stepped straight out of Barcelona's academy. They have spent their adult careers in the supremely international Premier League. So England has improved into one of the best European teams.

Look at Table 19.2, which shows the performances of all postwar England managers. Among the top four managers with the highest win percentages are the three most recent incumbents—Capello, Hodgson, and Southgate—along with Alf Ramsey, winner of the World Cup of 1966.

Match for match, the winningest of all England managers is Capello. True, the Italian had the good luck of coaching in the aftermath of the breakups of the Soviet Union and Yugoslavia. There are now far more weak little countries in European soccer, the likes of Slovenia and Kazakhstan, which England generally beats. But the previous five regular England managers enjoyed the same advantage, and none of them has stats to match Capello's. He was the nominated scapegoat for the World Cup of 2010, but it is unfair to judge him on just four matches. Over his four-year reign, his results stand out.

What's also noticeable is how freely his teams scored. Like Southgate's, Capello's team beat their opponents by an average of about 1.4 goals a game, around half a goal better than teams under the typical modern England manager. Scoring was easier for prewar England sides, and for Walter Winterbottom's teams in the immediate postwar period, because many international sides in those days were terrible: in May 1947, for instance, Winterbottom's England won 0–10 away to Portugal, not a result that England has threatened to match since.

Table 19.3 confirms that the foreign managers and the "New England" of Hodgson and Southgate have outperformed insular "Old England." The improvement in win percentage began around 2001. It was visible in tournaments, too. Eriksson's and Capello's England teams

TABLE 19.2. England manager records

Manager	Tenure	Played	Wins	Ties	Losses	Goals scored	Goals conceded	Wpc	Average goal difference
Winterbottom	1946–1962	138	77	33	28	369	192	0.678	1.283
Ramsey	1963–1974	112	67	28	17	212	97	0.723	1.027
Revie	1974–1977	29	14	8	7	49	25	0.621	0.828
Greenwood	1977–1982	55	33	12	10	93	40	0.709	0.964
Robson	1982–1990	95	47	29	19	154	60	0.647	0.989
Taylor	1990–1993	38	18	13	7	62	32	0.645	0.789
Venables	1994–1996	24	12	9	3	35	14	0.688	0.875
Hoddle	1996–1999	28	17	4	7	42	13	0.679	1.036
Keegan	1999–2000	18	7	7	4	26	15	0.583	0.611
Eriksson	2001–2006	67	40	15	12	128	61	0.709	1.000
Maclaren	2006–2007	18	9	4	5	32	12	0.611	1.111
Capello	2008–2012	42	28	8	6	89	28	0.762	1.452
Hodgson	2012–2016	56	33	14	9	109	44	0.714	1.161
Southgate	2016–	61	39	12	10	122	40	0.738	1.344

always qualified for tournaments, never lost at the group stages, and reached three quarterfinals and one round of sixteen. By contrast, the Old England missed the 1994 World Cup and Euro 2008, and managed just one semi (at home at Euro '96), one appearance in the last sixteen, and two exits in the first round.

Only in 2018 did England start to excel at tournaments. Clearly, this has something to do with the team's improved long-term performance. But it also has to do with luck. At the World Cup in Russia in 2018, England finished fourth—its best performance at any World Cup since 1990—by beating Panama, Tunisia, and Sweden, tying with Colombia before going through on penalties, and losing to Belgium twice and to Croatia. In short, the team's record (excluding penalties) was Played 7, Won 3, Tied 1, Lost 3. That's not world-beating, particularly not if you consider the quality of Panama and Tunisia. Compare that with the World Cup 2006, when England exited in the quarterfinals amid the usual national despair. The team's record that tournament, again excluding penalties, was Played 5, Won 3, Tied 2. The euphoria in 2018 overlooked the vagaries of the World Cup's structure.

The win on penalties against Colombia that year was England's first in a shoot-out since 1996. England was rightly praised for its professional planning, which included complex analyses of Colombia's penalty takers. What this overlooked was that in the previous decade almost all other leading teams had begun preparing for penalties, too. England beat Colombia not so much because it had got more professional but because it got luckier.

And reaching the European final in 2020 didn't prove in itself that this was the best English team in fifty years. Rather, England had

TABLE 19.3. From Old England to New England

Manager	Tenure	Played	Wpc	Average goal difference	Qualified WC and Euros	WC and Euro games played	WC and EC win percentage
Old England	1990–2000, 2006–2007	126	0.647	0.881	4/6	15	0.500
Foreigners	2001–2006, 2008–2012	98	0.735	1.286	5/5	18	0.583
New England	2012–2021	117	0.726	1.256	5/5	25	0.580

discovered one of the great secrets to winning at sports: play at home. The book *Scorecasting* gives the percentages of games won by home teams from 2000 to 2009:

Major League Baseball	53.9 percent
National Hockey League	55.7 percent
National Football League	57.3 percent
National Basketball Association	60.5 percent
International soccer in Europe	61.9 percent

Scorecasting argues that home-field advantage is mostly a result of biased referees. However, psychological factors probably matter, too. We know that you will generally sleep better in your own bed and dive better in your own pool.

In an international tournament, every team except the host is playing away. But not every team is equally affected. Many national teams now consist chiefly of players who emigrated young to play abroad. That's true even of a country as rich as France: Antoine Griezmann moved to Real Sociedad in Spain at age fourteen and Paul Pogba to Manchester United at sixteen. These players join the international 0.01 percent and soon feel more at home in a first-class airport lounge than on the average street in their home country. Playing abroad becomes routine for them: if it's Wednesday, this must be Azerbaijan.

But none of that is true for British (i.e., not just English) players. When FIFA TMS analyzed international transfers of different nationalities from 2011 to 2013, it found that only 26 percent of transfers involving British players were to a club outside Britain. The only two countries in the world with more insular transfer histories in that period were Myanmar and Nepal: over that time, both reported a grand total of zero foreign transfers (and just two domestic ones each). In short, few English players have much experience playing outside England.

This is another case of English insularity undermining English competitiveness. Most leading English players get their first taste of soccer abroad in their twenties, when they start to play in the Champions League and for England. But even on the national team, they build up limited foreign experience because England from 2000 to 2014 played just 40 percent of its friendlies abroad. That's in the lowest decile of all the countries on Earth.

Instead, England's main strategy for winning World Cups lately has been to bid to host the thing. Had England been awarded the 2006 or 2018 competitions (which, knowing what we now know about FIFA, was never going to happen), that might well have paid off. Of the three tournaments the English have hosted, they won the 1966 World Cup, reached the semifinals of Euro '96 , and then reached the final in 2021. In none of those three tournaments did they lose a game in open play, but only on penalties.

Yes, England has gotten better. But its luck turned, too.

20

TOM THUMB

The Best Little Soccer Country on Earth

In 1970, when Brazil won its third World Cup, it got to keep the Jules Rimet trophy. The little statuette of Nike, then still known chiefly as the Greek goddess of victory, ended up in a glass case in the Brazilian federation's offices in Rio de Janeiro. One night in 1983, the trophy was stolen. It has never been seen since.

It's a particular shame, because Brazil deserves the Jules Rimet. The fivefold world champion is still the best country in soccer history. Our question here is a different one: Which country is best after taking into account its population, experience, and income per capita? If Brazil is the absolute world champion, which is the relative one, the biggest overperformer? That overachieving country deserves its own version of the Jules Rimet trophy—call it the Tom Thumb. And which countries are the worst underachievers relative to their resources?

First of all, if we are dealing with statistics, we have to construct our arguments on the basis of large numbers of games played. There were only twenty-one World Cups from 1930 through 2018, and most of these hardly involved any countries from outside Europe and Latin America. So crunching the numbers from World Cups might at best tell us something about the pecking order among the long-established big soccer nations. But when the difference between, say, Argentina's two victories and England's one comes down to as little as Maradona's "hand of God" goal, or the difference between Italy's four and France's two to a comment by Marco Materazzi about Zidane's parentage, then the statistician needs to look elsewhere. Thankfully, national teams play a lot of games, so we have plenty of data. As in the previous chapter, we will rely on Mart Jürisoo's database of international matches.

The number of games between countries has soared over time. Between the foundation of FIFA in 1904 and World War I, the number rose quickly to fifty per year. After 1918, growth resumed. By the eve of World War II, there were more than one hundred international matches a year. But this was still a world dominated by colonial powers, and only with the independence movement after the war did international competition mushroom. In 1947 there were 107 international matches; by 1957, there were 203; by 1967, there were 308. Few new countries were founded in the next two decades, but the number of international matches continued to rise thanks to the jet plane, which made travel less of a pain and more financially worthwhile. In 1977 there were 368 international matches; in 1987 there were 393. At that point international soccer seemed to have reached some sort of stable equilibrium.

But then the Soviet Union broke up into fifteen separate states, and Yugoslavia collapsed. The new countries flocked into FIFA. At the same time the commercial development of soccer meant that cash-hungry national associations were eager to play lucrative friendlies. In 1997 there were 850 international games, more than double the figure of a decade before. Since 2000, the number seems to have stabilized around an average of about 940 international games per year.

If we concentrate just on games in the first two decades of this century, then a list of the most successful teams features the usual suspects. In Table 20.1 we rank the top ten countries by the percentage of games won or, given that around one-third of matches are ties, by the "win percentage" statistic calculated by valuing a tie as worth half a win.

The best teams are much as you would expect. As we saw in Chapter 19, Spain in this period was one of the handful of best international teams in the history of soccer. And even in a time when Brazil was struggling to reinvent its national playing style, its win percentage was over 75 percent. That equates to bookmakers' odds of three to one, or about as close as you can get to a sure thing in a two-horse race.

TABLE 20.1. Top ten countries in the world by win percentage: 2000–2021

Team	Played	Won	Tied	Wpc	GD
Spain	281	193	56	0.786	1.463
Brazil	309	201	65	0.756	1.414
France	288	178	65	0.731	1.083
Iran	294	174	73	0.716	1.190
Netherlands	260	157	57	0.713	1.196
England	257	153	60	0.712	1.121
Argentina	272	159	67	0.708	0.904
Germany	293	175	62	0.703	1.225
Portugal	272	157	68	0.702	1.151
Italy	272	147	80	0.688	0.816

If we look at Brazil's win percentage over time, some interesting insights emerge. Table 20.2 shows the team's results by decade.

Viewed in the light of history, it's little wonder that Brazil lost at home to Uruguay in the World Cup final of 1950. The Brazilians simply

TABLE 20.2. Brazil's results

	Played	Won	Tied	Lost	Goals for	Goals against	Wpc
1910s	15	6	4	5	28	24	0.533
1920s	24	10	4	10	35	34	0.5
1930s	22	14	1	7	60	49	0.659
1940s	43	23	7	13	127	68	0.616
1950s	96	62	18	16	229	100	0.74
1960s	115	78	16	21	275	134	0.748
1970s	101	65	27	9	188	62	0.777
1980s	117	73	28	16	222	83	0.744
1990s	166	108	38	20	366	137	0.765
2000s	157	96	36	25	323	118	0.726
2010s	139	94	28	17	298	89	0.777

weren't that good then. Their hubris at that tournament had no historical basis. It's only in the 1950s that Brazil turned into soccer's superpower. Indeed, in the fifty years after that, the team's performance was strikingly consistent: Brazil's winning percentage (counting ties as worth half a win) hovered between 73 percent and 78 percent in each of the past six decades. If you had to pick a particular golden age, it would probably be 1964 to 1985, but our main finding is great stability of performance, even in the supposedly fallow twenty years after 1970. World Cups, as we have seen, usually turn on a couple of crucial matches, which are usually decided by one goal each. The pundits then investigate these crucial matches for meaning, when in fact the best explanation for the outcome of such a tiny sample of games might be chance. The broader story of Brazil between the late 1950s and today is consistent excellence.

Still, Brazil now risks sliding out of the top unless it can plug into the Western European knowledge networks. In the last four World Cups it has often looked slow (or worse) against leading European teams. It ought to consider the revolutionary step of hiring a Western European manager. Imagine a Brazil coached by Pep Guardiola (as a few Brazilians were suggesting ahead of the 2014 World Cup). But it seems that even now, Brazilians are too proud of their own soccer tradition to try to learn from foreigners.

There's just one other finding of note. Brazil historically performs better in World Cup years. It wins about 5 percent more often in years with a World Cup, and the difference is statistically significant. That sounds counterintuitive: after all, the team tends to face tougher competition in those years. However, the sordid truth is that, most of the time, Brazilian internationals coast a little. They don't raise their game for qualifiers against Bolivia or Nike-inspired friendlies against Asian countries. In these off years, weary stars sometimes cry off claiming injury, and agents sometimes finagle places in the team for players who need a foreign transfer. But in a World Cup year, when everyone is playing for his place, Brazil is usually at its best.

Then there's Portugal, which deserves particular praise for making the global top ten. The country has only 10 million inhabitants, compared with the 47–83 million of the large European nations and Brazil's 213 million. The Portuguese victory in Euro 2016 was a merited reward for long-standing national overachievement. And England's sixth place in the global twenty-first-century rankings suggests that its reputation as "notorious underachiever" is undeserved.

One thing that Table 20.1 illustrates is Western Europe's dominance of international soccer. The region is home to seven of the ten best countries. We have seen that this is partly thanks to Europe's unmatched knowledge networks. Those networks rest on tradition: European nations are generally older, and have played international soccer longer, than the rest of the world. It may also help that until very recently, control of global soccer largely remained in Europe. FIFA makes the rules of the game from a posh suburb of Zurich, and little Western Europe hosted eleven out of twenty-one World Cups through 2018. (A mark of how power in global soccer is shifting is that the 2006 tournament in Germany may turn out to have been Western Europe's last for a very long time.)

But tradition does not in itself secure dominance. If it did, then British companies would still dominate industries like textiles, shipbuilding, and carmaking. Dominance is transitory unless producers have the resources to stay ahead of the competition. The key resource in soccer is talent. Generally speaking, the more populous countries are more likely to have the largest supply of talented people. We have also seen that rich countries are best at finding, training, and developing talent. In short, as we've mentioned, it takes experience, population, and wealth to make a successful soccer nation.

The easy bit is recognizing this. The hard work is assembling the data to answer our question: Which countries do best relative to their resources of experience, population, and wealth?

Now we'll run the multiple regressions we described in Chapter 19, using the Jürisoo data (to determine a country's level of experience) and the Penn World Tables (to determine a country's income). Our aim is to find the connection between goal difference per game and our three key inputs while also allowing for home advantage. Then we can identify soccer's most overachieving nations.

In the ranking in Table 20.3, we compensate all the world's national teams for that trio of factors beyond their control: experience, population, and income per head.

TABLE 20.3. The top ten overachieving national teams in the world, allowing for population, wealth, and experience, all games: 2010–2019 (countries with more than 75 games)

Country	Played	Won	Tied	Wpc	Goal difference	Goal difference outperformance
Croatia	115	59	30	0.643	0.6	1.362
Bosnia and Herzegovina	87	34	20	0.506	0.069	1.176
Palestine	99	33	29	0.48	0.051	1.118
Spain	131	87	23	0.752	1.221	0.916
Ukraine	109	56	28	0.642	0.55	0.91
Brazil	147	100	29	0.779	1.51	0.904
Portugal	132	73	33	0.678	0.879	0.856
Uruguay	126	60	32	0.603	0.563	0.846
Slovakia	96	47	17	0.578	0.365	0.836
Colombia	118	61	33	0.657	0.678	0.827

Remarkably, two neighboring countries finish at the top of our over-achievement table: Croatia and Bosnia-Herzegovina. To some degree they are one unified soccer culture: Croatia has long recruited players among Bosnian Croats, and Bosnia regularly fields ethnic Croats and Serbs. Importantly, the countries also share a broader inheritance: both are heirs to the great Yugoslavian soccer tradition.

When Yugoslavia was a united country, from 1918 until the start of the 1990s, it won gold in the Olympics of 1960 and finished runner-up in the European Championship that same year, and again in 1968. But the Yugoslavs impressed most for their high-skill style, becoming known as "the Brazilians of Europe." They also benefited from living in the most open communist country. The southern bit of the Iron Curtain was po-rous, and for much of the communist era, Yugoslav players were allowed to leave for Western clubs at age twenty-eight. That gave them at least some access to the sport's Western European knowledge networks.

The gruesome civil war of the 1990s broke up the country into six independent republics, chief among them Serbia and Croatia. Bosnia suffered most in the war: about 700,000 Bosnians, overwhelmingly Muslims, fled to the West, chiefly to Europe, North America, and Australia.

When the six newly independent republics then set out into international soccer, each carried the Yugoslav tradition with it. Zvonimir Boban, who started his career playing for Yugoslavia in 1988 and after the country's breakup captained Croatia, told us: "We have this Balkanic school that was created by the Yugoslavian federation of football, which we inherited and we somehow brought forward. Our football school is based a lot on freedom of creativity, talent. 'Feel the ball!' is a refrain from my childhood, what our coaches were saying. We are less good in the tactical side."

But, Boban notes, the Yugoslav footballers who came before him were hampered by going abroad late: "If you stay in Yugoslavia until twenty-eight, you can't develop, especially tactical skills and professionalism." The country's collapse allowed his generation of players to leave young. Boban joined Milan at the age of twenty-one, and his Croatian contemporary Robert Prosinecki went to Real Madrid, where Davor Suker later played, too. "We all had these brilliant experiences in the top European leagues," says Boban. "And we knew then how to implement it in our national team." In 1998 Boban, Suker, and Prosinecki starred on the Croatian side that finished third at the World Cup.

In 2014 Bosnia qualified for its only World Cup. Some of the frightened Bosnian children who had accompanied their parents into exile had become soccer players. Almost all the Bosnian players who went to the 2014 tournament had grown up outside the country. Goalkeeper Asmir Begovic, who left Bosnia at four, came of age in Edmonton, Canada, and the striker Vedad Ibisevic became a star of high school football in St. Louis, Missouri. If only Bosnia could also have fielded Zlatan Ibrahimovic, son of a Bosnian Muslim father, but the boy chose to play for his country of birth, Sweden.

Bosnia's coach in 2014, Safet Susic, a great Yugoslav player of the 1980s, told us, "We've kept the game of the ex-Yugoslavs: the players are all very good technically. Our weakness is our mentality, like always. When we hit a difficult moment, we let our heads drop." Still, the Bosnians, like the Croats, overachieved spectacularly given that we credited them with the experience of the Yugoslav national teams. (They did, after all, inherit the country's long-standing soccer structures when Yugoslavia collapsed.) In other words, although these countries are small and poor, we counted them as pretty experienced.

Once a country builds a history of soccer success, that becomes a light to later generations. Boban says of Croatia's 1998 triumph: "Luka Modric, when he was the best player of the world, was mentioning that they have been dreaming to repeat our result. He said, 'They put this aim in front of our eyes.'" In 2018 Modric's Croatia reached the World Cup final. The best of Yugoslavia lives on the soccer field.

Continuing down our list of overachievers, who would have predicted Palestine in third place? The poor country, mostly occupied by Israel, is still fighting just to be recognized as a state. Yet, against all odds, it has succeeded in soccer.

In 1998, very soon after becoming president of FIFA, Sepp Blatter recognized Palestine. It was "a bold move," comments James Montague, author of *When Friday Comes: Football, War and Revolution in the Middle East*, because at the time the Palestine Authority was merely counted as an "observer entity" (not even a "non-member observer state") at the United Nations.

Palestinians have long been crazy about soccer (more later about the general Arab love of the game). But their national team's success also has something to do with the quest for statehood. There is a famous parallel in club soccer: Catalonia isn't a state, so Catalans have invested a lot of their emotion and resources into FC Barcelona. De facto, the club flies the Catalan flag around the world. The Palestinian national team does the same for Palestine. A lot of private money has gone into coaching and facilities, and into the West Bank's professional clubs, which represent the country every time they play in an Asian competition.

After joining FIFA, Palestine did what many small national teams do: it recruited from its diaspora. Before the qualifiers for the 2006 World Cup, the country's soccer federation put an advertisement in the German magazine *Kicker* appealing to Palestinian-origin players. The team could also draw on an entire Chilean professional club: Palestino, started by Palestinian immigrants in 1920, plays in the Palestinian colors and is committed to a Palestinian state with pre-Israel borders.

But in recent years, Palestine has come to rely more on local players— or at least on some of them. The team's big problem (and arguably the country's) is Israel's blockade of the Gaza Strip. Gaza is Palestine's soccer hotbed, with a long tradition of beach games. Yet Gazans have a terrible time just trying to get to the Palestinian West Bank. One talented young Gazan, Mahmoud Sarsak, traveling to the West Bank to join a professional team there, was arrested by the Israelis, accused of being linked to Islamic jihad (which he denied), spent two and a half years in prison, and almost died after going on a hunger strike. He was finally released in 2012 after Blatter and former players, including Eric Cantona and Lilian Thuram, appealed on his behalf, but his soccer career never recovered.

It's so difficult for players to travel that Palestine has sometimes even struggled to put a team together for World Cup qualifying matches. Then there are the Israeli raids that have destroyed Gazan stadiums. (Israel says the stadiums were used as launch sites for rockets aimed at Israeli civilians.) Even watching a game on TV can be dangerous. During the 2014 World Cup, an Israeli missile killed nine young Palestinians enjoying the Argentina-Netherlands semifinal in a beach café.

No wonder Palestine's national team in recent years has largely been drawn from the West Bank (a place with its own problems), supplemented by some Israeli Arab players who don't even all speak Arabic. Palestine's physical proximity to Europe, the leading soccer continent, is no help anymore. "It might as well be on the moon," says Montague.

Given all that, the country's overachievement is astonishing. From 2010 to 2019, Palestine scored over a goal a game more than we would have forecast given its population, its income per capita, and its very short experience of international soccer. In 2015 and 2019, it qualified for its first ever Asian Cups. We would prophesy a bright soccer future for the country except that there seems to be zero prospect of the Israeli-Palestinian conflict ever sorting itself out.

Like Yugoslavia, western Arabia is a troubled region with an exceptional soccer culture. Jordan, which appears twenty-first in the outperformance rankings, is something of a second Palestine. So many Palestinian refugees have fled to the little country since 1948 that today somewhere between 50 and 80 percent of Jordan's population is Palestinian. (It's impossible to give an exact number because many families are mixed.)

Anyone who has witnessed anti-immigrant sentiment in Europe and the US will guess that it wasn't always easy to integrate Palestinians and

Jordanian "East Bankers." Each ethnic group has its own big professional soccer team (al-Wihdat for the Palestinians, al-Faisaly for the Jordanians), and games between the two are often fraught. The two teams provide most of the players for Jordan's national team, al Nashama ("The Brave"), so tensions have sometimes spilled over.

Another Middle Eastern nation that appears high on our list of overachievers is Syria at twenty-eighth, even though it spent the 2010s being destroyed by civil war. At the start of the century, Syria had entered a soccer golden age. Until then, the league had been dominated by the army and police clubs. They nabbed all the best players, so other clubs scarcely bothered. But then the Syrian soccer federation put a stop to this by making the sport professional. Money poured in. Players' salaries rose, facilities improved, and the federation got better at scouting and training youngsters. Syria started to do well in youth World Cups.

Tragically, the country was doomed. In 2011 the war broke out. Some of those talented youngsters made the long, dangerous walk to Europe. Others were killed at home.

Syrian soccer had enough juice left to win the West Asian championship in 2012. But the team's decline was inevitable (and just about the least important thing going wrong in the country). Syria's winning percentage from 2000 to 2010 was 52.3 percent (counting ties as worth half a win); from 2011 through 2014, it fell to just 42.5 percent. The team has recovered since and came close to making it to the 2018 World Cup, reaching the fourth round of qualifiers before narrowly going out to Australia.

Some of that Syrian soccer talent might yet come through, but probably not in the country's national team. Rather, Syrian refugees and their children may start popping up in European national teams.

When three neighboring countries such as Palestine, Jordan, and Syria are significant overachievers, there's obviously something about the region that makes it special; these are not three completely separate national stories. Note, too, that Egypt, separated from Gaza only by a steel barrier, only missed out by one place on our top ten of the world's winningest teams.

Indeed, when we carried out a similar study covering the period 1990–2010 for an earlier edition of this book, we identified yet another country in the region, Iraq, as a big overachiever. Those twenty years—which featured two Gulf Wars, massacres, sanctions, Saddam Hussein, and something close to a civil war—were not happy ones for Iraqis. Nonetheless, in that period the Lions of Mesopotamia scored nearly a goal a game more than you would expect given the country's resources. As Iraqi supporters used to chant (often while firing bullets into the air), "Here we are Sunni—yah! Here we are Shiite—yah! Bring us happiness, sons of Iraq!" Even Kurds supported the Lions. Montague calls the team "arguably the last symbol of national unity left in Iraq."

The Middle East has a remarkable soccer tradition. The region's proximity to Europe means that the game arrived here long before it reached bigger, richer East and South Asian countries such as China, Japan, and India. (Soccer may be the one activity in which Jordan can beat China and Palestine can beat India.) The Syrian-French journalist Henri Mamarbachi sent us his memories of the Israeli invasion of Lebanon during the 1982 World Cup:

> Day and night for weeks, Beirutis were under constant bombardment by sea, air, and land, there was no electricity and therefore no way to watch TV during whatever respite they could get in the evening. And this was worse than the shelling and the unbearable heat, for they were now deprived of watching what was more important than anything else. So, every evening, you could see under each house car hoods open for the purpose of linking the batteries to whatever portable generator they could get hold of. Watching the World Cup in the streets, with colorful foreign flags often hanging from the windows—those were the only moments Beirut was not totally isolated, totally desperate, and the enemy almost forgotten.

Montague writes (and one must never tire of quoting the classics): "In the Middle East there was the mosque and the terrace, and little in between."

Still, we're not claiming that these Arab nations are world-beaters. We have merely shown that they massively overachieve inside Asia. After all, they hardly ever play teams from anywhere else. In the first twenty years of the century, Syria played teams outside the Asian Football

Confederation just twice (Venezuela and Zimbabwe), and Palestine met only Chile, Mauritania, and Tanzania. It's hard to imagine any of the Arab countries beating the global big boys.

Furthermore, GDP statistics for poorer countries outside Europe (especially countries in the midst of war or sanctions) are notoriously unreliable. In general, there is more "noise" in all the data for countries outside Europe, meaning that we struggle to pick up the influence of the factors we are interested in. It's like listening to a radio with poor reception: many of the words are hard to make out.

It therefore makes more sense to focus on Europe alone. Europe is a more homogeneous place than the world as a whole, meaning that differences, especially in income and experience, tend to be smaller. Second, the data are better: Europeans have been collecting them longer, and they have a relatively long history of transparent record keeping (although there are some very suspicious European statistics, too). Last, most of the world's dominant teams are grouped together in Europe, playing against pretty much the same set of opponents. It all adds up to a fairly accurate picture of how well each European team performs.

Let's first rank the best European teams on their absolute performance, without taking into account their populations, experience, or incomes. Table 20.4 presents the "absolute" top ten ranked by win percentage. Little Belgium deserves applause for finishing the 2010s second behind Spain, presumably benefiting from being an open country with access to the world-class soccer cultures of neighboring countries. In 2006, during a fallow period for the "Red Devils," the national team, Simon appeared on a Belgian TV program with several senior soccer officials who bemoaned how far their neighbors had shot ahead. The men went on about how the Germans were setting up innovative academies, the Dutch were producing attacking soccer, and the French were finding talent in the poor suburbs of their big cities. Listening to this, Simon thought: *You know so much about global best practice that soon you'll catch up.* And Belgium did.

In the years after that TV program, the Devils jettisoned the traditional Belgian counterattacking game and copied the Dutch-German attacking style. A new generation emigrated young to the country's cutting-edge neighbors: Eden Hazard grew up just across the French

TABLE 20.4. Top ten European teams by win percentage: 2010–2021

Team	Played	Won	Tied	Wpc	GD
Spain	151	101	31	0.772	1.543
Belgium	132	89	24	0.765	1.462
England	140	86	33	0.732	1.179
France	151	93	32	0.722	1.007
Germany	153	93	32	0.712	1.248
Portugal	145	83	37	0.700	1.131
Netherlands	138	81	26	0.681	1.138
Italy	145	75	45	0.672	0.883
Croatia	133	69	31	0.635	0.647
Switzerland	123	63	30	0.634	0.732

border in Lille's academy, Jan Vertonghen and Toby Alderweireld were schooled at Ajax Amsterdam, and Romelu Lukaku, Kevin De Bruyne, and Thibaut Courtois joined Chelsea near the start of their professional careers. Imagine if the best American kids had had those opportunities.

Good club teams are almost inevitably better than national teams, Belgium's coach Roberto Martínez told us in 2018. A club team trains and plays together far more often, and it typically experiences less pressure than a national team. He might have added that big clubs can buy players to fill uncovered positions, whereas nations have to make do.

Martínez's Red Devils became the closest thing in international soccer to a good club side. Many of his players had known each other since boys' football and then played together their whole adult careers. The only six men in Belgian history to have notched up one hundred or more international games all debuted for the Red Devils between 2007 and 2011, and Courtois may have joined them by the time this book appears. As this generation starts exiting the stage, in the 2020s, we can say with confidence that Belgium will decline.

Now let's assess European countries by their overachievement relative to their resources. Table 20.5, the European efficiency table (the only one of its kind, as far as we know), may be the most telling we have, so we rank every team for which we have data. Again, the most important

TABLE 20.5. Ranking of European national teams, correcting for population, wealth, and experience, all games between two European opponents: 2010–2019

Team	Played	Won	Tied	Wpc	Goal difference	Goal difference outperformance
Croatia	82	42	24	0.659	0.622	1.061
Bosnia and Herzegovina	60	26	15	0.558	0.300	1.010
Iceland	80	27	16	0.438	–0.288	1.009
Montenegro	68	19	17	0.404	–0.397	0.977
Belgium	77	48	17	0.734	1.130	0.975
Portugal	87	50	20	0.690	0.920	0.924
Netherlands	84	46	13	0.625	0.964	0.827
Spain	81	51	16	0.728	1.160	0.662
Slovakia	79	38	13	0.563	0.291	0.529
Germany	86	53	19	0.727	1.291	0.523
Slovenia	67	23	14	0.448	0.000	0.476
North Macedonia	68	21	14	0.412	–0.338	0.463
Albania	76	24	14	0.408	–0.237	0.449
Sweden	98	45	23	0.577	0.490	0.445
Serbia	66	26	15	0.508	0.045	0.401
Denmark	80	33	23	0.556	0.350	0.366
Georgia	64	21	14	0.438	–0.250	0.337
Switzerland	68	35	17	0.640	0.544	0.269
Czech Republic	78	36	14	0.551	0.256	0.209
Ukraine	85	45	20	0.647	0.541	0.190
Austria	74	35	14	0.568	0.338	0.118
France	97	61	19	0.727	0.948	0.084
England	83	48	18	0.687	0.940	0.072
Poland	81	40	24	0.642	0.617	–0.029
Greece	77	32	24	0.571	0.104	–0.064
Armenia	67	16	11	0.321	–0.806	–0.114

Team	Played	Won	Tied	Wpc	Goal difference	Goal difference outperformance
Romania	81	28	28	0.519	0.086	−0.145
Finland	84	29	15	0.435	−0.250	−0.157
Italy	89	44	31	0.669	0.562	−0.173
Hungary	74	28	17	0.493	−0.203	−0.206
Bulgaria	69	22	14	0.420	−0.507	−0.238
Norway	85	33	18	0.494	−0.129	−0.281
Estonia	85	18	18	0.318	−1.047	−0.292
Moldova	67	3	19	0.187	−1.209	−0.332
Belarus	78	21	22	0.410	−0.513	−0.411
Cyprus	61	8	12	0.230	−1.213	−0.463
Israel	59	18	9	0.381	−0.288	−0.471
Latvia	74	11	21	0.291	−1.054	−0.518
Russia	74	36	20	0.622	0.635	−0.522
Malta	69	4	11	0.138	−1.725	−0.616
Turkey	89	40	21	0.567	0.258	−0.628
Luxembourg	77	13	12	0.247	−1.506	−0.845
Lithuania	78	10	15	0.224	−1.359	−0.930
Azerbaijan	62	9	17	0.282	−1.065	−0.959
Kazakhstan	64	8	16	0.250	−1.219	−1.425

number is in the last column: each country's "goal difference outperformance." Three of the top four countries—this time with Montenegro joining the Croats and Bosnians—are from the former Yugoslavia.

The top of our rankings also show that the starring roles of Iceland and Portugal at Euro 2016 didn't come out of the blue. By contrast, our table is less flattering to most of Europe's trophy-winning nations. Germany and France barely overachieve relative to their considerable resources, whereas Italy was actually underachieving slightly before it won Euro 2020 and went on to complete a world-record thirty-seven-game unbeaten run. It failed to qualify for the World Cups of 2018 and 2022.

These are large, well-connected countries, all of them richer than the European average. They only do about as well as they should.

Now that we've reviewed all the evidence, who gets the Tom Thumb trophy—the poor, small, inexperienced man's Jules Rimet—for being the relatively best team on Earth? Which country does best allowing for experience, population, and income? One day we'd like to see this played out on grass. Let's have a World Cup in which teams start with a handicap, settled by a panel of econometricians chaired by Professor Gerrard. But until that great day comes, all we have is our model. It shows that former Yugoslavia, the Middle East, and the Iberian Peninsula are the world's overachieving hot spots. Whether you think our award should go to Croatia, Portugal, or Palestine is a matter of judgment.

Only one question remains: Which is the relatively worst team on Earth? Table 20.6 shows the worst underperformers relative to their population, income, and soccer experience.

A constant refrain in India, the world's second-most-populous country, is: "We are 1.35 billion. We can't even find eleven players," reports Nikhil Paramjit Sharma, author of *India's Football Dream*. "Sleeping giant," the standard term for Indian soccer, feels too polite.

TABLE 20.6. Worst underperformers, entire world (of 119 teams with more than 75 games played): 2010–2019

Team	Played	Won	Tied	Wpc	Goal difference	Goal difference outperformance
India	98	35	18	0.449	−0.347	−1.320
Luxembourg	93	13	18	0.237	−1.505	−1.253
Indonesia	83	30	17	0.464	−0.337	−1.194
Malta	78	6	11	0.147	−1.705	−1.161
Lithuania	87	14	17	0.259	−1.184	−0.800
Singapore	116	31	24	0.371	−0.560	−0.795
Malaysia	108	33	28	0.435	−0.269	−0.761
Kenya	114	33	33	0.434	−0.184	−0.704
Tanzania	130	36	43	0.442	−0.308	−0.660
Latvia	87	13	23	0.282	−0.977	−0.610

The country's failure on the field seems odd given its venerable soccer history. Colonial British troops and missionaries carried the game around the subcontinent. In 1911 the barefooted Mohun Bagan club of Kolkata humiliated a booted British Army team and became a symbol of Indian nationalism. In 1950 India was invited to participate in the World Cup in Brazil, with all expenses paid. However, the Indians stayed home. The usual story is that they refused to go when they heard they couldn't play barefoot, but in fact they probably wanted to focus their limited resources on the 1952 Olympics. In 1951 they won gold in the first Asian Games in Delhi and in 1956 came fourth in soccer at the Melbourne Olympics. The 1950s and 1960s are still known as Indian soccer's "golden era," says Sharma.

But India just then was closing itself off from the world. Near-autarky may have its virtues, but it makes you bad at the international game. Indians barely ever saw the world's best soccer, let alone played against it. While the country was shut off, the cricket national team became a rare source of Indian unity. That itself was a mark of Indian isolation: elsewhere, cricket has usually faded after other sports arrived.

The soccer dream did live on. One summer night in 2001, India's national team visited East London to play their motionless old men's football against tiny Leyton Orient. While the visitors were holding the mighty Orient scoreless, a group of ten Indian fans chanted, "Are you watching, Pakistan?" But then Orient scored. When a chubby Indian named I. M. Vijayan equalized just before time, he disappeared beneath a pile of teammates as if he'd just won the World Cup.

The game continued to thrive in the country's few soccer hot spots, notably Kolkata, Goa, and Kerala. Elsewhere, even after a national professional league started in 2007, crowds mostly remained minute.

Perhaps the biggest problem for Indian sports is that something like two-thirds of the population live in isolated rural villages where traditional agriculture takes up all the time. Many rural Indians never encounter soccer or indeed play any sport at all. Even in the cities, where an estimated 11 percent of inhabitants are diabetic (often without even knowing it), sedentariness remains a problem.

Nevertheless, Indian soccer is now finally rising, boosted by TV broadcasts of the Premier League in particular. Growing numbers of urban

Indians can bore you to tears about Manchester City. More people are starting to play, too, often in English or Spanish team tops, embracing a sport that requires little equipment or even a proper field. "Baby leagues have sprung up in every major city," writes Sharma. "Greater Mumbai has more than two hundred five-a-side pitches. Recreational football for people across ages now rivals cricket and badminton in parts of the country." Ever more Indian soccer coaches are being trained and certified. Even the national team's results are slowly improving: as of March 2022, India ranked 106th in the world, only just ahead of tiny Kosovo, yet up from its long-term average ranking of 130th.

But, adds Sharma, sadly, Indian players and coaches still get too little soccer. The Indian Super League's season only lasts four or five months. It also features just twenty-two professional clubs, compared with the several hundred in the highest leagues of much smaller Europe. And when India hosted the under-seventeen World Cup in 2017, its team's players had only played about one hundred official games each in their careers, compared with nearly seven hundred for the visiting English.

For now, Indian soccer remains horribly weak. Our model says that India, given its population, soccer experience, and national income, ought to have had a positive goal difference in the 2010s. But it scored 1.3 goals a game less than it should have. India gets our *Soccernomics* award for the relatively worst soccer team on Earth.

21

THE FUTURE

The Best of Times—and the Streaming Service

As we finish this book, in early 2022, soccer clubs face the greatest financial crisis in their histories. COVID-19 has ripped the heart out of their balance sheets. UEFA sketched the scale of the problem in its licensing benchmarking report of May 2021. Normally, these documents take a fairly upbeat outlook for European clubs, but not this time. As if to rub in the seriousness, the background of the pages is shaded black. UEFA estimated that Europe's top-division clubs, whose combined revenues were $26 billion in 2019, would see a revenue shortfall of between $8 billion and $9 billion by the time the pandemic ended, mostly because of lost gate receipts while stadiums were closed.

Almost every professional club in Europe has survived COVID-19, as they have survived nearly every crisis over the last century or so, but most have been left battered. TV rights, which had been growing like Topsy for years, took a pause during the pandemic, as broadcasters hesitated to invest in an uncertain future. And without spectators, clubs' debts mounted. By late 2021, Barcelona alone owed more than $1.5 billion. The usual voices of doom went up, saying that the soccer economy was a bubble and that COVID-19 had burst it. These people were expressing a broadly felt disquiet: that the sport's transfer fees, debts, wages, ticket prices, spoiled players, and general hype have gotten out of hand.

We disagree. We don't think there is a soccer bubble. On the contrary, we think the game will continue expanding. Viewers from San Francisco to Chennai are tuning in to soccer, and they seem to be making the transition from the old medium, television, to the new one: streaming. Players will probably keep getting more spoiled and "overpaid" for a while yet.

Over the last thirty years, sports have been the fastest-growing segment of the entertainment business, and soccer has been the fastest-growing sport. Most of this happened thanks to TV. When clubs became de facto producers of TV content, the game had to smarten itself up. Run-down stadiums full of misbehaving fans no longer cut it. It's no coincidence that the refurbishing of English stadiums and the first sale of the rights to satellite TV happened almost simultaneously in the early 1990s. In the TV era, with comfortable stadiums, soccer hooliganism declined in the game's economic heartland of Western Europe. Since 2002, the build-up to World Cups has no longer been overshadowed by angst about thugs.

On the field, too, violence has been taken out of the game. In the past, creative players had it hard. The tackles that George Best endured on Manchester United's right wing in the 1960s almost resembled the sackings of NFL quarterbacks. In 1966 Pelé limped out of the World Cup, in 1983 Diego Maradona's time at Barcelona was ruined by an assault by Andoni Goikoetxea ("The Butcher of Bilbao"), and in 1992 Marco van Basten's career was effectively ended by injuries at the age of twenty-eight. But in the TV era, the authorities cracked down on thuggish defending. Before the World Cup of 1998, FIFA made the tackle from behind a sending-off offense. These curbs have freed the game's stars. Lionel Messi, Cristiano Ronaldo, and Zlatan Ibrahimovic have been able to thrill viewers week in, week out into their mid-thirties or even forties, almost unhindered by injuries or fear.

No wonder that since about 2000, people beyond Europe have been switching to European games. For instance, Manchester United started life as a club in Manchester. It soon became a club in England, later it grew into a club in Europe, and today it is a global club.

Perversely, the televising of games has made actually going to the stadium even more attractive. Perhaps because people now spend so much of their lives in a virtual world (even before the pandemic), they are willing to pay a premium for peak real-life experiences such as attending big soccer games. Of course, fans complain about English ticket prices. Yet in twenty years' time, when stadiums are packed with Asian tourists paying $500 for their tickets, they may well look back and say, "Can you imagine that in 2022 you could get into a game for $100 and have money left over for a pint?"

Soccer is now, by a large and constantly growing margin, the planet's favorite game. There was a landmark moment in 2009 when the Champions League final overtook the Super Bowl as the world's most watched sporting event: 109 million viewers versus 106 million, according to the Futures Sport & Entertainment consultancy. Even in the Canadian prairie city of Edmonton, crowds swarmed downtown to celebrate Barcelona's victory over Manchester United.

The soccer economy is not a bubble, because as long as stadiums are open, clubs' higher spending is funded by higher revenues and by rich men desperate to throw money at the game. In 2016 Manchester United could afford to pay $116 million for Paul Pogba because its annual revenues had jumped sixfold in the previous eighteen years to about $700 million. A year later, it wasn't really PSG that signed Neymar for $263 million (still an all-time world record)—it was Qatar, the tiny state that is the world's largest exporter of liquid natural gas. With all that money coming in, of course star players are earning enormous salaries and becoming spoiled. These are the problems of success.

It's perfectly reasonable to make a moral critique of the new soccer. You can say, "I remember when my local team consisted of local boys earning the same sorts of wages as most people in our town. I don't like the moneyed soccer of today, especially not when it's funded by evil billionaires." That's fair enough. You can still find the old, local soccer if you drop down a division or two, but perhaps you want to watch Real Madrid or Manchester United and find everything much as it was in 1974, and you can't. It's reasonable to resent that. After all, most of us like soccer because it connects us with our childhood. But it's illogical to jump from a moral judgment ("Soccer has lost its soul") to an economic prediction ("This is a bubble that's going to burst"). You might loathe today's big soccer, but that doesn't mean it's doomed.

In the 1960s the soccer agent Ken Stanley told his client George Best: "Think about what football will be like when it's truly a world game.

Think of the size of America. Think of every boy in Africa having a team shirt and a ball at his feet. Think about China and Japan and the rest of the Far East. There are billions of people out there, George. The game is still growing. They'll be watching you on television in Peking and Calcutta before long."

Stanley's prophecy is now coming true, even as Peking and Calcutta have become Beijing and Kolkata. Global TV has changed soccer. The game is only just beginning to penetrate the world's four most-populous countries—China, India, the US, and Indonesia—which between them account for about 45 percent of humanity.

Then there are the large economies of Japan, Canada, and Australia, where soccer is also growing fast. One measure of the game's unrealized potential is that the Premier League still probably earns more from TV rights inside England (about $6 billion total from 2022 through 2025) than in the rest of the world put together (a bit under $6 billion). Those numbers won't stay that way for long. European soccer has entered the global export business. As Gerard Piqué, the Barcelona defender-cum-entrepreneur, told us, "There are markets to exploit, and I think that football will still grow much more. And the big clubs will get much bigger. Barcelona and Real Madrid will increase their revenues." And other clubs outside Spain probably even more so.

Soccer now faces a tricky transition: scarily for a sport that turned itself into TV content, more and more people have stopped watching television. Global TV viewing of sports peaked in 2012. After that, the amount of time spent watching TV typically fell by a few percentage points a year, said the Futures Sport consultancy.

With ever more channels, and ever fewer viewers, most TV programs now cater to tiny niches. In fact, reported Future Sports in 2017, "One-third of all sports programs are watched by no one. That's to say, when the official TV audience reporting bureaus around the world report upon the audience for that event, their best estimate is zero viewers. There simply aren't enough sports fans, or people in the world in general, to go round to watch all televised sport."

Even soccer struggles to charge consumers to watch games. If you can mess around on social media for free and if your smartphone habit has slashed your concentration span, then why pay to sit down and watch a ninety-minute game that might be boring, especially now that websites package the best moments into free videos?

But as Johan Cruyff said, "Every disadvantage has its advantage." The decline of TV and the rise of streaming and social media may actually benefit soccer. Since the 1870s and possible even earlier, there have always been more fans interested in following a game than can be squeezed into a stadium. For this reason, new technologies that spread the action beyond the stadium have always created more revenue. To begin with it was the newspapers, printing reports that were avidly consumed across the country. Then came the telegraph, which enabled people to follow a game from afar while it was being played (and gamble on the outcome). Film added a little too, by allowing people to see the action in the most famous stadiums. Radio did much more, enabling play-by-play commentary to reach millions. Next came television, first on free-to-air and then on cable, first with analogue and then digital technologies, all steadily enhancing the breadth and depth of sports coverage and pouring ever more money into sport organizations. Now we are at the beginning of the social media era, with content reaching fans in new formats with new features. There is much talk about the threat that this poses to revenues from TV contracts. But that's like complaining that TV undermined the revenues from radio. We doubt that social media will prove to be a revenue loser for sports. Rather, it will open up new opportunities to squeeze money out of fans. Some new ways of engaging supporters, such as NFTs (nonfungible tokens), might prove to be mere fads, but others could end up being lucrative.

The rise of streaming offers the sport another opportunity: for the first time ever, viewers no longer need a television set to watch football. They can now choose their platform: mobile phone, computer, tablet, or Xbox. Online streaming tends to be cheaper than pay TV. It also allows people to watch on the subway, in the café, or while pretending to look after their children in the playground. Italy's Serie A sold its media rights from 2021 through 2024 to the sports streaming service DAZN. Phone operators in several countries have been buying soccer rights, and Amazon has bought streaming rights for Premier League games, as well as tennis and the NFL. Even if streaming rights end up selling for a touch less than the bubbly TV deals of the late 2010s did, that would still be enough to keep soccer players and agents in their multimillionaire lifestyles. And it may be that once most people on Earth can buy a live game on their phone for a dollar or two whenever the fancy takes them, the market for sports viewing will expand to hitherto unimagined levels.

These prospects continue to attract rich investors to the game. Sheikhs and oligarchs are more interested than ever now that UEFA has effectively ditched its Financial Fair Play policy, which stopped them from sticking their own money into their clubs. In recent years a newer breed of profit-seeking private-equity investor has joined the sugar daddies. We applaud the willingness of these people to burn their cash on entertaining the rest of us. If the private-equity firms imagine they will make profits in soccer, we suspect they will end up as disappointed as almost all previous investors who arrived with the same fantasy. This sport might live forever, but we doubt it will ever become a good business. And it's so much the better for that.

ACKNOWLEDGMENTS

Dozens of people helped make this book possible. We would like to thank Peter Allden, Dave Berri, Victor Bichara, Joe Boyle, Edward Chisholm, Dennis Coates, Bastien Drut, Rod Fort, Bernd Frick, Julien Bracco Gartner, Brian Goff, Sunil Gulati, Jahn Hakes, Pauline Harris, Brad Humphreys, Paul Husbands, Kai Konrad, Dan Kuper, Markus Kurscheidt, Mike Leeds, Ben Lyttleton, Wolfgang Maennig, Issa Martinez, Roger Noll, Andrew Oswald, Holger Preuss, Skip Sauer, Philip Soar, Henk Spaan, and Lia Na'ama ten Brink.

We got ideas and information from Kevin Alavy, Rob Baade, Rob Bateman, Joel Becker, Vendeline von Bredow, Carl Bromley, Tunde Buraimo, Pamela Druckerman, Gavin Fleig, Mike Forde, Rod Fort, Russell Gerrard, Matti Goksoyr, Ian Graham, Norbert Hofmann, Mart Jürisoo, Ted Knutson, Adam Kuper, Hannah Kuper, Marc McElligott, Kieran Maguire, Jean-Pierre Meersseman, Kaz Mochlinski, Christian Muck, James Nicholson, Ignacio Palacios-Huerta, Frank Pelosi III, Ian Preston, Antoinette Renouf, Placido Rodriguez, Mark Rosentraub, Andreas Selliaas, Simon Wilson, Axel Torres Xirau, and Paul in 't Hout; from Benjamin Cohen, Jonathan Hill, Mark O'Keefe, and Alex Phillips at UEFA; and from David O'Connor and Andrew Walsh at Sport+Markt.

The following were fantastic collaborators: Kevin Alavy, Wladimir Andreff, Giles Atkinson, Tunde Buraimo, Luigi Buzzacchi, Filippo dell'Osso, Christian Deutscher, Bastien Drut, David Forrest, Pedro Garciadel-Barrio, Steve Hall, David Harbord, Takeo Hirata, Tom Hoehn, Todd Jewell, Georgios Kavetsos, Stefan Késenne, Melanie Krause, Tim Kuypers, Umberto Lago, Stephanie Leach, Neil Longley, Victor

Matheson, Susana Mourato, Susanne Parlasca, Thomas Peeters, Ian Preston, Steve Ross, Nicolas Scelles, Rob Simmons, Ron Smith, Marko Terviö, Tommaso Valletti, Daniel Weimar, Guy Wilkinson, Jason Winfree, and Andy Zimbalist.

Gordon Wise and Kate Cooper were hardworking and imaginative agents. Carl Bromley—then at Nation Books—thought from the start that this book should appear in the United States, and he, Sandra Beris, Jennifer Crane, Antoinette Smith, Alessandra Bastagli, and Annette Wenda helped make the American edition much better than it would have been without them. For this edition, Hillary Brenhouse, Donald Pharr, and Michelle Welsh-Horst took over the reins with patience and competence.

We also want to thank all the interviewees quoted in the text.

NOTES

CHAPTER 2: GENTLEMEN PREFER BLONDS

1. In statistics, the measure of correlation can be squared in order to derive a percentage of the variation that is explained. Thus if the correlation (called "r") between league position and wages is +0.84, then the "r squared" is 0.7 or 70 percent.

CHAPTER 4: SAFER THAN THE BANK OF ENGLAND

1. The three lost clubs are Merthyr Town, Aberdare (disbanded 1928), New Brighton (which folded in 1983, was then reborn, but folded again in 2012), and South Shields (taken over by Gateshead in 1930). Both Merthyr and Aberdare are small towns that still possess a club today. Several other clubs have folded and been reborn, such as Accrington Stanley, Bradford Park Avenue, Durham City, Halifax Town, Merthyr Town, Nelson, and Newport County.

CHAPTER 11: THE ECONOMIST'S FEAR OF THE PENALTY KICK

1. You can watch it at www.facebook.com/Catenaccio.nl/videos /1159047960806155.

CHAPTER 14: HAPPINESS

1. Paul Dolan, Georgios Kavetsos, Christian Krekel, Dimitris Mavridis, Robert Metcalfe, Claudia Senik, Stefan Szymanski, and Nicolas R. Ziebarth, "The Host with the Most? The Effects of the Olympic Games on Happiness," CEP Discussion Paper No. 1441, 2016.

SELECT BIBLIOGRAPHY

BOOKS

Anderson, Chris, and David Sally. *The Numbers Game: Why Everything You Know About Football Is Wrong*. London: Viking, 2013.

Andreff, Wladimir, and Stefan Szymanski, eds. *Handbook on the Economics of Sport*. Cheltenham: Edward Elgar, 2006.

Andrews, David L. *Manchester United: A Thematic Study*. London: Routledge, 2004.

Ball, Phil. *Morbo: The Story of Spanish Football*. London: WSC, 2001.

Bellos, Alex. *Futebol: The Brazilian Way of Life*. London: Bloomsbury, 2002.

Bennetts, Marc. *Football Dynamo: Modern Russia and the People's Game*. London: Virgin, 2008.

Biermann, Christoph. *Die Fußball-Matrix: Auf der Suche nach dem perfekten Spiel*. Cologne: Kiepenheuer & Witsch, 2009.

Bose, Mihir. *The Spirit of the Game: How Sport Made the Modern World*. London: Constable & Robinson, 2011.

Burns, Jimmy. *Hand of God: The Life of Diego Maradona*. London: Bloomsbury, 1996.

Burns, Jimmy. *When Beckham Went to Spain: Power, Stardom, and Real Madrid*. London: Penguin, 2004.

Campomar, Andres. *¡Golazo! A History of Latin American Football*. London: Querkus, 2014.

Carragher, Jamie. *Carra: My Autobiography*. London: Corgi, 2009.

Cole, Ashley. *My Defence: Winning, Losing, Scandals, and the Drama of Germany 2006.* London: Headline, 2006.

Conn, David. *The Fall of the House of FIFA.* London: Yellow Jersey, 2017.

Cox, Michael. *The Mixer.* London: HarperSport, 2017.

Dobson, Stephen, and John Goddard. *The Economics of Football.* Cambridge: Cambridge University Press, 2001.

Dorsey, James. *The Turbulent World of Middle East Soccer.* London: Hurst, 2016.

Drogba, Didier. *"C'était pas gagné…"* Issy-les-Moulineaux: Éditions Prolongations, 2008.

Drut, Bastien, and Richard Duhautois. *Sciences Sociales Football Club.* Louvain-la-Neuve: De Boeck, 2015.

Epstein, David. *The Sports Gene: What Makes the Perfect Athlete.* London: Yellow Jersey, 2013.

Exley, Frederick. *A Fan's Notes.* London: Yellow Jersey, 1999.

Ferguson, Alex. *Managing My Life: My Autobiography.* London: Hodder and Stoughton, 2000.

Ferguson, Alex. *My Autobiography.* London: Hodder and Stoughton, 2013.

FIFA TMS Global Transfer Market 2012. Zurich: FIFA TMS, 2013.

Foot, John. *Calcio: A History of Italian Football.* London: Fourth Estate, 2006.

Gerrard, Steven. *Gerrard: My Autobiography.* London: Bantam, 2007.

Ginsborg, Paul. *A History of Contemporary Italy.* London: Penguin, 1990.

Gladwell, Malcolm. *Outliers: The Story of Success.* London: Allen Lane, 2008.

Goldblatt, David. *The Ball Is Round: A Global History of Football.* London: Viking, 2006.

Gopnik, Adam. *Paris to the Moon.* New York: Random House, 2000.

Hall, Matthew. *The Away Game.* Sydney: HarperSports, 2000.

Hamilton, Aidan. *An Entirely Different Game: The British Influence on Brazilian Football.* Edinburgh: Mainstream, 1998.

Hamilton, Duncan. *Immortal: The Approved Biography of George Best.* London: Century, 2013.

Hill, Declan. *The Fix: Soccer and Organized Crime.* Toronto: McLelland and Stewart, 2008.

Holt, Richard, and Tony Mason. *Sport in Britain, 1945–2000.* London: Wiley-Blackwell, 2000.

Honigstein, Raphael. *Das Reboot: How German Football Reinvented Itself and Conquered the World.* London: Yellow Jersey, 2015.

Hopcraft, Arthur. *The Football Man: People and Passions in Soccer.* London: Aurum, 2006.

Hornby, Nick. *Fever Pitch.* London: Indigo, 1996.

Kapuściński, Ryszard. *The Soccer War.* New York: Vintage International, 1992.

Kok, Auke. *1974: Wij waren de besten.* Amsterdam: Thomas Rap, 2004.

Kolfschooten, Frank van. *De bal is niet rond.* Amsterdam: L. J. Veen, 1998.

Lampard, Frank. *Totally Frank.* London: HarperSport, 2006.

Lever, Janet. *Soccer Madness.* Chicago: University of Chicago Press, 1983.

Lewis, Michael. *Moneyball.* New York: W. W. Norton, 2004.

Lyttleton, Ben. *Edge: What Business Can Learn from Football.* London: HarperCollins, 2017.

Mandela, Nelson. *The Long Walk to Freedom.* London: Abacus, 1995.

Montague, James. *When Friday Comes: Football in the War Zone.* London: deCoubertin, 2013.

Mora y Araujo, Marcela, and Simon Kuper, eds. *Perfect Pitch 3: Men and Women.* London: Headline, 1998.

Nieuwenhof, Frans van de. *Hiddink, Dit is mijn wereld.* Eindhoven: De Boekenmakers, 2006.

Norridge, Julian. *Can We Have Our Balls Back, Please? How the British Invented Sport and Then Almost Forgot How to Play It.* London: Penguin, 2008.

Oliver and Ohlbaum Associates and Fletcher Research. *Net Profits: How to Make Money Out of Football.* London: Fletcher Research, 1997.

Orakwue, Stella. *Pitch Invaders: The Modern Black Football Revolution.* London: Victor Gollancz, 1998.

Peace, David. *The Damned United.* London: Faber and Faber, 2006.

Perarnau, Martí. *Pep Confidential.* Edinburgh: Arena Sport, 2014.

Rooney, Wayne. *My Story So Far.* London: HarperSport, 2006.

Silver, Nate. *The Signal and the Noise: Why So Many Predictions Fail—But Some Don't.* London: Penguin, 2012.

Simons, Rowan. *Bamboo Goalposts: One Man's Quest to Teach the People's Republic of China to Love Football.* London: Macmillan, 2008.

Szymanski, Stefan. *Money and Soccer: A Soccernomics Guide.* New York: Nation, 2015.

Szymanski, Stefan. *Playbooks and Checkbooks: An Introduction to the Economics of Modern Sports*. Princeton, NJ: Princeton University Press, 2009.

Szymanski, Stefan, and Tim Kuypers. *Winners and Losers: The Business Strategy of Football*. London: Penguin, 1999.

Szymanski, Stefan, and Andrew Zimbalist. *National Pastime: How Americans Play Baseball and the Rest of the World Plays Soccer*. Washington, DC: Brookings Institution Press, 2005.

Taylor, Peter. *With Clough by Taylor*. London: Sidgwick and Jackson, 1980.

Tomkins, Paul, Graeme Riley, and Gary Fulcher. *Pay as You Play: The True Price of Success in the Premier League Era*. Wigston: GPRF, 2010.

Turnbull, John, Thom Satterlee, and Alon Raab, eds. *The Global Game: Writers on Soccer*. Lincoln: University of Nebraska Press, 2008.

Varley, Nick. *Parklife: A Search for the Heart of Football*. London: Penguin, 1999.

Vergouw, Gyuri. *De Strafschop: Zoektocht naar de ultieme penalty*. Antwerp: Uitgeverij Funsultancy, 2000.

Vergouw, Gyuri. *When Saturday Comes. Power Corruption and Pies: A Decade of the Best Football Writing from "When Saturday Comes."* London: Two Heads, 1997.

White, Jim. *Manchester United: The Biography*. London: Sphere, 2008.

Williams, Damien J., and Fergus G. Neville. "Sport-Related Domestic Violence: Exploring the Complex Relationship Between Sporting Events and Domestic Violence." In M. F. Taylor, J. A. Pooley, and R. S. Taylor (eds.), *Overcoming Domestic Violence: Creating a Dialogue Around Vulnerable Populations. Social Issues, Justice and Status*. New York: Nova Science, 2014.

Wilson, Jonathan. *The Anatomy of England: A History in Ten Matches*. London: Orion, 2010.

Wilson, Jonathan. *Inverting the Pyramid: A History of Football Tactics*. London: Orion, 2008.

Wortmann, Sönke. *Deutschland. Ein Sommermärchen: Das WM-Tagebuch*. Cologne: Kiepenheuer & Witsch, 2006.

Zirin, Dave. *A People's History of Sports in the United States*. New York: New Press, 2008.

ARTICLES AND RESEARCH PAPERS

Anderson, Christopher. "Do Democracies Win More? The Effects of Wealth and Democracy on Success in the FIFA World Cup." Paper presented at the annual meeting of the Midwest Political Science Association, Chicago, 2011.

Baade, R. "Professional Sports as Catalysts for Metropolitan Economic Development." *Journal of Urban Affairs* 18, no. 1 (1996): 1–17.

Berlin, Peter. "Playing by the Numbers." *Financial Times*, February 1, 1992.

Bryson, Alex, Babatunde Buraimo, and Rob Simmons. "Time To Go? Head Coach Quits and Dismissals in Professional Football." IZA Institute of Labor Economics, Discussion Paper Series, March 2017.

Dickson, Alex, Colin Jennings, and Gary Koop. "Domestic Violence and Football in Glasgow: Are Reference Points Relevant?" *Oxford Bulletin of Economics and Statistics* 78, no. 1 (February 2016): 1–16.

Feenstra, Robert, Robert Inklaar, and Marcel P. Timmer. "The Next Generation of the Penn World Table." 2013. www.ggdc.net/pwt.

Gabaix, Xavier. "Zipf's Law for Cities: An Explanation." *Quarterly Journal of Economics* 114, no. 3 (August 1999): 739–767.

Hicks, Joe, and Grahame Allen. "A Century of Change: Trends in UK Statistics Since 1900." House of Commons Library Research Paper 99/111. London: House of Commons Library, December 1999.

Hirshleifer, J. "The Paradox of Power." *Economics and Politics* 3 (1991): 177–200.

Kavetsos, Georgios, and Stefan Szymanski. "National Well-Being and International Sports Events." *Journal of Economic Psychology* 31, no. 3 (April 2010): 158–171.

Kirby, Stuart, Brian Francis, and Rosalie O'Flaherty. "Can the FIFA World Cup Football (Soccer) Tournament Be Associated with an Increase in Domestic Abuse?" *Journal of Research in Crime and Delinquency* 51, no. 3 (2014): 259–276.

McGrath, Ben. "The Sporting Scene: The Professor of Baseball." *New Yorker*, July 7, 2003.

Palacios-Huerta, Ignacio. "Professionals Play Minimax." *Review of Economic Studies* 70, no. 2 (2003): 395–415.

Peeters, T. L., B. M. Mills, E. Pennings, and H. Sung. "Manager Migration, Learning-by-Hiring, and Cultural Distance in International Soccer." *Global Strategy Journal* 11, no. 3 (2021): 494–519.

Peeters, Thomas, and Stefan Szymanski. "Financial Fair Play in European Football." *Economic Policy* 29, no. 78 (2014): 343–390.

Peeters, Thomas, Stefan Szymanski, and Marko Terviö. "The Survival of Mediocre Superstars in the Labor Market." *Journal of Law, Economics, and Organization*, November 22, 2021, doi.org/10.1093/jleo/ewab035.

Peeters, Thomas, Victor Matheson, and Stefan Szymanski. "Tourism and the 2010 World Cup: Lessons for Developing Countries." *Journal of African Economies* 23, no. 2 (2014): 290–320.

Quigg, Zara, Karen Hughes, and Mark A. Bellis. "Effects of the 2010 World Cup Football Tournament on Emergency Department Assault Attendances in England." *European Journal of Public Health* 23, no. 3 (2012): 383–385.

Szymanski, Stefan. "Entry into Exit: Insolvency in English Professional Football." *Scottish Journal of Political Economy* 64, no. 4 (2017): 419–444.

Szymanski, Stefan. "Income Inequality, Competitive Balance, and the Attractiveness of Team Sports: Some Evidence and a Natural Experiment from English Soccer." *Economic Journal* 111 (2001): F69–F84.

Szymanski, Stefan. "A Market Test for Discrimination in the English Professional Soccer Leagues." *Journal of Political Economy* 108, no. 3 (2000): 590–603.

Szymanski, Stefan, and Daniel Weimar. "Insolvencies in Professional Football: A German Sonderweg." *International Journal of Sport Finance* 14, no. 1 (2019): 54–68.

Szymanski, Stefan, and Guy Wilkinson. "Testing the O-Ring Theory Using Data from the English Premier League." *Research in Economics* 70, no. 3 (2016): 468–481.

Tapp, A. "The Loyalty of Football Fans—We'll Support You Evermore?" *Journal of Database Marketing and Customer Strategy Management* 11, no. 3 (April 1, 2004): 203–215.

Tapp, A., and J. Clowes. "From 'Carefree Casuals' to 'Professional Wanderers': Segmentation Possibilities for Football Supporters." *European Journal of Marketing* 36, no. 11 (2002): 1248–1269.

Taylor, Matthew. "Global Players? Football, Migration and Globalization, c. 1930–2000." *Historical Social Research* 31, no. 1 (2006): 7–30.

Van Ours, Jan C., and Martin A. van Tuijl. "In-Season Head-Coach Dismissals and the Performance of Professional Football Teams." *Economic Inquiry* 54, no. 1 (2016): 591–604.

MAGAZINES AND WEBSITES

De Correspondent (Netherlands, with a special mention for journalist Michiel de Hoog, who has produced some of the most intelligent articles on soccer in recent years. If he were writing in English, you might never have heard of *Soccernomics*.)

Hard Gras (Netherlands)

Johan (Netherlands, now defunct)

So Foot (France)

Voetbal International (Netherlands)

INDEX

ABOUT THE AUTHORS

Simon Kuper is the award-winning author of *Soccer Against the Enemy; Ajax, the Dutch, the War: The Strange Tale of Soccer During Europe's Darkest Hour; The Barcelona Complex*; and, with Stefan Szymanski, the international bestseller *Soccernomics*. He writes a weekly column in the *Financial Times* and has previously written soccer columns for the *Times* and the *Observer*. In 2007 he won the annual Manuel Vazquez Montalban prize for sports writing, awarded by the Colegio de Periodistas de Catalunya and FC Barcelona's foundation. He lives in Paris, France.

Stefan Szymanski is the Stephen J. Galetti Collegiate Professor of Sport Management at the University of Michigan's School of Kinesiology. In addition to his academic work, Szymanski writes occasional columns for the *New York Times*, the *Guardian*, and others, including the *Soccernomics* blog. He acts as a consultant to governments, federations, and sport businesses, and has been called as an expert witness in sports litigation in both the US and the UK. With Simon Kuper, he has been coauthor on all previous editions of *Soccernomics*. He lives in Ann Arbor, Michigan.